The
Left's War
Against GOD!

and

The Right's
RULES FOR ANTI-RADICALS!
A Call To ACTION!

Whether The Left Calls Themselves Liberals, Fascists, or Progressives ... *The Left's War Is Against GOD!*

Dr. Rhéma el Yérak Sr.

The Left's War Against GOD! and The Right's RULES FOR ANTI-RADICALS!: A Call To ACTION!

Dr. Rhéma el Yérak Sr.

Copyright © 2019 by the Third Awakening Foundation
Second Edition
All rights Reserved
Printed in the United States of America

ISBN: 978-0-578-53927-0
Library of Congress Control Number: 2019909071

Third Awakening Foundation Publishing
ThirdAwakeningFoundation.com
ThirdAwakeningFoundation@gmail.com

Cover photo: Gustave Doré (1832–1883) *The Triumph Of Christianity Over Paganism* (c 1868)

All scriptures are from the *Holy Bible* Authorized Version

TM

Third Awakening Foundation

The Left's War Against GOD!

DEDICATION

I am dedicating this book to my beautiful, wise, insightful, and GODly wife, the GODliest woman I have ever known. You are my anchor in this world and have been faithfully by my side to complete this book. This work would not have been possible without your support, inspiration, and dedication. I am eternally grateful. I love you and thank you!

And to my sons to whom I hope to leave them a legacy as a GOD-fearing man who chooses to stand in the Truth with humility and unshakable steadfastness no matter the Evil that threatens us. It truly is better that we should die on our feet charging the Enemy, than to live on our knees in surrender to Evil.

And not the least I dedicate this work to GOD. GOD who has chosen me before the foundation of the world. Of which I am wholly unworthy but wholly grateful to Him nonetheless.

The defining characteristic of the Left can be most easily conceptualized using a quote borrowed from the mid-Nineteenth Century French poet Charles Baudelaire and used in the Hollywood movie *The Usual Suspects*:

> "...You never knew. That was his power. The greatest trick the Devil ever pulled was convincing the world he didn't exist".

If Evil does not *actually* exist, then there can be no Right and no Wrong… and people are free to choose any path and make any decisions free from all moral constraints. If there is no actual Evil, then there is no basis for determining Wrong. However if as life itself attests all around us, Evil does *actually* exist, the Devil is real, and the Left is Evil! The Left has convinced the world that it only has good intentions while h   objectives, which can only be defined as... *Evil*.

FORWARD

I was concerned a few years ago when I started researching this book that it may be difficult for some to believe its contents. That some may consider some of its facts as exaggerated or hyperbole. Since then the Left has come out... *demons screaming.* The real-life demonstrable examples of the Left's Nazi tactics now fill the pages of every media source in America! The Left has publically embraced Evil in ways that before they only spoke in whispers behind closed doors. All critical points of this book have been painstakingly detailed and documented inline and in over 700 footnotes. There is simply *no* way to over-exaggerate the Left's Evil, Evil actions, and Evil intentions! If this book does not scare you Right then you are simply a compromised instrument of Evil in *The Left's War Against GOD!*

Table of Contents

DEDICATION... 5

FORWARD 9

1. DEFINING THE WAR: EVIL AGAINST GOD, LEFT AGAINST RIGHT: 15

2. UNDERSTANDING THE BATTLE....................................... 41

3. JESUS, CHRISTIANS, AND POLITICAL ACTIVISM: DEBUNKING THE LIE OF EVIL AND THE LEFT 55

4. THE COALITION OF THE UNLIKELY: THE TIE THAT BLINDS 69

5. UNDERSTANDING THE TWO FACES OF THE ENEMY............................. 77

6. THE PROGRESSIVE FACE OF THE LEFT 81

7. BAIT AND SWITCH: THE RE-NAME-GAME: 93

8. AMERICA'S WAR/THE LEFT'S WAR AGAINST AMERICA'S JUDEO-CHRISTIAN FOUNDATIONS...115

9. TACTICS FOR THE LEFT'S SUBVERSION AND TAKEOVER OF AMERICA: 133

    HAIL CAESAR OBAMA! 148

    INFILTRATE AND DESTROY FROM WITHIN:............................149

10. LIES, LIES, LIES! 155

11. SHADES OF GRAY 179

12. The "Fairness" Doctrine..181

13. Emotion Based Politics 189

14. TOLERANCE 199

    TOLERANCE TO ACCEPTANCE: 214

15. THE LEFT IS A RELIGION! 217

16. LEGISLATING MORALITY...267

17. P. C. POLICE:...275

18. EVIL IN OUR SCHOOLS..279

19. FASCISM AND THE LEFT IN AMERICA: KINDRED SPIRITS AND FAMILIAR BEDFELLOWS: 289

20. The Democrat Party Platform As Leftist Doctrines All OPPOSE God... 409

21. THE OBAMAS: THE EPITOME OF THE LEFT: 437
OBAMA AS A RACIST: 452
OBAMA AS A MUSLIM OR MUSLIM SYMPATHIZER:................................ 456
OBAMA WAS INTENTIONALLY AND PURPOSELY EMPOWERING ISLAM AND ITS MUSLIM TERRORIST IDEOLOGY: 464

22. IGNORANCE IS NO EXCUSE FOR THE LAW........................ 475

23. FIGHTING TO WIN!: HOW DO WE FIGHT THE WAR? THE RIGHT'S RULES FOR ANTI-RADICALS! A CALL TO ACTION! 477

24. PRACTICAL WAR STRATEGIES: THE RIGHT'S RULES FOR ANTI-RADICALS! A CALL TO ACTION!.................................. 485

25. RULES FOR ANTI-RADICALS: SPECIFIC WAR STRATEGIES:.................... 517

26. CONCLUSION 523

POSTSCRIPT: FOR THE SINNER WHO FINDS HIMSELF ON THE WRONG SIDE OF GOD IN THE LEFT'S WAR AGAINST GOD: 535

The *Holy Bible*:

"But if it be of God, ye cannot overthrow it; lest haply ye be found even to fight against God." – The *Holy Bible*, Acts of the Apostles 5:39

"let us not fight against God" – The *Holy Bible*, Acts of the Apostles 23:9

"These shall make war with the Lamb" – The *Holy Bible*, Revelation 17:14

"The fight for freedom is GOD's fight. Freedom is an eternal law of GOD. Men cannot break it with impunity, but can only break themselves upon it. When a man stands for freedom, he stands for GOD. As long as he stands for freedom, he stands with GOD. And were he to stand alone, he would still stand with GOD. Any man will be eternally vindicated and rewarded for his stand for freedom". – Ezra Taft Benson

"He who will not reason is a bigot; he who cannot is a fool; he who dares not is a slave". -- William Drummond

"It is when people forget GOD that tyrants forge their chains." – Patrick Henry

"We hold these truths to be self-evident, that all men are created equal, that they are endowed by their Creator with certain unalienable Rights, that among these are Life, Liberty and the pursuit of Happiness.--That to secure these rights, Governments are instituted among Men, deriving their just powers from the consent of the governed, --That whenever any Form of Government becomes destructive of these ends, it is the Right of the People to alter or to abolish it, and to institute new Government, laying its foundation on such principles and organizing its powers in such form, as to them shall seem most likely to effect their Safety and Happiness." – The United States Declaration of Independence, 1776

"It does not take a majority to prevail ... but rather an irate, tireless minority, keen on setting brushfires of freedom in the minds of men". – Samuel Adams

"When the people fear the government, you have tyranny. When the government fears the people, you have freedom". – Thomas Pain

1. DEFINING THE WAR: EVIL AGAINST GOD, LEFT AGAINST RIGHT:

Chapter 1

A working definition of "the Left" has defied explanation to virtually all who have attempted to discover one. How do you define the Leftist alliance in America so eclectic as to embrace Islam with its male dominated gross-brutality against women, and the same Leftist alliance which equally embraces in its faithful the militant-Feminists whose entire existence is to glorify the superiority of women over men? Political ideology cannot explain such an alliance because Islam and Feminism are in conflict at the very core of their individual belief systems. The only commonality that exists between the varied factions of the Left is... *Evil.*[1] This Evil can be explained as a common opposition to the One true GOD[2] of Christianity and Judaism. The Left by definition opposes *everything* upon which GOD and GOD's inerrant Words, as contained in His *Holy Bible*, firmly stand. This is driving force and shrieking hysteria of *The Left's War Against GOD*!

This book is not intended as a treatise on Christianity, but as an unmasking of the hidden agenda of the *Left* and its *War Against GOD*, especially in its targeting of America's Christian foundations in its attempt to *fundamentally transform America*, as Barack Hussein Obama, Jr. so dogmatically preached[3]. In such a comparison between GOOD and Evil, references to the Christian Faith are unavoidable. As will be seen, the only definition of GOOD is a direct association with the GOD of The *Holy Bible*. The Battle between GOOD and Evil is not

---

[1] For a broader discussion of Evil as the commonality of the Left see the chapter: *The Coalition of the Unlikely: The Tie That Blinds*.

[2] The "One true GOD" is GOD *JEHOVAH* of the Christian *Bible*, the Three in One of the Triune GODhead. The small-caps "GOD" will be used throughout this book, as was used in the Old Testament of the *Holy Bible*, to distinguish the Christian GOD *JEHOVAH* from all other imposters. When using quotes from others, the representation of "God" as "GOD" will be maintained for accurate representation of the source. The word GOOD with small-caps will be used throughout to signify this association to GOD the only source of GOOD.

[3] See following chapter *The Obamas: The Epitome of the Left* for fuller discussion.

a philosophical construct, but as will be clearly demonstrated, a real, historically verifiable, life-and-death struggle!

This discourse is presented in the terms of "Left" and "Right" because these terms are historically verifiable, widely recognized, and best encompass the varying complexities of each side of the political spectrum. These two terms also demonstrate the clear and irreconcilable division that stands between these two ideologies and two corresponding kingdoms. To state the obvious: You cannot be *Right* and *Left* at the same time. The terms have a Biblical precedent as GOD is always *Right*[4], and those who oppose[5] GOD are always *Left* or literally *Wrong* and as will be clearly shown historically, the opposite of GOD is *Left*.

The etymologically of the word "right" clearly shows that "Right" is synonymous with "correct":

>Definition of right[6]
>1 : righteous, upright
>2 : being in accordance with what is just, good, or proper
>   right conduct
>3 : conforming to facts or truth : **correct**
>   the right answer
>4 : suitable, appropriate
>   the right man for the job
>5 : straight
>   a right line
>6 : genuine, real

The term *Right* is self-defining. The very definition of Right is the representation of GOD Who *is Right*eousness. GOD, and GOD alone, *is Righteousness*[7]. Most of us today fail to make this simple connection,

---

[4] i.e. The *Holy Bible:* Genesis 18:25; Nehemiah 9:13; Is 45:19; Matthew 25:33-34.
[5] i.e. The *Holy Bible:* Matthew 25:33, 41-46; Notice that the term *left* in scripture when not talking about a direction often has the very negative connotation of *abandoning* GOD (i.e. Genesis 11:8; 2 Kings 17:16) or GOD *abandoning* evil people (i.e. Jeremiah 12:7; Luke 17:34-36).
[6] https://www.merriam-webster.com/dictionary/right (emphasis added)
[7] The *Holy Bible:* e.g. Romans 14:17; 1 Corinthians 1:30; Hebrews 1:8.

but it is a necessary and historically demonstrable truth. America's Founding Fathers reiterated this *Biblical* truth in America's Declaration of Independence, "We hold these truths to be self-evident, that all men are created equal, that they are endowed by their Creator with certain unalienable **Rights**…". Our Creator GOD is synonymous with our GOD-given "**Rights**". (It must also be noted that Christians are *righteous* not because of any effort of their own, but because Christians vicariously receive GOD's *Righteousness*[8] from GOD when a person becomes a Christian.)

The Left tries to counterfeit its own unGODly "righteousness" and in doing so falls for the *Big Lie* "ye shall be as gods"[9] propagated by the Serpent in the Garden of Eden at the beginning of time. Only GOD defines what constitutes true *Righteousness* because *Righteousness* is the very nature and being of GOD. Man's attempt to create his own righteousness outside of GOD is not a new sin, "For they being ignorant of GOD's righteousness, and going about to establish their own righteousness, have not submitted themselves unto the righteousness of GOD"[10]. GOD compares man's attempts to be *Righteous* outside of GOD as works equivalent to "filthy rags"[11]. To get a better mental picture from the original Hebrew text of "filthy rags" is literally… a discarded, used, bloodied tampon! This is a graphic self-defining representation of GOD's view of those on the Left who would attempt to establish their own counterfeit "righteousness" aside from GOD's true righteousness…. the Left and those who follow it are as repulsive to GOD as we are repulsed by a discarded, used, bloodied tampon!

The word "Left" has always been associated in the English language with the term *sinister* in deviance from GOD's *Righteousness* and a perversion of Christian morality:

> "The left hand has long been associated with deviance. The word 'sinister' originally meant 'to the left' in Latin. The word

---

[8] The *Holy Bible:* Ps 4:1; Romans 3:22.
[9] The *Holy Bible*: Genesis 3:5.
[10] The *Holy Bible*: Romans 12:3
[11] The *Holy Bible*: Isaiah 64:6

'left' comes from the Old English word lyft, which literally meant 'weak, foolish'"[12]. [Also notice that the root of "sinister" is "sin" and sin is uniquely and literally defined as an offense *Against GOD!*]

Here is the 1828 Webster's Dictionary definition of *sinister* as originally defined:

1. *Left*; on the left hand, or the side of the left hand; opposed to dexter or right; as the *sinister* cheek; or the *sinister* side of an escutcheon.
2. *Evil*; *bad*; *corrupt*; *perverse*; *dishonest*; as *sinister* means; *sinister* purpose. He scorns to undermine another's interest by any *sinister* or inferior arts.
3. Unlucky; inauspicious.[13]

Here is the current Webster's Dictionary of *sinister* which has gone almost totally secular, and has undergone several revisions to purge Webster's Dictionary from any Christian influence:

1 archaic : unfavorable, unlucky
2 archaic : fraudulent
3 : singularly evil or productive of evil
4 a : of, relating to, or situated to the *left* or on *the left side* of something; especially : being or relating to the side of a heraldic shield at the left of the person bearing it
b : of *ill omen* by reason of being on the *left*[14]

The editors of the bastardized modern version of Webster's first tell you that the word *sinister* is archaic or "of, relating to, or characteristic of an earlier or more primitive time"[15]. In other words, the use of the word sinister as related to *evil* was only used by primitive peoples and we modern people no longer believe that. Secondly, notice that the first two definitions of sinister in the modern Webster's dismiss the

---

[12] Dictionary.com; October 21, 2014
[13] http://webstersdictionary1828.com/Dictionary/Sinister June 3, 2018 (emphasis added)
[14] https://www.merriam-webster.com/dictionary/sinister (emphasis added)
[15] https://www.merriam-webster.com/dictionary/archaic

word altogether as a functioning word. Thirdly, the evil definition is pushed down to number 3. The Left always redefines evil, or as we shall see, *Renames* it in their *Rename-Game*!

The "name-game" or more accurately the "*Re-Name-Game*"[16] of the Left is always employed by the Left when the public recognizes the true Evil nature and goals of the Left under its historically current self-identifying label:

> "To avoid the negative and superstitious associations of the left side, many languages used euphemisms for it. In Old English the left side was called winestra, which meant 'friendlier'"[17].

When the Left's game is discovered, they simply change their identification from "Left" to "friendlier". What exactly is "friendlier"? Friendlier than what? We know what a friend is. We know what a friendly person acts like. But again, what exactly is "friendlier"? It is important to note that the Left's *Re-Name-Game* always involves a vague or indefinite word like "change" or "hope" or "friendlier". No one can ever really define a Leftist's beliefs or vision using the Left's meaningless self-labeling. This of course is the unGODly doxology of the Left's deceitful tactics as preached by Saul Alinsky and his radical acolytes who taught: "The issue is never the issue. The issue is always the [Leftist] revolution[18]". The Left's "revolution" *is* revolution *Against GOD!*

The term "Left" began to be widely used as a *political* and *religious* ideology during the French Revolution of the 1790's. It was picked up particularly by the Jacobins whose intent was to establish a purely *democratic*[19] government in France. Eventually, and for a time, the Jacobins came to power by the force-of-arms and established their

---

[16] See the chapters: *The Progressive Face of The Left* and *Bait and Switch: The Re-Name-Game*.
[17] Dictionary.com; October 21, 2014
[18] More on this in the chapter *America's War/The War Against America's Judeo-Christian Foundations*.
[19] The evils of a democracy as the Left defines it will be further discussed below.

"pure democracy", but as all democracies go they are short-lived[20], horrifyingly destructive[21], and require eliminating the opposition in an attempt to recreate a society in the image of the Leftist Utopian ideal. The hallmarks of the Jacobin government were the establishment of a new Religion, the *Cult of Reason*, literally worshipping the ancient Pagan goddess *Reason*, in specific rejection of the Christian GOD JEHOVA; and secondly the mass execution of tens-of-thousands of Christians in Paris and much of France. This is when and how the guillotine was institutionalized and dubbed the *National Razor* of France with its widespread use[22]. This period of time of the Left is known in our history books as the *Reign of Terror*! This was the path the Left used in France in the 1790's and the same path that the Left in America is also currently lunging down today. The Left is in the final stages of implementing its attempt at creating a *Christian-free* Leftist Utopia in America today.

President Donald Trump may have temporarily obstructed the Left's plans for America, but make no mistake the Left is still working behind the scenes in Congress, the judiciary, and the Deep State waiting like a coiled serpent ready to strike at its earliest opportunity. Evil never sleeps and never gives up. The Devil may hide himself well, but the Devil's and his minions' tactics and goals of *Terror* and death have never changed since the beginning of time.

The familiar terms "reach across the aisle" and "the left side of the aisle" all derive from the French Revolutionary political system of separating the Left from the Right by a literal isle. Today even the US Congress is seated according to party affiliation mirroring the Left/Right system established in the French Parliament which inevitably led to *The Reign of Terror* of the French Revolution. Today in the United States Congress, the Republicans sit on the Right and the Democrats on the Left! There is no coincidence there.

---

[20] Sept. 5, 1793, to July 27, 1794 (9 Thermidor, year II).

[21] See later discussion of a Republic vs. a democracy.

[22] It is no coincidence that the *Bible* alludes in Revelation 20:4 to the mass execution by guillotine of millions of Christians by the Antichrist who is possessed by Satan. Satan is merely conducting dress rehearsals in preparation for the final showdown against GOD and His people.

The age-old question "is man inherently good or inherently evil?" is easily answered by real-world observation. All that we have to do is watch the daily news which is packed beginning to end with stories of violence and tragedies that testify to the inherent sinful and therefore evil nature of man. If man where in fact inherently good, the world would be filled with goodness, as would be reflected in the daily news. Those Leftist ideologues who preach the inherent goodness of man have nothing but a Utopian viewpoint of "hope and change", a hope and change that is not supported in *all* of history by any real-world experience. It is insightful to understand that the word *utopia* actually means... *nowhere*[23]!

It is also interesting to note that the opposing forces *Against GOD* have often self-identified themselves as *Leftists*. The American Left proudly picked up the Leftist label. The Obamas, the Clintons, Pelosi, Schumer, Schultz, Warren, Sanders, Schiff, Kaine, *ad nauseam*... all proudly proclaim themselves to be "Leftists". The Left leadership inherently understands the term "Left", but the ignorant masses who blindly follow the Evil of the Left are merely useful idiots and means to the Left's elite's evil ends. These are the *Kookaphants* of the Left today!

At this point we need to recognize the Left's usurpation of the term "liberal" using their *Re-Name-Game* and claiming the term as their own. "Classic Liberalism" is, and always has been, a manifestation of the Right and Conservative school. Shocked? Well... read on. The Left shrewdly *Re-Named* itself "Liberal" to use chameleon-like tactics to confuse the masses, steal the definition from the Right in order to deceive, and usurp power. The Left must continually *Re-Name* itself and steal the terms from the Right to keep the masses from fully comprehending the Left's true nature of *Evil*. The Right has always been for the individual's freedoms and opposed to the empowering of the State over the individual. Classic Liberalism stood against the power of kings and all totalitarian régimes. The Left has *always* been in favor of kings, monarchs, tyrants, and dictators. The Right, as

---

[23] Webster's Dictionary Online; www.merriam-webster.com/dictionary/utopia; *Utopia* literally means *no place* or *nowhere*.

Classic Liberals, opposed the Leftist dictatorial usurpation of the Jacobins in the French Revolution, Communist China, Soviet Russia, Fascist Germany and Italy, Imperialistic Japan, and myriad other Leftist manifestations. It is the Right alone who stands against these same dictatorial designs of the Left in America today. The Left, who is always for State empowerment and dictatorial powers, started calling themselves "liberals" in their propagandistic effort to deceive the people into believing that the Left is "the Party of the people". Like their Communist masters before them, the Left has bastardized the term "Liberal" for their own *Evil* ends.

Even the modern Leftist Hillary Rodham-Clinton acknowledges the distinction between the Classic Liberalism of the Conservative school verses the modern Leftist Liberalism:

> "You know… Liberal… is a word that originally meant that you were for freedom … that you were willing to stand against big power and on behalf of the individual. Unfortunately, in the last 30, 40 years, it has been turned up on its head, and it's been made to seem as though it is a word that describes big government, totally contrary to what its meaning was in the 19th and early 20th century…".[24]

The definition of "Classic Liberal" is the foundation of the Right and the Conservative movement. Throughout this book, I will emphasize the distinctions in the use of "Classic Liberalism" and "Leftist Liberalism". Where the term "Liberal", or one of its variants are used, it pertains to "Leftist Liberalism" unless a note, usually in brackets [Classic Liberalism], is used to indicate otherwise.

It should also be recognized early on that *politics is the enforcement-wing of the Left*, and as such will by necessity play a prominent role in this discussion. Politics is the primary engagement point at which the Right *must* confront Evil in the Battle for America! Politics is the natural realm where the *Left's War of Evil Against GOD* is fought. To *not* fight the political War is to cede victory to Evil. Evil abhors a

---

[24] CNN/YouTube sponsored Democrat presidential debate; July 23rd, 2007.

vacuum. As Edmund Burke so astutely observed: *All that is necessary for evil to triumph is that good men do nothing*! Inaction against Evil is a sin *Against GOD*[25]. This is the crux of Jesus' admonition "He that is not with me is against me"[26]. To not act to advance GOOD is in fact to give aid to the advance of Evil! *Only* GOOD stops and turns back Evil. To not act *politically* in support of GOOD is to aid the advance of Evil. The Left's agenda can only be implemented through *politics*. Is it any wonder that Left constantly demands that the two subjects that must never be discussed are religion and *politics*? As will be clearly demonstrated, religion and politics are inseparably linked. The Left understands this and the Right has been blind to that fact. Politics, including political Leftist-activist judges, political elected office, political activism, political appointments, the Deep State, and many other areas of Leftist political activism, is the modern safe-house of the Left and Evil in America today.

The "separation of Church and State" has been the clarion call of the Left and the anvil upon which the Left has hammered out the drumbeat of *The Left's War Against GOD* and forged the foundation for its now emerging Anti-GOD caliphate in America. It will become clear through the discourse to follow that the Left's demand for "the separation of Church and State" is virtually exclusive to the disenfranchisement of the influence of the Christian Religion from American politics. The Christian Religion is the *only* religion that has a unique relationship at the core of who we are as Americans. What will become equally apparent is that the Left is not eliminating religious influence from American society and government, but replacing America's Christian religious foundations with the Left's own Evil Religion[27].

As was previously mentioned, the Left has preached incessantly that the two issues never to be discussed in public are "religion and politics". This is no coincidence nor a random association. Today the Left has shifted from a voluntary compliance to its Politically Correct

---

[25] The *Holy Bible*; James 4:17.
[26] The *Holy Bible*; Matthew 12:30.
[27] See chapter: *The Left is a RELIGION!*

(P.C.) mandates, to an iron-fisted enforcement to compliance to Leftist mandates in the pattern of the *Reign of Terror* of the Leftist Jacobins' Revolutionary France! Today a non-compliant person to the Left's P.C. mandates can lose their job, business, family, and even be jailed for violating the Left's *religious* P.C. edicts! The Left's programs are always voluntary until they have gained enough power to demand that they are no longer voluntary, but compulsory and enforced by the absolute power of the State.

By definition "religion", *without historical exception*, is the common, basic-held beliefs of *every* society in history, as accepted and promoted by the State; and "politics" is the enforcement-wing of *every* State's religion. It is "religion and politics" which are the two most important and inextricable questions which affect every human being on earth and to which every human being has a moral obligation to get the answer right![28] Ultimately we will all answer to GOD for our conclusions and subsequent choices to these two vital questions. What the Left does not want you to know is that "religion and politics" are fundamentally linked and absolutely inseparable. It is just a matter of choice between GOD and the Left's Anti-GOD Religion which historically has *always* determined mankind's contemporary politics.

Until recently America's religion has always been the Christian Religion of GOD and the *Bible*. America's accelerated shift to the Religion of the Left and of Evil is at its core responsible for the downward spiral of America's economics, culture, and families. *Evil always destroys*!

Starting diligently in the 1960's the Left demanded that the Right to stay out of the bedroom, but the Left brought the bedroom out into the public by sanctioning sexual perversion, and politicized it! To the Left *everything* is politics: sex, gender, religion, *Bibles*, speech (which is no longer free), motives (hate crimes assume motives not just actions), race (some protected for political advantage), what you eat (trans-fat), what you drink (criminalizing 32 oz. Sodas and straws), wearing a seatbelt, putting your child in a car seat, health insurance, even

---

[28] See chapter: *Ignorance Is No Excuse For The Law*

thinking! Yes, you can be arrested for *thinking* about committing a crime and for even *disagreeing* with the Left's doctrines. Nothing is sacred in the traditional Christian sense in a Leftist Utopian America. Yet in an Orwellian self-contradiction of the Left's new Religion, everything is sacred and therefore needs to be controlled by the State! Every man, woman, and child belongs to the State and therefore must be controlled by the State. Of course we need to be controlled by the State "for our own good", which is another Orwellian *Lie* of the Left as it re-defines the "greater good"[29]. If this sounds eerily familiar, it should as it comes directly from the pens of Engels and Marx, but with a modern Leftist poisonous mix of "we care".

Don't be fooled by the Left's rhetoric concerning the Left and Right of "we all have the same good goals at heart, just different methods of reaching those goals". Nothing could be further from the truth! Jesus said it best, "the thief cometh not but to steal, and to kill, and to destroy"[30], again as we will see, this the true hidden agenda of the Left[31]. The Left cannot afford to be exposed for its true *Evil* nature and intent in opposing GOD, so the Left creates rhetoric that is nothing more than cleverly camouflaged *Lies*. *Lies* are the common language of the Left[32]!

Jesus, who is GOD in the flesh[33], warned all of mankind that there is *NO* gray area[34], "He that is not with me is against me"[35]. Notice there is no "middle" or "moderate"[36] ground, no "gray areas" in GOD's eyes. GOD says that there are only two categories: those "with" GOD, and

---

[29] See the more thorough discussion of the Left's "greater good" in the chapter: *The Left Is a RELIGION!*.

[30] The *Holy Bible*: John 10:10

[31] See the following discussion especially Saul Alinsky and his *Rules For Radicals*.

[32] See the Chapter: *Lies, Lies, Lies!*

[33] Incarnate means that GOD in the Person of Jesus Christ took human form in order to live on earth in the flesh and live a perfect, sinless life in order to be the Perfect Sacrifice for all human sin. Thus paving the way for sinful man to enter into Heaven for those people who accept Jesus as their GOD and Savior.

[34] The subject of "gray areas" will be addressed more fully in the later chapter *Shades of Gray*.

[35] The *Holy Bible:* Matthew 12:30

[36] See broader discussion in the chapter *Fighting To WIN!: How Do We Fight The War? The Right's RULES FOR ANTI-RADICALS! A Call To ACTION!* and the subcategories: *Compromise Kills!* and *Moderates*.

those "against" GOD! The Left by Jesus' definition then, are those who are "*Against*" GOD[37]. Satan would have us believe that truth is relative, that everything is in a "gray area" to be decided by the individual. To further emphasize this, Jesus continues, "…and he that gathereth not with me scattereth abroad". To "scatter" is to divide and destroy, which as we will see, is the statecraft of the Left. The true *underlying* battle is not, *per se*, a political or philosophical ideology, but the Epic War of *Evil Against GOD*!

The Left has force-fed the concept that "all truth is relative" and "situational ethics" as a mechanism to *redefine* "truth" to the Left's religious and political advantage! If there is no right or wrong by GOD's definition, then the Left is free to redefine what is in their best interest "good and acceptable". The Left has forced this into its public schools using public schools and public and private universities as their indoctrination camps. By its very definition, either truth is absolute and unchangeable, or it's *not* truth! If it's not truth it is a *Lie* of the Left and Evil!

It is no coincidence that the Left envisions Christianity as the Left's *only* true enemy. For instance, children are regularly punished and even suspended for bringing a Christian *Bible* to a Leftist dominated public school. Have you ever heard of a child being disciplined for bringing a Satanic "bible", Ouija board, a Wicca Witchcraft "bible", a Muslim Koran, a Hindu Bhagavad Gita, or Buddhist Zen "scriptures" to school? The answer is of course… *never* as these religions are all Leftist and totally and often violently oppose GOD!!

Yet it is commonplace today for Christians to be ritualistically targeted by the Left! This even while our children are being preached to by the Left that the children are literally "gods" and that there are no absolute criteria by which to judge right or wrong. As a "god" our children are told that they are free to determine each for themselves what is "right" and what is "wrong". Even Abraham Maslow, the Left's grandfather of schoolchildren's self-esteem and "godhood",

---

[37] You do not necessarily have to be an activist of the Left to be "against" GOD, you simply have to be not "with" GOD.

discovered that his theory of "self-actualization", or full attainment of one's own "godhood", only leads to chaos and self-destruction as demonstrated on his test subjects in the classroom. When Maslow tried to implement his theory in an actual classroom setting, all sense of order abruptly vanished as the children realized that, if they were in fact "gods", then there was no "right" or "wrong" by which they could be held accountable. The children acted accordingly. Chaos inevitably ensued as each child chose his own set of self-created and self-centered "morals". Maslow was forced to abandon his experiment and conclude that self-actualization was neither a realistic nor a workable model. In the late 1960's Maslow even worried over the fact that his speculations were being too eagerly accepted by the Left as literally "*gospel*" rather than as a discredited sociological theory[38].

However the Left continues today to foist Maslow's principles upon our children. Why? Because it is the goal of the Left to create chaos and destruction by creating a vacuum of moral standards into which the Left can appear as the "savior" and implement its own Evil standards and "rescue" society. (notice the definite religious overtones) Rescue society from the very situation which *the Left itself has created* specifically for this Evil ends (See later discussion of Rahm Emanuel and *"You never want a serious crisis to go to waste"*). We see this tactic being used by the Left today in virtually every area of American society. For example, the Left's answer to teen pregnancy in the 1960's was sex education in schools, which led to more sexual promiscuity and more teen pregnancy[39]. The Left's "answer" to this new rise in teen pregnancy was... more sex education, which of course led to higher teen pregnancy! They have added to this cycle: birth control pills, then condoms handed out in our schools, then abortion coaching couched as "advice", then promoting the homosexual agenda disguised as "counseling" and more recently as "anti-bullying"[40] campaigns (The list of course is much longer, but these

---

[38] Maslow, Abraham H.; *Critique of Self-Actualization Theory*; edited by Edward Hoffman; The Journal of Humanistic Education and Development; Volume 29, Issue 3; pgs. 103-108, March 1991.
[39] For further discussion see the chapter: *The Progressive Face of The Left*.
[40] See the full discussion in the chapter: *Tolerance*.

examples are sufficient to make the point). The cycle of "fixing" evil with more evil is a doxology of the *Religion of the Left*!

Maslow himself admitted that his beliefs that he peddled were in fact a "religion" which Maslow identified as a "common faith"[41] saying, "...all religions are the same in their essence and have always been the same"[42]. This is a direct contradiction of the Christian Faith in which Jesus clearly says "I am the [*only*] way"[43] and that "no man cometh unto the Father, but by me". Maslow believed in a "Taoistic" religious transcendence based on the Hindu religious system which he believed could be achieved by a psychotherapy short-cut using LSD[44]. (Yes you read that correctly! LSD!) According to Maslow, those people not properly prepared for this "religious transcendence", the highest point of "self-actualization" and godhood of which Maslow preached, risked that "a peak experience could... lead to *insanity*[45]"! Our public schools are controlled by the priests and priestesses of the Left's totalitarian régime and have been turned into temples of Leftist ideology[46]. This is no Leftist accident, nor a modern Leftist phenomenon as David Horowitz[47] points out:

> "One kind of hell or another is what radicalism has in fact achieved since the beginning of the modern age when it conducted the first modern genocide during the French Revolution. The Jacobins who led the revolution changed the name of the cathedral of Notre Dame to the '*Temple of Reason*' and then, in the name of Reason, proceeded to slaughter every [Christian] man, woman and child in the

---

[41] Maslow: *Religions, Values, and Peak Experiences*; pg. 39.

[42] Maslow: *Religions, Values, and Peak Experiences*; pg. 20.

[43] The *Holy Bible*: John 14:6

[44] Wisniewski, Theodore; Experimenting with Power: *Liberal Psychologists and the Challenge of Social Reform: 1945-1975*; 2008; pgs. 136-137.

[45] Wisniewski, Theodore; Experimenting with Power: *Liberal Psychologists and the Challenge of Social Reform: 1945-1975*; 2008; pg. 137. See the broader discussion of insanity in the chapter *The Left Is a RELIGION!*.

[46] This effort to subvert the schools and thereby our children, was hallmarked by Dewey an icon of the Left.

[47] I quote from David Horowitz, but depart significantly from many of his ultimate conclusions, specifically my primary conclusion that this is the Epic War of Evil Against GOD. Horowitz fails to see the ultimate motivation and power of Evil that stands behind the Left.

Vendee region to purge religious "superstition" from the planet. The Jacobin attempt to liquidate [Christians] and their faith was the precursor of Lenin's destruction of 100,000 churches in the Soviet Union to purge Russia of reactionary ideas. The *'Temple of Reason'* was replicated by the Bolsheviks' creation of a "People's Church" whose mission was to usher in the "worker's paradise". This mission led to the murder not of 40,000 as in the Vendee [Jacobin France], but 40 *million* before its merciful collapse - with progressives[48] cheering its progress and mourning its demise. The radical fantasy of an earthly redemption takes many forms, with similar results"[49]. (emphasis and brackets added)

At the core of the Left's religious zeal, many Leftists believe themselves to be building a Utopian *paradise* on earth. The same goals and tactics as the Jacobins used in their *Reign of Terror*. As will be restated and more fully expanded upon in a later chapter:

"It is the Left's same false comparison between America and an imagined Leftist utopian state that deceptively manages to make America appear to be unfair, racist, bigoted, etc. David Horowitz comments, 'If the radicals' utopia were actually possible, it would be criminal *not* to deceive, lie, and murder to advance the radical cause which is, in effect, a redemption of mankind. If it were possible to provide every man, woman and child on the planet with food, shelter and clothing as a right, if it were possible to end bigotry and human conflict, what sacrifice would not be worth it?'"[50].

David Goldman makes an interesting observation along these lines in reviewing a book which analyzes Dostoevsky's literary work *The Brothers Karamazov* in concluding:

---

[48] More on Leftists as "Progressives" in the chapter *The Progressive Face of The Left*.
[49] Horowitz, David; *Commentary on Rule For Radicals*; pg. 20.
[50] See chapter *America's War/The War Against America's Judeo-Christian Foundations*

"And if we try to force fallible humans to live in an earthly paradise, ultimately we shall have to kill them all for their failings"[51].

This is inevitably what happens with all historical manifestations of the Left. They kill everyone who does not, or cannot, comply to their imagined perfect Utopia standard. This accounts for the *hundreds of millions* of deaths in the Twentieth Century inflicted by *every* Leftist régime that has come to power! We will return to this subject repeatedly throughout this discussion.

The Right, as expressed through Conservativism, demands the accountability of the government to the people, whereas Leftism demands the accountability of the people to the government. William Blackstone, author of the most comprehensive law reference books *Blackstone's Commentaries*, states the underlying truth of governments thirst for power, "power, when undefined, soon becomes unlimited"[52]. The law of the Leftists is that there are no limits. The Right always wants less for the government and the Left always demands more! With Leftism, subjection of the people and totalitarianism is inevitable!

The Left can and does rationalize every evil deed done in its cause of creating a "Utopian Paradise" on earth. The Left's various factions may disagree on exactly how this Utopia is to look, but the Left is in full harmony with *using any and all means*[53] at their disposal to accomplish such a self-aggrandized "laudable" goal.

The Left preaches diametrically opposed contradictions with a straight face and expects them to be happily and unquestioningly accepted and followed. One such irreconcilable contradiction is the "inclusion of exclusivistic groups" into the Left's tent of "inclusivism". Many of the

---

[51] David Goldman; Book Review of Angels and Inquisitors: *A Point in Time* by David Horowitz; Asia Times Online; Dec 22, 2011
[52] Blackstone, Sir William, St. George Tucker, Edward Christian; *Blackstone's Commentaries: With Notes of Reference, to the Constitution and Laws, of the Federal Government of the United States, and of the Commonwealth of Virginia*; 1803; pg. 154.
[53] Remember Alinsky's directives to Leftist rebel "In **war**, the end justifies almost *any means*...".

Left's core groups illustrate this point quite succinctly. Black Liberation Theology groups are exclusive to blacks. *La Raza*, "The Race", is exclusive to the Hispanic race, primarily the Mexican race[54]. The Left welcomes all exclusive groups into its fold of ***privileged inclusivism***[55], except of course the group called Christians! Christians just do not fit in the Left's all-inclusive tent. Have you ever stopped to ask yourself... Why? The answer is because the ***inclusive*** tent of the Left is only inclusive of *Evil*! If your "group" opposes anything in the *Bible* you are welcomed with open arms into the not-so-all-inclusive, "inclusive" tent of the Left. The more they oppose GOD, the higher their clout and influence is touted by the Left and your leadership is sought! This was highlighted in the 2012 Democrat Convention as Muslims, Feminists, atheists, black Leftists, abortionists, and every other group in the Democrat Party voted to remove any mention of the Christian GOD of the *Bible* from its Party platform!

The Left's ideal of ***Privileged Inclusivism*** is, not coincidently, a *religious* term and intentionally deceiving. While sounding very "inclusive" Privileged Inclusivism is in fact a cleverly crafted ambiguity of the Left's P.C. "tolerance" police . Privileged Inclusivism mirrors the Left's political program of "tolerance", which the Left will tell you is "inclusive of all groups" in their so-called big tent, except this "***excludes all groups that exclude***". This of course is absurd and meaningless P.C. double-speak[56]. Because this places the P.C. Police in the awkward position of themselves ***excluding*** and violating their own mandate. They create a clever name to mask their "self-righteous", Anti-GOD, and hypocritical position by naming it "**Privileged**". After all who does not want to be "*privileged*" and "*inclusive*"? Right? Again to any reasonable person the P.C. catch-

---

[54] Note that neither Hispanics nor Mexicans are actually a "race", but are dubbed so by the Left for political reasons. Hispanics is a designation of those who natively speak the Spanish language who include primarily the white or Caucasian race, but also include all other races as well.

[55] Johnson and Gleason; *Reforming or Conforming? Post Conservative Evangelicals and the Emerging Church*; pg. 200

[56] Doublespeak, or double-speak, is the verbalization of what George Orwell dubbed DOUBLETHINK which is defined by Webster's as: language used to deceive usually through concealment or misrepresentation of truth. Doublespeak is more thoroughly discussed in the chapter: *Lies, Lies, Lies!*.

phrases are empty, meaningless, and absurd, but they effectively serve the Left's designed purpose in bludgeoning non-conformists, the Right and primarily Christians, into conformity and the acceptance of Evil! The Left's "tolerance" only goes one way![57]

This contrivance of **Privileged Inclusivism** masquerading as "tolerance" is being promoted by Brian McLaren a spokesman for the Leftist and Anti-GOD religious organization calling themselves the *Emergent Church Movement*. McLaren says, "To be truly inclusive, the Kingdom must exclude exclusive people"[58]. Not only does McLaren not identify his "Kingdom" as the Kingdom of GOD, but this is obviously double-speak and a self-contradicting, and thereby a logically self-defeating statement designed to sound "inclusive" but by their very admission "*excludes*" anyone who does not agree with them! Sound confusing? That's OK it's designed by the Left to be confusing! Just as it is impossible to be right and left at the same time, it is impossible to be *inclusive* and *exclusive* at the same time! By "*exclusive* people" the thinly veiled threat applies exclusively to those of the true Christian Faith, who by GOD's definition, must be exclusive to GOD as the One and only true GOD[59]. This in direct opposition to the Left which calls its devil gods by myriad of inclusive names. Likewise, the Christian Church cannot be exclusive and inclusive simultaneously. Being exclusive literally *defines* the Christian Church. This is of course the true rub of Evil's opposition, which has deeply infiltrated many within the Christian "community" today demanding the Christian Church be inclusive and tolerant of the Left and Evil! If a Christian Church tries to be "inclusive" of Evil it is no longer a Christin Church!

It is also interesting to note that McLaren and his followers embrace exclusivistic religions such as Islam. How much more "exclusive" can a "people" be than those who kill all other religious people who refuse to convert to Islam?! Obviously the *Emergent Church Movement* is an attack on true Christianity by Evil from within by those *claiming* to

---

[57] See chapter: *Tolerance*
[58] Johnson and Gleason; *Reforming or Conforming? Post Conservative Evangelicals and the Emerging Church*; pg. 200; Quoting Brian D. McLaren; Secret Message of Jesus; pg. 168
[59] i.e. The *Holy Bible:* Isaiah 45:5, 21; Hosea 13:4

be Christians. Unfortunately, many in the Church today are afraid to call the religious Left… *Evil*. They fear the backlash from outside the Church by the world and from within the Church by weak, backslidden, and many who are counterfeit Christians. GOD is not just the GOD of love, but also the GOD of truth, judgement, rebuke, justice, correction, chastisement, excommunication, and damnation! These are the Inconvenient Truths of which the Left would have us either ignorant of, or afraid to speak.

Not coincidently, these modern tactics of the Left were the same Fascist[60] tactics used by Hitler in Nazi Germany against the Jews and Christians alike. What the Left has carefully hidden in its revisionist history is that it was not just the Jews which Hitler murdered, but even more so… the Christians! The Nazis under Hitler murdered 5 million Jews, but over 7 million Christians![61]

Christianity, as the earthly expression of GOD, is the Left's primary target of its angst *Against GOD*. Evil cannot touch GOD directly, but Evil can reach GOD's heart through His people!

It will not be difficult for the Left to find willing accomplices in the pews of Christianity to aid their Evil in attacking the foundations of truth in this book. The Church has been infiltrated at every level by those willing to compromise and destroy the institutions of the Church. Evil and the Left place a special focus on the Christian *Bible*, the Holy Word of GOD, which is the written manifestation and representation of Jesus Christ Himself.[62] Many who call themselves "Christian" today have no real association with GOD, or GOD's Church. Neither calling oneself a Christian, nor church membership, or even being an ordained minister qualifies one as a Christian. The only qualification according to GOD in His Word is accepting Jesus Christ as one's personal GOD and Savior, by the subsequent

---

[60] The subject of the Left's blood-tie with Fascism is further discussed in the chapter: *Fascism and the Left in America: Kindred Spirits and Familiar Bedfellows.*
[61] See a deeper discussion in the following chapter: *Fascism and the Left in America: Kindred Spirits and Familiar Bedfellows.*
[62] See Jesus' accounting of this in the *Holy Bible* Luke 24:27. Also Jesus is called "the Word" in John 1:1, 14 which is the Greek *Logos* or the Written Word of the *Holy Bible*.

indwelling of the Holy Spirit, and by the will of the Father. Sell-outs, imposters, and apostates are commonplace today among those claiming the title of "Christian".

Given the current pre-programmed Leftist P.C. climate, some of the language in this book may be considered a bit "extreme", or so the Left would have us believe, but this book is an honest and truthful assessment that defies the same P.C. shackles as demanded by the Left. Defiance of the Left, is in and of itself, enough to have the Left spitting burning sulphur and howling at the moon. The Left by definition is the most viral form of extremism and the Left cannot be identified without discussing the Left in its own extreme terms.

The author anticipates the anger and attack which will certainly follow from the publication of this unmasking of the Evil behind the Left's hidden agenda. The Left's reaction to exposure to the truth is predictable: ridicule, anger, righteous indignation, *Lies*, scoffing, derision, attack, destroy, and diversion. These are all tell-tale signs that the Left's collective nerve has been effectively tapped and their demon masters enraged. Shakespeare identified this reactionary nerve when he commented in Hamlet through the lips of Queen Gertrude "methinks...the lady doth protest too much". The guilty in general, and Evil in particular, always "protest too much" in attempting to deflect the guilt of their deceptions. In psychology it is called "transference". Transference is shifting the blame from oneself onto another in order to avoid having to answer to the truth and attempting to avoid the appearance of guilt.

The Left screams not because these things are not true, but precisely because they *are* true! You can be sure that the collective nerve of the Left has been struck by the deafening shriek of the Left to truth being spoken against them, which is meant to drown out the voices of Truth and strike fear into the hearts of the Truth-bearers. This is a favorite tactic of Leftists in debates and political discussions where the Leftist over-talks or over-shouts his opponent, diverts to another subject, or resorts to childish temper tantrums and meaningless name-calling. Almost all of us know people who control those around them with fits of anger and rage. "Better not to disturb the beast and avoid the conflict", we rationalize to ourselves. This is the tactic of the Left in subduing America. Again as Edmund Burke so astutely observed: **All that is necessary for evil to triumph is that good men do nothing!** ... and I would append, good men who are made too afraid to take a stand against Evil!

Evil's aversion to public exposure can be best epitomized by the line of the French poet Charles Baudelaire "the finest trick of the devil is to persuade you that he does not exist". The Left has embodied this deceit by parading as "change" agents for "good", while cloaking their true intentions to promote Evil with *Lies*, deceptions, and treacheries. The "change" they offer and the "change" they deliver bear no resemblance one to the other as they employ a sleight of hand, *Bait-and-Switch* game in implementing their Evil agenda[63].

Anyone who chooses to join in the Battle against Evil can be sure to encounter the collective wrath of Evil whether it be through Leftist politicians, the Deep State, Anti-GOD theologians, the Leftist controlled media machine, academia, the mindless Hollywood elite, and even "Christian" imposters! Of course the only alternative to enjoining the War is to wait for the Left to amass enough power and show up at your door and drag you and your family into the street for reeducation and eventually the inevitable... extermination! (Of course the Left's creative history as word masters will call it something like "compassionate euthanasia".) Until the Left gains complete control such as they enjoyed in Nazi Germany, these Leftist individuals and organizations will present themselves as concerned individuals and "good" citizens representing the "collective good" which the Left also likes to euphemize as the "greater good", but the Left are in fact the ambassadors of *Evil*. Ronald Reagan articulated this point most profoundly when he commented, "The nine most terrifying words in the English language are, 'I'm from the government and I'm here to help'"[64]!

---

[63] See especially the following chapter: *Bait and Switch: The Re-Name-Game.*
[64] President Ronald Reagan's News Conference, August 12, 1986.

Have you ever stopped to ask yourself: How could the Left only see oppression today in America, the same America which enjoys the greatest freedoms of any Country in the history of the world? The answer is that Freedom is the arch-enemy of the Leftist Religion! The Left's world and worldview are upside down. We are constantly warned by the change-agents of the Left that it is Christianity that wants to turn the world upside down, when in fact the world is already upside down as the tragic result of the Fall of man into the sin of self-righteousness. GOD is simply wanting to restore the fallen and perverse condition of man back *right*-side-up as when GOD first created man. The Left is guilty of calling Evil as good and GOOD as evil[65].

In a world without GOD, any Leftist fantasy seems possible: global warming could wipe out the human race; the human race can be reprogrammed to achieve a Utopian Paradise on earth; and a multitude of other Leftist *Lies*. Global Warming/Climate Change and its purported apocalyptic predictions by the Left is itself a degradation to a Pagan religious worldview. It is *literally* a pronouncement by the Left that GOD does not exist. These Leftist fantasies are only conceivable if there is no GOD. A GOD Who is all-knowing and can see the future would make allowances for every human eventuality even before it happens and would create a built-in mechanism of Creation which prevents any man-caused global cataclysmic event. Only the Christian GOD makes these claims and therefore must be "destroyed", or at least marginalized, as an obstacle to the Leftist agenda of Evil. Leftist *Lies* meant to control the lives of all humans cannot be believed in the context of an all-knowing, all-seeing, GOD.

Let me restate that. The very idea that manmade "climate change" can cause any man-caused global cataclysmic event is a spitting in the face of GOD! If GOD is GOD, then GOD would see all future events and have prepared His Creation to be resilient to all of the tinkering of mortal men. GOD as GOD would have created a planet capable of avoiding any apocalyptic events. The Left-Wing wackos have cavalierly

---

[65] The *Holy Bible*: Isaiah 5:20

dismissed GOD as a factor in human events. ***Without GOD every Leftist fantasy <u>seems</u> possible!***

Until the Right learns to recognize the Battle for what is: *The War of Evil Against GOD*, the Right will remain in a state of delusion (most of which is self-inflicted) and continually find themselves in a position of defeat. GOD has promised us as His representatives of the Right, ultimate victory in this War, but we can still lose the Battle for America. Victory in America requires diligence and a reawakening of the Right!

Evil never sleeps and never gives up. The Left are emissaries of Evil and fight a no-holds-barred *War Against GOD* and His people! Sadly the Right for the most part has reduced their tactics to a laughable level of conciliation, compromise[66], and reasoned debate. (Newsflash: You cannot reason with the evil insane![67]) "In time liberalism remakes conservatism in its own image by forcing it to give up everything distinctive for the sake of consensus".[68] The Left is eagerly willing to accommodate those terms which the Left knows will make the Right... *dead* right! Somehow the Right feels that if they can just win a "reasoned" debate that that will win the battle. (Newsflash: You cannot reason with the unreasonable!) Reasoning assumes that both parties are using truth by which to argue their side. However, Lucifer set the stage in the beginning salvo of *The Left's War Against GOD* in the Garden of Eden laying the foundation for the Left's tactics of "rationalization" to usurp reasoning with Eve the mother of all mankind. Lucifer used *Lies* couched as truth to persuade Eve to eat of the Forbidden Fruit. (Newsflash: You cannot reason with a Liar!)

Actually, Eve was not so much deceived as Lucifer simply told Eve what she wanted to hear. A tactic of Evil. Eve wanted to feel justified to sin, which is the definition of rationalization. Eve was convinced

---

[66] See broader discussion in the chapter *Fighting To WIN!: How Do We Fight The War? The Right's RULES FOR ANTI-RADICALS! A Call To ACTION!* and the subcategories: *Compromise Kills!* and *Moderates:*.
[67] See the broader discussion of insanity in the chapter *The Left Is a RELIGION!*.
[68] Kalb, James; Modern Age Quarterly; *The Tyranny of Liberalism: The Iron Heel of Freedom*; Summer 2000.

because Eve wanted to be convinced. This is what the Left has continued to do throughout all of history. Evil uses rationalizing to justify sin *Against GOD*. The Left re-creates language in which it redefines Evil as good. Today we call this P.C., or Politically Correct, speech. At the core of Politically Correct speech is the acceptance and *normalizing of sin* Against GOD. Once sin is accepted as normal, all restraint of the Evil is removed. ***Selling permission to sin is the merchandise of the Left!***

If you do not identify and acknowledge the Enemy, you cannot defeat the Enemy. The Enemy does not want to be recognized for its true nature of Evil. Evil would rather that the world goes on believing that there is no such thing as Evil. The Devil wants us to believe that he does not exist. A non-existent Enemy is not a threat. All we have to do, however, is look around us to see that Evil really does exist and Evil is obsessed with destroying everything and everyone. The Left has sold its soul to Evil for thirty pieces of silver. That has never worked out well in history for those who have tried!

It is time for the Right to wake up from its malaise of misguided, lazy, and deadly delusions! The very hearts and souls of America and our children depend upon it! We as the Right must learn to recognize that this is a literal and historically demonstrable Epic *fight to the death* of Evil *Against GOD*! The Right in America today is at the end of a long slow march to the Left's guillotines and gas chambers! As Jesus Himself clearly stated, Evil comes not but to steal, kill, and destroy[69]. If we cannot learn to see the true Enemy for who he is – *Evil* – then we cannot hope to turn back Lucifer's human army of the Left's Evil! This is *not* a game or a simple intellectual exercise. We need only look to history's repeated lessons with its hundreds of millions of dead victims. The Left means to conquer GOD's representatives of GOOD on earth, and eventually when Evil has had time to position itself in power, to literally *kill* them! Dietrich Bonhoeffer, a German pastor martyred by the Nazis, warned the Christians of Nazi Germany of the true Evil nature of the GODless Nazi régime, but they refused to

---

[69] The *Holy Bible*; John 10:10.

recognize the true Enemy behind Hitler[70]. Seven million GOOD Christian men, women, and children were murdered by the Left. All because they did not recognize the nature of Evil and *fight* vigilantly against it.

Christian Germany lost the Battle against Evil and over 7 million Christians were murdered by the Left simply for being a Christian. Islam has murdered millions of Christians simply for being Christians. *Religion and politics matter!* Politics is inseparable from religion and Right. This is not just a theory, but a thousand-fold repeated *fact* of history. What the Left seeks to do is not separate religion from politics, but to separate Christianity from politics, as Christianity is the *only* religion that stands in opposition to the Left's Evil agenda. German Christians in large part refused to believe that a Christian genocide could happen in their country. Seven million German Christians died because they bought the *Lie* of the Devil and the Left that the Devil did not really exist and Evil was an imaginary construct of the weak minded. The *Lie* of the Left has not changed. America is now plunging headlong down the same road of surrender to the same Evil which brought about the Jewish and Christian Holocaust in Nazi Germany. The Left will always do what the Left has always done; to believe otherwise is to ignore all of the *facts* of history!

This is not yet a call to arms, but a clarion wake-up call to the Right to start *fighting* the political *War* as if our very lives depended upon it! If history is any indicator and the Left has its way... our lives and the lives of our children may very well, and soon depend upon it!

The Left's War Against GOD is real and the only plausible explanation for the Left's calculated Evil actions is the *Left's War Against GOD*, and by extension GOD's people. The otherwise seemingly erratic behavior of the Left is unexplainable. As Rand Paul identified "There is a war on Christianity, not just from liberal elites here at home, but worldwide"[71]. In the following chapters I will lay out the facts that

---

[70] See wider discussion on Fascist Nazi Germany parallels in the following chapter: *Fascism and the Left in America: Kindred Spirits and Familiar Bedfellows* .

[71] Brody, David; CBN.com; *Rand Paul's Message To Evangelicals: "There is a war on Christianity"*; 6/13/2013.

support and lead to the unavoidable conclusion that the Left are the willing, though sometimes naïve, servants and promoters of *Evil* in *The Left's War Against GOD!*

2. UNDERSTANDING THE BATTLE

Chapter 2

The United States of America was founded as a Republic *NOT* a democracy[72]. Not only would virtually every college student be stunned by this statement, most reading this book are no doubt equally taken aback. The Left has pounded home the term "democracy" and painted any association with the term Republic and Republican as something to be disdained, scoffed at, feared, and even hated. A Republic is a representative form of government where the people elect representatives to uphold the standards of a *constitution*, which is the law of the land. In a democracy the people directly vote their every selfish whim into existence and thereby self-destroy the democracy which has no unmovable standard of law by which to restrain corruption[73].

The basis for a Republic is *liberty*, whereas the basis for a democracy is *freedom*[74]. Liberty and *freedom* are at odds one against the other. *Liberty* says you can, but you don't[75]. *Freedom* says you can, and you do. Because there are no Christian moral constraints on *freedom* as the Left preaches *freedom*, not only do those who advocate *freedom* "do" everything that they "can", but they do everything without restraint or conscience. Notice that the word "can" pertaining to a democracy implies "permission" from the government. The Left gives "permission", or the *freedom*, to sin in exchange for your *liberty*. *Liberty* is self-control, with GOD as the source, whereas *freedom* is a loss of self-control, in defiance of GOD with man as its source.

---

[72] It is interesting to note that a Republic has a capital "R" and a Republic is an empirical reality whereas a democracy is always in lower case and is simply a utopian idea, an always unrealized and elusive idea.

[73] See below.

[74] The term freedom as discussed here is the postmodern definition peddled by the Left in America today of legalizing the immoral to be free to act without the restraint of the Christian standards on which America was founded.

[75] The *Holy Bible*: Galatians 5:13

It is also important to note that *liberty* implies keeping the government out of the lives of Americans to the greatest extent possible. The *freedom* offered by the Left on the other hand, requires that the government become involved in the controlling of every human activity.

The *only* world religion that teaches *liberty* is Christianity through the *Bible*[76]. Even the U. S. Supreme Court acknowledged the Christian foundation of America as it ruled, "The morality of the country is deeply engrafted upon Christianity, and not upon the doctrines or worship of other religions. In people whose manners are refined, and whose morals have been elevated and inspired with a more enlarged benevolence, it is by means of the Christian religion"[77].

The American *Constitution* references freedom only once and is limited only to the phrase "freedom of speech", but *liberty* is expounded upon as our GOD-given right three times and guarantees *liberty* broadly to all Americans. *Liberty* is specified at the very beginning of the Constitution's preamble establishing the principle of *liberty* on which the remainder of the *U.S. Constitution* is built. The Holy Spirit, the Third Person of the Trinity of GOD, is the Spirit of Liberty[78] to Whom the Christian surrenders himself and thus acts under voluntary restraint, or *liberty* of the Holy Spirit. Only the *liberty* that GOD offers can truly set a person free[79]. Freedom without liberty is a trap of the Left!

Those who advocate *liberty* and the Republican government promote "the pursuit of happiness". Thomas Jefferson, who penned the Declaration of Independence, was asked to explain his meaning in his use of "the pursuit of happiness" as Jefferson recorded it in the Declaration of Independence. Jefferson responded, "the pursuit of happiness is not pleasure or material satisfaction, but the higher good,

---

[76] e.g. Authorized Bible: Leviticus 25:10; Isaiah 61:1; Luke 4:18; Romans 8:21; 2 Corinthians 3:17; *et al*

[77] The United States SUPREME COURT, *People v. Ruggles*; 1811; 143 U.S. 457, 12 S. Ct. 511

[78] The *Holy Bible*: 2 Corinthians 3:17

[79] The *Holy Bible*: Galatians 5:1

joy a sense of wellbeing, a life of virtue and excellence". A Republic exemplifies self-restraint of the individual and the restraint of the government by the people and the promoting of the general welfare of others over our own sinful self-interests. The same principles are found in the *Bible* in Jesus' words: "Thou shalt love the LORD thy God with all thy heart, and with all thy soul, and with all thy strength, and with all thy mind; *and thy neighbor as thyself*[80] (*emphasis added*).

In opposition to liberty, *"freedom"* as promoted by the Left and as the Left advocates *"democracy"*, is nothing more than unrestrained Hedonism. Hedonism that is expressed as an obsession with self-pleasure. ***The Left actually takes away true freedom in exchange for a license to sin!*** This Leftist concept of "democracy" *always* leads to a totalitarian dictatorship. On this Cycle of Dictatorship, Alexander Fraser Tytler (1747-1813) is quoted,

> "The average of the world's great civilizations [democracies] before they decline has been 200 years. These nations have progressed in this sequence: From bondage to spiritual faith; from faith to great courage; from courage to liberty; from liberty to abundance; *from abundance to selfishness*; from selfishness to complacency; from complacency to apathy; from apathy to dependency; from dependency back again to bondage"[81]. (emphasis added)

As will be noted below, "bondage" is defined by Tytler as the enslavement by a Leftist style "dictatorship". As documented in chapter one, a *pure democracy* in the French Revolution yielded the *Reign of Terror* and tyranny, whereas America's pure Republic established at the American Revolution yielded the freest, fairest, and most prosperous Nation in the history of mankind!

---

[80] The *Holy Bible*: Luke 10:27
[81] Alexander Fraser Tytler, Lord Woodhouselee (1747-1813) was a Scottish lawyer, writer, and professor at the University of Edinburgh, Scotland. Tytler was an historian in Greek and Roman Antiquities and was intimately familiar with the Greek democracy and the degradation of the Roman Republic into democracy, then into dictatorship. There is some question to the origin of this quote which was first published in America on December 9, 1951 in an article by Elmer T. Peterson in *The Daily Oklahoman* and credited to Tytler. It has since been quoted and attributed to Tytler by dozens of people including Ronald Reagan.

(As an important side note: There has been a sustained effort to subtly *Re-Name* or Re-Brand the Left as the "Democrat*ic* Party". The Left Stream Media bolsters this *Lie* of the "Democrat*ic* Party" as though it is the sole upholder of a "democratic free society", when in fact it is public enemy number one to a true free society! The Left does represent what Robespierre implemented as a "pure democracy"[82] which became known as the *Reign of Terror*! We all know the murder, and pain inflicted in the name of "pure democracy" in Revolutionary France. In this sense the Democrat Party is "democrat*ic*", but certainly not in the sense of "democracy" as colloquialized representing America's Constitutional Republic. The Right must begin to challenge this misrepresentation at every opportunity. Remember… words do hurt, and unrestrained… eventually kill!)

There is a reason that the Left continuously demonizes our Founding Fathers who wrote and ratified our Republican Constitution. Here is what John Adams (Founding Father, our first Vice President and second President of the United States, and who also assisted Thomas Jefferson in drafting the *Declaration of Independence* in 1776) said:

> Remember, democracy never lasts long. It soon wastes, exhausts, and murders itself. There never was a democracy yet that did not commit suicide.[83] -John Adams

The Left continually screams that our Founding Fathers were racists, homophobes, elitists, and generally bad people. Why? Because the Left *must* undermine and destroy the *Constitution* in order to implement the Left's evil agenda. Remember as previously noted, Obama stated that our Republican *Constitution* is "Generally, the Constitution is a charter of negative liberties" or restraints. What Obama failed to mention is that our *U.S. Constitution* is a charter of restraints against evil, restraining the evil of government and its tyrannical tendencies and the inherent evil in men!

---

[82] See the discussion in the chapter: *Defining The War: Evil Against GOD, Left Against Right.*
[83] From a letter from John Adams to John Taylor, 17 December 1814.

A *Constitution* is the *restraining* guardian of a Republican representative form of government. A *Constitution* is a voluntary agreement and a binding contract between the governed and the government to *restrict* the power of the government, as the governed originally defined and empowered it in a written constitution. If the contract can be altered then there is no contract but a constant repositioning by the government for increased power to usurp control over those it governs. This is the hidden agenda of those on the Left who advocate a "living Constitution". By "living" they mean "changeable" at the whim and advantage of the Left. To adopt a policy of a "living Constitution", as the Left advocates, renders the *U.S. Constitution* both meaningless and worthless, a thing to be manipulated at will by the Left for the Left's advancement of Evil.

A rental agreement or home mortgage is a binding contract, akin to a personal constitution, where the renter or home owner voluntarily enters into a contract with the landlord under the binding terms agreed upon before the commencement of the contract. If your landlord or banker were then free and unrestrained to alter the terms of the lease or mortgage contract, how long would it be before he would increase your payments beyond your means to pay, he would take everything you owned, and he would in essence *own* you? Would any sane person advocate for a "living mortgage" or "living lease agreement" for himself? It has been profoundly noted, "A 'living Constitution' means the death of our Republic".

The Left must destroy the *U.S. Constitution* in order to free itself from the Constitution's inherent *restraints* on the power of the Federal government. The primary function of the *U.S. Constitution* was the protection of individuals from the tyranny of an unrestrained national government. The *Constitution* did not give power as much as *restrain* national power. The *U.S. Constitution* was established as a Judeo-Christian document with individualism and private rights, foremost private property rights, as laid out in the *Bible*. The *Bible* recognizes the inherent evil in men and lays out laws by which this inherent evil must be *restrained*.

A small civics lesson is probably in order here on American Federalism. Federalism has long-since been banned from public education as it wholly opposes the Left's attempt at the National-centralization of power. The State controlled Leftist/Progressive education system has eliminated the teaching of Federalism since the time of the militantly Anti-GOD and Anti-Christian educator John Dewey and the rise of the Progressive Movement from the 1890's to the 1920's. How can I say this with such authority? Do you know exactly what Federalism is? Do you know why it is so critical to the defense of the American governmental system? No? Neither can virtually any American. The reason that practically no American knows what Federalism is, is that the Left has banned the teaching of Federalism from the public education system. The United States was founded as a *Federal* Republic.

Federalism was designed by the Founders to be the core of our Republic as the ultimate defense against National tyranny. When we hear someone reference the "Federal Government" it is a direct reference to the National government in Washington DC. However the Founders created a Constitutional Federal System whereby power was divided between the National government and the States. What powers that were not given to the Federal government, as specifically enumerated in the Constitution, were reserved for the States. This acted as a built-in *restraint* against the natural inclination of a National government to usurp total control over the states. This has often been referred to as "States Rights". The Tenth Amendment to the *United States Constitution* established Federalism:

> The powers not [specifically] delegated to the United States by the Constitution, nor prohibited by it to the States, are reserved to the States respectively, or to the people.

The basis for American Federalism is a Constitutionally *restrained* National government. Federalism is meant to prevent a National usurpation of powers over the States that would ultimately lead to a tyrannical National dictatorship. This is what we are facing today in the Left's consolidation of power in the National government in denying the States their Constitutionally mandated *restraining* powers. Remember that it was the States that originally empowered the Federal government into existence, and the States alone that have the power to alter the *U.S. Constitution* which places restraint on the Federal government. We have seen the Supreme Court under its occasioned Leftist majority usurp National control over the Constitutionally guaranteed States Rights in defiance of the United States Constitution. Therefore it is vitally important to elect Presidents like President Trump to ensure that all vacating Supreme Court Justices are replaced with *Constitutional* Conservatives. The *restraining* force of Federalism has all but disappeared in America today as a tactic for a Leftist takeover of our Federal Republic and the repercussions are obvious and everywhere.

The Left preaches that man is inherently good and that a properly ordered Leftist society will allow man's potential to be realized. The Left sees that "evil", as such, is environmental and caused by the suppression of man's potential by the Judeo-Christian restraints. This is why the Left's Pagan ideals worship the environment and Mother Earth (Gaia) as a means to return to an imagined pristine past. A past which predates an imagined Judeo-Christian contamination of the world. (This by no coincidence was the identical position of Hitler and Nazi Germany further vetted in the chapter: *Fascism and the Left in America: Kindred Spirits and Familiar Bedfellows*.) The truth is however that the Edenic Paradise of GOD was destroyed when Evil was introduced into the world by the Fall of man into sin *Against GOD*. Man's Fall into sin infected not only man's nature, but also the planet's very nature.[84]

The Left buys concessions from the American people by removing any moral restraint placed on the people by the Christian principles used to establish our American Federal Republic. John Adams, a Founding Father, signer of our Constitution, and our second President, and a devout Christian wrote "Our Constitution was made only for a moral and religious people. It is wholly inadequate to the government of any other". Benjamin Franklin wrote, "Only a virtuous people are capable of freedom. As nations become corrupt and vicious, they have

---

[84] The *Holy Bible*; Genesis 3:11-19

more need of masters". Unrestrained *freedom*, as the Left promises it, only leads to enslavement of the American people to the national government and the Left as the resultant chaos in the total breakdown of society demands the "need of masters" or Leftist dictators to restore order[85]. *Freedom* here in the Leftist incarnation, is better described as "freedom from any restraint", or *lawlessness*. Lawlessness is the total abandonment of GOD's Laws. Lucifer himself is described in the *Bible* as the epitome of "lawlessness"[86]! The Left's endgame is total and absolute lawlessness from GOD. This is the trap which many Libertarians fall into who call for the dismantling of many of America's moral laws such as legalizing drugs[87] and prostitution.

The Scottish historian Tytler again deftly recognizes, "A democracy cannot exist as a permanent form of government. It can only exist until the voters discover that they can vote themselves largesse from the public treasury. From that moment on, the majority always votes for the candidates promising the most benefits the public treasury with the result that a democracy always collapses over lousy fiscal policy, always, as predicted by the Cycle of Dictatorship, is followed by a dictatorship"[88]. ***Moral bankruptcy always precedes fiscal bankruptcy***. Does this ring a familiar bell as America's National Debt exceeds **$20,000,000,000,000**? That is twenty trillion with a "t" followed by *12* zeros!

To help get our minds around such an inconceivable figure as **20,000,000,000,000** consider this: Comparing one million to one billion to one trillion we can use a conversion of dollars to seconds. If one dollar equals one second of time, then going back in time one *million* seconds would take us back almost 12 days. Not bad so far. Now one *billion* seconds would take us back in time almost 32 years. A large amount of time, but still in the conceivable range. Now what

---

[85] See the following discussion of Alinsky's *Rules For Radicals* and the Left's cycle of control in creating a "crisis", demanding their solution, implementing their agenda which makes the "crisis" worse, and demanding more of their solutions, repeating the cycle again, *ad nauseam*.
[86] The *Holy Bible*: 2 Thessalonians 2:8, Wicked or Lawless one.
[87] For the discussion of drugs see the chapters: *Fascism and the Left in America: Kindred Spirits and Familiar Bedfellows* and *The Democrat Party Platform As Leftist Doctrines ALL OPPOSE GOD*.
[88] Tytler, Alexander Fraser, op. cit.

would you imagine for one *trillion* seconds? ...come on take a guess... one *trillion* seconds would take us back in time.................. 31,710 years!

Now multiply 31,710 years by 20 and what do you get? Wait for it... wait for it... it would take us back 634,200 years!!!!!!! That is longer than even the evolutionists[89] tell us that modern man has existed on earth! Did "the voters discover that they can vote themselves largesse from the public treasury"? Has our Federal Republic morphed into a lawless democracy paving the way for our own doom?

For the Left to claim ignorance of the dangers of such a looming National debt is an outright and intentional *Lie*. Here is what then Senator Barack Hussein Obama said in 2008 about President Bush and America's debt crises:

> "The way Bush has done it over the last eight years is . . . [he] added $4 trillion by his lonesome, so that we now have over $9 trillion of debt that we are going to have to pay back.... *That's irresponsible. It's unpatriotic*"[90].

Of course when the debt accumulation under Obama exceeded that of Bush in only three years, Obama's tone changed dramatically as Obama quipped,

> "I don't remember what the number was precisely... We don't have to worry about it short term".

Convenient memory lapse or gross ignorance? Compiling this kind of debt can only be explained either by gross ignorance of the Left, on the level of an adult who still believes in the tooth fairy, or as an intentional scheme of the Left. An intentional scheme that Obama's then White House Chief of Staff Rahm Emanuel admitted was to

---

[89] This is not an endorsement of the Left's doctrine of evolution in any of its unbiblical and therefore Anti-GOD manifestations including macro-evolution, the Gap theory, theistic evolution, or any other Leftist promoted religious doctrine meant to undermine American's belief in the trustworthiness of the Christian *Bible*.

[90] *The Wall Street Journal* online; Updated Oct. 26, 2012 5:46 p.m. ET

"create the appearance of an imminent catastrophe, use Chicken Little style tactics to scare America to a pre-prescribed action, then use the fear of this imagined catastrophe to step in and rescue America from sure destruction that will result from inaction or any action other than that demanded by the Left[91]". Here is the Left's crisis/action template:

1) Use a tragedy as a crisis, or create a crisis where none exists.
2) Paint the crisis with as much emotion as possible, and throw logical analysis out the window.
3) Propose the one and only solution to the problem, which just happens to coincide with what you've wanted to implement for many years.
4) Paint anyone who opposes your one and only solution as evil, uncaring, not smart enough to understand the nuanced brilliance of your solution, or in the pockets of .... you pick the evil entity.
5) Force the solution on the people by any means, whether legislatively, by executive order, or through the legal system.
6) When the unintended consequences of your solution rear their ugly head, use them as a reason for more brilliant solutions to made-up crises[92].

This of course is the formula outlined in the Radical Left's godfather Saul Alinsky's *Rules For Radicals* and implemented by the Left as prominently as the response to the banking "crisis". The "subprime mortgage crisis" that was caused by the Left as spearheaded by Senator Barney Frank in passing laws, the Community Reinvestment Act and others, which forced banks to give mortgages to poor and minorities who could not afford to pay them back. Then the Dodd-Frank Act stepped in and instead of making lending laws more secure, just made the situation worse needing further intervention. Notice the pattern? Additionally, in response to this crisis, the Federal government stepped in and forced all of America's major banks to accept "bailout" money as a way of indebting our financial institutions to the Federal government, thus forcing government control over our

---

[91] See the telling adlib comment by Rahm Emanuel in following paragraph.
[92] Austrianaddict.com; December 18, 2012; you-never-let-a-serious-crisis-go-to-waste

private banking system. The only way for the Left to take over the historically unprecedentedly successful American capitalistic system is to first bankrupt it! Remember the $20,000,000,000,000 and climbing National debt?! The Left even under President Trump keeps agitating for more debt!

This tactic is typified in an adlib statement and Freudian slip made again by Obama's then White House Chief of Staff Rahm Emanuel speaking of the shooting of US House of Representatives Congressman Gabby Giffords in Arizona as reported in *The Wall Street Journal* online:

> "This opportunity isn't lost on the new president and his team. **'You never want a serious crisis to go to waste,'** Rahm Emanuel, Mr. Obama's new chief of staff, told a Wall Street Journal conference of top corporate chief executives this week. He elaborated: **'Things that we** [*the Leftist elite in America*] **had postponed for too long, that were long-term, are now immediate and must be dealt with. This crisis provides the opportunity for us to do things that you could not do before'"**[93].

It is also notable that Emanuel then ticked off this to-do list: "some areas where he thought new doors were opening: energy, health, education, tax policy, regulatory reforms". This list is virtually verbatim from the old Soviet plan to takeover America from within. These points were the few remaining points that the Left had not yet successfully implemented in their quest to usurp America. More importantly these few "areas" were virtually all that remained of the Soviet plan to be implemented from the original list of the 45 identified by the U.S. Congress in 1963[94].

(An interesting side-note here, how many of you were offended by the use of the word "Soviet"? The Left has conditioned Americans to

[93] Seib, Gerald F.; *The Wall Street Journal* online; *In Crisis, Opportunity for Obama*; Updated Nov. 21, 2008 12:01 a.m. ET.
[94] ***Congressional Record***; January 10, 1963; **Appendix, pp. A34-A35**; see also: Skousen, Cleon; *The Naked Communist*; 1958.

respond with disdain those who would dare use such myopic terms as "Soviet", "Communist", or "Socialist" as if these words were just a construct of an inferior mind and lacking any connection with the real world in which we live. We could easily add to the list of their condemned and reactionary terms words such as "Leftist"", "Liberal", "Progressive", *et al.* Again, Evil cannot tolerate being identified for what it really is… Evil!)

Make no mistake it *is* the Left's intention to bankrupt America and to build its envisioned Leftist Utopia upon the ashes. There is no other plausible explanation for their otherwise seemingly reckless behavior. The Left is either naïve to the point of a mentally retarded child or its actions are intentional. (Some days it seems a hard call between mentally retarded and intentionally evil, but the latter is the absolute answer with the former also applying in most cases!) The Left must by force of circumstance make all Americans dependent upon the Left for their very survival. This has been the plan of the Left from the beginning in their otherwise grossly failed programs of the welfare State. (Remember the Obama campaign's 2012 cartoon depiction of "The Life of Julia" from age 3 to age 67 and their cradle-to-grave socialist utopian proposals?)

The Left's programs only bring enslavement, especially of minorities, with programs such as food stamps, public education, and nationalized healthcare. The Left's agenda of cradle-to-grave welfare is to control every conceivable activity of every American and exclude GOD in the process of re-fashioning every citizen of the State into its own image of Evil.

(It is no coincidence that the Bible tells us that a global economic collapse brings about the implementation of a global currency under the person of the Antichrist, Evil incarnate, which in turn allows Evil to control the activities of all the peoples of the world. Evil has played out this scenario since the beginning of time in anticipation of the day when the catastrophic worldwide conditions allow for Evil to seize control of the entire world as GOD foretold in the *Bible's Book of Revelation.*)

Here we come back to dictatorship. As previously quoted President Ronald Reagan warned Americans 30 years ago, "The nine most terrifying words in the English language are, 'I'm from the government and I'm here to help.'", which Reagan spoke with his usual wit about the Left's dictatorial tendencies and tactics. The Left's way of seizing control is to present itself as "here to help".

As we have begun to witness in America, once the Left are allowed in the door they will show what George Carlin aptly termed their deceitful "smiley-face fascism". Once the Left has gained entrance, the Left's true vicious nature of totalitarian theocratic Fascism will be unmasked!. Make no mistake, the Left's ultimate goal is the absolute control of America in an iron fisted dictatorship. Again the Left's *any means to the ends*[95] is a sleight-of-hand deception in fostering a national desire for a *pure democracy*[96], which as history proves always devolves into chaos, a chaos from which the Left plans to step in to "rescue" America, and by necessity to restore order and install a dictatorship[97]. (For our own good of course… ☺) The Left may couch its objectives as a benevolent religion-free Utopia, but its intention is to create a Leftist dictatorial theocracy[98]! This is *the Left's War Against GOD!*

---

[95] Alinsky's directives to Leftist rebel "In **war**, the end justifies almost ***any means***...".

[96] For *pure democracy* and the evil that it represents see chapter one *The Coalition of the Unlikely/The Tie That Binds*.

[97] See the discussion of the Cycle of Dictatorship in chapters: *The Coalition of the Unlikely/The Tie That Binds* and *Understanding The Battle*.

[98] See the discussion in the chapter *The Left Is A Religion*.

3. JESUS, CHRISTIANS, AND POLITICAL ACTIVISM: DEBUNKING THE LIE OF EVIL AND THE LEFT

Chapter 3

To those who say that Jesus was not political, Jesus and the *Bible* say that that is absolutely *a Lie of the Devil*!, *a Lie of Evil*!, and *a Lie of the Left*! Jesus regularly confronted and condemned the corrupt and Evil Jewish *political* establishment. For any who doubt this they should be reminded that Jesus continuously and publically confronted and even condemned the Jewish *politicians* and said that they were going to burn in Hell![99] I would say that that qualifies Jesus as a *political* dissident! For those who need further convincing... read on!!!

We need to define *religion* here early in this discussion, and religion's inseparable link to *politics*. The definition of "religion" is: The common, basic held beliefs, of *each* historical society as accepted and promoted by the State; and "politics" is the enforcement-wing of every historical State's religion. It is "religion and politics" which are the two most important and indivisible questions which affect every human being on earth, and to which every human being has a moral obligation to get the answer right! Ultimately we will all answer to GOD for our conclusions and subsequent choices to these two questions. What the Left does not want you to know is that "religion and politics" are intrinsically linked at their core and absolutely inseparable. It is just a matter of choice between GOD and the Left's Anti-GOD Religion, which choice always determines mankind's contemporary politics.

Is America a Christian Nation? If not, then *why* until the past few years have all Presidents, Congressmen, Legislators, and judges still lay their hand on GOD's *Christian Bible* when taking the oath of office?

How about Congress?

---

[99] The *Holy Bible*; Matthew 5:20; 23:15.

PUBLIC LAW 97-280—OCT. 4, 1982   96 STAT. 1211

Public Law 97-280
97th Congress

Joint Resolution

Authorizing and requesting the President to proclaim 1983 as the "Year of the Bible".

Oct. 4, 1982
[S.J. Res. 165]

Whereas the Bible, the Word of God, has made a unique contribution in shaping the United States as a distinctive and blessed nation and people;

Whereas deeply held religious convictions springing from the Holy Scriptures led to the early settlement of our Nation;

Whereas Biblical teachings inspired concepts of civil government that are contained in our Declaration of Independence and the Constitution of the United States;

Whereas many of our great national leaders—among them Presidents Washington, Jackson, Lincoln, and Wilson—paid tribute to the surpassing influence of the Bible in our country's development, as in the words of President Jackson that the Bible is "the rock on which our Republic rests";

Whereas the history of our Nation clearly illustrates the value of voluntarily applying the teachings of the Scriptures in the lives of individuals, families, and societies;

Whereas this Nation now faces great challenges that will test this Nation as it has never been tested before; and

Whereas that renewing our knowledge of and faith in God through Holy Scripture can strengthen us as a nation and a people: Now, therefore, be it

Resolved by the Senate and House of Representatives of the United States of America in Congress assembled, That the President is authorized and requested to designate 1983 as a national "Year of the Bible" in recognition of both the formative influence the Bible has been for our Nation, and our national need to study and apply the teachings of the Holy Scriptures.

Year of the Bible.

Approved October 4, 1982.

LEGISLATIVE HISTORY—S.J. Res. 165:
CONGRESSIONAL RECORD, Vol. 128 (1982):
    Mar. 31, considered and passed Senate.
    Sept. 21, considered and passed House.

PUBLIC LAW 97-280—OCT. 4, 1982 96 STAT. 1211

Public Law 97-280
97th Congress
Joint Resolution

Authorizing and requesting the President to proclaim 1983 as the "Year of the Bible".
Oct. 4, 1982

[S.J. Res. 165]
Whereas the Bible, the Word of God, has made a unique
contribution in shaping the United States as a distinctive and
blessed nation and people;
Whereas deeply held religious convictions springing from the
Holy
   Scriptures led to the early settlement of our Nation;
Whereas Biblical teachings inspired concepts of civil
government
   that are contained in our Declaration of Independence and
the
   Constitution of the United States;
Whereas many of our great national leaders—among them
   Presidents Washington, Jackson, Lincoln, and Wilson—
paid
   tribute to the surpassing influence of the Bible in our
country's
   development, as in the words of President Jackson that the
Bible
   is "the rock on which our Republic rests";
Whereas the history of our Nation clearly illustrates the value
of
   voluntarily applying the teachings of the Scriptures in the
lives of
   individuals, families, and societies;
Whereas this Nation now faces great challenges that will test
this
   Nation as it has never been tested before; and
Whereas that renewing our knowledge of and faith in God
through
   Holy Scripture can strengthen us as a nation and a people:
Now,
   therefore, be it
Resolved by the Senate and House of Representatives of the
   United States of America in Congress assembled, That the
   President is authorized and requested to designate 1983 as a
   national "Year of the Bible" in recognition of both the
   formative

influence the Bible has been for our Nation, and our national need
to study and apply the teachings of the Holy Scriptures.

Approved October 4, 1982.

LEGISLATIVE HISTORY—S.J. Res. 165:
CONGRESSIONAL RECORD, Vol. 128 (1982):
   Mar. 31, considered and passed Senate.
   Sept. 21, considered and passed House.

The U. S. Supreme Court flatly declared of the United Sates "this is a Christian nation"[100]. Justice David J. Brewer quoted language from many Colonial and State Charters and the US Declaration of Independence which *all* referenced its foundations and reliance on the Christian GOD of the *Bible*.

With that in mind, how is it that when Obama said "our prayers are with the families of the victims" that the Left Stream Media (LSM) bows its collective heads in reverence to Obama, but when those on the Right tweet almost identical condolences that the Left Stream Media in concert goes berserk? Does the Left Stream Media instinctively understand that Obama's "god" and the 2016 Republican Presidential candidates GOD were not the same God?! I submit that the Left absolutely understands!

Obama declared emphatically of the 2015 Oregon mass shooting "our thoughts and prayers are not enough. It's not enough". Hum... it doesn't take a genius to figure out that Obama wanted a Leftist political solution and Obama's reference to prayer was intentionally deceptive.

Jesus consistently, *publically*, and loudly preached against the Jewish politicians and confronted their Evil on many, many occasions. The closest *political* enemy to Christ and Christianity was the *political*

---

[100] The United States Supreme Court, *Church of the Holy Trinity v. United States*, 143 U.S. 457 12 S. Ct. 511, 36 L.Ed. 226

Jewish *Sanhedrin*. The *Sanhedrin* was the ruling Jewish National *religious* and *political* government in Israel at the time Jesus was on earth as a man. (Remember *all* governments are both *political* and *religious*!) The Jewish *Sanhedrin* answered only to Rome and all Jews in Israel answered to the *Sanhedrin*. Ultimately Jesus was crucified at the *political* demands of the leadership of the *Sanhedrin*.

Jesus' only political interaction with the government of Rome was not until the time of His Crucifixion. At that time Jesus made it clear that it was the Roman government in Jerusalem that was doing the will of GOD in crucifying Jesus, *not* Jesus being subjugated to the Pagan politics of Rome! Jesus was *the political* Authority above all earthly politics. Ultimately as the *Book of Revelation* in the *Bible* clearly tells us Jesus' ultimate victory over Evil will be inclusive of the final destruction of Evil *politics*. Evil *politics* as will be embodied in the Antichrist and the false Religion of the Left as embodied in the False Prophet the third person of Satan's false trinity, an Evil imitation of GOD's Trinity. Notice the inseparable relationship of "politics and religion" in the kingdom of Evil! So is the relationship of "politics and religion" inseparable in the Kingdom of GOD. Remember GOD created politics! GOD created politics and set up its proper arrangement and function. This is the template used by our Founding Fathers in establishing America's political system!

Now the Left would have us to believe that GOD has abandon all interest in the politics… the same politics which GOD Himself created and ordained?! Really? The answer from GOD to the Left is simple… NO! Here is what Jesus says about all things which GOD has established, "What therefore God hath joined together, let not man put asunder."! GOD has certainly and inseparably joined "religion and politics" together and given His people, the Right, on earth the responsibility to establish, maintain, and defend it!

Satan is the great imitator of GOD, but imitated only just enough to make evil *appear* as "good". The Devil himself, as the essence of Evil, can be looked at for the antithesis of what is GOOD and Right. (Have you ever noticed that the word "*evil*" is derived from the name "D*evil*"?) Even logic tells us the opposite of Right is Wrong. Satan's tactics and ends are the exact opposite of GOD's. A person's motives can be discovered not only by his friends and his actions, but equally by his enemies. Evil has spent countless time and energies to keep Christians and the Right *out of politics*. Have you ever asked yourself... Why? If Christian, or Right, influence is not important to the support and defense of the American political system, why then does the Left in general, and Evil specifically, frantically spend so much time, energy, and money to remove the Right's influence? It is their obsession! What Evil works so hard to prevent is what GOD works to so diligently to establish, maintain, and defend. The P.C. drumbeat of the Left demands that the Right *not* talk about only two things, which are not by coincidence *religion* and *politics*!

Jesus did set the example in His lifetime of dealing with an Evil *political* system... Confront, Resist, and overthrow! To accept the Left's conclusion that "Jesus would never be involved in politics" is to surrender GOD's work on earth to Evil. That is what the Left desperately wants and is frantically working to convince the Right of accepting! Tragically the Right in general has fallen for evil's Big Lie!

To not actively oppose Evil and the Left is to tacitly give aid and comfort to the Enemy in *the Left's War Against GOD*. Evil triumphs when good men do nothing. Jesus speaking as our GOD and King said of this, "Verily I say unto you, Inasmuch as ye have done it unto one of the least of these my brethren, ye have done it unto me"[101]. Just in case you think GOD left you a little wiggle room, Jesus also stated it in the reverse concerning inaction, "Verily I say unto you, Inasmuch as ye did it *not* to one of the least of these, ye did it *not* to me"[102]. GOD takes inaction against Evil *personally*!

There is clearly a GOD-given absolute command when the *Bible* commands us to, "**Resist** *the devil and he will flee from you*"[103]! To "resist" is to actively and physically confront, fight, and defeat evil! Here is Webster's 1828 Dictionary definition:

---

[101] The *Holy Bible*: Matthew 25:40.
[102] The *Holy Bible*: Matthew 25:45.
[103] The *Holy Bible*: James 4:7.

RESIST, *verb transitive* rezist'. [Latin resisto; re and sisto, to stand.]

1. Literally, to stand against; to withstand; hence, to *act* in opposition, or to oppose. a dam or mound resists a current of water passively, by standing unmoved and interrupting its progress. An army resists the progress of an enemy actively, by encountering and defeating it. We *resist* measures by argument or remonstrance.

Why doth he yet find fault? for who hath resisted his will? Romans 9:19.

2. To strive against; to endeavor to counteract, defeat or frustrate.

Ye do always *resist* the Holy Spirit. Acts 7:51.

3. To baffle; to disappoint.

God resisteth the proud, but giveth grace to the humble. James 4:7.

RESIST', *verb intransitive* to make opposition.

Notice that the 1828 Webster's Dictionary even quotes GOD's Word using the *Bible* three times in defining "resistance" and as an *active* "*act* in opposition" and "An army resists the progress of an enemy *actively*, by encountering and defeating it"! (emphasis added) Active Resistance to evil is a Christian concept ordained by GOD! The Devil is the Commander of evil! Remember that *evil* is the root of D*evil*! Let me repeat the GOD-given absolute command as Christians are to, "***Resist** the devil and he will flee from you*". We on the Right are commanded by GOD to resist evil!

As we have seen and circumstances around us demonstrate, the Left *is* literally the Devil's Advocate! We need to see beyond the colloquialism of the term "Devil's Advocate". The Left Advocates for *all* that is Evil. Literally! GOD made no distinction between politics and religion in His command to "Resist the devil"! The Left always acts as the dissident in refusing to uphold the law based on GOD's principles, so why then when the Left rewrites the law and renders the law unConstitutional and Anti-GOD, does the Right cow down and follow an UnConstitutional and unGODly law?!

When Pontius Pilate, the Governor of Israel and curator of Rome, sought to interrogate Jesus before His Crucifixion[104], Jesus *refused* to answer as *required* by Roman Law. Jesus refused to comply with Evil. Jesus broke, defied, and *resisted* the overlying Roman Law! Likewise Jesus was taken before King Herod[105], the regional King of all greater Palestine who was appointed by Rome, and questioned. Again Jesus openly defied the Evil political system! Here again Jesus *resisted* against evil and broke the law! Jesus is our example[106] by which we are to *resist* Evil *political* representatives and laws. Jesus *resisted*, refused to comply, and ultimately overthrew Evil. We on the Right are *commanded* in the *Bible* to follow Jesus' example. Let's get going on that!

As stated earlier, it should be emphatically restated that **politics is the Enforcement-Wing of the Left and its Religion**, and as such, by necessity politics will play a prominent role in this discussion. *Politics is the engagement point at which the Right must confront Evil in the battle for America.* GOD tells us: "Ye that love the LORD, *hate* evil"[107]. (Not a verse that one often hears quoted and *never* acknowledged by the Left! Yes we are to *HATE* Evil!) Hate here is *not* a mental exercise, but a clarion call from GOD Himself to the Right for *action* against Evil and its modern-day Leftist Stormtroopers! Politics is the natural realm where the Left's War of Evil Against GOOD is fought. To *not* fight the *political War* is to cede earthly victory to Evil!

Evil abhors a vacuum! Again as Edmund Burke so astutely observed: All that is necessary for evil to triumph is that good men do nothing! **According to the *Holy Bible*, GOD's *Holy Word*, inaction against Evil is a sin**: "Therefore to him that knoweth to do good, and doeth it not, to him it is sin"[108]! Did you catch that? It bears repeating: According to the *Holy Bible*, GOD's *Holy Word*, inaction against **Evil** is a **sin** *Against GOD*! GOD demands *action* against Evil. This is what

---

[104] The *Holy Bible*: Luke 18:28-19:15.
[105] The *Holy Bible*: Luke 23:1-12.
[106] The *Holy Bible*: Jn 13:15, 17:18-20; 1 Pet 2:21; 1 Jn 2:6, 4:17.
[107] The *Holy Bible*: Psalms 97:10.
[108] The *Holy Bible*; James 4:17.

the Left frantically tries to hide from the Right in general, and Christians in particular. This is the crux of Jesus' admonition "He that is not with me is against me"[109]. To not *act* to advance GOOD is in fact to give aid to the advance of Evil! Only GOOD stops and turns back Evil. To not act *politically* in support of GOOD is in fact to aid the advance and triumph of Evil. The Left's agenda can only be implemented through *politics*. Again, remember that *politics is the implementation point of Evil!* Leftist politics is implemented through: Leftist-activist judges, elected office, political activism, political appointments, public schools, the Deep State, and many other areas of the American *political* system. The Right *must* engage Evil on the only practical point of engagement Against Evil, which *is **politics***! Politics is the *only* point of engagement on the Battlefield of *The Left's War Against GOD!*

Another "go to" argument of the Left against Christian involvement in politics was Jesus' statement to "render therefore unto Caesar that which is Caesar's". Concluding that Jesus submitted wholly "unto Caesar", Caesar being the "government" in the Left's *Lie*. However, the Leftists conveniently leave out the rest of the verse, "Render therefore unto Caesar the things which be Caesar's, *and unto God the things which be God's*"[110]. Jesus made a clear distinction between the boundaries of government and the boundlessness of all things which belong to GOD. (GOD's things clearly supersede Caesar's things.) Jesus was specifically talking about *taxes*... it does not address *any* restrictions on voting, opposing Evil, running for office, surrendering to Evil, or any other forms of Christian and Right involvement in government and confrontation in opposing Evil. Under the Left's self-serving definition (*Lie!*), even Christianity could be abolished by the simple edict of "Caesar", or the government, that Christians must simply kill themselves in order to be a "good Christian"! This is not just suicidal but Biblically *insane*! It is also interesting to note that the Left willingly associates itself with "Caesar" one of the most brutal and murderously Anti-Christian succession of dictators the world has ever known!

---

[109] The *Holy Bible*: Matthew 12:30.
[110] The *Holy Bible*: Luke 20:25.

There are also those who will use the "love your neighbor" argument to dissuade Christians from getting involved in politics. Their argument typically goes something like this: "Since we are to love our neighbors as ourselves as commanded by God, and politics and the confrontation of Evil is not love, therefore Christians should quietly and privately serve God and leave politics to others". On the outside this might appear to some as "reasonable". However, it is *not* Biblical and as we have seen it contradicts the Biblical example that Jesus Himself set for us in the Gospels with Jesus' vehement confrontation of the Evil in *politics*! First let me say that the command to "love your neighbor" is in the context of a Christian's *evangelical* responsibility, not his societal/political responsibility. This is also a thinly veiled argument which not so coincidently benefits *only* the Left and the Evil which the Left serves as being the self-defined, and self-serving, "others" in their argument. The argument is bogus and wholly unBiblical. Secondly, who in the Hell do the Left think they are quoting the Christian *Bible* to Christians! The same *Bible* that the Left seeks to destroy all vestiges of from American society and thought! Here is a clue, hey Left... *do not* try to interpret our *Bible* to us on the Right, our *Bible* which only can be interpreted by the Holy Spirit of GOD Who is the mortal enemy of the Left!

The Left also demands that "religion is strictly a private matter". A "private" faith is not a Christian Faith. The *Bible* clearly tells us that "faith without works is *dead*"[111]! Christianity demands public *action* in society in both its public manifestations of *religion* and *politics*. Otherwise it is a "dead" faith and *not* Christianity at all! The Left is always anxious to tell the Right what the *Bible* "says", which is always a well-crafted... *Lie*! We should take notice that in every European country that has bitten the poison apple of the Left's "religion is strictly a private matter", Christianity has virtually disappeared. This is the formula of Evil, for Evil, and directly *Against GOD*!

The Left's intentional misquote of the *Bible* that Christians are to "Judge not" is just another attempt to *disarm* Christians in *The Left's*

---

[111] The *Holy Bible*: James 2:20-26.

War Against GOD. Here again the Left loves to quote a small fragment of Scripture and deliberately leave out any qualifying text. What the *Bible* actually says is that as a Christian we are to judge as we want to be judged. The whole text reads: "Judge not, that ye be not judged. For with what judgment ye judge, ye shall be judged: and with what measure ye mete, it shall be measured to you again". The Left also intentionally confuses "judging" with "passing judgement". To "judge" is to discern Right from Wrong and to "pass judgement" is to condemn to Hell. It is the "judgement" of condemnation that is GOD's alone. Further the *Bible* absolutely commands all Christians *to* judge[112]. Yes, you read that right! The *Bible* commands all Christians to judge! It is amazing to me that any Christian would let any non-Christian try to tell him what the *Bible* really says! The *Bible* emphatically states that *only* Christians can discern the Scriptures[113]. Being non-Christian the Left is always speaking from a bias of *Evil*. Christians should keep that bit of wisdom clearly in mind in *The Left's War Against GOD!*

Furthermore, GOD Himself certainly did not apply non-confrontation to the *Bible*'s hundreds of examples of *political* situations when GOD's people were faced with annihilation by an Evil *political* enemy. If this were the case all remnants of GOD's people would have been wiped out by Evil before civilization had even had a chance to begin. In defense of this I note again that Evil comes "but to kill, steal, and destroy". Any other conclusion stands in opposition to all facts!

What is the definition of Western Civilization? Western Civilization is the Region of the world where Christianity, Christian ethics, and the Christian GOD are at the Foundation and center of the culture. The whole meaning of Civilized here is Christianized! What happens when Western Nations who were once the bedrock of Western Civilization give up their Christian Foundations? In Canada, England, France, Netherlands, Australia, *et al*, Christians are arrested and prosecuted for speaking GOD's Word. This persecution is exclusive Against the Christian religion, GOD's Word, and of course GOD

---

[112] The *Holy Bible*: 1 Corinthians 2:15.
[113] The *Holy Bible*: 1 Corinthians 2:14.

Himself. These nations have reverted to paganism as a religion, which again by definition, is barbaric in nature and deadly to Christians!

Those Christians who believe in the Separation of Church and State are they really suggesting that we approve going back to the Roman Empire where Christians were persecuted, fed to the lions, and executed on a Cross! Which is exactly what these misguided Christians are suggesting and the Left intends to see be executed!

The celebrated Soviet dissident and refugee Alexander Solzhenitsyn has pointed out that the reason that Russians had been subjugated to the unGODly Soviet Left was because the Russian people had "forgotten God. That's why all this has happened". That is the current trajectory that America has set for itself today. Unless we remember GOD, and put GOD back at the center of American life, Americans will soon be asking ourselves "What happened?". The answer will be the same "we have forgotten God" and we have lost the ability to "*resist* Evil"!

To accept the Left's demands that Christians abstain from politics would be as absurd as demanding that in the last days Christians who live under the Satan-possessed Antichrist, who for a short time in the Apocalypse will be the world-dictator, must never politically oppose the Antichrist's Evil commands! Absurd! Absurd and wholly in contradiction to GOD's Word, commands, and example. The Evil at work today in America is the same Evil as that which will possess the Antichrist at the end of time. The Book of Revelation, the last Book of the *Bible* that foretells of earth's last days, is filled from start to finish with examples of GOD's people who are told by GOD to stand and oppose all that is evil in politics and religion. **They are specifically instructed by GOD to oppose all that is Evil in politics and religion** including the Antichrist who will be the world's evil *political* leader, the False Prophet who will be the world's evil *religious* leader, and all of the followers of Evil! GOD is the same yesterday, today, and forever[114]! GOD told us in the *Bible yesterday* to oppose and overcome evil in the days past, and GOD will clearly have

---

[114] The *Holy Bible*: Hebrews 13:8.

His people do so in the *future* which is clearly depicted in the Book of Revelation, and clearly GOD *commands* us to so do *today*!

Apparently the Left understands the inseparability of *religion* and *politics* explicitly where the Right by-in-large is clueless. Certainly the Left never heeds its own advice given to its enemies in this matter. Anyone who allows the Enemy to set the terms of engagement deserves the certain defeat that follows! As an icon of the Left so deftly observed it is the "survival of the fittest". There are no allowances in War for stupidity, naiveté, or ignorance. GOD gave us His *Bible*, His *Book* on the rules of engagement Against Evil, and if we do not entirely familiarize ourselves with these rules we *will* suffer loss, setback, and defeat, and ultimately we will have no one to blame but ourselves!

As a personal aside, it is amazing to me that those who call themselves "Christian" and loudly advocate Christian non-participation in politics, themselves preach involvement in Leftist endeavors through the Left's evil "Social Gospel" movement. Newsflash: Jesus was neither a refugee nor homeless! These are common *Lies* of the Left used in an attempt to commandeer Christianity to the Left's imagined "Social Gospel"! These fake "Christians" will actively seek congregational participation of the Left's endeavor of "creating a heaven on earth", a sentiment which *totally* opposes GOD's Holy *Bible* and GOD's Gospel! These Leftist "Christian" fakers will work programs of feeding the hungry, helping the homeless, seek partnerships with local governments, work to eliminate poverty, advocate for nuclear non-proliferation, promote Environmentalism, talk about world peace, let Leftist politicians speak at their churches, but "God forbid" that any Christian participate in Right political endeavors! (Not by coincidence they seldom, if ever, follow-up with a Gospel message of Salvation and creating a personal relationship with GOD.) These are not accidents, nor Christians, but Leftist infiltrators who seek to destroy the work of GOD. GOD's plan is to create a personal relationship with Him which will allow a person to reach Heaven in eternity, not to create a delusional impossible man-made "heaven on earth". You know people by their actions and by the company that they keep; these fakers are not Christians, but wolves in sheep's clothing!

In the meantime, Jesus commands us as Christians, as the earthly representation of Right, to stand in Christ's stead[115], GOD's place on earth, and to *Fight* the epic Battle Against Evil. As we have seen, the Right is by definition the only earth-bound representatives of GOOD against the powers of Evil. To shirk this GOD-given responsibility is to empower Evil in the imminent power void that is created. It is an age-old taunt of the Left to convince the Right that the two unbreechable subjects for public discussion are "religion and politics". As we have clearly seen "religion and politics" are the two inseparable Battlefronts on which the triumph of GOOD over Evil depends!

We must remember that ultimately Jesus was Crucified by Evil and killed for His interference in Jewish and ultimately Roman *politics*! Those who suggest that Jesus was never political, are in fact teaching, preaching, and acting *Against GOD*!

---

[115] The *Holy Bible*; 2 Corinthians 5:20.

4. THE COALITION OF THE UNLIKELY: THE TIE THAT BLINDS

Chapter 4

Every sub-group of the Left's power-base is ideologically at odds one with the other. Islamists, Feminists, Abortionists (especially Planned Parenthood), Children's Rights Advocates, Homosexual Activists, Leftist-minded Black Activists, Atheists, Leftist-minded Jews, Leftist Billionaires, the Leftist-minded "poor working class", are all seemingly at irreconcilable odds one to another. Yet there they all are as a collective Democrat Leftist Confederation. Why?

Let me demonstrate what I mean. Let's consider a few of the obvious examples as a representative sampling of the Democrat Leftist Confederation as a whole. Islamists subjugate women and sell young girls into sexual slavery; while Feminists denigrate men and Suprematize women. How are these two groups compatible in the same Democrat Leftist Confederation? Abortionists (especially Planned Parenthood) kill babies and children by the tens-of-millions; while Children's Rights Advocates claim to be the protector of babies and children. How are these two groups compatible in the same Democrat Leftist Confederation? Feminists promote women's rights and the protection of women, while Abortionists (especially Planned Parenthood) kill baby girls by the tens-of-millions. How are these two groups compatible in the same Democrat Leftist Confederation?

Planned Parenthood Founder Margaret Sanger began Planned Parenthood in large part as a means to eradicate all the blacks in the West, one black baby at a time, while Leftist-minded Black Activists promote the idea of Black Supremacy and the "right" of abortion to black women. How are these two groups compatible in the same Democrat Leftist Confederation? Atheists militantly demand that there is no GOD[116] and that all vestiges of religion be irradiated,

---

[116] By the way how do you execute a War Against something that you claim does not exist? Atheists say that GOD does not exist, but then they unleash Hell upon and person, organization, and symbols of a "non-existent GOD". Hummm... maybe the Atheists are not exactly being truthful with us?

forcefully if necessary, from the planet, while Leftist-minded Jews hold onto at least some semblance of religion. How are these two groups compatible in the same Democrat Leftist Confederation? Leftist Democrat Billionaires supposedly exploit the working-class (a prime example being George Soros), while the Leftist-minded "poor working class" fight against the rich as evil subjugators of the masses. How are these two groups compatible in the same Democrat Leftist Confederation? Islamists kill Homosexuals. How are these two groups compatible in the same Democrat Leftist Confederation? We could go on-and-on, but this serves as a sufficient relative sampling.

Here is the *only* plausible answer to these seemingly irreconcilable disparities: The Lowest Common Denominator of all these groups is… *Evil*! What do Islamists have in common with Feminists? *Evil*. What do Abortionists have in common with Children's Rights proponents? *Evil*. Islamists and Homosexual Activists? *Evil*! What do Abortionists have in common with Leftist-minded Black Activists? *Evil*! Let's be a little more specific. Over 79% of Planned Parenthood abortion slaughterhouses are located within walking distance of minority neighborhoods, especially targeting Blacks! Blacks who represent less than 12.5% of the American population, represent nearly 40% of all babies killed by abortions each year; Coretta Scott-King, who is black, accepted the Margaret Sanger Award posthumously on behalf of her Black husband Martin Luther King Jr. for King's Black Activism, and for all Blacks in general. How are these groups able to coexist in the same Democrat Leftist Confederation? *Evil*! Their commonalities are manifested in the *Evil* that they inflict upon Americans and all of humanity. Islamists cut the heads off of children… so does Planned Parenthood! They are equally… *Evil*! These Evil Leftist groups are the core of the Left's implementation of their imagined *Evil* "Kingdom of Paradise on Earth".

The Leftist is obsessed with building their "kingdom on earth". GOD is focused on getting as many people as possible to His Kingdom in Heaven *after* our life on earth. The two philosophies are absolutely irreconcilable! Here are Horowitz's comments as an ex-radical Leftist:

In his own mind the radical is building his own kingdom, which to him is a kingdom of heaven on earth. Since a kingdom of heaven built by human beings is a fantasy - an impossible dream - the radical's only real world efforts are those which are aimed at subverting the society he lives in. He is a nihilist.[117]

Obama, who is a student and protégé of the godfather of the modern Left Saul Alinsky, espouses the same radical rhetoric as Alinsky:

"I am confident that we can create a Kingdom right here on Earth.[118]"

Notice that Obama's "Kingdom" cannot be a Biblical Kingdom as only GOD can bring Heaven to earth. Obama was talking about "creating" this Leftist "Kingdom" himself, of course, at least in theory, with the assistance of fellow Leftist sojourners. Another glaring and intentional omission is any reference to whose kingdom Obama refers! No Christian omits a reference to "GOD" using either the "Kingdom of GOD" or "GOD's Kingdom". Here Obama references his envisioned kingdom as "a" kingdom, which Obama intentionally left undefined. The use of "a" could mean anything except "the" Kingdom of GOD. Obama is referring to his mentor Saul Alinsky's reference in *Rules For Radicals* to Lucifer's kingdom: "Lest we forget at least an over-the-shoulder acknowledgment to the very first radical...the first radical known to man who rebelled against the establishment and did it so effectively that *he at least won his own kingdom — Lucifer*.[119]"!

---

[117] Horowitz, David; Commentary on Rules For Radicals; pg. 16.

[118] Hamby, Peter; CNN.com; *Obama: GOP doesn't own faith issue*; October 8, 2007.

[119] Alinsky, Saul; *Rules for Radicals*; dedication page.

Here is the actual page from Alinsky's book *Rules For Radicals* dedication page:

> *Lest we forget at least an over-the-shoulder acknowledgment to the very first radical: from all our legends, mythology, and history (and who is to know where mythology leaves off and history begins— or which is which), the first radical known to man who rebelled against the establishment and did it so effectively that he at least won his own kingdom —Lucifer.*
>
> —SAUL ALINSKY

By their own admission, the Left has their own Religion which unites the many streams of Evil into a single force. As we have documented, the Religion of the Left is the Religion of *Lucifer*, a Kingdom of Evil which is vehemently and militantly opposed to GOD and His Christian Religion. This Kingdom of Evil otherwise referred to here as the Religion of the Left, or the Left's Religion, will be much further exposed and detailed in the later chapter: *The Left Is a RELIGION!*. If the idea of the Left as a Religion haunts you now, feel free to skip ahead to that chapter and settle the matter before proceeding further here. (Don't worry we'll be here waiting to continue when you return..........)

This discussion begs the question: Why does the Left appeal to the basest of men who are in fact... *Evil*? Here is one of the most succinct non-religious explanations for the mass appeal of Evil to those on the Left. Bear in mind that this almost prophetic piece was written in 1945 by a contemporary to the events of the rise of Nazi Fascism and that it, almost without variance, precisely describes the Left in America today, with particular homage to the modern Democrat Party:

> There are three main reasons why such a numerous group, with fairly similar views, is not likely to be formed by the best but rather by the worst elements of any society.
>
> First, the higher the education and intelligence of individuals become, the more their tastes and views are differentiated. If

we wish to find a high degree of uniformity in outlook, **we have to descend to the regions of lower moral and intellectual standards where the more primitive instincts prevail**. This does not mean that the majority of people have low moral standards; it merely means that the largest group of people whose values are very similar are the people with low standards. [I would not be so kind here to the Left, as even the Über-Leftist philosopher and Hitler's mentor Friedrich Nietzsche saw that the ranks of the Socialists tended toward "the logical conclusion of the tyranny of the least and dumbest[120]" and Vladimir Lenin murderer of millions in the name of Socialism referred to the rank and file Socialists as "useful idiots".]

Second, since this group is not large enough to give sufficient weight to the leader's endeavours, he will have to increase their numbers by converting more to the same simple creed [of useful idiots]. He must gain the support of the docile and gullible, who have no strong convictions of their own but are ready to accept a ready-made system of values if it is only drummed into their ears sufficiently loudly and frequently. [The Big *Lie* of Hitler discussed at length in other chapters.] It will be those whose vague and imperfectly formed ideas are easily swayed and whose passions and emotions are readily aroused who will thus swell the ranks of the totalitarian party.

Third, to weld together a closely coherent body of supporters, **the leader must appeal to a common human weakness** [Read *sin*]. It seems to be easier for people to agree on a negative programme – on the hatred of an enemy, on the envy of the better off – than on any positive task. The contrast between the 'we' and the 'they' is consequently always employed by those who seek the allegiance of huge masses.

Advancement within a totalitarian group or party depends largely on a **willingness to do immoral things**. The principle

---

[120] Nietzsche, Friedrich; *Will to Power*; New York, Vintage Books; 1968; pgs. 51, 125.

that **the end justifies the means** [Remember Saul Alinsky Obama and Hillary's mentor], which in individualist ethics is regarded as **the denial of all morals**, in collectivist ethics becomes necessarily the supreme rule. **There is literally nothing which the consistent collectivist must not be prepared to do if it serves 'the good of the whole'**, [See the index for the Left's trumpeting of their "common good".] because that is to him the only criterion of what ought to be done. **Once you admit that the individual is merely a means to serve the ends of the higher entity called society or the nation, most of those features of totalitarianism which horrify us follow of necessity**. From the collectivist standpoint intolerance and brutal suppression of dissent, deception, and spying [the Deep State of the Left], the complete disregard of the life and happiness of the individual are essential and unavoidable. Acts which revolt all our feelings, such as the shooting of hostages or the killing of the old or sick, are treated as mere **matters of expediency**; the compulsory uprooting and transportation of hundreds of thousands becomes an instrument of policy approved by almost everybody except the victims. **To be a useful assistant in the running of a totalitarian state, therefore, a man must be prepared to break every moral rule he has ever known if this seems necessary to achieve the end set for him**. In the totalitarian machine there will be special opportunities for the ruthless and unscrupulous. Neither the Gestapo nor the administration of a concentration camp, neither the Ministry of Propaganda nor the SA or SS [or their Russian counterparts] are suitable places for the exercise of humanitarian feelings. Yet it is through such positions that the road to the highest positions in the totalitarian state leads[121]. (Emphases, bold, underline, and comments added)

Dostoevsky in his novel *The Brothers Karamazov* through his character Ivan Karamazov, puts it this way:

---

[121] Hayek, Friedrich A.; *The Road to Serfdom with The Intellectuals and Socialism* (Readers Digest Condensed version); 1945; pgs. 52-54.

"If God does not exist, everything is permitted".

This *War* is a conflict to the death of *Evil Against GOD*! Humans are simply Evil's collateral damage strewn along the pages of history. Whether the Right realizes it or not, we are the primary targets of Evil, and Evil will stop at *NOTHING* to Win! As such, the Christian, his family, and the Church are in Evil's crosshairs! America was established as a Christian Nation and has been a target of Evil since its conception.

In another ironic and horrifyingly tragic twist, one of the specific examples Obama gave as his means to "transform this Nation" was, as President, Obama would act by the force of the Federal government in legalizing every type of abortion which Obama specified to include the most grotesque form, partial-birth abortion! (For a more graphic description of partial-birth abortion see the chapter *The Obamas: The Epitome of the Left*) Speaking to Planned Parenthood of its fight to legalize all forms of abortion Obama said, "When we have achieved as one voice a strong call for that kind of more fair and more just America, then I am absolutely convinced that we're not just going to win an election ***but more importantly we're going to transform this nation***."[122]. Paradoxically, Obama in building up to his point cites the event of Planned Parenthood's first Margaret Sanger Award that was given to Martin Luther King Jr. The "award" was accepted posthumously in 1966 by King's widow Coretta Scott-King. In a surreal irony it should be noted that it was Margaret Sanger's intended goal in establishing Planned Parenthood and promoting "planned parenthood" to ideally eliminate, or at least greatly eradicate, the undesirable segments of society specifically targeting the black race:

> "As her organization grew, Sanger set up more clinics in the communities of other 'dysgenic races'—such as Blacks and Hispanics. Sanger turned her attention to 'Negroes' in 1929 and opened another clinic in Harlem in 1930. Sanger, 'in

---

[122] Transcribed by Laura Echevarria, www.lauraechevarria.com; Barack Obama before Planned Parenthood Action Fund, July 17, 2007.

alliance with eugenicists, and through initiatives such as the Negro Project ... exploited black stereotypes in order to reduce the fertility of African Americans... Sanger believed the 'Negro district' was the 'headquarters for the criminal element' and concluded that, as the title of a book by a member of her board proclaimed, *The Rising Tide of Color Against White World Supremacy*, was a rise that had to be stemmed.... **'to limit or even erase the black presence in America'**"[123]. (emphasis added)

In a letter to Clarence Gable in 1939, Sanger wrote:

"We do not want word to go out that **we want to exterminate the Negro population,** and the minister is the man who can straighten out that idea if it ever occurs to any of their more rebellious members" (Margaret Sanger commenting on the 'Negro Project' in a letter to Gamble, Dec. 10, 1939)[124]".

A full 36% of abortions are on black babies when in America the black population is less than 13%. A full 79% of Planned Parenthood abortion clinics are within walking distance of minority neighborhoods. Does Planned Parenthood still target blacks for extermination? You do the math!

Oh what strange bedfellows the Left embraces! A black President who praised Planned Parenthood and its founder Margaret Sanger who supported the eugenic ideals that target the black race for extermination! Only *Evil* can explain such a coalition. This is *The Coalition of the Unlikely: The Tie That Binds* and is the Left's noose around the necks of the Right in America today!

---

[123] Bergman, Jerry; Journal of Creation; *Birth control leader Margaret Sanger: Darwinist, racist and eugenicist*; Volume 22, Issue 3; December 2008.
[124] Grossu, Arina; Washington Times online; *Margaret Sanger, racist eugenicist extraordinaire*; May 5, 2014.

5. UNDERSTANDING THE TWO FACES OF THE ENEMY

Chapter 5

The Right in America has been baffled by the all-embracing success of the Left's *War* Against the Right. Innumerable explanations have been posited for the Left's seemingly unexplainable success, but none have adequately, nor nearly explained, nor accounted for this phenomenon of the Left's systematic success *Against* the Right. An honest and all-encompassing assessment of this *War* is *absolutely* necessary in order to confront and overcome the unseen assaults of the Left *Against* the Right. The Right has been continually blindsided by the bludgeoning blows from an unseen fist. The Right staggers around stupefied with no idea what has hit them. The blows of the Left are relentless and without mercy. The Left, whether the Right realizes it or not, is simply waging a two-front *War*. One front is visible and the other front is invisible. Defeat is guaranteed when one faces two enemies, of which only one is seen and recognized. As such the unseen source of the assaults cannot be actively defended against nor can the *War* even be waged on that front! We are sitting ducks totally unaware of the imminent demise that awaits us. This is where the Right stands today, completely undefended on one front of a two-front *War*!

Keep in mind the elitist leadership of the Left themselves today acknowledge that their spiritual power comes from Lucifer. Remember again Saul Alinsky, the godfather of the Leftist elite today, references Lucifer's kingdom as their spiritual collaborator in *Rules For Radicals*: "Lest we forget at least an over-the-shoulder acknowledgment to the very first radical...the first radical known to man who rebelled against the establishment and did it so effectively that *he at least won his own **kingdom** — Lucifer.*[125]"! (For those scoffers reading this who do not believe in a literal evil "Lucifer", is it not frightening enough that the Left *does* believe and follows the evil as set forth by what is attributed as "Lucifer"?!)

---

[125] Alinsky, Saul; *Rules for Radicals*; dedication page.

It has never been so clear that this *War* cannot be understood by the surface definitions of simply "Left Against Right" or "Liberal Against Conservative", but must inescapably be differentiated as *"Evil Against GOD"*! The Left's unseen spiritual presence of Evil is the power behind the Left and its second front in this *War*. This second front is the hidden "religious" aspect of the Left's wildly successful *War* strategies against the Right. (see especially the following chapter: *The Left is a RELIGION!*) Again we are reminded of the line of the French poet Charles Baudelaire "the finest trick of the devil is to persuade you that he does not exist". If we cannot see the invisible Enemy, Evil incarnate, the Devil, behind our visible enemy for who and what he really is, then we are powerless to resist and defend against Evil's strategies. The Right has attempted to Fight this *War* as if Evil "does not really exist". This has been the deadliest of mistakes and miscalculations of the Right in attempting to Battle back against *The Left's War Against GOD!*

The *Bible* tells us that "though we walk in the flesh, we do not *war* after the flesh"[126], but the *War* is against demonic "powers, against the rulers of the darkness of this world, *against **spiritual** wickedness* in high places". The true *War* is on the "religious", *spiritual* level and spills over into the second arena of the physical world of *politics*. The Left has been Fighting the spiritual warfront of this *War* all along, while the Right has been almost absolutely oblivious and humiliated into surrender on this front. After all, the Left reminds us, what idiot believes in an *unseen* Evil power; only the dim-witted and superstitious imbecile believes in the Devil. Really? The Left believes! We *must* carry on the Fight on both the *physical* and *spiritual*, the *seen* and the *unseen* fronts, ever considering that the true *power* of Evil comes from the *unseen*, *spiritual* realm. If we neglect, or deny, the *spiritual* side of the *War*, the Battle for America will be lost!

---

[126] The *Holy Bible:* 2 Corinthians 10:3 (emphasis added).

The Devil, who Jesus tells us is the father of *Lies*[127], never intentionally reveals his true nature, but always comes behind the façade of the "greater good". The Devil offers the Forbidden Fruit to us, and we too often discover too late that what we bite into is actually the Poison Apple! The drugs that Evil offers are poison pills. The free sex is a deadly disease and a destroyed home. Nothing that the Left offers us is in the spiritual realm as it appears in the natural world. It is all cloak and dagger, smoke and mirrors, an upturned grin, and death!

Only GOD can break the downward cycle, Win the Battle, and as He has ultimately done, Win the War! Fighting only the enemy we can see unaided from Heaven is a deadly game of certain defeat. The *War*, whether we choose to recognize it or not, must be fought on two simultaneous levels, both the *spiritual* and the *natural*, which is the religious and the political. To ignore, or be ignorant of, the *spiritual* War is to guarantee defeat! This is a fact of which we must be made painfully aware. The Devil's unseen assault, combined with the Left's visible attacks, have been the undoing of what was uniquely American. We must recognize and Fight on both the spiritual and the natural fronts if the Right is to prevail Against the Left in the Battle for America!

---

[127] The *Holy Bible:* John 8:44 (emphasis added).

6. THE PROGRESSIVE FACE OF THE LEFT

Chapter 6

The word "Progressive" has become the code word among Leftists to self-identify themselves to fellow Leftist conspirators in much the same way that Masons have their secret handshakes and gang members flash their secret gang signs. Much of America is oblivious to the true message and beliefs that these "Progressives" are conveying in their secret passwords. Remember to the Left, "The issue is never the issue. The issue is always the revolution[128]". Newsflash... those who need to keep their associations secret... have something to hide!

There is a direct correlation between the Left's "*Re-Name-Game*"[129] and an attempt to hide the true Evil inherent in the outworking of Leftist ideologies. The Left must continually *Re-Name* itself to avoid detection of their true Evil nature and intentions with all its historically associated Evil precedents. While some of the overly-sensitive might find the following example somewhat offensive, their Pavlovistic reaction will only serve to further highlight the point. Before we begin let me first state that this example is not in and of itself evil, but the process has been championed by Left to soften the acceptance of later *Re-Name-Game* tactics which are themselves Evil. Politically Correct euphemisms have become so commonplace that Stephen Pinker in his 2003 book *The Blank Slate* coined the name "euphemism treadmill" to describe the process. A euphemism is of course an attempt to *Re-Name* something to make it seem somehow better than it really is and/or as an attempt to somehow avoid stigmatization.

---

[128] More on this in the chapter: *America's War/The War Against America's Judeo-Christian Foundations*.
[129] For further discussion see the chapter: *Bait and Switch: The Re-Name-Game*.

The example of the ultimate circular reasoning[130] *Re-Naming* is the designation of the "retarded" individual. To the Leftist leaning, the moniker "retard" sounded, well, too much like... *retarded*. So through various "evolutions" the euphemistic treadmill began: retard, idiot, mongoloid, slow, slow minded, mentally retarded, mentally handicapped, mentally challenged, mentally impaired, mentally disabled, intellectually challenged, intellectually disabled, intellectual disability, learning disabled, severely diminished mental capacity, developmentally disabled, special, special needs, now they want to call them "gifted". Guess what? When it comes right down to it, they are still... retarded! Changing names does not change the condition originally described!

Progressivism of the Left in America today reflects this *retarded* Re-Name-Game tactic. The Left simply continues to *Re-Name* itself to keep ahead of discovery of the true Evil nature of the Left, which ultimately comes full-circle back to the starting point of Evil. "Progressives" have Re-Named themselves through a continual *Re-Name-Game*. All the manifestations of Progressives were at one time very much in vogue and considered a modern intellectual movement worthy of success *at any cost*, so much so in their own estimation, that the very survival of mankind depended upon it!

The meaning of the word "Progressive" is self-defined for us by modern-day Leftists leaving no question, that at its core, Progressivism is the Left's means to *radicalize* and *"transform"* America into the Left's imagined Leftist Utopia. Make no mistake the Left's attempt to "transform" America is a P.C. doublespeak for destroying America as we know it! The Left's "story" is being written and warped into the Leftist dream (Read *nightmare*!). We need look no further than Michelle Obama's 2015 Memorial Day address to graduates at Oberlin College:

> I want to urge you to actively seek out the most *contentious, polarized, gridlocked* places you can find. Because so often,

---

[130] For a brief discussion of Circular Reasoning see chapter Emotion Based Politics.

throughout our history, those have been the places where *progress* really happens.

And, graduates, climate change, economic inequality, human rights, criminal justice — these are the *revolutions* of your time. And you have as much *responsibility* and just as much *power* to wake up and play your part in our great American *story*.

The use of the words "*contentious, polarized,* and *gridlocked*" are particularly telling. To be *contentious* is to be mean-spirited and vicious by nature, *polarized* is to be violently without compromise, and gridlock means to intentionally take a position from which you will not move and, if your opponent will not compromise, some disaster looms. This is the position from which the Left operates (and again of which the Left accuses the Right. See broader discussion in the chapter: *Lies, Lies, Lies!*).

Have you ever wondered about the obsession of the Left with "climate change, economic inequality, human rights, and criminal justice"? It is the drumbeat and means to seize control of America and Americans by playing on the human fears of "inevitable doom" and a supposed "inequality" caused by the "inherent evil" in traditional America. By their very definition the Left mocks GOD by presuming that GOD cannot save the world form "inevitable doom" and that GOD's ways cause "inequality". When in fact it is the Left who has brought about the very possibility of the "inevitable doom" and "inequality", which they now claim to be trying to correct! (Remember the discussion on Rahm Emanuel's "Never let a crisis go to waste…" and the discussion of the Left's "solution" to teen pregnancy as a cloak to promote sexual sin.) "Progressivism" in the Leftist use means to "correct" all the perceived evils of the Right that the Left imagines and tells us exist. "Progressivism" is the path to total domination and "cradle to grave" control of Evil over all Americans, hidden in the smokescreen of the "we care" *Lie* of the Left! Truly "Progressivism" is a *progression* to total abandonment of America to Evil!

A women's workout clothing company began using a flower to represent a woman's size to avoid "size-shaming". However, we all intuitively know that any particular woman's "flower" size, representing a women's size 24, still means she's fat! Do you think that's harsh? OK. The *Bible* calls her a "glutton". Does that make the Left's *Lie* "feel" better? The *Lie* does not work any more than a man putting on a dress or having "sex change surgery" makes a man a woman! A man's gender is predetermined by GOD and *embedded in his DNA*. You cannot change the gender that is embedded in DNA! No matter how many cosmetic changes, a man can *never* be a woman. *Never*. It's all Leftist attempts at self-delusion and trying to make a person "feel" better about their *sin Against GOD*! Remember the Left's goal is always to circumvent and control by making *sin Against GOD* irrelevant in their *War Against GOD*.

The road from and to Progressivism looks like this: From Progressives to Socialists to Communists to Fascists to Liberals to Leftists to Environmentalists, and now back to Progressives. Of course the move back to "Progressive" could only occur without a public mutiny after the government-run public school system has dummied-down civics to the point beyond which the meaning of the term "Progressive" has long since been erased from the collective American mind.

The term "Progressive" sounds very *avant-garde*, very cultured, very modern. However, few people outside of the Left's Elite have actually stopped to consider what the word "Progressive" actually means and implies. To be "progressive" means "to move beyond". But ask yourself: Move beyond what? The very word Progressive is to work to destroy every foundation upon which America was built, and "move beyond" it! Our success, our Freedoms, Christianity, unprecedented opportunity for all citizens, protections from government tyranny, independence, individual incentive, and the greatest economy in the history of the world… these are what are in the crosshairs of the "Progressive" Left. These American freedoms are antithetic to the Left's "progressive" mindset and goals.

Progressive, Liberal, New Left, Socialist, Fascist, Populist, Collectivist, Marxist, Communist, Democrat, Environmentalist, New

Ager, Communitarianist, Jacobin, *ad infimum*, all trace directly back to Paganism, which itself ultimately traces back to the Tower of Babel and the establishment of the Religion of the Great Whore of Babylon, the Religion of Satan[131], or as Alinsky identified him *Lucifer*! The Biblical reference to the "Whore" also helps us understand the Left's obsession with the sexual in areas like "sexual freedom" being based in the Religion of the "Great Whore of Babylon" or Lucifer.

Think this link to the Great Whore of Babylon is a stretch? Let's let Paul Goodman, a *secularist* American novelist, playwright, poet, *open homosexual*, psychotherapist and self-avowed "anarchist philosopher" describe the 1960's Leftist movement in retrospect:

> I had imagined that the worldwide student protest had to do with changing political and moral institutions, and I was sympathetic to this. But I now saw that we had to do with a **religious** crisis. Not only all institutions but all learning had been corrupted **by the Whore of Babylon**, and there was no longer any salvation to be got from Works[132]. (emphasis added)

Even secularists, who like Paul Goodman who are presumably irreligious, can recognize that the Left is a *religious* movement. Goodman even goes as far as to call the religious nature of the 1960's movement a "New Reformation", clearly using historically Christian language to refer to the modern machinations of the Left.

David Horowitz sums up the "*Re-Name*" game from his own personal experience this way:

> "The many names of Satan [Lucifer] are also a model for the way radicals camouflage their agendas by calling themselves at different times Communists, socialists, new leftists, liberals, social justice activists and most consistently *progressives*. My parents, who were card-carrying Communists, never referred

---

[131] The *Holy Bible:* Revelation 17:1-6; 19:2
[132] Goodman, Paul; *New Reformation: Notes of a Neolithic Conservative*; 1970; pg. 48.

to themselves as Communists but always as *"progressives,"* as did their friends and political comrades. The "Progressive Party" was created by the Communist Party to challenge Harry Truman in the 1948 election because he opposed the spread of Stalin's empire. The Progressive Party was led by Roosevelt's vice president, Henry Wallace, and was the vehicle chosen by the Communists to lead their followers out of the Democratic Party, which they had joined during the "popular front" of the 1930's. The progressives rejoined the Democrats during the McGovern campaign of 1972 and with the formation of a hundred-plus member Progressive Caucus in the congressional party and the ascension of Barack Obama to the presidency have become its most important political force"[133]. (emphasis added)

It should be remembered here that it was the 1968 Democrat Convention in Chicago where the Leftist-Progressives took over the Democrat Party by *force*. While the Leftist radical foot soldiers battled the police outside the Democrat Party nomination convention, the Leftist radical elites pulled off their own *coup* inside. So as Horowitz rightly points out, the 1972 Democrat Convention was controlled by the Leftist *Progressive* radicals who continue to control the Democrat Party today! This is easily evidenced by the current Democrat Party chairman Debbie Wasserman-Schultz, herself an über-Leftist radical, remarked about how the avowed Socialist Bernie Sanders is a welcome member of the modern Democrat Party and as the Presidential candidate for the Democrat Party saying of Sanders' rise in popularity "we think it is fantastic!". Sanders makes it clear that there is no difference between a Socialist and a Progressive, by which title Sanders refers to himself interchangeably.

The French Revolution's Leftist and Progressive "achievements" were enshrined in *The Declaration of Rights of Man and the Citizen*. Several basic "rights" were contrived and codified by the Left here. In a radical departure from GOD-given rights, to man-bequeathed rights, divorce was legalized and **so was, not surprisingly, homosexual sex**.

---

[133] Horowitz, David; *Commentary on Rules For Radicals*; pgs. 18-19.

As will be documented at length in the chapter *Fascism and the Left in America: Kindred Spirits and Familiar Bedfellows* and other places, homosexuality is always the *avant-garde* in *The Left's War Against GOD!* The psychoanalyst Jean Artarit diagnoses Maximilien François Marie Isidore de Robespierre, the tyrant who created the Anti-GOD *Reign of Terror* of the French Revolution, as a "repressed homosexual with a castration complex, a misogynist, and pathological narcissist"[134]. Laurent Dingli, French biographer of Robespierre, makes a direct association between the pathological personalities of Leftists Robespierre, Stalin, Lenin, and Hitler[135]. A "right" is by its very definition "GOD-given". It cannot be bought, earned, given, or bequeathed; a right exists because GOD exists. It just IS! Rights exist as naturally inherent in GOD's Creation. *No one* has a GOD-given "right" to equal pay, a job, welfare, cell phones, or healthcare. We *do* have a GOD-given right to life, liberty, and the *pursuit* of happiness as is enshrined in the GOD-based American Declaration of Independence. The Left always wants to play "god" and take credit for creating what they misrepresent as "rights":

> Contemporary liberalism [Progressive Leftism] is not so limited a view. It is a comprehensive governing philosophy that determines the whole of public morality [religion]. While it sounds permissive, comprehensive solutions are usually intolerant in practice and liberalism [Progressive Leftism] is no exception. Contemporary liberalism [Progressive Leftism] sets forth categorical demands it calls **rights**, and rejects balancing principles such as respect for natural tendencies and settled [religious] understandings [of Christianity]. Without balancing principles [Progressive Leftist] abstract demands expand without limit. As a result, liberal [Progressive Leftist] standards have become all-embracing to the point of **tyranny**[136]. (Brackets added)

---

[134] McPhee, Peter; *Robespierre: A Revolutionary Life*; 2013; pg. 230.
[135] Dingli, Laurent; *Robespierre*; Paris (Flammarion); 2004, 605 S.
[136] Kalb, James; Modern Age Quarterly; *The Tyranny of Liberalism*; 2000; pg. 243.

On the Leftist doctrine of the *right to work*, the imagined and man-made "right" to State guaranteed employment, as Alexis de Tocqueville the French Historian of America astutely observed in 1848 in his speech to the French Assembly titled: *Discours prononcé à l'assemblée constituante le 12 Septembre 1848 sur la question du droit au travail* (Speech to the constituent Assembly on September 12, 1848, on the question of the right to work):

> "Democracy [modern republicanism] extends the sphere of individual freedom, socialism [Progressive Leftism] restricts it. Democracy [modern republicanism] attaches all possible value to each man; socialism [Progressive Leftism] makes each man a mere agent, a mere number. Democracy [modern republicanism] and socialism [Progressive Leftism] have nothing in common but one word: equality. But notice the difference: while democracy [modern republicanism] seeks equality in liberty, socialism [Progressive Leftism] seeks equality in restraint and servitude"[137].

It cannot be overemphasized that the Nazi movement named the *Nationalist **Socialist** German Worker's Party*, or the "Nazi Party" which is its acronym in English, was a ***Socialist*** party! Socialism is purely a Leftist phenomenon. One thing that can be stated with absolute certainty is that the Nazi ideology was neither Right, nor Conservative, but very much a Leftist, Liberal, Progressive, ***Socialist*** movement.

Arguably the first openly Progressive President of the United States was Woodrow Wilson who has been adequately described as:

> "In his unintentionally chilling 1890 essay, *Leaders of Men*, Wilson explained that the 'true leader' uses the masses like 'tools'. He must not traffic in subtleties and nuance, as literary

---

[137] Frères, M. Lévy; *Oeuvres complètes d'Alexis de Tocqueville, vol. IX: Étude économiques, politiques et littéraires*; 1878; pg. 536.

men do. **Rather he must speak to stir their passions**, not their intellects.[138]"

Hillary Rodham-Clinton says she doesn't really like the descriptive word "liberal", preferring to be characterized as a "Progressive":

"You know... Liberal... is a word that originally meant that you were for freedom ... that you were willing to stand against big power and on behalf of the individual. Unfortunately, in the last 30, 40 years, it has been turned up on its head, and it's been made to seem as though it is a word that describes big government, totally contrary to what its meaning was in the 19th and early 20th century... **I prefer the word 'progressive,'** *which has a real American meaning*, going back to the progressive era at the beginning of the 20th century. **I consider myself a modern progressive**".[139] (emphasis added)

The duplicitous self-*re-naming* of Progressivism to Liberalism was spearheaded by Progressive/Leftist John Dewey, the Left's "father of modern education", to avoid the negative connotations that had become associated with Progressivism and hijack the positive connotations then associated with classical liberalism. In an equally deft sleight of hand, classical liberalism became known as Conservatism making its own negative association of Conservativism with European monarchies. So Hillary Rodham-Clinton has come full circle "going back to the *progressive* era at the beginning of the 20th century" and its association with Leftist Progressive Totalitarianism!

Let's let an ex-militant Progressive leader tell us what Progressive means:

"If someone has supported an idea or movement that he comes to see as destructive, the first thing he will want to do when he

---

[138] Goldberg, Jonah; *Liberal FASCISM: The Secret History of the American Left From Mussolini to the Politics of Meaning*; 2007; pg. 89.
[139] CNN/YouTube sponsored Democrat presidential debate; July 23rd, 2007.

abandons it is to repudiate and warn others against it. If he [or she] does not do that, it is apparent that he [or she] has not left the movement or abandon the idea but has *just put another face* **on the same destructive goals**. Instead of calling himself [or herself] a communist or socialist, he [or she] will call himself [or herself] a liberal and progressive. In fact, as I have just noted, this camouflage is very old. As a young man, I never heard my parents or their communist Party friends refer to themselves as communists. They were **progressives**.[140]"

Hillary Rodham-Clinton hides her Evil Leftist philosophies behind euphemisms as illuminated in her book titled "It Takes a Village: And Other Lessons Children Teach Us". This euphemism of the *"Global Village"* is a Leftist, One World government Utopian idea common to all Leftist manifestations. The One World community or *"Global Village"* united under the Left, is the mantra most commonly associated with Communism, but it is the common thread of Progressivism, Fascism/Nazism, Socialism, New Age, Environmentalism, Collectivism, and all other Leftist self-identifications that seek to "unite" the world under Leftist Anti-GOD control. This is the endgame of Hillary Rodham-Clinton and *all* Progressives. This is what the Left is *progressing* towards! The downward trajectory of Evil is predictable and given opportunity, inevitable! Progressivism is always "progressive" towards more and greater... *Evil*!

Here is the common motivation uniting all organized strains of the Leftist plague through history:

> "But therein lies the common principle: the State *should* be allowed to get away with anything, so long as it is for "good reasons". This is the common principle among fascism, Nazism, Progressivism, and what we today call liberalism [Leftism]. It represents the triumph of Pragmatism in politics in that it recognizes no dogmatic boundaries to the scope of government power. The leader and his anointed cadres are

---

[140] Horowitz, David; *Take No Prisoners: The Battle Plan For Defeating The Left*; pg. 40.

decision makers above and beyond political or democratic [Christian] imperatives"[141].

Obama has not moderated his Leftist ideology in any sense and has always identified himself in personal reference as a Leftist, a Liberal, a Progressive, a New Party (Socialist/Marxist), and a Democrat. Obviously *all* of these evil Leftist identities are synonymous and interchangeable!

Many people have watched first-hand the seamless transformation from having called what was Socialism into calling it Fascism. A contemporary to this decent of evil into Fascism was Friedrich Hayek who put it this way:

> **"To many who have watched the transition from socialism to fascism at close quarters the connection between the two systems has become increasingly obvious**, but in the democracies the majority of people still believe that socialism and freedom can be combined. They do not realize that democratic socialism, the great utopia of the last few generations, is not only unachievable, but that to strive for it produces something utterly different – the very destruction of freedom itself[142].

Progressivism seeks to prevent reasoned thinking and relies on rampant emotion alone to drive the Leftist movement forward. This language of the Progressive Left of yesterday reverberates today from beyond the grave in the words of Saul Alinsky and his instructions to the aspiring modern radical Progressive Leftist agitator:

> "I hope that these pages [in Alinsky's *Rules For Radicals*] will contribute to the education of the **radicals** of today, and to the conversion of **hot, emotional, impulsive passions** that are

---

[141] Goldberg, *Jonah; Liberal FASCISM: The Secret History of the American Left From Mussolini to the Politics of Meaning*; 2007; pg. 131.
[142] Hayek, Friedrich A.; *The Road to Serfdom with The Intellectuals and Socialism* (Readers Digest Condensed version); 1945; pg. 44.

impotent and frustrating to **actions that will be calculated, purposeful, and effective.**[143]"

Recently on MSNBC's Hardball when then Democratic National Committee Chairman Debbie Wasserman-Schulz was asked by Leftist anchor Chris Matthews, "What is the difference between a Democrat and a Socialist?" Ms. Wasserman-Schulz could not state even a single difference between a Democrat and a Socialist![144] Matthews did not let it pass so easily and asking again, "You're the chairman of the Democratic Party. Tell me the difference between you and a Socialist". Ms. Leftist-Schultz was stumped. This is the head of the Democrat Party in America today! Is this just a random miscue by Democrats? Hardly! When asked a few months later by Chris Matthews on "Hardball", Hillary Rodham-Clinton could not define the difference between a Democrat and a Socialist! Why? Because there is no difference! The Left is just stumped on crafting a believable *Lie* to redefine Socialism as something different than, as Hillary defines herself, that of the *Progressive Democrat*! There is *no* difference today between a Democrat, Socialist, Progressive, or Fascist. They are all the same... Evil!

---

[143] Alinsky, Saul; *Rules For Radicals*; pg. 6.
[144] MSNBC's Hardball with Chris Matthews; July 30, 2015.

7. BAIT AND SWITCH: THE RE-NAME-GAME:

Chapter 7

There is a direct correlation between the Left's "*Bait and Switch: Re-Name-Game*" and an attempt to hide the true Evil inherent in the outworking of the Left's ideologies.[145] This chapter and *Lies, Lies, Lies!* are closely related but they are important enough to warrant their own chapters. The Left must continually *Re-Name* itself to avoid detection of their true Evil nature and intentions with all its associated Evil history.

While some of the overly-sensitive might find the following example somewhat offensive, their Pavlovistic reaction will only serve to further make the point. Before we begin let me first state that the following example is not in and of itself evil, but the process has been championed by Left to soften the acceptance of later *Re-Name-Game* tactics which ends are themselves Evil. Politically Correct euphemisms have become so commonplace that Stephen Pinker in his 2003 book *The Blank Slate* coined the name "euphemism treadmill" to describe the process. A euphemism is of course an attempt to *Re-Name* something to make it seem somehow better than it really is and/or as an attempt to somehow avoid negative stigmatization.

The example of an ultimately circular *Re-Naming* is the designation of the moniker of a "retarded" individual. To the Leftist-leaning, the moniker "retard" sounded, well, too much like… *retarded*. So through various "evolutions" the euphemistic treadmill began: retard, idiot, mongoloid, slow, slow minded, mentally retarded, mentally handicapped, mentally challenged, mentally impaired, mentally disabled, intellectually challenged, intellectually disabled, intellectual disability, learning disabled, severely diminished mental capacity, developmentally disabled, special, special needs… now they want to

---

[145] We begin this chapter by reiterating several points from the previous chapter. The tactics of Evil and the Left are so intertwined that when discussing their tactics it becomes totally impossible to separate the discussion of Evil from that of the Left.

call them "gifted"! Gifted? Guess what? When it comes right down to it, these unfortunate individuals are still… retarded! *Renaming* something does not change the condition originally described.

Progressivism reflects this *retarded* Re-Name-Game tactic of the Left. The Left simply continues to *Re-Name* itself to keep ahead of discovery of the true Evil nature of the Left, which ultimately comes full-circle back to the starting point. "Progressives" have *Re-Named* themselves through a continual *Re-Name-Game*. All of the manifestations of Progressives were at one time very much in vogue and considered a modern intellectual movement worthy of success at any cost, so much so in their own estimation that the very survival of mankind depended and continues to depend upon it. When in truth only the survival of the Left depends on the deception!

As we have seen, Progressives become Socialists, Socialists become Communists, Communists become Fascists, Fascists become Liberals, Liberals become Leftists, Leftists become Environmentalists, and Environmentalists are now back to self-identifying as… Progressives. Each *Bait and Switch and Re-Name* is a step in the circular deception of Evil. The Left, as with Lucifer, acts as though its previous manifestation of Evil does not now, nor ever exist. For example, the Left in public totally disassociates itself from Fascism. (and even tries to associate Fascism with the Right!) But Fascism now (e.g. Antifa) and Fascism in Nazi Germany are and have always been Socialists/Leftists! Aided by the Left Stream Media and Leftist education system the revisionist history erases all knowledge of the Evil of the Left from the collective minds of Americans. This is the tactic of the Left in recreating itself with every new generation in the Left's *Re-Name Game*!

Leftist doctrines are necessarily contradictory at their very core. The Left tells us that it is a priggish Right who condemns overweight young girls, however it is the Leftist-inspired school teachers who send notes home to parents telling them that their child's body-mass index (BMI) is too high and that this is unhealthy and that the child needs to lose weight! The Left wants it both ways. They want to impugn the Right for something that the Right actually does not do,

94

while the Left regularly practices doing it themselves. This is the ploy which is to transfer Leftist guilt away before they can be labeled with the negative stereotype which they are themselves guilty of, and in fact are themselves doing.

The Left will scream about the Right and their conjured-up "stereotypes", however it is the Left who as a planned strategy uses collective stereotypical pejoratives like "the vast rightwing conspiracy"! The Left even effectively uses stereotypes to consolidate its power-base like "African-Americans", "Hispanics", "homosexuals", "transgenders", etc. as though these groups on the Left were absolutely monolithic in their beliefs, morals, and desires. To buck the Left's stereotypes is to be targeted for destruction by the Left! Cases in point include Supreme Court Justice Clarence Thomas, Secretary of State Condoleezza Rice, and Secretary of Housing and Urban Development Ben Carson.

Let's review some blatant recent examples. The Left pays Leftist agitators to infiltrate Tea Party rallies and commit acts of violence, then the Left screams how violent that the Right is because the rallies are violent! The Left pays Leftist agitators to infiltrate Trump rallies and commit acts of violence, then the Left screams how violent that the Right is! The Left calls the rioters against Trump "protestors" exercising their "First Amendment constitutional rights" and encourage the rioters to continue attacking people, rioting, and looting. The Left pays rioters to riot in the streets against Conservatives and Trump, they then accuse the rioters of being "alt-Right" agitators. This is straight out of the Nazi takeover playbook which violently took over Germany[146] and as adopted by Saul Alinsky to violently take over America!

It is not that the Left doesn't understand that they violate laws, it's just that they don't care! (Remember Saul Alinsky's by all means necessary?!) The Leftist "protesters" hide behind the Constitution's First Amendment when they violently protest by attacking people, beating people, threatening those who oppose them, and dozens of

---

[146] See the chapter: *Fascism and the Left in America: Kindred Spirits and Familiar Bedfellows.*

other criminal activities. The Left's objective is not "free speech", but shutting the Right's Free Speech down! The Left only touts the *Constitution* when they can hide behind it. We should not allow the Left to use "Free Speech" when they are espousing destroying the Constitution, the same *Constitution* of which the Left fights to destroy! Make no mistake that the Left is complicit in the violence of the Left and its minion minority groups! Do you doubt this? Then why is it that since Donald Trump became President that there has been no widespread violence in the streets as was under Obama? Humm… because Barack Hussein Obama is no longer there to instigate the Left's thugs to violence and then protect their violent "protesters" with the Federal authorities not the least of which was the Obama Attorney General's Office and FBI! The Left fears having to answer to the Law and frighteningly are seldom called into account for their criminal behavior (Hillary Clinton, Barack Hussein Obama, Loretta Lynch, James Comey, Eric Holder… *ad nauseam*!).

Let's also consider the Left's frantic attempt to accuse President Donald Trump of "collusion with the Russians". Here is a clue… Trump did not collude with the Russians! However, Barack Hussein Obama absolutely *did* collude with the Russians! Remember in 2012 when as President Obama was caught on an open mic telling Russian President Dmitry Medvedev to tell Medvedev's successor Vladimir Putin:

> "On all these issues, but particularly missile defense, this can be solved, but it's important for him to give me space," Mr. Obama could be heard saying to Mr. Medvedev, according a reporter from ABC News, who was traveling with the president. "Yeah, I understand," the departing Russian president said. "I understand your message about space. Space for you … ." Mr. Obama then elaborated in a portion of the exchange picked up by the cameras: "This is my last election. After my election I have more flexibility." "I understand. I will transmit this information to Vladimir," Mr. Medvedev said,

referring to Prime Minister Vladimir V. Putin, who just won an election to succeed Mr. Medvedev.[147]

Oops! But of course the Left will not admit Obama Russian collusion even when we can all watch it for ourselves!

And then there are the Clintons and their Clinton Foundation who also absolutely did collude with the Russians! Hillary Rodham-Clinton in 2010 while Secretary of State used her influence to arrange for approval the sale of Uranium One to "a state-owned Russian energy giant — which gave it control of one-fifth of U.S. uranium supplies" whilst "the FBI was actively investigating that company for extensive criminal activity designed to expand Russia's footprint in the U.S. uranium business." Further:

> "And shortly after the Russians announced their intention to acquire a majority stake in Uranium One, Mr. Clinton received $500,000 for a Moscow speech from a Russian investment bank with links to the Kremlin that was promoting Uranium One stock."[148]

> The Clintons and their foundation raked in a cool $145 million in donations and "speaking fees" just from Uranium One and Rosatom-affiliated donors while Secretary of State Hillary Clinton was supposedly keeping all Clinton Foundation business at "arm's-length." As we reported in July, Clinton official emails show extensive connections between Hillary, the Clinton Foundation and donors during her time as secretary of state, a kind of criminal conga-line of people asking for favors from Hillary and donating to the foundation.[149]

---

[147] Goodman, J. David; New York Times online; obama-caught-on-microphone-telling-medvedev-of-flexibility; March 26, 2012.

[148] Becker, Jo and McIntire, Mike; The New York Times; Cash Flowed to Clinton Foundation Amid Russian Uranium Deal; April 23, 2015; published online April 24, 2015.

[149] Investor's Business Daily; Yes, The Russia Scandal Is Real — And It Involves Hillary Clinton; 10/17/2017.

Again, the Left *always* accuses the Right of what the Left has already done! The Left is manifestly guilty of collusion with the Russians! President Trump is not!

The Left continuously *Re-Names* itself as the general population discovers the guise behind each previous incarnation of the Left in the *Re-Naming* of Evil from generation to generation. It is the goal of the Left to use the *Bait and Switch*, sleight of hand illusion to make Evil appear as "GOOD" and thereby be accepted by the public in general. Thomas Paine, a Patriot and Founding Father of America, characterized the Left's plot this way: "a long habit of not thinking a thing wrong, gives it a superficial appearance of being right"[150]. The Left can never just be truthful of their Evil intentions as they would never be accepted in mass as is necessary for a total takeover of every aspect of American life! Mussolini's maxim concerning the takeover of pre-Fascist Italy can be equally applied to the Leftists in America today:

> *"Our programme is simple. We want to rule Italy"*. As I have argued at length elsewhere, that is the real program of any Leftist. But Mussolini had the honesty to be upfront about it[151].

The honest modern American Leftist equivalent would simply be "We will use any means necessary to rule America"! Oh that's right... that is exactly what Saul Alinsky did say to his proselytes like Obama and the Clintons, "In **war**, the end justifies almost any means..."!

How about the radical Left using their *Bait and Switch: Re-Name Game* claiming the rainbow as their own moniker for every sort of sodomite Evil. (There are so many acronyms that it stalls the mind to remember all of the evil manifestations: LGBT (lesbian, gay, bisexual, transgender), LGBTQ, LGBTTQQIAAP (lesbian, gay, bisexual, transgender, transsexual, queer, questioning, intersex, asexual, ally, pansexual (aka what a joke!), LGBTQIA, GSM (Gender and Sexual Minorities), GNC, MSM, CD, MAAB/FAAB/UAAB,

---

[150] Paine, Thomas; *Common Sense*; 1776.
[151] Carsten, F.L.; *The Rise of Fascism*; London: Methuen; 1967, pg. 62.

CAMAB/CAFAB, SSM, *ad vomitum, ad absurdum*!) Talk about confused! Even the homosexuals cannot decide who they really are!) However the Rainbow was *created by* GOD after the Flood as GOD's promise to never destroy the earth by flood again. The Left has usurped the Rainbow of GOD with the rainbow of EVIL!

As mentioned earlier, we need to recognize the Left's usurpation of the term "liberal" using their *Re-Name-Game* and claiming the term as their own. "Classic Liberalism", as it is now called to clarify it from "Leftist Liberalism", is, and always has been, a manifestation of the Right and Conservative school. The Left must continually *Re-Name* itself and steal the terms from the Right to keep the masses from fully comprehending their true Evil nature. The Right has always been for the individual's freedoms and opposed to the empowering of the State over the individual. Classic Liberalism stood against the power of kings and all totalitarian régimes. The Right as Classic Liberals opposed the Leftist dictatorial usurpation of the Jacobins in the French Revolution, Communist China, Soviet Russia, Fascist Germany and Italy, Imperialistic Japan, and all other Leftist manifestations. The Left who is always for the State empowerment started calling themselves "Liberals" in their propagandistic effort to deceive the people into believing that the Left is "the Party of the people". Like their Communist masters before them the Left has bastardized the term "Liberal" for their own Evil ends!

Even the Über-Leftist Hillary Rodham-Clinton acknowledges the distinction between the Classic Liberalism of the Conservative school verses the modern Leftist Liberalism:

> "You know... Liberal... is a word that originally meant that you were for freedom ... that you were willing to stand against big power and on behalf of the individual. Unfortunately, in the last 30, 40 years, it has been turned up on its head, and it's been made to seem as though it is a word that describes big government, totally contrary to what its meaning was in the 19th and early 20th century... I prefer the word 'progressive,' which has a real American meaning, going back to the

progressive era at the beginning of the 20th century. **I consider myself a modern progressive"**.[152]

Even the term "patriot" has been redefined in order for Leftists to claim to be American "patriots". The Left operates under their new definition while Americans still interpret it by the old Right meaning. This deceit is a bald-face *Lie* and the American people are being duped. The real controversy started in earnest when Obama refused to wear an American Flag lapel pin during the 2008 presidential elections:

> "the Flag pin... became a substitute *for I think* [is] *true patriotism*... I decided I won't wear *that* pin on my chest. Instead, I'm going to try to tell the American people what I believe *will make* this country great, and hopefully that will be a testimony to *my* [new definition of] *patriotism*.[153]" (emphasis added)

Even the considerably Über Leftist PolitiFact.com called Obama's remarks on his flag pin statements "FALSE" on their "TRUTH-O-METER". The Left's *Re-Definition*, *Re-Naming*, of "patriotism" is not a reflection of what most Americans understand as "patriotism", but a *Bait and Switch* substitute definition, or *Lie*!

Obama described the Left's new form of "patriotism" to radically "remake this nation" in "each successive generation" in a speech full of his racist remarks in Selma, Georgia:

> "What greater expression of faith in the American experiment than this; **what greater form of patriotism is there; than the belief that America is not yet finished**, that we are strong enough to be self-critical, that *each successive generation* can look upon our imperfections and decide that **it is in our power**

---

[152] CNN/YouTube sponsored Democrat presidential debate; July 23rd, 2007.
[153] Drobnic-Holan, Angie; Tampa Bay Times, PolitiFact.com; *Obama contradicts previously stated pin philosophy*; April 18th, 2008

> **to remake this nation** to more closely **align with our highest ideals**?[154]".

Notice that the Left wants to "**remake this nation** to more closely **align with our highest [Leftist] ideals**"! America was and always has been a fundamentally Right Nation. Obama was then talking about "**remaking**" a former Right America into a new Leftist Paradise that will then "align with the highest [Leftist] ideals"! Otherwise there is no way to make Obama's remarks make any sense. As will be discussed further later, Common Sense is an enemy of the Left!

The Left can seem honest when they claim to be a "patriot" because they have simply *redefined* it as a Leftist euphemism! Leftist "patriotism" is not to America, but to an imagined Leftist Utopian global community! The reason that Obama would not wear a patriotic pin was because it had the American flag on it. If the pin had had the United Nations flag on it he certainly would have worn it in full regalia with his new Leftist definition of "patriotic pride"!

Here is an example of Obama's hypocrisy as it is represented in the Leftist doctrine of "patriotism". During Obama's 2008 presidential run, Obama emphatically promised, "I will never question the patriotism of others in this campaign"! Then Obama turned around during the campaign and said, "The way Bush has done it over the last eight years is . . . [Bush] added $4 trillion by his lonesome, so that we now have over $9 trillion of debt that we are going to have to pay back… That's irresponsible. It's *unpatriotic*". To Obama he had not lied but was speaking from his new euphemistic *Re-Definition, Re-Naming*, of "patriotism". In both instances Obama was speaking from the Left's redefinition; Obama would not question anyone's patriotism concerning that of the global Leftist Utopian redefinition. While most would view these statements as a contradiction, Obama was not speaking of a loyalty to a sovereign America, but to the creation and advancement of the Leftist *Global Community* synonymous with Hillary Rodham-Clinton's Global "Village". Bush was being attacked by Obama because Bush was not loyal to the

---

[154] Obama's speech in Selma, Alabama on March 7, 2015.

Leftist Global Utopian goals of Obama and the Left. Had Bush been spending the trillions of American dollars to further the Leftist global agenda, then of course Obama could have not said that Bush was "unpatriotic". When it was Obama's turn, then Obama as President under the Leftist definition of "patriotism", could spend trillions *more* than Bush advancing the Leftist agenda and pass it off as "nothing to worry about":

> "I don't remember what the number was precisely that I [have spent in deficit]... We don't have to worry about it short term".
> -President Obama, September 2012

Obama has put America in more debt more than *all* previous American Presidents *combined*, in the more than 240 years since the founding of the United States of America! Which of course to the Left is not unpatriotic, but ultimately "patriotic" and therefore heroic and laudable in the "progress" of creating the Left's imagined Global Utopian Paradise! To the Left it is not a matter of truth, but *Re-Defining* terms to match their agenda and creating an alternate "truth" akin to the Nazi Ministry of Propaganda and in the ultimate Orwellian sense. The Left does *not* "love America" any more than the Left are Patriots! You do not plot and fanaticize to destroy nor preach against what you love! This is the Big *Lie* of Hitler and a sin *Against GOD*! This defines the Left's agenda of the *Bait and Switch: The Re-Name-Game*!

The Left co-opts the terms, institutions, and symbols associated with the Right: As briefly discussed in the chapter *Defining The War: Evil Against GOD, Left Against Right*: "liberal" vs. "Classic Liberalism". Classic Liberalism, is in fact Right and Conservative! The color 'red' was the banner under which the Left associated itself in virtually every murderous régime like the flags of the Soviet Union, North Korea, North Vietnam, Pol Pot's Khmer Rouge in Cambodia, and Communist "Red" China. Now the Left uses the color red to signify the Republican Party in its designations such as the Republican "Red States". (and the Right helped the Left in accepting this *Lie*!) The Left euphemizes, with some hocus pocus, abracadabra, or some other witch's incantation, and voilà... "Pro-abortion" becomes "pro-choice", promoting the perverted homosexual agenda becomes a "civil rights" campaign, Leftism becomes the epithet *A Brave New World* (who does not want to be seen as "Brave"?), "Intolerance" becomes a Leftist Crusade for a *Re-Defined* "Tolerance" campaign. The examples of the Left's deceitful *Re-Name-Game* are endless…!!!

A blatant example of the Left's witchery is the Left's contrived "War On Women" of which it accuses the Right. The Left acts as if there are two Americas, a women's America that has had war declared against it by the men's America! How insanely absurd is that?![155] In essence the Left is saying that men have declared wholesale war on their mothers, sisters, wives, and daughters! Again, in fact it is the Left who has literally declared a War on Women! The Left demands abortion which kills tens-of-millions of unborn women! The Left supports euthanasia which kills women. The Left supports doctor assisted suicide, which kills women. *The Left has declared war on women and have in fact killed millions of women!* The Left's battle-cry of "the Right's war on women" is meaningless drivel (double-speak meant to confuse and deceive) and covering fire for its own *documentable* "Leftist War On Women". The falsified "Right's war on women" elicits nothing more than an emotional rallying point for the Left and its radical Storm Troopers. With the obvious stated, meaningless emotional appeals work! The Right needs to wise-up and employ similarly powerful emotional appeals (call-to-arms language) of its own, but appeals founded on *truth*. Truth and emotion will trump *Lies* and emotion every time!

Liberals love to use deceptive titles to project a false persona for themselves and their projects. Obamacare was titled "The Affordable Care Act" of which there is nothing "affordable" about it. Obama promised thousands of dollars in savings for the American family which now cost Americans additional thousands. Obama's promise that we could "keep your doctor" was another one of numerous *Lies*. The Left intentionally mislabels things as a way of deception. Instead of calling it "Nationalized Healthcare", which it really is and was argued as such by the Obama Administration before the US Supreme

---

[155] See the broader discussion of insanity in the chapter: *The Left Is a RELIGION!*.

Court, it is labeled the "Affordable Care Act". As Johnathan Gruber later admitted, that if Americans really knew what was in it, they would never have allowed it to pass. This is a tactic of Evil since the beginning of time and the political Left since it was founded in the Garden of Eden. Lucifer did not present Eve with the Forbidden Fruit and say "Here, eat this and you will surely die!". Satan used *subtlety*, which is complicated language intended to *deceive*[156]. The Left as inheritors of Evil employ these same tactics. Subtlety and deception are the trade language of the Left!

Remember über-Leftist Democrat Nancy Pelosi when she was the Speaker of the House of Representatives commenting on the impending Obamacare legislation, that if you want to know what's in the Obamacare bill, Congress will have to pass it so Americans can find out. This is an identical tactic used in Nazi Germany to fool the Germans into buying into their Leftist, Anti-GOD agenda. The German Fascists used the *Bait and Switch Re-Name-Game* and deceptively named Nazi death cult programs with titles such as "*The Charitable Foundation for Curative and Institutional Care*". (For a broader discussion see the chapter *Fascism and the Left in America: Kindred Spirits and Familiar Bedfellows*.) All Leftists use deception, subtlety, and *Lies* to advance their agenda and usurp power in their *Bait and Switch, Re-Name Game*!

Leftist "tolerance" is only intended to go one way. Tolerance in the Leftist sense is meant only for those on the Right pertaining to their thoughts and actions, or inaction as is the case, against the Left. Leftist "tolerance" is really "*in*tolerance against the Right" and as Barack Hussein Obama tells us, intolerance is violence: "It's time to heed the words of Gandhi: 'Intolerance is itself a form of violence and an obstacle to the growth of a true democratic spirit'"[157]. Leftist intolerance is always expressed in violent terms against the Right and often with physical violence by one of their modern Storm Trooper enforcement organizations like the SEIU (Service Employees

---

[156] The *Holy Bible*, 2 Corinthians 11:3.
[157] Obama, Barack ; White House Press Office; Remarks by the President to the United Nations General Assembly; September 25, 2012.

International Union). As long as we allow the Left to define the "rules of engagement", the Right will *never* be successful in its defense and persecution of *The Left's War Against* the Right and *GOD!*

The Left's propaganda machine today rivals Hitler's *Reichsministerium für Volksaufklärung und Propaganda* or the Reich Ministry of Public Enlightenment and Propaganda. Do you like the *Re-Name* euphemism of "enlightenment"? The Orwellian Ministry of Truth whose job was to "rewrite history to change the facts to fit Party doctrine for propaganda effect" defines the Democrat "Party" of today! The Left uses deceiving names to disguise its Evil intents. The Democrat Party calls itself the "Democrat*ic*" Party in an attempt to associate themselves with what is actually a Republican principle, and by definition… Right!

The term "mainstream" is the Left's new code-word for "Leftist"! The Left argues that any Supreme Court nominee made by President Trump must be "mainstream". It sounds so "normal" but it is *not* normal, it is simply *Leftist*. The Main Stream Media is in fact the *Left Stream Media* (LSM), the Left Wing Propaganda department of the Democrat Party!

On January 11, 2017 in one of Donald Trump's famous tweets, President Trump correctly compared the Leftist collusion between the Main Stream Media (Left Stream Media or LSM) and U.S. Intelligence Agencies to the Nazi Propaganda efforts. Of course the Left erupted in loud and unified wail in response. (Me thinks… she doth protest too much!) During the brief reign of the Third Reich the Nazi Office of Propaganda and the Nazi SS Office of Intelligence worked hand in hand to create, validate, and promote the Leftist agenda just as is the Left Stream Media's and Intelligence Complex had been doing in America under Obama. This Leftist "Deep State" has been outed repeatedly for its corruption and illegal manipulation of the resources of the Federal government for the benefit of their Leftist cause.

Remember screaming when Bush 43 refused to fight back against the insane accusations of the Left? Well finally we have someone in

President Trump who is willing to fight back! Tweet, baby tweet! Only the Left and the Leftist "Republican" RINOs are yelling for Trump to stop tweeting.

The idiot Republicans and RINOs who respond to the Left's attacks on the Right by parroting the attacks on Republicans in hopes of themselves avoiding condemnation will eventually suffer the same attacks after the Left has destroyed all of those around them. This scapegoat strategy is akin to the Jews of WWII who sold out their fellow Jews to the gas chambers to save their own lives! Hey idiots, this only works temporarily! Soon these traitors will suffer the same fate. When British Prime Minister Chamberlain conceded Sudetenland to Hitler under a peace agreement that was supposed to stop Nazi aggression, after which Chamberlain declared this was "peace for our time". Five months later the Nazis invaded Czechoslovakia and six months after Poland! When will the Right learn… Evil is *NEVER* appeased!

The Republican's self-imposed trap of "civility" is killing the Right! When your opponent is a lawless animal then "civility" is suicide! It is literally going to War armed only with a good speech! Civility did not work against the Nazis, and civility will not work against the Left today! Civility allows our enemy the Left to savagely attack the Right while civility limits the Right's response to high-minded words. Again, it is political *suicide*!

The Left has always bullied Republican Presidents for decades by defining "Presidential" behavior, which the Democrat presidents *never* themselves follow. Remember Alinsky's 4th Rule, "Make the enemy live up to their own book of rules. You can kill them with this, for they can no more obey their own rules than the Christian church can live up to Christianity"?

Trump has destroyed the Left's narrative by creating a new "modern day Presidential" behavior with a Tweet!

> **Donald J. Trump** ✪
> @realDonaldTrump
>
> Follow ⌄
>
> My use of social media is not Presidential - it's MODERN DAY PRESIDENTIAL. Make America Great Again!
>
> 3:41 PM - 1 Jul 2017
>
> **6,113** Retweets **18,314** Likes
>
> ○ 9.0K ⤵ 6.1K ♡ 18K ✉

President Donald Trump is not playing by the *Rules* that the Left has created for him and the Left is coming unglued! Why? Because Trump's refusal to play by the Left's *Rules* is working to tear apart the Left's playbook!

Do you question that Leftists define Republican Presidential Behavior? Here's a recent demand for President Trump's Behavior from the Editorial Board of the Über-Leftist New York Times May 13, 2017 titled "The Republican's Guide to Presidential Behavior":

> It wasn't so long ago that Republicans in Congress cared about how a president comported himself in office. They cared a lot! The president is, after all, commander in chief of the armed forces, steward of the most powerful nation on earth, role model for America's children — and he should act at all times with the dignity his station demands.

Notice the ironic sarcasm dripping in the last several sentences where these Leftists grossly exaggerate the Republican's reaction to Obama's disrespectful behavior in the Oval Office? The Left *never* had a negative reaction to Obama's behavior as President. Now the Left wants to create a *de facto* code of conduct that only applies to Republicans and the Right! The gall of the Left to try to hold

Republicans to a standard to which they would *never* except for a Democrat President! Thank GOD that we have a President that refuses to play by the Democrat Left's *Rule* book! That is exactly why President Donald Trump is Winning Against the Left and Evil! GODspeed President Trump, GODspeed!

MSNBC's Morning Joe's Bonnie and Clyde, Joe Scarborough "Psycho Joe" and Mika Brzezinski "low I.Q. Crazy Mika", have constantly and viciously attacked President Trump. They have called President Trump, "mentally ill", "a narcissist", "ignorant", "completely racist", "delirious", "out of his mind", "stupid", Trump's statements "ridiculous, cartoon-like, kindergarten-like", Trump tells "lies, and misinformation", "an idiot", "a schmuck", "a thug", partially responsible for the assassination attempt of Congressman Steve Scalise, "Neurotic and not very bright", "a soft and flaccid man", "extremely damaging to our democracy", not a "Christian", and on-and-on *ad nauseam*! When President Trump finally tweets back against these MSNBC buffoons, the Left comes unglued! The Left's *Rules* have been violated! Tweet Trump, TWEET! We must fight back or get slaughtered in our "civility"! BREAK THEIR *RULES*!

Republican House Speaker Paul Ryan's in response to President Trump's Tweet slapping back at MSNBC's Morning Joe's Bonnie and Clyde attacks:

> "Obviously, I don't see that as an appropriate comment," said House Speaker Paul D. Ryan (R-Wis.). "What we're trying to do around here is improve the civility and tone of the debate, and this obviously does not do that."

This is as stupid as the British Red Coats lining up in formation, because of their "civility", as the Americans hid behind trees and rocks and picked the British regulars off! Guess who won that War?!

During a lively discussion on February 22, 2017 centered on fears that President Trump is "trying to undermine the media," MSNBC's Mika Brzezinski let slip the awesome unspoken truth that the media's "job" is to "actually control exactly what people think."

SCARBOROUGH: "Exactly. That is exactly what I hear. What Yamiche said is what I hear from all the Trump supporters that I talk to who were Trump voters and are still Trump supporters. They go, 'Yeah you guys are going crazy. He's doing -- what are you so surprised about? He is doing exactly what he said he is going to do.'"

BRZEZINSKI: "Well, I think that the dangerous, you know, edges here are that he is trying to undermine the media and trying to make up his own facts. And it could be that while unemployment and the economy worsen, he could have undermined the messaging so much that he can actually control exactly what people think. And that, that is our job,"

The representatives of the Right always concede to the Left in consistently giving the Left the "benefit of the doubt". The Right has abandoned their Fight in the Left's *Bait and Switch Re-Name Game*. How is it that the Left constantly usurps names and *Re-Defines* terms to fit their Evil agenda, and the Right stands by without even raising an objection? Even worse, how is it that the Right stands by and allows the Left to *Re-Label* and *Re-Define* the Right's own historical associations at will? Was there an uproar and refusal to comply when the Left changed the color association of the Left from Red to Blue? Does the Right scream on live television when the Left Stream Media calls the Democrat Party the Democra*tic* Party? Why does virtually every person on the Right refer to the Pro-Death groups as "pro-choice"? Why does the Right comply with the Left's mandated *Bait and Switch Re-Name-Game*!!!!? Conceding to the Enemies *Bait and Switch Re-Name-Game* empowers the Enemy's Leftist Propaganda and Enlightenment War! Here is some news: You cannot win if you don't even fight! WISE UP people, THIS IS A WAR!

In the Left's Propaganda War, Taxes become "investments". Obfuscation becomes "transparency". *Lies* become "truth". Truth becomes "Lies". Baby Murder becomes "Planned Parenthood". Baby parts harvesting becomes "Planned Parenthood". Targeted murder of black babies also becomes "Planned Parenthood". No choice becomes "pro-choice". Pro-abortion becomes "pro-choice". Pro-Death becomes "Pro-Choice". Isn't it about time to draw an immovable line before the Left and start defending our territory?!

In the 2015 Colorado Planned Parenthood clinic shooting, the shooter afterward was reported to say "No more baby parts". The Left said that the "incendiary language" of the Right's Pro-Life Movement caused a man to shoot a dozen people in a Planned Parenthood baby killing factory. When it was the "incendiary *actions*" of the Left that caused this man to do so! The Left blames the Right for *talking* about the murder that the Left commits by the tens-of-millions in its abortion mills!

The Left screams about the person who killed the adults who kill thousands of babies, not about the Leftists themselves who are killing ten-of-millions of babies! I am certainly not advocating that everyone picks up arms and attack abortion mills, but come on, to blame the *language* of the Right which expose the *actions* of the Left is *insane*!

If the Right points out the crimes of the Left, the Left accuses the Right of being "divisive". The Left refuses to take responsibility for their own actions and divert to accusing the Right of "divisiveness". Using the Muslim terrorist motivated mass shooting in San Bernardino, Über-Leftist David Goodfriend lectured Conservative Angela McGlowan on Fox News[158] "You can't say on the one hand that we shouldn't be divisive and then point your finger at one group and say well they're being divisive. What you said is divisive". (This is circular reasoning nonsense to a level of insanity!) The radical-Leftist Goodfriend is the one being divisive by doing *exactly* what he was wrongfully accusing McGlowan of doing. Goodfriend was calling a Conservative divisive for simply *speaking* the truth! This is the *Lies*! of the Left. [159]

It is the ultimate *Lie* wrapped in the "Do as I say, not as I do" hypocrisy. Obama literally said of politicizing the gun debate after a

---

[158] Fox News, December 3, 2015.
[159] For a brief discussion of Circular Reasoning see chapter Emotion Based Politics.

major mass shooting in Oregon that gun control is "is something we *should* politicize". This while the Left acts in its Shakespearean Iago role falsely accusing the Right of "divisive" language and *politicizing* tragedies!

Let us take on a sacred doctrine of the Left... marriage. When you attempt to change GOD's definition of marriage you open "marriage" up to a litany of insane redefinitions such as polygamy (multiple partners in any combination of ways), bestiality ("marriage" to animals), homosexuality, and now according to Good Housekeeping, marriage to one's self[160]! Sound ridiculous? Well each of these has already been done! Yet these are all self-delusions of the Left because when all is said and done, marriage is still only between one man and one woman just *as GOD Himself created marriage*! A person can scream over and over until they pass out that they are a potato, but they will *never* be a potato! (Of course there are those who resemble a potato in looks and mental capacity but they are genetically still *homo sapiens*!)

Homosexual "marriage" is *not* about "equality". Homosexuals were always "equal" and free in their ability to marry, just not someone of the same sex. The homosexuals' demanded to *Re-Define* marriage to fit their own perversion, a perversion of the marriage that GOD Himself created and instituted at the beginning of time, is an intentional and directed spit in the face of GOD! Only Evil perverts what GOD has ordained! (By the way perversion of GOD's ways IS the very *definition* of Evil!) The homosexual "marriage" issue was always about *The Left's War Against GOD* in attacking, rejecting, and redefining marriage as GOD created and ordained!

The Left *Re-Names* homosexual couplings to "gay marriage", and voilà... homosexuality becomes gay marriage! (But marriage is still a sacred union created and ordained only by GOD between one man and one woman!) But answer this, if homosexuality is not a perversion of the GOD's natural creation, then why do lesbians use dildos (artificial

---

male penises!)? Why do sodomite "couples" generally pair up in "butch" and "fem" combinations? These "pairings" are bastardized and Evil imitations of the GOD created and ordained "one man and one woman" couplings of marriage! If homosexuality were a "natural" phenomenon, then there would be none of these imitation "male/female" pairings which are so universal in the homosexual community. Homosexuals can snort, stomp, scream, and *Re-Name* as much and as loud as they can, but is does not change the fact that homosexual behavior is an abomination to the GOD created and ordained "one man and one woman" marriage! However, homosexuals will not address this fact. Homosexuals get better results being grossly over-dramatic, which tends to get people to shut up and let them have their way. Hyperbole has replaced facts in the Leftist mantra. The Right has given up the Fight and the Leftist homosexuals now make the Right cower in fear. It's time to re-engage the Fight and seize the ground that we have seceded to Evil!

There will be an expanded discussion in the chapter *Tolerance* of the Left's deceptive coopting of terms to advance their homosexual agenda on our schoolchildren, but here is a preview as it pertains here:

> "If the Radical Right can succeed in portraying us as preying on children, we will lose. Their language – '**promoting homosexuality**' – is laced with subtle and not-so-subtle innuendo that we are '**after their kids**'. We must learn from the abortion struggle, where the clever claiming of the term 'pro-life' allowed those who opposed abortion on demand to frame the issue to their advantage, to make sure that we do not allow ourselves to be painted into a corner before the debate even begins"[161].

The Left always tries to *Re-Name* their agenda and issues before they can be identified as Evil. Constitutional law attorney Edwin Vieira Jr. judiciously characterizes the Left's deceptive wordplay this way:

---

[161] Contrada, Amy; MassResistance Special Report; Kevin Jennings – Author of 1993 Education Report to the Massachusetts Governor's Commission on Gay and Lesbian Youth: Template for Homosexual and Transgender Activism in Schools across the U.S.; May 2011.

"Simply by transmogrifying definitions, entirely new sets of legal rights, powers, privileges, immunities, duties, exposures, and liabilities can be created out of essentially nothing more than plays on words. For example, prefixing the noun 'speech' with the pseudo-adjective 'hate' creates the novel legalistic category of 'hate speech,' which supposedly is not protected by the First Amendment, and therefore can be subjected to pervasive governmental regulation. With no greater difficulty than that, public officials can arrogate to themselves a license to impose censorship and to penalize individuals who expatiate vehemently on prohibited subjects. This process is also capable of aggregating such synthetic powers. For instance, once 'same-sex marriage' receives a legalistic imprimatur, those who express a strong aversion to it can be condemned for 'hate speech'".[162]

Giving up the *Word Game* to the Left has cost the Right dearly and the bodies of the Left's victims of the Left's *Word Games* are strewn along the way. Like Revolutionary France, Nazi Germany, Communist China, the Soviet Union, and *every single* manifestation of State-sponsored Leftist Evil, the *Word Games* of the Left *always* precede the total physical domination of the Evil which they represent in the physical world. The Right *must* engage the Nazi-like Propaganda machine of the Left and take back our terms and definitions which *Rightfully* and singularly belong only to the Right! Words hurt, words destroy, words kill! We must engage the Propaganda *War* of the Left. If we as the Right will not tell the truth to the people... who will? The childish "sticks and stones may break my bones, but words will never hurt me" attitude toward the Left's *Bait and Switch Re-Name Game* is *killing* us, *killing* America, and will soon *kill* our sons and daughters. Literally! Just like in Nazi Germany and *every* other Leftist manifestation in history! Will you step up and engage the *Fight* to push back and destroy Evil in America?

[162] United States Senate Committee on the Judiciary Subcommittee on Oversight, Agency Action, Federal Rights and Federal Courts, Hearing on July 22, 2015, "With Prejudice: Supreme Court Activism and Possible Solutions".

I leave you with a sage quote credited to different men from Rabbi Hillel the Elder and to the poet John E. Lewis. Regardless of its origin, it remains sage quizzical wisdom:

"If not us, then who?
If not now, then when?"

8. AMERICA'S WAR/THE LEFT'S WAR AGAINST AMERICA'S JUDEO-CHRISTIAN FOUNDATIONS

Chapter 8

The Leftist Elite has sold their soul to the Devil for thirty pieces of silver and the common citizen's soul for a bowl of red pottage. The Left offers State endorsement of Evil and all of its associated sins to individuals, in exchange for our GOD-given inalienable rights and freedoms. GOD-given inalienable rights and freedoms from oppression without which follows the subsequent bondage to the Evil State. Leftism in all of its manifestations is *not* a benign philosophy for the "greater good"[163], but a malignant cancer of Evil that eats at the soul of a nation until it is wholly consumed and destroyed by Evil…one life at a time! It is no coincidence that the rise of the Left in America is paralleled exactly with the rise of Evil in America. Escalating murder rates, abortion, and even an economy spiraling out of control are the necessary results and reflection of a people who have sold their collective souls to Evil. Trump has turned around the economy that Obama and his Democrat cohorts almost destroyed, but the Left salivates at its next opportunity to finish the job. The constraint of Evil in America's Judeo-Christian society is fundamental to the preservation of freedoms which were before unknown in the history of the world. When the constraints of Evil are removed, life and freedom are its inescapable casualties.

The Left has sold its bill of goods as a competitive means to "a similar goal" alongside that of the traditional American values of the Right. This is simply a repackaged *Lie* of Satan, as Satan rationalized evil with Eve in the Garden of Eden questioning "Yea, hath GOD [really] said…?". GOD does *not* place constraints on Evil to deprive man of "freedoms", but to protect man from the sure destruction and the *total loss of freedom* that results from embracing Evil. Leftist Totalitarian

---

[163] See the more thorough discussion of the "greater good" in the chapter: *The Left Is a*

Dictatorships are the inescapable result of the Left's "freedom" to sin campaigns!

The *United States Constitution* was specifically structured by our Founding Fathers upon the *Bible*'s use of constraints upon evil. (i.e. "Our *Constitution* was made only for a moral and religious people. It is wholly inadequate to the government of any other" John Adams: Assisted in drafting the US Constitution, Founding Father, and second President of the United States.) Barack Hussein Obama called the *U.S. Constitution* "a charter of negative liberties"[164] of which Obama lamented that "we have not broken free" from the "essential constraints that were placed by the Founding Fathers in the Constitution". These "negative liberties" are the moral constraints of the *U.S. Constitution restraining the State and Federal governments'* actions against its citizens and limiting the individual actions of its citizens against other citizens. Obama simply acted to empower the Federal Government's power over the individual rights! Moral, that is Christian, constraints *always* hinder the "progress" of evil and by extension the Left. Obama sees the American *Constitution* as chains that restrain "positive liberties" offered the Left. Positive liberties are deceptively intended to "free" America from the Founding Father's Judeo-Christian restraints inherent in the Constitution. To be "free" of the Constitution's protections is to be enslaved to the State! Enslavement of the people *is* the endgame of the Left!

We begin here by building upon the previous chapter's theme of the Left's *Bait and Switch: Re-Name Game.*

Liberalism *is* the classic *Bait and Switch: Re-Name-Game* by which the Left offers "freedom", not in the traditionally understood sense, but "freedom" from GOD's moral constraints! This is the Left's Re-definition of "freedom". It is only under GOD's moral restraints from Evil that we are provided the environment in which true freedom can exist! GOD says it clearly: "Woe unto them that call evil good, and good evil..."[165]. *It is not merely Left verses Right, but Wrong verses*

---

[164] Obama 2001 interview with Chicago public radio station WBEZ-FM.
[165] The *Holy Bible*: Isaiah 5:20.

Right, Evil against GOOD, Evil against GOD! Unless and until the Right recognizes the true nature of the *Fight*, defeat is inevitable. Evil may change its face and name, but Evil remains Evil, Evil with evil intentions! Here is an example from 1945 written from amongst the ashes and carnage of the resultant horrors of World War II of the results of the Left's so-called "freedoms":

> "To allay these suspicions and to harness to its cart the strongest of all political motives – *the craving for freedom* – socialists began increasingly to make use of the promise of a *'new freedom'*. Socialism was to bring 'economic freedom' without which political freedom was 'not worth having'. To make this argument sound plausible, *the word 'freedom' was subjected to a subtle change in meaning*. The word had formerly meant freedom from coercion, from the arbitrary power of other men. Now it was made to mean freedom from necessity, release from the compulsion of the circumstances which inevitably limit the range of choice of all of us. Freedom in this sense is, of course, merely another name for power or wealth. The demand for the new freedom was thus only another name for the old demand for a redistribution of wealth[166]". (emphasis added)

In case you think that this "economic freedom" selling point of the Left does not exist today, let me remind you of Barack Hussein Obama's opining, "I'm not optimistic about bringing about major *redistributive change* through the courts"[167]. (emphasis added) Obama also asked this question in a 1998 Loyola University interview, "How do we structure government resources that pool resources and hence facilitate some *redistribution* [of wealth]? Because I actually believe in *redistribution* [of wealth]…" (emphasis added). The Left and its Evil agenda *never* change!

Liberty is another word which the Left has co-opted and bastardized:

---

[166] Hayek, Friedrich A.; *The Road to Serfdom with The Intellectuals and Socialism* (Readers Digest Condensed version); 1945; pgs. 47-48.
[167] Obama 2001 interview with Chicago public radio station WBEZ-FM.

The most effective way of making people accept the validity of the values they are to serve is to persuade them that they are really the same as those they have always held, but which were not properly understood or recognized before. And the most efficient technique to this end is *to use the old words but change their meaning*. Few traits of totalitarian regimes are at the same time so confusing to the superficial observer and yet so characteristic of the whole intellectual climate as this *complete perversion of language*.

The worst sufferer in this respect is the word **'liberty'**. It is a word used as freely in totalitarian states as elsewhere. Indeed, it could almost be said that wherever liberty as we know it has been destroyed, this has been done in the name of some *new freedom* promised to the people. Even among us we have planners who promise us a 'collective freedom', which is as misleading as anything said by totalitarian politicians. 'Collective freedom' is not the freedom of the members of society, but the unlimited freedom of the planner to do with society that which he pleases. This is the confusion of freedom with power carried to the extreme.

It is not difficult to deprive the great majority of independent thought. *But the minority who will retain an inclination to criticize must also be silenced*. Public criticism or even expressions of doubt must be suppressed because they tend to weaken support of the regime[168]. (emphasis added)

Here is another warning from a contemporary observer of the Leftist, here Fascist, program to "silence" all opposition to the Left, which ultimately and inevitably leads to eliminating (killing!) the opposition! Remember David Goldman's warning: "And if we try to force fallible humans to live in an earthly paradise, ultimately we shall have to *kill them all* for their failings"? Karl Marx, the founding father

---

[168] Hayek, Friedrich A.; *The Road to Serfdom with The Intellectuals and Socialism* (Readers Digest Condensed version); 1945; pg. 55.

and icon of the modern Left in the West, stated emphatically, *"Everything that exists deserves to perish"*. The essence of what it means to be a *radical* is thus summed up in Alinsky's praise for Satan (Lucifer) is according to the Left: "to be willing to destroy the values, structures and institutions that sustain the society in which we [as Americans] live", or not live as is emphatically implied! The examples that could be employed here to further bolster the point are legion, but the preceding examples should be sufficient to make the point.

James Kalb describes the inevitable destruction which is always brought about by the implementation of the Leftist ideas:

> "In [Leftism as in Communism] the motive has been to *eliminate human nature* as an obstacle to re-creation of the world [as a Leftist Utopia]. The difficulty has been that destruction in concept of fixed and rooted human nature has led repeatedly to the concrete destruction of very large numbers of actual human beings [genocide]. The sequence seems natural. If man does not exist, why should it matter whether men exist? [Leftists] do not take the threat of such inferences seriously, but it is not clear why. If human is content-free, so it becomes a social classification the point of which is determined politically, and if it is irrational to recognize a radical difference in rights between a man and a dog, both of which seem to be the emerging [Leftist] views, the stage seems rather clearly set for horrors"[169]. (emphasis and clarifications added)

(The preceding quote was written in 2001. Have you noticed even since then the subtle and hyper-elevation of the "plight" of homeless and abused animals, especially dogs? Not that there is anything inherently evil in taking care of animals, but animal welfare has been elevated to a level of importance even higher than that of the human! For example, we are instructed by the Left that killing unborn babies is a civic and honorable duty and that seeing to the protection of

---

[169] Kalb, James; Modern Age Quarterly; *The Tyranny of Liberalism: The Iron Heel of Freedom*; Summer 2000.

unborn dogs is a moral duty represented in advertisements complete with the faces of sad dogs in the background and emotionally weighty music. The Left truly turns the world upside-down!)

Centralization, on which Leftism depends, has been a wholly alien idea in America until the turn of the last century. In a strange turn of events the Leftist minority has bribed, cajoled, and bludgeoned the majority of Americans through oppressive P.C. campaigns into not only accepting, but exponentially expanding the dictatorial powers of the Left!

Alexis de Tocqueville, the French historian on American exceptionalism, warned us in 1835 of the dangers and eminent collapse of the uniquely American system and Judeo-Christian society if the "Tyranny of the majority" were to gain acceptance in America. In de Tocqueville's *magnum opus, Democracy In America*, he wrote of the "Absence of Administrative Centralization" and *"Of What Tempers Tyranny of the Majority in the United States"*. Tocqueville penned, "The national majority does not have the idea of doing everything. —It is forced to use town and county magistrates in order to carry out its sovereign will…

> "… Previously I distinguished two types of **centralization**; one, I called governmental, and the other administrative. Only the first exists in America; the second is almost unknown there. **If the power that directs American societies** found these two means of government at its disposal, and combined, with the right to command everything, the ability and the habit of carrying out everything by itself; if, after establishing the general principles of government, it entered into the details of application, and after regulating the great interests of the country, it **could reach as far as individual interests, *liberty* would soon be banished from the New World"**. (emphasis added)

In the [original] manuscript, the paragraph is written as follows:

"The Americans must consider themselves fortunate that this is so: *if the majority in the United States found the one, like the other, in its hands in order to compel obedience to its will, and if it combined, with the right to do everything, the ability and the habit of carrying everything out by its agents, its power would be, so to speak, without limits*"[170]. (emphasis added)

What was unheard of in America in 1835, *Leftist/Socialist* Centralization of Power, has now become the "Power… without limits" in a Leftist dominated America!

It is equally no coincidence that the rise of the Left in America exactly corresponds with the decline of America. This can be seen in microcosm in the cities of America. The cities which are controlled by Leftist politicians are those which are notoriously corrupt, and morally and financially bankrupt. This corruption is manifest in deteriorating roads, declining government services, intolerance of Christian symbols, escalating unemployment, lawlessness, nepotism, and theft by government officials. This is epitomized in the 2013 Detroit bankruptcy.

This is also evident in the individual states in America. Leftist run states like California are on the verge of financial bankruptcy as a direct result of having long since sold their collective souls to Evil in supporting virtually every abomination named in the *Bible* and rejecting every blessing offered by GOD. Contrast this with states like Texas, which at least to some degree, has retained the Christian moral structure that America was founded upon. Businesses are fleeing California and going to Texas. Coincidence? Hardly. But what happens when there are no safe havens which the Left has not destroyed? What happens when the Left has finally established itself as the supreme totalitarian dictatorship over *all* of America?

---

[170] Tocqueville, Alexis de; DEMOCRACY IN AMERICA; Historical-Critical Edition of *De la de´mocratie en Ame´rique*; a Bilingual French-English edition, Volume 2; Edited by Eduardo Nolla, Translated from the French by James T. Schleifer; Liberty Fund, Inc.; Indianapolis; 2010; pgs. 427-428.

Pat Robertson was vehemently condemned by the Left when he linked Haiti's devastation in the January 12, 2010 earthquake and its plagued past to Haiti's having held a voodoo dedication ceremony dedicating Haiti to the Lucifer. This was done at the beginning of the Haitian revolt against French occupation, foundationally dedicating Haiti to the Lucifer in return for demonic "spirit" help and victory over the French occupation. This backlash of the Leftist media, aside from what Pat Robertson said, was a well-documented historical fact. Even the Prime Minister of Haiti at the time agreed to the historicity of the foundational voodoo covenant. While the Prime Minister equivocated, he did not in any way dispute the facts of Robertson's statement. Facts being defined as truth.

Again facts mean nothing to the Left. It is the exposure to the truth that the Left will not tolerate, especially when it exposes the true Evil behind their movement and motivations. The Left does not out-rightly deny the voodoo ceremony where a pig was sacrificed to the "spirits", but the Left tries to dismiss any association of their State sanctioned voodoo spirit worship being tied to devil worship. Yet this is the exact correlation that the *Bible* makes when it states that "they sacrificed to devils"[171]. The voodoo practitioners, or vodouists, are in the French called *vodouisants*, literally "servants of the spirits" who's highest calling as a faithful voodooist is to yield oneself to become "spirit possessed", which the *Bible* clearly identifies as "devil possession".

Some have tried to argue that the Haitian "pact with the Devil" made in 1791 "expired" 200 years later in 1991, yet in 2003 voodoo was declared by the President of Haiti to be a nationally recognized religion. A pact with the Devil does not simply "expire". A pact with the Devil *can only* be terminated by coming into agreement with GOD and can only be severed by the Power of GOD! Again the Left's tactic is generally one of simply dismissing facts and thereby dismissing the existence of Evil as defined by GOD. Here, again, the Left's circular reasoning[172], which is based on a denial of Biblical truth, goes like

---

[171] The *Holy Bible:* 1 Corinthians 10:19-22; see also Exodus 34:12-16; Leviticus 17:7; Deuteronomy 32:17.

[172] For a brief discussion of Circular Reasoning see chapter Emotion Based Politics.

this: "The Devil does not exist, so voodoo cannot be of the Devil, therefore Christians are crazy for trying to associate Haiti's misfortune with an imaginary Devil". This is not just a violation of logic, but an intentional deception meant to delude and thereby manipulate the hearers.

The *Bible* gives a clear message from GOD directly associating a nation's turning away from GOD and its punishment beginning with national catastrophes and ending with their destruction as a direct result of its *rebellion* against GOD. The *Bible* not only records this resultant destruction against Egypt, Tyre, Philistia, Edom (Petra), Assyria, Babylon, Greece, the Roman Empire, and myriad others, but also against Israel who the *Bible* names as GOD's *chosen people*! Israel will ultimately repent and turn back to GOD and be restored, but has suffered immensely in the meantime for its various rebellions *Against GOD*. If even GOD's very chosen nation Israel is not exempt from the wrath of GOD against its rebellion, what arrogance would make any American think that GOD would not do the same or more against the rebellion of America *Against GOD*? No nation of the world has exceeded America's sins *Against GOD*. America's window of opportunity to repent before GOD is quickly closing. What we choose to do now will determine GOD's ultimate response to America's Leftist conspiracy of Evil.

The Left are not "well-meaning" Liberals working for the "greater good"[173] any more than the Fascists of Nazi Germany were striving for their stated purpose of working for the "greater good". These are Leftist, Progressive, Anti-GOD Fascists who have sold out theirs and their children's souls to Evil for personal gain and sexual indulgences. And we, at least until now, for the most part have remained blind to their tactics by the public façade of the "greater good". The Left's evil ruse and hidden masters must be unmasked and exposed for the hidden wickedness that lurks just under the surface. Our choice is perpetual enslavement to Evil or freedom from Evil. We may still have a short window of choice. Given some Americans' current

---

[173] See the more thorough discussion of the "greater good" in the chapter: *The Left Is a RELIGION!*.

general reluctance and some Americans' inability to repent from Evil, our children may no longer have a choice but may be enslaved by our collective choices now!

It is the Left's same false comparison between America and an imagined State created Utopian Paradise that deceptively manages to make America appear to be unfair, racist, bigoted, etc. David Horowitz comments:

> "If the radicals' utopia were actually possible, it would be criminal *not* to deceive, lie, and murder to advance the radical cause which is, in effect, a redemption of mankind. If it were possible to provide every man, woman and child on the planet with food, shelter and clothing as a right, if it were possible to end bigotry and human conflict, what sacrifice would not be worth it?"[174].

Horowitz answers the question "Why would the Left want to destroy America?" with his personal experience among these Leftists:

> This is something that conservatives generally have a hard time understanding. As a former radical, I am constantly asked how radicals could hate America and why they would want to destroy a society that compared to others is tolerant, inclusive, and open, and treats all people with a dignity and respect that is the envy of the world. The answer to this question is that radicals are not comparing America to other real world societies. They are comparing America to the heaven on earth - the kingdom of social justice and freedom - they think they are building. And compared to *this* heaven even America is hell. In my experience conservatives are generally too decent and too civilized to match up adequately with their radical adversaries, at least in the initial stages of the battle. They are too prone to give them the benefit of the doubt, to believe there is goodness and good sense in them which will outweigh their determination to change the world. Radicals talk of justice and

---

[174] Horowitz, David; *Commentary on Rules For Radicals*; pg. 45.

124

democracy and equality. They can't really want to destroy a society that is democratic and liberal, and more equal than others, and that has brought wealth and prosperity to so many people. Oh yes they can. There is no goodness that trumps the dream of a heaven on earth. And because America is a real world society, managed by real and problematic human beings, it will never be equal, or liberal, or democratic *enough* to satisfy radical fantasies - to compensate them for their longing for a perfect world, and for their unhappiness in this one[175].

Horowitz goes on to quote Karl Marx, the founding father of the modern Left in the West, "*'Everything that exists deserves to perish.'* The essence of what it means to be a *radical* is thus summed up in Alinsky's praise for Satan (Lucifer): to be willing to destroy the values, structures and institutions that sustain the society in which we [as Americans] live". Everything the Left controls, the Left destroys! Everything the Left controls is an abject and abysmal failure on a catastrophic human level. Every education system the Left controls, every American city controlled by the Left (Detroit, Los Angeles, Chicago, New York, Columbus, *ad nauseam*), every State controlled by the Left (California, New York, Illinois, all bankrupt financially and morally), and on and on.

Nobody wants to admit that it could be happening in their country. The Germans didn't, the Italians didn't, and Americans don't! Ignoring evil empowers evil!

Programmed destruction is a common theme of the Left from the French Revolution to even Italian Fascism under Mussolini who made its relation to Evil as a weapon clear:

> "The plebes, who are *excessively Christianized* and humanitarian, will never understand that a higher degree of **evil is necessary** so that the Superman might thrive... The

---

[175] Horowitz, David; *Commentary on Rules For Radicals*; pgs. 16-18.

Superman knows **revolt** alone. **Everything that exists must be destroyed**[176]". (emphasis added)

This was and is the same ongoing goal of Barack Hussein Obama who declared "But the way this plan achieves those goals would lead to a *fundamentally different America* than the one we've known throughout most of our history", in describing his plan to "fundamentally transform America"[177]. Again, make no mistake the Left's attempt to "transform" America is a P.C. doublespeak for destroying America as we know it!

Only Evil destroys for the sake of destroying. As has been previously quoted, the Devil "cometh not but to steal, and to kill, and to **destroy**"[178]! This is the Evil Voice behind the Students for a Democratic Society (SDS) delegate to the 1967 meeting who screamed "Tactics? It's too late... Let's break what we can. Make as many answer as we can. Tear them apart"[179]. The Voice no doubt was not his own, but the shriek of Evil lashing out to commit destruction for destruction's sake!

In the Left's rejection of the One true GOD of the Christian *Bible*, they seek to replace GOD's eternal Paradise in Heaven with an earth-bound substitute paradise ruled by Lucifer (Not an exaggeration, Remember Alinsky's over the shoulder acknowledgement of Lucifer as the Left's original Rebel?), to which even the Left is forced to co-opt the Biblical term *paradise* because the term is meaningless outside of GOD. Satan, or Lucifer, always counterfeits GOD's truth with a look-alike shell that only contains perverting evils and death. The Forbidden Fruit that Satan tempted Eve with looked amazing on the outside, it was "pleasant to the eyes" and "to be desired to make one wise"[180], but as Evil goes, it was only a concealing shell filled with suffering and

---

[176] Goldberg, Jonah; *Liberal FASCISM: The Secret History of the American Left From Mussolini to the Politics of Meaning*; 2007; pg. 178.
[177] Obama's plan to destroy America and build a new Leftist Utopian paradise upon the ruins is more fully examined in the following chapter *The Obamas: The Epitome of the Left*.
[178] The *Holy Bible*: John 10:10.
[179] Goldberg, Jonah; *Liberal FASCISM: The Secret History of the American Left From Mussolini to the Politics of Meaning*; 2007; pgs. 178-179.
[180] The *Holy Bible*: Genesis 3:6.

death[181]! With Satan what you see is *not* what you get. The Devil's true motives, as with the Left's, are *always* concealed in an appealing wrapper, "The issue is never the issue. The issue is always the revolution." which translates for the Left, "In other words the cause - whether inner city blacks or women - is never the real cause, but only an occasion to advance the real cause which is the accumulation of *power* to make the revolution [*Against GOD*]. *That* was the all-consuming focus of [the Left]"[182].

This is a drumbeat carried over from Hitler's Leftist-Nazi régime as observed from an expatriate Nazi "For National *Socialists* there was and is no aim they would not take up or drop at a moment's notice, their only criterion being the strengthening of the movement"[183]. The Left is in lockstep, or goosestep as the case may be, with Nazi methodologies.

Individualism is at the core of our traditional American culture. In 1945 economist Friedrich Hayek put it this way:

> "*Individualism*, in contrast to socialism and all other forms of totalitarianism, *is based on the respect of Christianity* for the individual man and the belief that it is desirable that men should be free to develop their own individual gifts and bents"[184].

The US Supreme Court's decision to mandate Homosexual "marriage" to every state can only be seen as an act of treason against America in total offense to the US Constitution. The offending Justices *must* be removed and our Federal Republic restored! This is clearly a right given to us by GOD and enumerated in the United States Declaration of Independence, the Founding Document of America:

---

[181] The *Holy Bible*: Genesis 3:4.
[182] Horowitz, David; *Commentary on Rules For Radicals*; pgs. 8-9.
[183] Goldberg, Jonah; *Liberal FASCISM: The Secret History of the American Left From Mussolini to the Politics of Meaning*; 2007; pg. 55; quoting Hermann Rauschning.
[184] Hayek, Friedrich A.; *The Road to Serfdom with The Intellectuals and Socialism* (Readers Digest Condensed version); 1945; pg. 42.

We hold these truths to be self-evident, that all men are created equal, that they are endowed by their Creator with certain **unalienable Rights**, that among these are Life, Liberty and the pursuit of Happiness.--That **to secure these rights**, Governments are instituted among Men, **deriving their just powers from the *consent of the governed***, That *whenever any Form of Government becomes destructive of these ends, it is the Right of the People to alter or to abolish it*, **and to institute new Government,** *laying its foundation on such principles and organizing its powers in such form, as to them shall seem most likely to effect their Safety and Happiness*. Prudence, indeed, will dictate that Governments long established should not be changed for light and transient causes; and accordingly all experience hath shewn, that mankind are more disposed to suffer, while evils are sufferable, than to right themselves by abolishing the forms to which they are accustomed. *But when a long train of abuses and usurpations, pursuing invariably the same Object evinces a design to reduce them under absolute Despotism, it is their right, it is their duty, to throw off such Government, and to provide new Guards for their future security*. (emphasis added)

You don't read that in any Leftist inspired and approved text books! No wonder that the Left hates the *U.S. Constitution* and *Declaration of Independence* and has worked tirelessly to destroy it! There are still a few lingering steps to take by which we can reclaim our Great Nation, but these grow fewer and weaker by the day. The Leftist juggernaut is on its final goosestep march for the full conquest of America! It may be that in the words of Thomas Jefferson that the Tree of liberty may have to once again be, "refreshed… with the blood of patriots and tyrants", but we pray
that this will not now or ever be the necessary.

It is shocking to compare the grievances of the 1776 American *Declaration of Independence* against the British Monarchy [Leftist Dictatorship] and the grievances we hold against the Left's totalitarian usurpation of power today. See for yourself if we have the GOD-given right, documented authority, and responsibility before our Sovereign GOD to defend our Constitutional Republic against Leftist tyranny just as the 1776 Colonial Americans threw off the yoke of oppression from the British Empire. Here is the list as enumerated in the *Declaration of Independence*:

> Such has been the patient sufferance of these Colonies; and such is now the necessity which constrains them to alter their former Systems of Government. The history of the present King of Great Britain [King George III] is a history of repeated injuries and usurpations, all having in direct object the establishment of an absolute Tyranny over these States. To prove this, let Facts be submitted to a candid world.
>
> He [King George III] has refused his Assent to Laws, the most wholesome and necessary for the public good.
>
> He [King George III] has forbidden his Governors to pass Laws of immediate and pressing importance, unless suspended in their operation till his Assent should be obtained; and when so suspended, he has utterly neglected to attend to them.
>
> He [King George III] has refused to pass other Laws for the accommodation of large districts of people, unless those people would relinquish the right of Representation in the Legislature, a right inestimable to them and formidable to tyrants only.
>
> He [King George III] has called together legislative bodies at places unusual, uncomfortable, and distant from the depository of their Public Records, for the sole purpose of fatiguing them into compliance with his measures.
>
> He [King George III] has dissolved Representative Houses repeatedly, for opposing with manly firmness of his invasions on the rights of the people.

He [King George III] has refused for a long time, after such dissolutions, to cause others to be elected, whereby the Legislative Powers, incapable of Annihilation, have returned to the People at large for their exercise; the State remaining in the meantime exposed to all the dangers of invasion from without, and convulsions within.

He [King George III] has endeavoured to prevent the population of these States; for that purpose obstructing the Laws for Naturalization of Foreigners; refusing to pass others to encourage their migrations hither, and raising the conditions of new Appropriations of Lands.

He [King George III] has obstructed the Administration of Justice by refusing his Assent to Laws for establishing Judiciary Powers.

He [King George III] has made Judges dependent on his Will alone for the tenure of their offices, and the amount and payment of their salaries.

He [King George III] has erected a multitude of New Offices, and sent hither swarms of Officers to harass our people and eat out their substance.

He [King George III] has kept among us, in times of peace, Standing Armies without the Consent of our legislatures.

He [King George III] has affected to render the Military independent of and superior to the Civil Power.

He [King George III] has combined with others to subject us to a jurisdiction foreign to our constitution, and unacknowledged by our laws; giving his Assent to their Acts of pretended Legislation:

For quartering large bodies of armed troops among us:

For protecting them, by a mock Trial from punishment for any Murders which they should commit on the Inhabitants of these States:

For cutting off our Trade with all parts of the world:

For imposing Taxes on us without our Consent:

For depriving us in many cases, of the benefit of Trial by Jury:

For transporting us beyond Seas to be tried for pretended offences:

For abolishing the free System of English Laws in a neighbouring Province, establishing therein an Arbitrary government, and enlarging its Boundaries so as to render it at once an example and fit instrument for introducing the same absolute rule into these states

For taking away our Charters, abolishing our most valuable Laws and altering fundamentally the Forms of our Governments:

For suspending our own Legislatures, and declaring themselves invested with power to legislate for us in all cases whatsoever.

He [King George III] has abdicated Government here, by declaring us out of his Protection and waging War against us.

He [King George III] has plundered our seas, ravaged our coasts, burnt our towns, and destroyed the lives of our people.

He [King George III] is at this time transporting large Armies of foreign Mercenaries to compleat the works of death, desolation, and tyranny, already begun with circumstances of Cruelty & Perfidy scarcely paralleled in the most barbarous ages, and totally unworthy the Head of a civilized nation.

He [King George III] has constrained our fellow Citizens taken Captive on the high Seas to bear Arms against their Country, to become the executioners of their friends and Brethren, or to fall themselves by their Hands.

He [King George III] has excited domestic insurrections amongst us, and has endeavoured to bring on the inhabitants of our frontiers, the merciless Indian Savages whose known rule of warfare, is an undistinguished destruction of all ages, sexes and conditions.

In every stage of these Oppressions We have Petitioned for Redress in the most humble terms: Our repeated Petitions have been answered only by repeated injury. A Prince [King George III], whose character is thus marked by every act which may define a Tyrant, is unfit to be the ruler of a free people.

The crimes of the Tyrant King of England which forced America into the *Revolutionary War* are almost indistinguishable in the modern sense from those forced upon the American people by the Tyrannical Left in America today! The similarities are unavoidable. GOD help us that the same remedies are not necessary in order to reclaim our once great Republic!

9. TACTICS FOR THE LEFT'S SUBVERSION AND TAKEOVER OF AMERICA:

Chapter 9

In a March 30, 1961 speech before the Phoenix Chamber of Commerce Ronald Reagan, condemning socialized medicine, quoted Norman Thomas, Socialist Party Presidential Candidate in 1928, 1932, 1936, 1940, 1944 and 1948, co-founder of the über-Leftist, and wholly anti-American, American Civil Liberties Union (ACLU), on how Socialism would subjugate America to the Socialist Utopian agenda:

> "A short time ago, Norman Thomas, six times candidate for president on the socialist party ticket, gave a critique on the success of this program when he said the American people will never knowingly vote for socialism, but under the name of *liberalism* the American people will adopt every fragment of the socialist program".

Author Upton Sinclair an outspoken Socialist in a letter written to Norman Thomas wrote:

> The American People will take Socialism, but they won't take the label. I certainly proved it in the case of EPIC. Running on the Socialist ticket I got 60,000 votes, and running on the slogan to 'End Poverty in California' I got 879,000. I think we simply have to recognize the fact that our enemies have succeeded in spreading the Big Lie. There is no use attacking it by a front attack, it is much better to out-flank them".

Al Sharpton, in a rare moment of candor, on March 21, 2010 on Fox News said that "We have to say that the American public overwhelmingly voted for Socialism when they elected president Obama". The tactics of the Left never change.

My Dad was more right than he knew...

Throughout my childhood into my early adulthood I engaged in many ongoing discussions with my father on his belief in a Leftist Conspiracy to bring down the Conservative pillars of Western Civilization. I profoundly disagreed with his assessment of an unseen conspiracy lurking behind the scenes whose entire aim was to bring about the collapse and subsequent takeover of America. I instinctively rejected such a conspiracy as humanly impossible and argued vigorously against that possibility.

Over the years I gathered evidence in support of my argument. I often relied upon the wisdom of historians and philosophers that a conspiracy was doomed when more than two people were involved because someone always blabs and the conspiracy is always discovered and soon ruined. I even quoted Shakespeare's earnest warning that no conspiracy of more than two can be kept secret as the third or more is always apt to brag of their involvement as they are not as intimately tied to the secret conspiracy. Shakespeare in *Romeo and Juliet* spoke through the lips of Juliet's nurse, "Two may keep counsel putting one away!". Shakespeare repeats this timeless proverb in *Troilus and Cressida*, "Who shall be true to us, when we are so unsecret to ourselves?[185]". Conspiracies in my estimation were simply impossible. Benjamin Franklin also wisely noted that "Three can keep a secret... if two of them are dead!". Both of these historical sages agreed that a conspiracy of more than one was destined to fail. I attended the University and amassed many more philosophical and intellectual arguments against the possibility of a global Conspiracy. A mass conspiracy of the Illuminati, the Trilateral Commission, the Bilderbergers, and countless thousands others, was simply too unwieldy to establish, coordinate, and sustain.

I had it all figured out. Or so I thought...

Then it occurred to me, as what I can only describe as a revelation from GOD and after a nearly decade-long study of the history of the *Bible*, that such a conspiracy of global proportions was not only

---

[185] The exact quote is: "Who shall be true to us, when we are so eun secret to ourselves?".

possible, but in fact existed… with *Evil* at its epicenter: *The Conspiracy of Evil Against GOD and GOOD*! Suddenly all of the unanswerable questions had absolute answers. This Conspiracy of Evil was not merely a manmade conspiracy of Illuminati and Bilderbergers, but a Conspiracy centered around the secret connection of unbounded Evil empowering and cloaking the extended and intricate secret connections. Connections of which even the men involved in the conspiracy would not fully be able to discern. Men many of which were the Leftist useful idiots of Evil, and as such they would be wholly unaware of their involvement in the Conspiracy of Evil. (Most men, because of their Fallen and therefore corrupt evil natures, live in a perpetual state of "delusions of grandeur", which greatly aids in Evil's secret workings.) Men left to themselves are not capable, as Shakespeare rightly notes, of the necessary veiled secrecy to carry out such a Conspiracy of global proportions. (It also occurred to me some time later that Shakespeare also wrote of some of the most successful conspiracies in history including the assignation of Caesar by Brutus and his fellow conspirators. In Shakespeare's play *Julius Caesar* a soothsayer warns Julius Caesar "Beware the Ides of March" and Caesar ignores the warning and is assassinated later that same day. Conspiracies are always revealed, but their warnings are often ignored at our own peril!) However the Father of Evil is the only one capable of coordinating and implementing such an Anti-GOD Vast Left-Wing Conspiracy of secrecy and deceit!

My Father was more correct than he or I even realized at the time… let me explain.

There can be no such thing as a "Vast Right-Wing Conspiracy" as a "conspiracy" requires secrecy and subterfuge, the Right carries out their agenda proudly in the open appealing with reasoned pleas of Right and GOOD to the public. A conspiracy is by definition both *secret* and *concealed*. I had to laugh at Hillary Rodham-Clinton's contrived "Vast Right-Wing Conspiracy". (I should know, Hillary accused me of being the hidden hand of her contrived "Vast Right-Wing Conspiracy"! Wow it's so secret that I didn't even know that it existed or that I was a member!) The Right operates totally in the open and is *neither* secret *nor* hidden! The Right has no hidden agenda. As they say simply "it is what it is". What you see is what you get. The Right is proud of its agenda and openly espouses its goals and intentions. The Right's agenda is not secret, hidden, or even misrepresented, as is the Left's secret, hidden, and deceitfully disguised agenda. The Right operates openly in the Light and the Left operates shrouded in Darkness. As Sir Arthur Conan Doyle famously uttered through the lips of Sherlock Holmes: "When you have eliminated the impossible, whatever remains, however improbable, must be the truth". There simply is not and cannot be a Vast Right-Wing Conspiracy. Period.

We must remember that whatever the Left accuses the Right of doing is, almost without exception, what the Left is *actually* guilty of doing itself. Hillary Rodham-Clinton's conveniently imagined "Vast Right-Wing Conspiracy" was in fact the malicious working of the "Vast Left-Wing Conspiracy". The "Vast Left-Wing Conspiracy" is as old as Lucifer, Alinsky's original Leftist rebel *Against GOD*, in the temptation of Eve in the Garden of Eden manifesting in man's subsequent fall into sin. It is the Left who hides their agenda and not the Right; it is the Left's *secrecy* which *defines* a conspiracy! The Left simply cannot afford to be exposed for the Evil that underlies every aspect of their rebellion *Against GOD* and all that is GOOD. The Left and its sycophants by *preempting* the argument, seats in the minds of the public that the evils of the Left are actually the work of the Right. (Remember the homosexual activist who said that the Left must *pre-define* the so-called "Anti-Bullying"[186] Campaign before the Right had the chance to expose them with the truth that they were actually a pedophile movement aimed at young boys?!) This is the same genre of *Lies* of the Left as: the Right is the Party of the rich, the Party of the Wall Street fat cats, oppressors of the poor, the enemy of minorities, and standard-bearers of all that is loathsome.

There is, however, a documentable *Vast Left-Wing Conspiracy*! This Vast Left-Wing Conspiracy remains hidden only because the Father of *Lies*[187], who is Lucifer, the Devil, and the source and binding force

---

[186] See the full discussion in the chapter: *Tolerance*.
[187] The *Holy Bible*, John 8:44.

of *Evil…* empowering, coordinating, and effecting the Vast Left-Wing Conspiracy, remains cloaked in the shadows. (The greatest trick the Devil ever pulled was convincing the world he didn't exist.). In rare, candid moments, even the Left acknowledges the source and power of their Vast Left-Wing Conspiracy as *Evil*, and as we have documented elsewhere Saul Alinsky, the godfather of America's New Left, himself acknowledged the Left's Father as *Lucifer* himself. Some on the Left serve Darkness as willing accomplices for personal power; some are blinded by Evil with a missionary zeal to build an imagined Leftist Utopia; some as a means to live a lifestyle of sin in rejection of GOD in their attempt to live the *Lies* of Friedrich Nietzsche's "GOD is dead" delusion; and some as those whom fellow *Comrade* Vladimir Lenin aptly called them evil's "useful idiots". These are the *Kookaphants* of the Left today!

It is the *Vast Left-Wing Conspiracy* who conspires in the shadows while using its *Lies* to the public using every subterfuge and dark trick to get the Left's agenda implemented. The Left are by definition TERRORISTS *Against* GOD and GOOD! The *Vast Left-Wing Conspiracy* is… A Conspiracy of Evil!

It was Nancy Pelosi who looked condescendingly down the end of her nose and spit out "If you want to know what's in the Obamacare bill…", while it was those on the Right who tried to expose the Conspiracy hidden in the Dark behind the Left's *Lies*. It was the Right who tried to expose the Evil behind Obama's *secret* deal with Muslim Iran to allow Iran to get the nuclear bomb. *Comrade* Hillary Rodham-Clinton screams of the nonexistent "Vast Right-Wing Conspiracy" as a *preemptive* move to hide her commitment to the actual, existent "Vast Left-Wing Conspiracy". (See especially the chapter *Bait and Switch: The Re-Name-Game*)

It was the Leftist-Progressive Hillary Rodham-Clinton who in 1993 secretly plotted a hostile takeover of America's healthcare system along with her husband President Bill Clinton. It was dubbed "Hillary-Care" by the press. Even the Left Stream Media complained of the *secrecy* of the Clintons' appointments to the committee, and the *secrecy* surrounding the whole affair. It was Obama who in 2010 succeeded in a hostile takeover of our healthcare system by the means of a *secret* behind closed-doors conspiracy of the Leftist-Democrat Party. Remember it was Jonathan Gruber the "architect of Obamacare" who said after Obamacare passed that "Americans were too stupid [to recognize the conspiracy]" and if Americans had known what was in Obamacare "they would never have allowed it to pass"! It was the Leftist-Democrat House Speaker Nancy Pelosi who said if Americans wanted to know what was in Obamacare "Congress '[has] to pass the bill so [Americans] can find out what's in it"! This is the *secret* "Vast Left-Wing Conspiracy"?!

The logical question then becomes: What is the endgame of the Left? It can be found in the often overlooked remarks by Barack Hussein Obama Jr. in his speech outlining his plan to "fundamentally changing the United States of America...", however it is Obama's next words that give up the *conspiracy*: "We are five days away from fundamentally changing the United States of America. ... we will change this country, and we will **change the world**". This makes sense of Obama's "global tour" telling the world that America is not exceptional. The Left has always had global aspirations and for the last 240 plus years it was America's exceptionalism that stood, at times single-handedly, in the way. It has always been the goal of Evil since the beginning of time to establish global control. The Left in America today is the embodiment of that Evil!

The Left will sing in shrieking chorus a condemnation about the "hysterical" tone of this book. The Left will mock it as a delusional "conspiracy" theory, as if anyone believing in a conspiracy is crazy, delusional, or just plain paranoid. (Of course one can only be "paranoid" if the object of their fears is imaginary. But the Truth has never been an obstacle for the Left!) This book documents and stands on the *Truth*. The Left will conveniently forget about Hillary Rodham-Clinton's constant bellowing of her self-conjured "Vast Right-Wing Conspiracy", which was imagined solely for the political benefit of the Leftist cause. However no one would have considered a watchman on the Titanic as "hysterical" had he shouted a warning of an approaching iceberg! This book is meant as a shouted warning to the USS America for an immediate course correction as we are headed straight for an ideological iceberg that will shipwreck America and end the 240-year maiden voyage of the American dream!

Leftist Power Brokers
The majority of the rich donors and power brokers in America are Leftists: Bill Gates, Warren Buffett, George Soros, Tom Steyer, Michael Bloomberg, Fred Eychaner, Hank Paulson, Peter B. Lewis, Herb and Marion Sandler, Peter Lewis, Drummond Pike, *et al*, *ad absurdum*. Among them exists an Evil and documentable *Vast Left-Wing Conspiracy*.

These Leftist Democrat Billionaires control much of the U.S. economy and support Leftist causes through a coordinated series of *secret* organizations. A U.S. Senate Report identified one such Democrat based organization comprised of these missionary-minded Leftist billionaires:

> "The report details how an elite group of rich liberal donors such as Tom Steyer and Hank Paulson – "the Billionaire's Club" – is directing and controlling the far-left environmental movement, "which in turn lobbies and controls major policy decisions and lobbies on behalf of the Environmental Protection Agency (EPA)".
>
> The scale of the **conspiracy** "by a small group of powerful and active millionaires and billionaires who exert tremendous sway over a colossal effort" is so **vast**, the report admits, that it has barely been able to scratch the surface"[188]. (emphasis added)

The U.S. Senate report documents in detail the nefarious intentions of these Leftists supporting the Democrat agenda in a Nazi-like Fascist takeover of the U.S. economy:

---

[188] Delingpole, James; Breitbart London; Shock U.S. Senate Report: *Left-Wing 'Billionaire's Club' Using Environmentalism to Control the US Economy and Subvert Democracy*; July 30, 2014.

"... their tax deductible contributions **secretly** flow to a select group of **left wing** activists who are complicit and eager to participate in the fee-for-service arrangement to promote shared political goals"[189]. (emphasis added)

Further the U.S. Senate report continues in its indictment of the Nazi-like exploitation of Federal tax dollars to further fund the Leftist takeover in America:

"In fact, the Committee has uncovered evidence that proves President Obama and his EPA are pivotal partners in the **far-left** environmental movement. The Agency's leadership under President Obama is closely connected with the [Leftist] Billionaire's Club and their network of activists. These connections provide the Billionaire's Club with the opportunity to exploit the relationships, and in turn shape public policy and the disposition of government grants"[190]. (emphasis added)

Delingpole continues:

"These labyrinthine arrangements serve at least three functions. First, they enable left-wing donors to give large sums of money to aggressively political causes in the guise of disinterested, non-partisan, and tax-deductible charitable donations; second, they *mask* the vast scale of the sums being pumped into hard-left environmental activist causes; third, they help maintain the illusion that the numerous and *secretly* well co-ordinated NGOs which use green issues to agitate for more state intervention and regulation are in fact innocent, mom-and-pop grass roots organisations with widespread popular support". (emphasis added)

---

[189] United States Senate Committee on Environment and Public Works Minority Staff Report; *How a Club of Billionaires and Their Foundations Control the Environmental Movement and Obama's EPA*; July 30, 2014; pg. ii.
[190] United States Senate Committee on Environment and Public Works Minority Staff Report; *How a Club of Billionaires and Their Foundations Control the Environmental Movement and Obama's EPA*; July 30, 2014; pg. 23.

The Left's War Against GOD!

This Leftist "Billionaires Club" touts the *secrecy* of its *hidden* activities in promoting its Leftist/Socialist agenda:

> "This weekend, a **shadowy leftist** group named Democracy Alliance will meet in Chicago to figure out a way to thwart conservative rivals… While top liberal organizations blast the right for accepting dark money, **the Alliance's entire business model is based on maintaining _secrecy_ akin to the Illuminati**. 'Like a lot of elite groups, we fly beneath the radar,' Oakland lawyer and Alliance donor Guy Saperstein… The group requires some hefty financial backing. It costs $25,000 just to join, yearly dues of $30,000 and an additional $200,000 donation to Alliance causes. Donation recipients must sign **confidentiality [secrecy] agreements**, the Post reported. The Alliance was founded by a group of billionaires, including George Soros and philanthropist Peter B. Lewis... Its goal was to fund think tanks and media organizations to move societal change toward a more **socialist agenda**"[191]. (emphasis added)

The Left employs Ecosocialism as a means of seizing control of our lives. Christiana Figueres, executive secretary of the UN's Framework on Climate Change, in Brussels February, 2015 she said, "This is the first time in the history of mankind that we are setting ourselves the task of *intentionally*, within a defined period of time, to change the economic development model that has been reigning for at least 150 years since the Industrial Revolution." This is about Leftist ideology and destroying Capitalism as is has existed "for at least 150 years since the Industrial Revolution"! Doubt this? Figueres, added that "Communism is the best model to fight global warming"![192]

Australia's Prime Minister Tony Abbott, "the carbon tax was basically socialism masquerading as environmentalism"!

---

[191] Richards, Tori; Watchdog.org; *Taking a look inside the secret leftist billionaires club*; May 2, 2014.
[192] Wordpress.com , *There Is No Climate Change Crisis*, November 21, 2016

Climate policy has almost nothing to do anymore with environmental protection, says the German economist and U.N. Intergovernmental Panel on Climate Change's (IPCC) official Ottmar Edenhofer. *"The next world climate summit in Cancun is actually an economy summit during which the distribution of the world's resources will be negotiated."* – Ottmar Edenhofer

In an interview published in the *Neue Zürcher Zeitung*[193] on 14 November 2010, Ottmar Edenhofer, co-chair of IPCC Working Group III, said "The climate summit in Cancun at the end of the month is not a climate conference, but one of the largest economic conferences since the Second World War…. *one must say clearly that de facto we redistribute the world's wealth by climate policy…. One has to rid oneself of the illusion that international climate politics have anything to do with environmental concerns."* (emphasis added)

Why bother when the whole AGW thing is a fraud? To quote IPCC spokesmen themselves: "Prof. Dr H. Stephen Schneider, lead author in Working Group II of the IPCC (said in 1989): 'For these reasons we have to announce terrifying scenarios, make simplified, dramatic statements with no mention of any doubts whatever which we might have. In order to attract attention, we need dramatic statements leaving no doubt about what is said. Every one of us researchers must decide how far he would want to
be honest rather than effective."[194]

At least then-French President Jacques Chirac waited until the opening plenary session of the Kyoto talks in the Hague (COP-6) at about this time in 2000 to boast that Kyoto is "the first component of an authentic global governance."[195]

---

[193] https://www.nzz.ch/klimapolitik_verteilt_das_weltvermoegen_neu-1.8373227
[194] Bachmann, Hartmut; *Die Lüge der Klimakatastrophe* (the 'Lie of the Climate Catastrophe'), Frieling, Berlin, 5th edition 2008; p.28.
[195] Horner, Chris; *The American Spectator* online; And this Year's Chirac Award Goes to…; November 18, 2010, 8:24 pm

Obama was forced to admit that since he took office in 2009, as even reported by the Über-Leftist organization CNN, 95% of the income gains had gone to the top 1% of the richest in America[196]. What was missing was the fact that the vast majority of this wealth was filtered to Obama's Leftist cronies through government grants, favoritism to Leftist organizations, and especially the so-called *Trillion dollar* "stimulus" programs. As much as 80% of the stimulus bailouts went to Leftist organizations, especially unions, as payback for their campaign donations and PAC expenditures to support Democrats. (Is it a coincidence that the largest donor base to Democrats are unions which have donated hundreds of millions of dollars to Leftist causes and candidates?[197]) This is the defining characteristic of classic Fascism in harnessing crony-capitalism and diverting financial rewards to those businesses and businessmen who support the Leftist government in power. The Fascists called this Corporatism (also known as corporativism). The Left always takes the good from the Right and corrupts it and bends to its own Evil will. There is in fact a *documentable* Vast Left-Wing Conspiracy! My Dad was more right than he knew!

Education:

Evil has captured our educational system and is using it to "transform America" into its Leftist Paradise:

> "For the past several months, the NEA (National Education Association) website has recommended that its members read books by communist sympathizer Saul Alinsky. And, for a time, the website listed October 1 as a day for teachers and students to celebrate the anniversary of the Communist takeover of China by Mao Zedong. Saul Alinsky, who has been described by his biographer Sanford Horwitt as a "Communist fellow-traveler," wanted to transfer power from the so-called *Haves* to the so-called *Have-nots* and transform

---

[196] Yousuf, Hibah; CNN.com; *Obama admits 95% of income gains gone to top 1%*; September 15, 2013.
[197] Becker, Kyle; Independent Journal Review; *The Real Party of the Rich: Democrats Have More Top Donors, Millionaires in Congress*; Jan 30, 2014.

the U.S. into a communist state". Saul Alinsky's primary goal of revolution was to establish "the political paradise of communism"[198].[199] (*See this quote in Evil In Our Schools*)

It should be remembered that Mao murdered over 80 million[200] of his own people on the path to create the Left's imaginary communist Utopia which Saul Alinsky called "the political paradise of communism"! Mao starved over 30 million Chinese to death over his delusional agricultural policies and millions were denied food altogether because Mao deemed them too old, too sick, or otherwise undesirable[201]. Mao tortured and killed millions at a whim including all the teachers. Over 45 million were killed in only a four-year period in Mao's "Great Leap Forward"[202]. Many were simply killed to meet Mao's quota-based executions[203]. Some of Mao's most vicious atrocities especially those committed during China's "Cultural Revolution" were reserved for Christians who, by the very nature of Christianity, oppose the Leftist ideals and inherent oppression in the name of "progress". This is the same Mao Zedong that Anita Dunn, who Obama appointed as White House Communications Director, said was one of her "favorite political philosophers"! Of course Obama is also an admirer of Chairman Mao who murdered tens of millions in the name of creating a Leftist Utopia[204]. Remember the Obama White House Christmas tree which sported a Christmas bulb featuring the effigy of Mao?!

Entertainment:

The Left has taken a page from history of the Roman games where the Emperor who in order to deflect attention away from the stolen

---

[198] Alinsky, Saul; *Rules For Radicals*; pg. 10.

[199] Costello, Bill; AmericanThinker.com; *National Education Association Selling Its Saul*; August 21, 2010.

[200] Panné, Jean-Louis; *The Black Book of Communism: Crimes, Terror, Repression*; 1999.

[201] Mirsky, Jonathan; *A bleak anniversary: Mao the mass murderer*; New York Times; January 9, 2004.

[202] Akbar, Arifa; The UK Independent; *Mao's Great Leap Forward 'killed 45 million in four years*; Friday 17 September 2010.

[203] Wikipedia; The Great Leap Forward, Consequences.

[204] See further discussion in the chapter *The Obamas: The Epitome of the Left*.

freedoms of the Republic, implemented the sport of battling gladiators. In this ancient Leftist-style Roman dictatorship the favorite target of the Coliseum games were Christians to be killed for, you got it, their Christian faith! Today the Left has substituted sports, movies, gaming, and other various types of entertainment which are progressively more violent, mocking, demeaning, and dehumanizing in their villainizing of Christians. Obama's obsession as President with extending high-speed internet into rural America seems hard to explain, until of course one takes into account the corrupting nature of the vast majority of internet content and its "entertainment value" in distracting Americans away from the things which really matter in life.

Sexual "liberation" has always been at the core of the Left's plan to destroy people and nations. When Israel left the Evils of Egypt they wandered in the wilderness of Sinai for forty years because of unbelief. During this time of wandering the Israelites needed to pass through the land of Moab. Balaam was asked by Balak, the king of Moab, to prophesy against Israel. GOD Himself came to Balaam, in the pre-incarnate person of Jesus Christ, and forbid Balaam upon threat of death! Balaam instead instructed king Balak to send young prostitutes to sexually corrupt the Israelites and conquer them from within. That is exactly what happened and Israel was held in the wilderness until that whole adult generation died off and a new faithful generation rose up in its place. Today the Left does not even have to send in young prostitutes in person, they simply deliver them via the internet! The sin of Balaam is alive and corrupting to destruction today in America!

The internet is a conduit directly into our homes for filth, perversion, depravity, and all other forms of Leftist indoctrination and Evil. The Left does not want to limit the Evil content, but only limit the content which promotes GOD and the Right. Rural America today is the last bastion of the Right.

The Left not only wants to force Universal internet on every American, but it wants to simultaneously tax and regulate the content! This is a Leftist coordinated campaign that includes the "fairness doctrine", which would effectively eliminate all Conservative and Right commentary from the public airwaves, internet, and discussion! While the "fairness doctrine" certainly is a Leftist *religious* "doctrine"[205] it is in no way "fair" as it is designed to eliminate all opposition from the Right, to the Left's Evil agenda.

In sports in America today, it is forbidden for players to write a reference to a *Bible* verse about love on his face, but it is perfectively permissible to flash gang signs and tattoo vulgarities all over their bodies. It used to be commonplace to see sports teams pray before the beginning and after the end of a game. Now it is champagne corks popping and female sports reporters in locker rooms interviewing men parading around nude.

Movies from Leftist Hollywood portray Christians as perverts, sociopaths, murderers, and general thrill-killers. Much of the Left's antagonism towards Christianity is overt, while much is more subliminal like naming an evil character with his first name of "Christian" as in the evil, tormenting, and murderous character on *Agents of Shield* Christian Ward under the guise of an adaptation based on the Marvel children's comics.

Religion:

The Left will even invoke "religion" as a justifier to violate Biblical restrictions and to act in unGODly ways to supposedly accomplish "good" ends. By its very definition it is *impossible* to do "good" for one's own benefit and without GOD. GOOD is always, that is exclusively, done for the benefit of others. The Left does "good" under the guise of "helping" when it is only for the benefit of the Leftist elite at the expense of those they claim to be "helping".

On Fox News a Leftist apologist said that the Right should support then President Obama breaking the law in granting amnesty by Executive Order because most Hispanics are "religious"![206] Indeed the

---

[205] See the chapter: *The Left Is a RELIGION!*.
[206] Fox News November 22, 2014.

Leftist-Evil moniker *the ends justifies the means* has been the guiding principle of the Left as originally voiced by Satan to Eve in the Garden of Eden. This has been the tactics of the Left from the Fall of man into sin, to the French Revolution, and now reiterated in Saul Alinsky's *Rules For Radicals*. Even Leftist programs, such as "*outcome* based education" betrays this tactic. Outcome Based Education was a catastrophic failure in educating our children, however the Left's outcome was not intended to better educate our children, but to indoctrinate our children in Leftist propaganda which was a *coup* of monumental success.

Minorities:

The Left in America is designed to usurp power by their control of minority fringe elements. The Left continually drums for the recognition and empowerment of minority groups. When the Left cannot form a majority from its minorities-coalition, the Left simply further divides the Country and creates new groups of minorities! Do not be fooled, the goal is to destroy the Conservative majority which founded and has maintained the United States since its inception! The very concept of American Republicanism is *majority* rule. Every election in America is decided by a vote of the *majority*. Have you noticed the Left's monumental efforts to allow non-American minorities to vote in American elections? Hence the Left's attempt to *Re-Name* "illegal aliens" to "illegal immigrants", to "undocumented workers" to… voila "undocumented citizens"! Of course it is the right of every "citizen" to vote! The Left screams "come to America illegally and we'll give you the right to vote for us!". The Democrat Left allowing and even recruiting foreigners to vote in America is the absolute outworking of a One World government! Global Citizenship which allows illegals to vote is an admission by the Left that they support, promote, and violently demand a One World Government! The Left follows the dictates of the one who will be the only successful one in creating a One World Government… Lucifer![207] And the Left is working frantically to that end!

---

[207] The *Holy Bible:* Revelation 13:4-8.

The Soviets seized control and ruled the Evil Empire with only 5% of the population. The Soviets did it militarily. The Left in America today has not been able to seize control of the military so the Left has seized control of nearly all American institutions using a small Leftist minority. Education, economics, banking, the Media, and the Democrat Party are today all controlled by Leftist radicals. Watching the nightly news and television programing you would be left to assume that America is comprised of a majority of Leftists: Socialists, homosexuals, transgenders, feminists, anti-war, Antifa, Black Lives Matter, anarchists, and so forth. Even many Conservatives were shocked when Donald Trump won the White House. Where did all those votes for a Conservative agenda come from? From a silent and frightened Conservative majority! The Left through its Left Stream Media Propaganda Machine had convinced many of people that the new norm is Leftism! As the 2016 Presidential election soundly proved, America is still a Conservative Country! We, the Right, can still take back our Country from the Minority Left!

HAIL CAESAR OBAMA!

Only a tyrant rules by Executive fiat. Obama as President repeatedly told Congress "either do it my way or I will circumvent Constitutionally mandated Congressional approval and use the Emperor's magic pen and do it myself". Do you find the use of the term "Emperor" offensive here in this context? Well let's use Obama's own quote on the matter in connection to illegal aliens infiltrating America and his ability to act without Congress passing a law: "I am not the emperor of the United States. My job is to execute laws that are passed" and when Congress would not comply with Obama's directive Obama signed an Executive order that in Obama's own words made him the "Emperor" of America!

Here is the full quote:

> "This is something I've **struggled** with throughout my presidency. The **problem is** that I'm the president of the United

States, ***I'm not the emperor of the United States***. My job is to execute laws that are passed. And Congress right now has not changed what I consider to be a broken immigration system. And what that means is that *we have certain obligations to enforce the laws that are in place* even if we think that in many cases the results may be tragic. ... [W]e've kind of **stretched** our administrative flexibility as much as we can..."[208]. (emphasis added)

Notice that poor, poor Obama had painfully "struggled" against his Constitutional restraints and his admitted inability to usurp power, that is until Obama decided not to "struggle" any longer and assume the office of, in his own words, "Emperor"! Is this not conclusive enough for you? White House Press Secretary Josh Earnest added that Obama "wears the 'emperor' insult "as a badge of honor"! Only those willfully blind cannot see the dictatorial thread in all the Left's actions.

What was the response from the Left at Obama's illegal usurpation of power? Only silence or outright support! House Democrat Minority Leader Nancy Pelosi then commented that President Obama's forthcoming executive action on immigration was about "securing the border", completely ignoring the illegality of Obama's action. Acting against the law only concerns the Left when it becomes an opportunity to point a crooked finger at the Right. Regardless if it is deserved or not.

INFILTRATE AND DESTROY FROM WITHIN:

The Left took a page, literally, from Saul Alinsky's *Rules For Radicals* in teaching Leftists to "put on a suit" and infiltrate America's institutions and subvert America, just as the Soviet Communist dictator Nikita Khrushchev predicted, "from within". Here is what Alinsky advocated, "True revolutionaries do not flaunt their

---

[208] Wolking, Matt; Speaker.gov; *22 Times President Obama Said He Couldn't Ignore or Create His Own Immigration Law*; November 19, 2014.

radicalism… They cut their hair, put on suits, and infiltrate the system from within". Can someone say "Deep State"?! The Left's infiltration includes political office, the Deep State, judgeships, non-profits, churches, media outlets, education, NGOs, CEOs, entertainment, medicine, science, and myriad others. These infiltrators speak the Left's Word Game in unison which gives the appearance that an overwhelming majority of Americans are in lockstep with the Leftist agenda, but as the 2016 election proved… we aren't! We need to identify the Enemy beyond their coiffed haircuts and Armani suits and cut the cancer out of the heart of America!

Constitutional Law attorney Edwin Vieira Jr.:

> "By whatever means … *something* must be done – and soon – to bring reckless judges to heel. The present enthusiasm among all too many judges for legitimating 'same-sex marriage' indicates how far they are willing to go in aid of perverse 'social engineering' at this point in time. That vanishingly few people ever imagined that American judges would go even as far (and as fast) as they already have ominously suggests that they are more than likely to go farther still"[209]

The tactics of the Left began at the Fall of Lucifer into sin, when he was cast out of Heaven, by the Power of GOD and renamed Satan, the Devil. Satan's tactics always start using what the *Bible* calls *subtlety*[210], or Word Games which are deceiving language used to trick the hearer to sin, and which sin *always* leads to wholesale death and destruction. *Always*! The Word Games used by the Left really do act like "sticks and stones' and will *always* allow the Left to ultimately "break our bones" and will *always* "hurt us"! The contemporary Politically Correct campaigns through history have *always* turned into

---

[209] United States Senate Committee on the Judiciary Subcommittee on Oversight, Agency Action, Federal Rights and Federal Courts; Hearing on July 22, 2015; *With Prejudice: Supreme Court Activism and Possible Solutions*; Edwin Vieira, Jr., holds four degrees from Harvard: A.B. (Harvard College), A.M. and Ph.D. (Harvard Graduate School of Arts and Sciences), and J.D. (Harvard Law School).
[210] The *Holy Bible*: 2 Corinthians 11:3.

physical blows and incarceration, and ultimately, *always* into flying guillotine blades and gas chambers. Power corrupts, and absolute power corrupts absolutely! The denial of "it can't happen here" is a delusion from the Pit of Hell. We are already seeing a frightening escalation of Christians incarcerated for refusing to comply with a multitude of unConstitutional Politically Correct demands from the Left. The Left *always* begins by the usurping of power employing its P.C. Word Games, followed by an escalation of seized power with escalating incarceration, followed then by seizing absolute power and *extermination* of all opponents. *Always!*

Nietzsche, Goebbels, and Hitler used their Leftist Word Games and we got Nazi Germany and over 65,000,000 people dead. Engels, Marx, Lennon, and Stalin began and successively escalated their Leftist Word Games and we got Communist Russia and then the Soviet Union and 100,000,000 people dead. Mao began his Leftist Word Games and we got Communist "Red" China and 40,000,000 people dead. Kim Il-sung began his Leftist Word Games and we got Communist North Korea and 1,600,000 people dead. Hideki Tojo began his Leftist Word Games and we got a Leftist Dictatorship in Japan and over 5,000,000 people dead. Yahya Khan began his Leftist Word Games and we got a Leftist Muslim Dictatorship in Pakistan and over 2,000,000 people dead. Pol Pot began his Leftist Word Games and we got Communist Cambodia and 2,500,000 people dead. Ho Chi Minh began his Leftist Word Games and we got Communist North Vietnam and over 1,000,000 people dead. Yakubu Gowon began his Leftist Word Games and we got a Nigerian Dictatorship and over 1,000,000 people dead. Mengistu Haile Mariam began his Leftist Word Games and we got a Communist Ethiopian Dictatorship and 1,500,000 people dead. Mugabe began his Leftist Word Games and we got Communist Zimbabwe and 500,000 people dead. Idi Amin Dada began his Leftist Word Games and we got a Leftist Muslim Dictatorship in Uganda and 500,000 people dead. Saddam Hussein began his Leftist Word Games and we got an Iraqi Muslim Dictatorship and over 2,000,000 people dead. Ismail Enver Pasha began his Leftist Word Games and we got a Leftist Muslim Dictatorship in Turkey and 2,500,000 people dead. Omar al-Bashir began his Leftist Word Games and we got a Leftist Muslim

Dictatorship in Sudan and 400,000 people dead. The list of Leftist Word Game's resultant in mass genocide is nearly endless and *always* leads to unimaginable deaths and indiscriminate destruction! *Always*!

To the Left the above list is simply the necessary causalities of *War*, the necessary collateral damage on the road to realizing the Left's Utopian Paradise. Death to the Left is *not* a horrifying loss of life, but a necessary step in advancing toward victory in their *War Against GOD*. For the cynic that still thinks that "it can't happen here", let's go back to the fact that it *already is* happening here! The Left has already killed over 57,000,000 AMERICAN babies in the name of realizing its Leftist dream. Still think that it can't happen here? Not only is it happening here *now* in America, but you haven't seen nothing yet. The Left in America is just getting started!

The Left means to subvert all things in America that have traditionally made America unique born from its Conservative foundations. The Left's Word Game is the opening salvo in *Re-Naming* Evil as "good". The Tactics for *The Left's Subversion and Takeover of America* are keeping its agenda hidden through the *Lies* of Word Games, infiltrating and positioning people and organizations that have *secret* agendas to destroy America, and implementing a Leftist Utopia in its place. Everywhere we look we find Leftist infiltrators controlling: the US Supreme Court, Federal Appeals Courts, lower court judgeships, Corporations (CEOs), Church leadership in many "Christian" denominations, the Entertainment Industry, Education from our Universities down to the pre-school level, all Federal Agencies (e.g. the Deep State: CIA, FBI, State Department, Justice Department, *et al*!), our Political Parties (including the Republican Party (RHINOs)), the entire Left Stream Media, Non-Profits, Sciences, the Medical Industry, and on-and-on *ad nausea*! The Left's tactic of infiltrate and subvert has been wildly successful. The Left has been mostly successful because of the *secret*, hidden nature of Evil's *Vast Left-Wing Conspiracy*. We on the Right *must* publically identify each Leftist traitor to America and document each of their sins to Americans! Americans who generally are clueless to the Evil that lurks behind the Cheshire grins of theses Leftists and the horrors that are inevitable to their *secret* and hidden endgame! This is *Tactics for the Left's Subversion and Takeover of America* in *the Left's War Against GOD!*

10. *LIES, LIES, LIES!*

Chapter 10

Evil *must Lie* continually as a basic means of their survival. The Left *cannot* tell the truth as they would be instantly rejected by any sane person! If the Left, as the earthly manifestation of Evil, spoke the truth as "we will offer you legalization of sin *Against GOD* in exchange for destroying and enslaving you and your children" most would either run away screaming or stand and fight to eliminate this Evil. Satan did not offer death to Eve in the Garden of Eden; Satan camouflaged his offering of sin to Eve as "freedom" from GOD and to be herself like GOD. It was a *Lie* of Evil to death and destruction then in the beginning as it is today equally to death and destruction today!

The *Lies* of the Left are so often, and so innumerable, it almost becomes farcical to restate the obvious in calling them *Liars!* But of course that is part of the Left's deception, Hitler was as famous for lying then, as is Obama, Hillary, Pelosi, *ad infinitum* for lying now, "if you repeat it frequently enough people will sooner or later believe it". The Left actually produces daily "talking points" that are the *Lies* to be repeated in chorus by the Left's minions. **Leftism is by its nature and practice a Lie!** Here is the sad truth: It works! It works primarily because the Right cowers, afraid to confront the Left on its *Big Lies*! Hence the adage: *Evil Triumphs When Good Men Do Nothing.* It is time for GOOD men to stand up against Evil and take back America from the *Lies* of Evil!

It is time that the Left's rhetoric is called what it truly is: *Lies, Lies, Lies!* Congressman Joe Wilson was absolutely right when he called Obama a Liar shouting, "You Lie!" at the September 9, 2009 State of the Union Speech. The Left collectively came unhinged. How dare anyone expose a *Lie* of the Left, especially on live unedited National television! Newsflash: Barack Hussein Obama, Jr. is and was a pathological and unrepentant... *Liar*! This fact has been documented by dozens of respected sources, and amazingly, even some main-stream media outlets began to document Obama's *Lies* also!

The Left's collective insanity and their Chicken Little "the sky is falling" hysteria over their loss in the 2016 elections and Trump's victory can be easily explained. The Left had convinced itself that the 2016 election was in the bag for Hillary Rodham-Clinton and by extension the Left had secured their final "transformation" of America. In doing so the Left outed itself by proudly proclaiming many of their true evil intentions and motives. They went out on a limb in the election and the American people cut off that limb! The Left is in freefall and nearly totally exposed! The Left's position is indefensible and their only defense is to scream as loudly as possible their thousands of *Lies* against the Right and hope that something… anything… sticks!

The Left screams totally manufactured *Lies* about Russian collusion. When they are forced to admit that there is no evidence for collusion the Left begins screaming obstruction to which they can produce no actual evidence. Because it's all *Lies!* How many *Lies* of the Left Stream Media have been cloaked by nonexistent "unnamed sources"? These made up *Big Lies* will continue without end as long as the Left is in existence!

The Left collectively lives in an Orwellian fantasy from which reality never deters their Utopian delusion. Obama held up Yemen as an example of his foreign policy success and less than two months later Yemen falls to Islamic terrorists… and Obama still holds up Yemen as a success! Actual unemployment rates were somewhere between 11% and 18% and Obama bragged about "historically low unemployment rates", "If you like your doctor you can keep him", etc. This is truly Orwellian Doublespeak. Translate: *LIES!*

One overlooked phrase that was overshadowed in Obama's infamous 2008 "God and religion" speech in San Francisco is the preceding line where Obama laments: "the truth is, our challenge is to get people persuaded that we can make progress when there is no evidence of that in their daily lives". Obama wants to be "honest" ["the truth is"] to the Leftist faithful in the crowd, behind closed doors of course, about lying to the American people in public! This is the Leftist-imagined Utopia!

In a *Time Magazine* article titled: *"A Striking Admission of Political Dishonesty From the Keeper of the Obama Flame"* here is *Time*'s synopsis of David Axelrod's book *Believer: My Forty Years in Politics*:

> "Barack Obama *misled* Americans *for his own political benefit* when he claimed in the 2008 election to oppose same sex marriage for religious reasons, his former political strategist David Axelrod writes in a new book, Believer: My Forty Years in Politics."

> "I'm just not very good at *bullshitting*," Obama told Axelrod, after an event where he stated his opposition to same-sex marriage, according to the book.

> Axelrod writes that he knew Obama was in favor of same-sex marriages during the first presidential campaign, even as Obama publicly said he only supported civil unions, not full marriages. Axelrod also admits to counseling Obama to conceal that position for political reasons. "Opposition to gay marriage was particularly strong in the black church, and as he ran for higher office, he grudgingly accepted the counsel of more pragmatic folks like me, and modified his position to support civil unions rather than marriage, which he would term a 'sacred union,' " Axelrod writes.

> "Yet if Obama's views were "evolving" publicly, they were fully evolved behind closed doors. The president was champing at the bit to announce his support for the right of gay and lesbian couples to wed…"[211]. (emphasis added)

---

[211] Miller, Zeke J; Time Magazine online; *Axelrod: Obama Misled Nation When He Opposed Gay Marriage In 2008*; Feb. 10, 2015.

The Left's covering code phrases like "Dishonesty", "Misled", "bullshitting", "conceal", "modified his position", "parsing words", "It depends on what your definition of is, is", and "evolving" are what GOD (and most of us) calls *LIES!*

Further, in response to Axelrod's revelations, Obama told *Buzzfeed*, "I think David [Axelrod] is mixing up my personal feelings with my position on the issue", wasn't Obama in fact saying that he contradicts his own convictions for political expediency? Of course Obama was just trying to use one *Lie* to cover another, but what a poor choice of words! Obama's "personal feelings" have always been totally in line with his "position" in support of homosexual marriage and in defiance of GOD's definition of marriage! Obama knew then, and knows now that his support of the homosexual agenda and homosexual marriage spits in the face of GOD! Again, do you think this is a harsh, exaggerated, or an incorrect point of view? How about we check Obama's own statement from 2008 in Rick Warren's Saddleback Church while running for President about his convictions regarding homosexual marriage "that marriage could only extend to *heterosexual* couples" saying:

> "I believe that marriage is the union between a man and a woman," Obama said at the time. "Now, for me as a Christian — for me — for me as a Christian, it is also a *sacred* union. **God's in the mix**."[212]. (emphasis added)

Did you catch that? Obama concedes when "**God's in the mix**" that "marriage is [only] the union between a man and a woman"! That marriage between a man and a woman is *sacred* to GOD! Of course with Obama GOD is *not* "in the mix", because Obama is *not* a Christian![213] Obama stutters here over his *Lie* that he is a "Christian": "for me as a Christian — for me — for me as a Christian". Obama cannot quite seem to get it out as he chokes on his bald face *Lie!* If

---

[212] Miller, Zeke J; Time Magazine online; *Axelrod: Obama Misled Nation When He Opposed Gay Marriage In 2008*; Feb. 10, 2015.
[213] The *Holy Bible*; Matthew 7:15-20, "Ye shall know them by their fruits... a corrupt tree bringeth forth evil fruit". For a wider discussion see the chapter: *The Obamas: The Epitome of the Left* and the sub-section: *Obama as a Muslim or Muslim Sympathizer*.

you had not noticed before, without the aid of a teleprompter, Obama tends to stutter and stumble over his words when he *Lies*. After stuttering in front of Rick Warren's Saddleback Church when claiming to be a Christian, Obama might as well have said, "Alright I admit it, I'm *not* a Christian, Sorry folks as I confessed to David Axelrod, unfortunately as my stuttering betrays… 'I'm just not very good at bullshitting'"!

Here is the definitive statement of Jonathan Gruber, the chief architect of the Obamacare legislation, the largest tax increase in the history of the world, concerning the use of lying and deception used by the Obama Administration and the Democrats in Congress to get Obamacare passed:

> "This bill was written in a tortured way to make sure CBO did not score the mandate as taxes. If CBO scored the mandate as taxes, the bill dies. Okay, so it's written to do that. In terms of risk rated subsidies, if you had a law which said that healthy people are going to pay in – you made explicit healthy people pay in and sick people get money, it would not have passed… **Lack of transparency [LYING] is a huge political advantage**. And basically, call it **the stupidity of the American voter** or whatever, but basically that [**Lying**] *was really, really critical for the thing to pass*… Look, I wish Mark was right that we could make it all transparent, but I'd rather have this law than not.[214]" (emphasis added)

Notice the "I'd rather have this law than not" statement which uses the Alinsky tactic of "the ends justifies the means" deceptions of the Left? Is it any wonder that Nancy Pelosi chided the American people, "we have to pass the bill so you can find out what's in [the Obamacare bill]"? It was a thinly veiled charade, or as Peter Roff of *U. S. News and World Report* put it:

---

[214] Howley, Patrick; *Obamacare Architect: Lack of Transparency Was Key Because 'Stupidity Of The American Voter' Would Have Killed Obamacare*; dailycaller.com; November 09, 2014, 10:30 PM; A video of Jonathan Gruber's statement was uploaded to YouTube.com by AmericanCommitment with an upload stamp October 17, 2013.

"It has been said well and famously that **politicians only really commit a gaffe when they tell the truth without meaning to**. Add House Speaker Nancy Pelosi to the list.

Speaking Tuesday to the 2010 Legislative Conference for the National Association of Counties, Pelosi began the windup of her healthcare pitch by alluding to the controversies over the healthcare bill and the process by which it has reached its current state. Then, just after saying, 'It's going to be very, very exciting,' Pelosi gaffed, telling the local elected officials assembled that Congress '[has] to pass the bill so you can find out what's in it, away from the fog of controversy'"[215].

The "fog of controversy" is an allusion to the *Lies* being employed by the Left to cover up, or "fog" over, the truth. The Obamacare bill rhetoric was a *Lie*, which Jonathan Gruber exposed for all of America to see. Again for a second time, Gruber was caught on tape commenting on a Leftist conspiracy involving the

"then-Senator John Kerry came up with the idea of taxing the companies providing the Cadillac plans, rather than taxing Americans directly. Gruber told him that it was the same thing, and he didn't see why that's matter. 'You'll see,' responded Kerry. Sure enough, the provision passed, in Gruber's estimation because 'the *American people are too stupid to understand the difference*'"[216].

The term "stupid" is a bit loose in Gruber's use of it. The American people cannot be "stupid" of what is intentionally hidden from them. What Gruber is actually saying is that American's in general are too naïve in not instinctively assuming that **every action on the Left is Evil and hidden behind *Lies*!**

---

[215] Roff, Peter; usnews.com; *Pelosi: Pass Health Reform So You Can Find Out What's In It: The speaker has a surprise for voters*; March 9, 2010, 6:05 p.m. EST
[216] Griswold, Alex; dailycaller.com; *Yet Another Video Emerges Of Obamacare Architect Calling Americans 'Stupid'*; 11/11/2014.

Even über-Leftist organizations even then felt compelled to acknowledge the über *Lies* of Obama. PolitiFact, a Leftist oriented website, for 2013 awarded Obama their Lie of the Year Award for "If you like your health care plan, you can keep it". The Washington Post, another über-Leftist media organization, named Obama *the biggest Liar of 2013* with "The biggest Pinocchios of 2013" award. This is the Left's most revered messiah-In-Chief as the Biggest Liar as President of the United States! GOD help us!

Lying is the stock-in-trade of the Left! Because, as Jonathan Gruber so eloquently stated, the Left's position of "if the American people actually knew what the truth was behind the Left's agenda, Americans would never have voted for it or tolerated it"! The Left has convinced itself that they deceive Americans "for our own good". The Left has to *Lie* because the American people are too "stupid" to know what's "good" for them!

The Left often resorts to name-calling and emotional hyperboles. In their bible, *Rules For Radicals*, written by the Leftist icon Saul Alinsky, the Leftist activists are instructed:

> "RULE 5: Ridicule is man's most potent weapon. There is no defense. It's irrational. It's infuriating. It also works as a key pressure point to force the enemy into concessions" and

> "RULE 12: Pick the target, freeze it, personalize it, and polarize it. Cut off the support network and isolate the target from sympathy. Go after people and not institutions; people hurt faster than institutions."

Alinsky taught that in order for the Left to take over all opposing political viewpoints, "Marxism in America must move beyond the dialectical materialism of Marxism"[217]. In his 1971 book *Rules for Radicals*, Alinsky berated the Sixties Left for scaring off potential converts in middle-class America:

---

[217] Infed.org; Article: *Saul Alinsky: community organizing and rules for radicals.*

"'True revolutionaries do not flaunt their radicalism', Alinsky taught. 'They cut their hair, put on suits and infiltrate the system from within. Alinsky viewed revolution as a slow, patient process. The trick was to penetrate existing institutions such as **churches**, unions and political parties[218]'".

"The radical organizer", Alinsky explains that he "does not have a fixed truth...truth to him is relative and changing; *everything* to him is relative and changing. He is a political relativist"[219]. As previously stated, the Left has force-fed the concept that "all truth is relative" and their "situational ethics" through its public school indoctrination camps. Either truth is absolute or it's *not* truth! If it's not truth is the Left's *Lie*! Alinsky's teachings are so pivotal to the thinking of the Left and used so profusely by the Left to implement their *War* plans, that it will be often referenced throughout these pages.

Noted admirers and followers of Saul Alinsky's *Rules For Radicals* include Barack Hussein Obama and Hillary Rodham-Clinton as noted even by Leftist publications including National Public Radio, *The Washington Post*, and Salon.com[220]. Alinsky's biographer, Sanford Horwitt, makes this link between Alinsky and Obama in Horwitt's book *Let Them Call Me Rebel*. In a letter to Saul Alinsky in 1971, Hillary identifies herself as a fellow Leftist aligning her ideology with that of Alinsky's "New Left"[221].

A firmly held and proselytized belief of Alinsky was that "In **war**, the end justifies almost any means..." (emphasis added). This is the tightly held belief of virtually every Leftist leader since the beginning of Evil. The Left clearly sees its struggle as a "war" and are willing to employ

[218] Quoted from FreeRepublic.com; Poe, Richard Lawrence; November 26, 2007.
[219] Alinsky, Saul; *Rules For Radicals*; pg. 10-11.
[220] Cohen, Alex; Horwitt, Sanford; January 30, 2009; "*Saul Alinsky, The Man Who Inspired Obama*"; Day to Day, NPR.
Sugrue, Thomas; January 30, 2009; *Saul Alinsky, The Man Who Inspired Obama*; and Saul Alinsky: *The activist who terrifies the right*; NPR. Slevin, Peter; March 25, 2007; For Clinton and Obama, a Common Ideological *Touchstone*; The Washington Post. Sugrue, Thomas; February 7, 2012; Saul *Alinsky: The activist who terrifies the right*; Salon.com.
[221] This July 8, 1971 letter written by Hillary Rodham-Clinton to Saul Alinsky was suppressed by the Clintons until its release in 2014. Why would the Clinton's go to such lengths to hide Hillary Clinton's relationship with Saul Alinsky if she had nothing to hide?

"almost any means" to win their *War*, specifically *The Left's War Against GOD!*

Outgoing U.S. Senate Leader Harry Reid's self-righteous sneer after his admission of his own *Lies* about then Presidential candidate Mitt Romney, *Lies* which contributed significantly to Romney's loss against Obama: "Well, they can call it whatever they want," Reid sneered, "Romney didn't win, did he?". As Alinsky preached to the Left like Reid: "the end always justifies the means". The Left is proud of its *Lies* especially when those *Lies* result in the defeat of an opponent on the Right. Of course this is only a one way street for the Left. The Left would suddenly develop a case of "moral" outrage if this same Evil tactic was used against them!

Lying is one of the key deceptions that the Left employs to convince people that their intentions are good when in fact they are Evil. Saul Alinsky himself associates the goals of radicals and source of their inspiration with the original radical "Lucifer" saying, "Lest we forget at least an over-the-shoulder acknowledgment to the very first radical...the first radical known to man who rebelled against the establishment and did it so effectively that he at least won his own kingdom — Lucifer.[222]" Jesus tells us that Lucifer is the father of *Lies*[223]! If this is not enough to convince you of the Evil origins of Alinsky's teachings then how about this; in a 1972 *Playboy Magazine* interview Alinsky said, "if there is an afterlife, and I have anything to say about it, I will unreservedly choose to go to Hell. Hell would be heaven for me". *The Left's* War is truly *Against GOD* and all that is GOOD.

David Horowitz, who was once himself a radical Leftist, profoundly states:

> Alinsky's tribute to Satan [Lucifer] as the first radical is further instructive because it reminds us that the radical illusion is an ancient one and has not changed though the

---

[222] Saul Alinsky, *Rules for Radicals*.
[223] The *Holy Bible:* John 8:44 (emphasis added).

millennia. Recall how Satan tempted Adam and Eve to destroy their paradise: If you will rebel against God's command then "You shall be as gods." This is the radical hubris: *We can create a new world. Through our political power we can make a new race of men and women who will live in harmony and peace and according to the principles of social justice. We can be as gods.* And let us not forget that the kingdom the first radical [Lucifer] "won," as Alinsky so thoughtlessly puts it, was ***hell***. Typical of radicals not to notice the ruin they leave behind. This, in a nutshell, is why conservatives are conservative and why radicals are dangerous. Because conservatives pay attention to the consequences of actions, including their own, and radicals don't.[224]

This is exemplified in the most successful Leftist leaders in history, in addition to Lucifer, including Hitler, Mussolini, Mao, Lenin, Stalin, and now Leftists such as Schumer, Pelosi, Hillary Rodham-Clinton, and Barack Hussein Obama. In a letter praising Obama, Saul Alinsky's son David Alinsky wrote, "Obama learned his lesson well. I am proud to see that my father's model for organizing is being applied successfully beyond local community organizing to affect the Democratic campaign in 2008. It is a fine tribute to Saul Alinsky as we approach his 100th birthday." Obama while a law professor even "taught the Alinsky power tactics at the University of Chicago[225]". The Left does not follow the rules of common decency or truth. The Right must learn the "Rules" of the Left and learn to recognize them when they are being employed against the Right. The Right must formulate responses to these deceptive tactics of the Evil of the Left. When the common man can recognize the Left's tactics for the Evil they are, and the destruction they bring, then the common man can revolt against the Evil intentions of the Left, which Evil intentions are ultimately aimed at the enslavement of all of mankind. We need to expose the Left's "Rules" to the masses and turn the Left back on their heads using their own Rules against them.

---

[224] Horowitz, David; *Commentary on Rules For Radicals*; pg. 19.
[225] Shiver, Kyle-Anne; AmericanThinker.com; *Obama's Nazi Straw Man: An Old Alinsky Trick*; August 13, 2009.

The Left functions on telling Big Lies. The person who coined the term ***the Big Lie*** was Adolf Hitler in his memoirs *Mein Kampf (My Struggle)* Hitler defined the Big Lie as:

> "All this was inspired by the principle—which is quite true within itself—that in the big lie there is always a certain force of credibility; because the broad masses of a nation are always more easily corrupted in the deeper strata of their emotional nature than consciously or voluntarily; and thus in the primitive simplicity of their minds they more readily fall victims to **the big lie** than the small lie, since they themselves often tell small lies in little matters but would be ashamed to resort to large-scale falsehoods. It would never come into their heads to fabricate colossal untruths, and they would not believe that others could have the impudence to distort the truth so infamously. Even though the facts which prove this to be so may be brought clearly to their minds, they will still doubt and waver and will continue to think that there may be some other explanation. For the grossly impudent lie always leaves traces behind it, even after it has been nailed down, a fact which is known to all expert liars in this world and to all who conspire together in the art of lying." —Adolf Hitler, Mein Kampf, vol. I, ch. X

The Left's *Lies* are indistinguishable from Hitler's Big Lie. The Satan is the father of lies[226], and Satan told the first *Lie* in the history of the world when he questioned Eve as to whether GOD had really said what GOD had said about not eating of the Forbidden Fruit[227]. Then Satan went further and told Eve that her rebellion against GOD would actually make her a "god" because GOD understood both GOOD and evil.

Newsflash!: the Nazi's and Islam were *allies* in WWII in opposing Israel, killing Jews and Christians, and attempting to establish a

---

[226] The *Holy Bible*: John 8:44.
[227] The *Holy Bible*: Genesis 3:1-6.

Muslim caliphate in the Middle East, just like the Democrat Left is aligned with the Muslims today!

Why does the Left relentlessly defend and so closely embrace Islam? The Left has found a kindred *spirit* in Islam. The Muslim Hadith quotes their prophet Muhammad as saying, "The Prophet said, 'War is deceit.'"[228] Both Alinsky's modern day Leftist Stormtroopers, and Islam are at War with America and specifically America's Christian remnants. "Deceit" is treachery in *Lies* designed to conceal evil intentions behind a smile and a nod. This is the tactic adapted and preached by Alinsky and other Leftists today to advance their own Leftist jihadist cause. The Leftist activists today are nothing more than American Jihadists!

Muslims are *great* Leftists! They live by the Leftist creed "Listen to what I say and pay no attention to what I do!". Think that is a bit of an overreach? Let's see what Islam demands as a fundamental tenant of Islam...

Lying is at the center of both Islam and the Left. In Islam there are two interchangeable words "*taqiyya*" and "*muda'rat*"[229] by which Muslims are *commanded* to *Lie* by Allah in order to advance Islam. "The sixth Shiite imam, emphasized *taqiyya* as a political tool. 'Befriend people on the surface, and keep your grudges and intentions hidden... Being double-faced with one's own takes one outside the bounds of faith, but with others is a form of worship.[230]"! Sound familiar? The Left has refined treachery and Lying to an art form.

While much has been written on the imagined lies of the Right, these accounts are almost entirely nothing more than flights of fantasy with absolutely no empirical facts to back them up. Why no facts? Because they are contrived *Lies* of the Left not only intended to discredit the Right, but also to lay cover for the documentable *Lies* of the Left. Two such *Lies* should be sufficient for this point. The Left constructed a

---

[228] Bukhari, Sahih; Volume 4, Book 52, Hadith 269.
[229] The word "*taqiyya*" is the Shia, or Shiite, version where "*muda'rat*" is the Sunni version.
[230] Quoted: Fandy, Mamoun; Christian Science Monitor; November 22, 2009; pg. 28.

Lie that President George W. Bush was himself responsible for the 911 attacks on the Twin Towers. Several variations on this *Lie* exist but all are equally without a single documentable shred of evidence. Another flight of fantasy, pardon the pun, was the Left who claimed that George H. W. Bush before he became Ronald Reagan's Vice President secretly flew to Iran and negotiated with the ayatollah Khamenei to hold the American Embassy prisoners until after the election so that Reagan could defeat Carter in the 1980 election. When there was documented proof that there were only a few hours unaccounted for in Bush's schedule, the Left claimed that Bush must have flown the supersonic Lockheed SR-71 "Blackbird". The accusation was adding absurdity to insanity. The SR-71 required hundreds of hour of specialty training to be able to fly the specialized aircraft of which Bush had no experience an rendered him wholly unable to pull off such a feat. Of course, reality seldom hinders the Left.

There have been entire books and innumerable articles written documenting just a fraction of Obama's Big Lies[231]. How telling is that? Lying defines the *modus operandi* of Left. The Left's entire persona is fabricated on Lies.

Everything that the Left accuses the Right of is exactly what the Left is guilty of. (Vast Right-Wing Conspiracy; favoring the rich; enslaving the poor, minorities, women) The Left's *An Inconvenient Truth* turns out to be An Inconvenient Lie! Worth emphasizing again is the almost prophetic point-in-fact written in his 1949 book *Nineteen Eighty-Four* (1984), George Orwell's definition of what he named *DOUBLETHINK* is visionary example of the Left's and Al Gore's double-speak of Lies:

> "...since the essential act of the Party is to use conscious deception while retaining the firmness of purpose that goes with complete honesty. To tell **deliberate lies** while genuinely believing in them, to forget any fact that has become

---

[231] Skeptical? Try this: A Google search for "books, Obama, lies" on 10/11/2014 revealed 3,310,000 responses.

inconvenient, and then, when it becomes necessary again, to draw it back from oblivion for just so long as it is needed, to **deny the existence of objective reality** and all the while to take account of the reality which one denies"[232]. (bold added)

Doublespeak is the verbalization of what Orwell dubbed DOUBLETHINK. Orwellian DOUBLETHINK in its full description defines the *Lies* of the Left today:

"DOUBLETHINK means the power of holding two contradictory beliefs in one's mind simultaneously, and accepting both of them. The Party intellectual knows in which direction his memories must be altered; he therefore knows that he is playing tricks with reality; but by the exercise of DOUBLETHINK he also satisfies himself that reality is not violated. The process has to be conscious, or it would not be carried out with sufficient precision, but it also has to be unconscious, or it would bring with it a feeling of falsity and hence of guilt. DOUBLETHINK lies at the very heart of Ingsoc, since the essential act of the Party is to use conscious deception while retaining the firmness of purpose that goes with complete honesty. To tell deliberate lies while genuinely believing in them, to forget any fact that has become inconvenient, and then, when it becomes necessary again, to draw it back from oblivion for just so long as it is needed, to deny the existence of objective reality and all the while to take account of the reality which one denies — all this is indispensably necessary. Even in using the word DOUBLETHINK it is necessary to exercise DOUBLETHINK. For by using the word one admits that one is tampering with reality; by a fresh act of DOUBLETHINK one erases this knowledge; and so on indefinitely, with the lie always one leap ahead of the truth"[233].

---

[232] Orwell, George; *Nineteen Eighty-Four*; Martin Secker & Warburg Ltd, London; 1949; part 1, chapter 3, pg. 32.
[233] Orwell, George; *Nineteen Eighty-Four*; Martin Secker & Warburg Ltd, London; 1949; part 1, chapter 3, pg. 32.

Whenever the Left accuses the Right of wrongdoing, they are themselves guilty of exactly what they accuse others of! It should be an automatic reaction that when the Left accuses the Right, that the Right must search and find that very thing which Left is actually doing. It is a classic diversion tactic. The first one to spew the accusation has the assumed credibility and moral high-ground. So what of Hillary Clinton's secret personal email accounts while Secretary of State in the White House?:

Hillary Rodham-Clinton on the campaign trail on June 20, 2007:

> "Our constitution is being shredded. We know about the... secret White House email accounts. It is a stunning record of secrecy and corruption of cronyism run amuck. It is everything our founders were afraid of. Everything our constitution was designed to prevent".

Notice her shrieking pitch when leveling the accusation? And Hillary Clinton's instructions while secretary of State to all Diplomatic and Consular Staff under her authority in June 2011:

> "Sent to Diplomatic and Consular Staff in June 2011, the unclassified cable, with Clinton's electronic signature, makes clear to "avoid conducting official Department from your personal e-mail accounts" and employees should not "auto-forward Department email to personal email accounts which is prohibited by Department policy." The Cable was addressed to all diplomatic and consular posts with the subject line "Securing Personal E-mail Accounts." While the cable told employees to secure personal/home email accounts given increased targeting of government employees, it makes clear that these personal accounts should never be used for government business and cites the departure procedures which prohibit the practices"[234].

---

[234] McCarthy, Andrew C.; National Review online; *Hillary Clinton Banned Use of Private Email by State Department Employees ... While She Conducted All Her Business By Private Email*; March 5, 2015.

Have you ever noticed that shrieking insanity[235] is a hallmark of the Left? Michelle Obama *shrieked* the Communist slogan *"Power to the people"* and she is cheered by the Left. Most would consider this behavior *insane*.

Conservatives are not calling for an Islamic style jihad against the Left. The Left can still be stopped in the arena of politics and religion through established means. We *do* believe that the radical Left should face the criminal consequences of their unconstitutional and *illegal* actions. I am sounding a clarion call to act to destroy the Left by *all* Constitutional means at our disposal.

This jihad-style attack is what the radical Left would have us believe that the Right has planned, but as usual this is a *Lie* and exactly what the Left planed for the Right! The minions of the Evil Left are constantly calling for a physical confrontation and even death against those on the Right. Wanda Sykes calls Rush Limbaugh a 911 terrorist and says that Rush should be waterboarded and die. This at a White House event while Obama laughs hilariously! Then there is Jimmy Hoffa Jr., president of the Teamsters labor union, who said that the Left should kill all of those who oppose the Left and "take these sons of bitches out". Hoffa referred to it as a "war" and the union thugs were Obama's "army". All this at an Obama rally as Obama looked on approvingly and later said how "proud" Obama was of Hoffa!

A New Jersey homosexual activist threatens to kill Conservative Louisiana Governor Bobby Jindal and a constituent affairs employee on the staff of U.S. Rep. Michele Bachmann. Where is the Left's moral outrage? There is only silence[236]. Professor Otis Madison at the University of California, Santa Barbara said to his students "Ted Cruz-supporting 'teabaggers' to get the hell out of his classroom before he sent them home to their mother *in a body bag*"[237]. Liberal talk radio host Mike Malloy, a Leftist anti-gun activist, threatens to

---

[235] See the broader discussion of insanity in the chapter *The Left Is a RELIGION!*.
[236] John Hinderaker; powerlineblog.com; *New Jersey Liberal Threatens to Kill Republicans*; December 20, 2012.
[237] mrconservative.com; *Liberal Professor Threatens To Kill Tea Party Students*; 05/2014.

kill any board member of the NRA with his own gun, *"And you come, meet me someplace, and all of a sudden, see, we have stand your ground here, and all of a sudden I'm going to feel real goddamned threatened by you! And I will shoot you! If I feel threatened. The law says I can!"*[238].

Leftist actor Orlando Jones tweets for liberals to kill Sara Palin. Where is the moral outrage? None on the Left denounce these Leftist criminals. At best the Left makes excuses for this criminal behavior that they would never make for someone on the Right. The number of these examples is nearly as vast as number of Leftists radicals in America, but these examples will suffice as an accurate sampling. It is not the Right, but the Left who calls for literal violence and death against their opponents. Where is the moral outrage of the Left? The Left is continuously "outraged" about their own made-up accusations against the Right. It is certainly on the Left a form of mental insanity![239]

In the 1990's William Sapphire called Hillary Clinton a congenital Liar. (Some things never change!) The Left Press went insane! The Left will not, and in fact cannot, tolerate the truth. It is an existential issue for the Left to always *Lie*! The Truth always exposes and kills the evil and *Lies* of the Left!

The Democrats tell you that the Right does not want your vote to count. Yet it was the Left in the person of Barack Hussein Obama after the humiliating losses for the Democrats who responded:

> "Obviously, Republicans had a good night. And they deserve credit for running good campaigns. Beyond that, I'll leave it to all of you and the professional pundits to pick through yesterday's results. What stands out to me, though, is that the American people sent a message, one that they've sent for several elections now. They expect the people they elect to work as hard as they do. They expect us to focus on their

---

[238] Anderson, Brian; downtrend.com; *Liberal Radio Talk Show Host Threatens To Kill NRA Board Member*; March 28, 2014.
[239] See the broader discussion of insanity in the chapter *The Left Is a RELIGION!*.

ambitions and not ours. They want us to get the job done. All of us in both parties have a responsibility to address that sentiment. Still, as president, I have a unique responsibility to try and make this town work. So, to everyone who voted, I want you to know that I hear you. **To the two-thirds of voters who chose not to participate in the process yesterday, I hear you, too**"[240]!

Obama wants the votes of those who didn't vote to count! Of course this was because he did not want the vote of those who did vote to count. In addition the Obama Administration has gone out of its way to make sure that as many in the military as possible are denied the right to vote. The military overwhelmingly supports the Right in elections. Obama denies many in the military who are stationed overseas the right to vote.

Obama's Race baiting is another prime example of how the Left accuses the Right for what they are in fact guilty of to claim the "moral" high ground. Obama in his speech in March 7, 2015 Selma, Alabama spoke accusingly of "those seeking to play the 'race card'", while Obama was himself "playing the race card"! The last true bastion of Racism in America is black against white, sanctioned, promoted, and encouraged by the Leftist State!

Milwaukee County Sheriff David Clarke, a black sheriff, refers astutely to the "Black Lives Matter" movement as "Black LIES Matter". Sheriff Clark refers to this movement as the Left's "Frankenstein's monster". The whole front of Black Lives Matter is based on a Lie: "because it's the bastard child of the 'Hands Up, Don't Shoot' Lie, the whole thing is based on a Lie". Clark notes that the members of this Leftist front movement are "a conglomeration of misfits… the Occupy Movement, organized Labor, criminals, black racialists, cop haters, and anarchists". This is who the Left uses as its ramrod against traditional America. The "Black Lives Matter" movement is a Leftist movement that really says "*only* black lives

---

[240] Hayward, John; Human Events Online; *Obama on midterms: People who didn't vote matter more than those who did*; Thursday November 6, 2014 10:27 AM.

matter"! This of course is what Martin O'Malley was excoriated for when he said, "Black Lives Matter. White Lives Matter. All Lives Matter". Silence by Obama on the systematic killing of whites by blacks is Obama's silent approval! Obama is Hell-bent to try to make issue with whites supposedly doing harm to blacks a racist issue, so where is Obama on the deliberate blacks who are executing whites?

Even Sheriff Clarke puts the blame of the murders immediately tied to the "Black Lives Matter" directly on Obama and Obama's Administration saying, "I am too pissed off tonight to be diplomatic about what's going on and I'm not going to stick my head in the sand… I said last December that war had been declared on American police officers led by some high profile people one of them coming out of the white House [Obama] and one coming out of the US Department of Justice [black US Attorneys General Eric Holder and Loretta Lynch] and it's open season right now there is no doubt about it!". Of course Obama's response to Black Lives Matter leaders calling for the execution of white police officers was to invite them to the White House and celebrate their movement!

Here is a note to the Black Leftists: How dare you defy GOD in favor of a Black Supremacist Anti-GOD movement! What ever happened to Martin Luther King, Jr's Dream of a day when we would not look at people for their skin color? The color-blind, non-color Dream is a Conservative Dream of the Right today. It is the Leftist Democrats who want to constantly remind the black population of their color and keep them segregated by their color! The Left invented the Jim Crow Laws against blacks, along with segregation and fought vigorously against desegregation and Civil Rights. The Left wants to keep the blacks in America enslaved and beholding to the Left!

Of course the Left still excoriates those fugitive blacks who have escaped from their shackles and fled the Democrat Party Plantation. Leaving the democrat Party Plantation is an unpardonable sin to the Religion of the Left. Hillary Rodham-Clinton while Secretary of State wanted to impeach US Supreme Court Justice Clarence Thomas because Thomas was a Constitutionalist Justice who dared to uphold the Right foundations instilled in the Constitution.

This is a classic Bait and Switch tactic. The Left's *modus operandi* is always do as I say and pay no attention to what I do. The classic *Wizard of Oz* "pay no attention to the man behind the curtain" parlor trick. The Left consider themselves absolutely above the law. This behavior of the Left is nothing short of a *Lie!* Barack Hussein Obama Jr., Hillary Rodham-Clinton, Bill Clinton, Susan Rice, Eric Holder, Rahm Emmanuel, Al Gore, *ad infinitum*, are all Leftist *Liars* and the Right *must* take up against the Left's *Rules* and continually shout these violations of American conscience at every opportunity! For those on the Right, to not do so is to themselves condone and advance the Left's agenda. Evil triumphs when good men do nothing!

For examples: Hillary Clinton's comment concerning the murder of four Americans in Benghazi, Libya including U.S. Ambassador J. Christopher Stevens on Hillary's watch as Secretary of State, "What difference, at this point, does it make?" is a perfect example of the callousness of the Left. If it were the Clinton's child or loved one who were killed by Islamic terrorists could you *ever* imagine Hillary saying, "What difference, at this point, does it make?"! Of course not! The Left considers themselves above the law and their own mandates, especially when they are attempting to bury their own sins. Über-Leftist Al Gore who opposes school choice as Vice President quipped, "If I was the parent of a child who went to an inner-city school that was failing... I might be for vouchers too". The Left will stop at nothing to advance their collective cause and individual careers.

The Left *hates* school choice, vouchers, and home schooling. Why?... any rational person would ask. All of these public school options remove the central component of the Left's takeover plan: indoctrination! This indoctrination of our youth has been clearly documented since the early 80's beginning with Alan Bloom's *The Closing of the American Mind*.

The Left is the dread Party forewarned in George Orwell's 1984:

"If the Party could thrust its hand into the past and say of this or that event, it never happened -- that, surely, was more terrifying than mere torture and death?

... But where did that knowledge exist? Only in his own consciousness, which in any case must soon be annihilated. And if all others accepted the lie which the Party imposed -if all records told the same tale -- then the lie passed into history and became truth. **'Who controls the past,'** ran the Party slogan, **'controls the future: who controls the present controls the past**.' And yet the past, though of its nature alterable, never had been altered. Whatever was true now was true from everlasting to everlasting. It was quite simple. All that was needed was an unending series of victories over your own memory. 'Reality control', they called it: in Newspeak, 'doublethink'"[241].

In order to control people, the Left claims "history" as its own. It has become so common of the Left that we now have a term by which to identify it as "revisionist history". The Left is continually claiming: "We are on the right side of history", which of course implies that the Right is on the wrong side of their "history". With statements like this the Left attempts to give the sense of inevitability of the Left's actions and agenda. Anyone who knows even a small bit of history knows that the vast majority of history has been more Evil and wrong, then Right and GOOD.

Here are a few examples of how the Left has revised "history" to accommodate their Lies:

- Abraham Lincoln a Republican President who was willing to go to war to free the black slaves, the Democrat Left went to war to try to prevent it!
- Because of Republican President Abraham Lincoln's freeing of the black slaves, Malcolm X was a registered Republican!

---

[241] Orwell, George; *Nineteen Eighty-Four*, pgs. 23-24

- The Voter Rights Act of 1965 was passed by the Republicans and almost wholly opposed by the Democrats who are Leftists!
- Alabama Governor George Wallace, who opposed civil rights and whose Selma, Alabama march and speech Martin Luther King Jr. was primarily targeted against, was a Democrat, a Leftist!
- US Senator Robert Byrd of West Virginia, the longest serving US Senator, was a leader of the Ku Klux Klan was a Democrat!
- The Left today enslaves blacks and tells them that they are their only hope!

You do not hear those facts of history from the Democrat Left today. The Left would have you believe just the opposite of real history! This is why the Left must continually rewrite history to match their conveniently "evolving" [Lies!] statements and actions. Karl Marx said, "If I can steal their history, I can steal their country." This is why Michelle Obama said, "Barack knows that we are going to have to change our history"[242]. To "change" history is to simply dismiss any fact inconvenient to their current storyline.

Notice the startling similarities between Obama's and the Left's deny, deny, deny protocol with that of Communist Red China. China hacks US Defense computer systems and uses a program of deny, deny, deny, until the attention of the US is eventually focused elsewhere. China says it has no significant air pollution. China's leaders are so benevolent that only have an "all-consuming desire for people's welfare". Deny, deny, deny. The Left in America uses the same program of *Lies* and deny, deny, deny. Pelosi did not know what was in the Obamacare bill until it was passed. Harry Reed did not know he was lying about Romney's tax returns. Obama did not know he supported homosexual marriage. Hillary Rodham-Clinton did not know that it was illegal to destroy US government emails. Elizabeth Warren was a true-blue American Indian. Bernie Sanders, a self-avowed Leftist-socialist, says that the Social Security Trust Fund is

---

[242] See further discussion in the chapter: *The Obamas: The Epitome of the Left.*

not going broke but has a $2.8 trillion surplus. (It would require dozens of encyclopedic-sized volumes to fully exhaust the subject of the Left's *Lies*!) Then they deny, deny, deny the Lie. But then the truth comes out. But by then the publics' attention is elsewhere. As Hillary Rodham-Clinton says, that is so yesterday, such "old news". That is of course unless it was someone on the Right, then the imagined offense is without excuse or expiration date! Hypocrisy is a LIE! Obama Lies, Pelosi Lies, Reed lies, Sanders Lies, Warren Lies, Clinton Lies, Red China Lies… the Left LIES! When these people are the ones who want to have absolute authority over our lives, *Lies* matter!

The *Truth* hurts and is often offensive to manmade moral codes that parade as cheap imitations to GOD's perfect and righteous codes. This of course is why so many people live in a continual state of self-deception. If they refuse to acknowledge the *Truth*, then they can, at least on some level, fool themselves into believing the Left's convenient Lie. This is what the *Bible* means when it says "only the fool says in his heart there is no God"[243]. The heart is the spirit of man. A man lies to himself in a vain attempt to placate his conscience against his imminent guilt, guilt from the intentional violation of GOD's Word and nature, which the *Bible* says is *sin*. Lying to oneself does not make what is real, unreal. (Try jumping off the top of a 100-story building while telling yourself over and over that gravity is not real! What you accept as real has consequences!) The Left *Lies*, and *Lies*, and *Lies* to us, telling us what we want to hear to placate our consciences against our guilt of sin *Against GOD*. The Left panders to our basest, lowest, and most deprived inclinations in offering sexual perversion, self-indulgence, and "the pleasures of sin for a season"[244]… for our freedom, and ultimately our souls.

If the Right cannot even call the Left Liars who are pathological LIARS, how can we expect the common American to see the *Lies* of the Left? The Right must, as a matter of American survival and Truth, confront the Left and expose the Left's *Lies, Lies, Lies!*

---

[243] The *Holy Bible*: Psalms 14:1; 53:1.
[244] The *Holy Bible*: Hebrews 11:25.

11. SHADES OF GRAY

Chapter 11

The Left specializes in "Shades of Gray". As is clearly evidenced in the previous chapter, these "Shades of Gray" are nothing more than "Lies, Lies, Lies" of Evil. Shades of Gray are nothing more than rationalizations to commit evil. Rationalization is the process by which a person takes a situation which he knows to be wrong and twists it in his head until it appears right. This was the tactic that Satan used on Eve in the Garden of Eden when Satan twisted GOD's truth in asking the question of Eve, "Yea, hath GOD [really] said..."[245]. Shades of Gray are always a corruption of the truth. Jesus Himself, Who is the Truth[246], warned us of the effects of "leaven" or just a little Evil, as even the smallest amount of Evil will multiply and permeate the whole[247]. Leaven in His words were used to represent the corruption of the Pharisees who were the religious leaders at the time. The Apostle Paul later expounded on Jesus' words saying, "A little leaven leaveneth the whole lump" attributing this acceptance of "a little leaven" to the corruptions of "Satan"[248]. The Left would have us believe that "shades" are merely variants of truth rather than corruptions of Evil as GOD defines them.

Even common sense[249] tells us that a "shade" is a corruption of a pure color. A shade of "yellow" that has been mixed with "blue" is no longer a pure representation of "yellow", but now is called a "shade of green". A corruption of white with black is called "gray". If a "shade" was the same as the pure original, then the "shade" would be the same color as the pure color. A "shade" implies a corruption or

---

[245] The *Holy Bible*: Genesis 3:1.
[246] The *Holy Bible*: John 14:6.
[247] The *Holy Bible:* Matthew 16:6-12.
[248] The *Holy Bible:* 1 Corinthians 5:5-6.
[249] For a wider discussion of the Left's "common good" see the chapter: *Fighting To WIN!: How Do We Fight The War? The Right's RULES FOR ANTI-RADICALS! A Call To ACTION!*, Bolded Topic: Practical War Strategies, Bolded sub-Topics: THE LEFT IS NOT ABOUT COMMON SENSE!/Use Common Sense.

contamination of the pure. It must therefore by commonsense definition be different from the primary color.

A "shade" or "shadow" is represented in the *Bible* as a corruption of Darkness also called Evil. Evil always seeks darkness to hide itself within[250]. A "shade" or "shadow" is depicted in Scripture as being an evil corruption wholly apart from GOD and the presence of Death[251]. Renaming a corruption of Darkness as a "shade" somehow helps us rationalize capitulating with Evil. However, renaming Evil does not change it from being Evil[252].

Even in the Hollywood movie *Fifty Shades of Grey*, the "Shades" depict increasing levels of depravity. The Left uses Shades of Gray to slowly coax people into more and more depravity. Depravity is an evil quality or evil behavior. The Left teaches Shades of Gray as relativism which is there is no right or wrong but just an individual's personal choice and is embodied in the saying "if it feels good do it".

Anyone who has lived in the real world understands that there is real Evil and that real Evil is not simply a construct of the human mind. Evil is a force that always corrupts involving a downward spiral that ends in the Pit of Hell. The great English statesman Edmund Burke rightfully noted that "One that confounds (confuses) good and evil is an enemy to the good".

The Left is the Enemy of GOOD and of GOD.

---

[250] The *Holy Bible:* 1 Corinthians 4:5.
[251] The *Holy Bible:* James 1:17 and Luke 1:79 respectively.
[252] See the discussion in the chapters *The Progressive Face of The Left* and *Lies, Lies, Lies!*.

12. The "Fairness" Doctrine

Chapter 12

The "Fairness" Doctrine is actually a Leftist tactic to eliminate all opposing Conservative voices from the airwaves. However here we will concentrate on the Left's deceptive use of the word "fair" as a club to bludgeon opponents into submission.

The word "fair", as defined by the Left, is not found in Christian Doctrine, nor in the *Bible* [253]. It is an arbitrary term defined only by the Leftist user to subtly manipulate the hearer at will as it is neither anchored in truth nor reality. "Fair" is what the Left declares it to be at any given moment and changes definitions at their will, always being manipulated to their advantage and current viewpoint. GOD does what He does not because of convenience or contrivance, as the Left, but because it is the Right thing to do regardless of any individuals view of "fairness". The Left demands us to unquestionably accept their arbitrary view of fairness regardless of what is Right and true. The Left is only concerned with its Evil agenda and will always Lie, cheat, steal, and manipulate to get what it wants[254]. Leftist leaders can facilitate a male homosexual prostitution ring run out of their basement and when discovered no punishment ever comes[255]. In fact, they are afterward lauded the more and promoted within Leftist institutions. A non-Leftist accidentally taps a shoe under a bathroom stall and they are villianized by the Left and run out of town as a closet homosexual.

Conservatives are held to a "beyond all appearance of impropriety" standard by the Left, while the Left holds themselves to a standard of "arbitrary fairness", which is a sliding-scale designed to always favor the Leftists who have grossly violated all sense of truth and Rightness.

---

[253] The word "fair" as used in the *Bible* is that of referring to something as "beautiful" and has no association with the arbitrary meaning used by the Left.
[254] The *Holy Bible*: John 10:10.
[255] Democrat Congressman Barney Frank who later was promoted to Chairman of the House Banking Committee and who was largely responsible for the mortgage collapse of 2007-2009.

It is interesting to note two points here, first the basis of the term "beyond all appearance of impropriety" actually comes from the *Bible* in 1 Thessalonians 5:22 "Abstain from all appearance of evil". It is a Christian standard. The Left turns this Biblical standard upon its head by using the *Bible* to actually foster their Evil intentions! Second the Leftists, who are non-Christians by definition, use Saul Alinsky's *Rules For Radicals* Fourth Rule: "Make the enemy live up to their own book of rules. You can kill them with this, for they can no more obey their own rules than the Christian church can live up to Christianity". The Left intentionally conspires to create circumstances to box in the Right with the Right's own moral and Biblical constraints, while the Left is free to act any way which is expedient and convenient because the Left is admittedly neither moral nor "Christian", but Evil!

According to the Left, the Left is never "wrong" only a victim of unfortunate circumstances to which it is only "fair" to relieve the Left of any guilt and accusation. In fact, those most guilty of Evil on the Left become the most celebrated "victims" of the Left. (Bill Clinton, Barney Frank, Mark Spitzer, Ernesto "Che" Guevara, Fidel Castro, FDR, Dewey, Marx, Mao (Obama Appointees: (See List) Anita Dunn W.H. Communications Director; John Holdren Science Czar; Van Jones Ron Bloom Manufacturing Czar). The bigger the Liar, thief, pervert, anti-American, and especially anti-Christian, the bigger the praise, adoration, and promotion they receive from within the ranks of the Left. Leftist ideologies are directly responsible for the murder of over 200 million people in the 20th Century through the likes of Stalin, Lenin, Mao, Pol Pot, Castro, et al. Yet these remain the celebrated hallmarks of Leftist ideology. (To which should be added Hitler and Mussolini who through the Leftist media propaganda machine miraculously became associated with the Right, but were in fact celebrated Progressives or Leftists, praised pre-WW2 by such icons as Franklin D. Roosevelt) Even now this Evil is celebrated as the new "fairness" of "global population control" to set right the overpopulation "sins" against the planet. Hindu Earth worship or *Gaia* worship is openly promoted by Leftist spokesmen the likes of ex-vice president Al Gore author of *An Inconvenient Truth*. This the same Al Gore who claimed to have invented the internet and who has made tens of millions of dollars peddling Global Warming and selling carbon credits, all based on bogus science. The Left celebrates the evil spread by Gore not because it is "truth", right, or good, but because it attacks the only real Truth which is GOD as expressed through His *Bible* and through His Christian people.

Evil hates GOD and everyone and anyone that stands for GOOD. This is the common link of what otherwise are seemingly odd bedfellows of the Left. Evil links groups that for all intents and purposes would be enemies to each other such as Feminists who purport to represent "women's rights" with Islam who deny women virtually all rights. Evil is the glue that binds the Left together, the unseen Force that binds, guides, and controls the Left. The Left has literally sold their souls to Evil for thirty pieces of silver. Evil allows the Leftists to satiate their evil desires under the guise of "fairness" and "tolerance" to all. All, that is, except any who would dare oppose them and their Evil agenda. "Fairness" has become the umbrella argument which the Left evokes to stifle dissent. (e.g. gay marriage, taxes to crush Capitalism, attacks against Christianity especially any public acknowledgement or displays including Christmas, Ten Commandments, Not taxing the primary constituencies of the Left- the "poor" and "minorities", universal healthcare (since when is a US government program "universal" unless it is a global one-world movement?)). The "revolution" that Michelle Obama kept referring to is a communist slogan made popular by Karl Marx the founding voice of the violent movement. Marx's struggle was against any influence of Christian morality! Marx, a devoted homosexual, was vehemently opposed to Christian morals and foundations Capitalism! Capitalism is hated by the Left because Capitalism's foundations are directly from the pages of the Christian *Bible*!

Fairness is always couched by the Left in the guise of a financial "zero sum game". That is, the Left tells us that there are a defined and limited set of resources for which everyone must compete. If one person makes a million dollars a year they are, by the Left's accounting, taking someone else's "fair share". When in reality wealth is created and expanded through productivity. The wealth of the United States increased virtually every year since our founding. When the wealth did not increase it was under a Leftist President who fought to restrict our free Capitalistic system.

The "fairness" mantra has always occupied center stage in the Left's propaganda machine. Such slogans as "workers' rights", "bourgeoisie", "fair share", *ad nauseam*, are all designed to illicit sentiments of "unfair" circumstances and a cry for "fairness", which according to their rhetoric only the Left can be trusted to provide. Fairness to the Left is to bring everyone down into poverty and into government control where everyone's very life is dependent upon the Left.

The Left will agree that the actual term "fair" is not directly to be found in the U.S. Constitution, but the Left somehow convolutes the essence of "fairness" to exist in the "nature" of the Constitution. The Left will tell us that "The *U.S. Constitution* is far too old an antiquated for such a new and progressive concept". Supreme Court Justice Ruth Bader Ginsburg recommends the South African constitution as a good model with which to build the new Egyptian constitution under then Egyptian President Mohammed Morsi and the terrorist Muslim Brotherhood. A quote from the Marxist inspired South African constitution under the heading "Equality" speaks for itself as it illustrates this point quite well combining the Leftist "fairness doctrine" with Orwellian double-speak:

> "Discrimination on one or more of the grounds listed in subsection (3) is unfair unless it is established that the discrimination is fair.[256]".

This from a member of the U.S. Supreme Court sworn to uphold the *U.S. Constitution* of the United States! The word *treason* comes directly to mind. The paraphrase here is "Discrimination is not fair unless the government says it's fair", meaning that discrimination is discrimination unless it benefits the Leftist agenda of the day! Then discrimination by the Left is sanctioned and deemed legal, proper, and good! As discussed earlier, this is the same type of psychotic *double-*

---

[256] Wikipedia; Section Nine of the Constitution of South Africa.

speak Lie the Left pushes in the invented Utopian phrasing of "privileged inclusivism". You cannot be inclusive and exclusive at the same time, any more than you be discriminatory and non-discriminatory at the same time.

The focus of the Left's "Fairness" campaign is to criminalize all forms of "discrimination". That seems reasonable. On the surface who could disagree with that? However, what we think of as discrimination is not what the Left means by their Re-Definition. What the Left defines as "discrimination" is to make any rational judgment between any two options. Because to the Left all options are equal, except any choice which is reasonable and right, then to choose one option as better than another is to commit an act of "discrimination"! As Evan Sayet so profoundly states it:

> "The same is true of good and evil. Since nothing can deemed good, nothing can be deemed evil. That which society does recognize as **good must be the beneficiary of some sort of prejudice**. That which society recognizes as **evil must be the victim of that prejudice**. So, again, the mindless [Leftist] foot soldier will invariably side with whatever policy, mindlessly accept whatever policy seeks to tear down what is good--America, Israel, Wal-Mart--and elevate what is evil until everything meets in the middle and there is nothing left to fight about"[257].

This is the mindset of the Left and their mindless "useful idiots" when they demand that every child must receive a trophy who plays a sport. Because to not give a trophy to everyone would be to victimize failure! If you reward success that is prejudice and discrimination, to not reward failure is to make a victim of the loser. Sayet continues:

> What happens is, they are indoctrinated into what I call a "cult of indiscriminateness." The way the elite does this is by teaching our children, starting with the very young, *that*

---

[257] Sayet, Evan; Speech to The Heritage Foundation; *Regurgitating the Apple How Modern Liberals "Think"*; March 5, 2007.

rational and moral thought is an act of bigotry; that no matter how sincerely you may seek to gather the facts, no matter how earnestly you may look at the evidence, no matter how disciplined you may try to be in your reasoning, your conclusion is going to be so tainted by your personal bigotries, by your upbringing, by your religion, by the color of your skin, by the nation of your great-great-great-great-great grandfather's birth; that no matter what your conclusion, it is useless. It is nothing other than the reflection of your bigotries, and *the only way to eliminate bigotry is to eliminate rational thought.*

There's a brilliant book out there called *The Closing of the American Mind* by Professor Allan Bloom. Professor Bloom was trying to figure out in the 1980's why his students were suddenly so stupid, and what he came to was the realization, the recognition, that they'd been raised to believe that indiscriminateness is a moral imperative because its opposite is the evil of having discriminated. I paraphrase this in my own works: "In order to eliminate discrimination, the Modern Liberal has opted to become utterly indiscriminate."

I'll give you an example. At the airports, in order not to discriminate, *we have to intentionally make ourselves stupid.* We have to pretend we don't know things we do know, and we have to pretend that the next person who is likely to blow up an airplane is as much the 87-year-old Swedish great-great-grandmother as those four 27-year-old imams newly arrived from Syria screaming "Allah Akbar!" just before they board the plane. In order to eliminate discrimination, the Modern Liberal [Leftist] has opted to
become utterly indiscriminate [stupid].

The problem is, of course, that the ability to discriminate, to thoughtfully choose the better of the available options--as in "she's a discriminating shopper"--is *the essence of rational thought*; thus, the whole of Western Europe and today's Democratic Party, dominated as it is by this philosophy, rejects rational thought as a hate crime[258].

Most political analysts try to reason the *actions* of the Left and almost never attempt to assess the *motives* that are at the core of what the Left is. Only an idiot claims that we can never know the motivations of a person! We must recognize that the Left continuously assesses the motives of people. What else is a "hate crime", so vaunted by the Left? The Left pushing "hate crime" legislation is in effect telling us that motive of an action is worse than the action and a wrong motive deserves a more severe punishment! Somehow the Left has convinced us that motives are more criminal than the crime. The Left does this with specific intent with prejudice. The Left has expanded the "hate crime" to include "hate speech". Hate speech is then defined as anything said contrary or in opposition to the Left and its agenda!

Diversity is another Leftist code word for their Fairness Doctrine. However:

> "One of the big canards of Modern Liberalism [Leftism] is this notion of diversity, as if diversity is a virtue. Diversity is not a virtue; diversity is meaningless. Diversity just means "different." Without the critical moral judgment to say, "Yes, it's different and good," you're not only not supporting good, but you are invariably supporting evil."[259].

Who determines a "fair share"? The Left of course! As a weapon of the Left the "Fairness" Doctrine is intentionally employed as an arbitrary term for deliberate deception. The concept of "Fairness" is a Leftist concoction meant to manipulate truth and any rational thought process. This is what the *Bible* describes as Satan's "subtlety"[260] in confusing an individual to sin and making it seem GOOD. Fairness is not found in the *Bible* and is only used by Evil in their quest to destroy

---

[258] Sayet, Evan; Speech to The Heritage Foundation; *Regurgitating the Apple How Modern Liberals "Think"*; March 5, 2007.
[259] Sayet, Evan; Speech to The Heritage Foundation; *Regurgitating the Apple How Modern Liberals "Think"*; March 5, 2007.
[260] The *Holy Bible*: 2 Corinthians 11:3.

and subvert individuals to Evil. Here's the Truth of the matter: Life isn't fair. We can ensure opportunity but there is NO universal fairness. Fairness, like Utopia, is a Fools game!

13. Emotion Based Politics

Chapter 13

Only animals are wholly controlled by their emotions. Science has long acknowledged that the primary characteristic that separates man from animals is man's ability to *reason*. Yet, as we have discussed, reason is an anathema to the Left. The connection between the Left and unbridled animal savagery has been clearly documented in these pages, which documents the clear connection between the Left and unrestrained emotion devoid of all reason. Unrestrained emotion is nothing more than a base animal instinct which defies reason. The Right is intrinsically linked to *reason* as GOD calls for us to "Come now, and let us reason together, saith the LORD"[261]. The Left is inseparably linked to *emotion* and at War Against reason because of reason's intrinsic association with the very being of GOD. The very definition of a "radical" is being *emotionally* driven and *without Reason*!

You cannot have a reasoned discussion with a religious fanatic who relies on religious fervor and not logic, common sense[262], or real-life experience. Truth does not matter to the religious zealot. When you try to reason with the indoctrinated Leftist faithful, the best you can hope for is incoherent screaming and name-calling. The Left's Religion is wholly and savagely unreasonable! Reason is the foundation of all civilized societies. Irrationality is emotion based and the antithesis of reason, and the foundation for chaos, self-destruction, and all that is the Left. Lyle H. Rossiter, Jr., M.D. author of *The Liberal Mind: The Psychological Causes of Political Madness* puts it this way:

---

[261] The *Holy Bible*: Isaiah 1:18.
[262] For a wider discussion of the Left's "common good" see the chapter: *Fighting To WIN!: How Do We Fight The War? The Right's RULES FOR ANTI-RADICALS! A Call To ACTION!*, Bolded Topic: Practical War Strategies, Bolded sub-Topics: THE LEFT IS NOT ABOUT COMMON SENSE!/Use Common Sense.

Only an irrational agenda would advocate a systematic destruction of the foundations on which ordered liberty depends. Only an irrational man would want the state to run his life for him rather than create secure conditions in which he can run his own life. Only an irrational agenda would deliberately undermine the citizen's growth to competence by having the state adopt him. Only irrational thinking would trade individual liberty for government coercion, then sacrifice the pride of self-reliance for welfare dependency. Only an irrational man would look at a community of free people cooperating by choice and see a society of victims exploited by villains.[263]"

Here is a dose of the reality of the Big *Lies* of the Left which everyone should understand instinctively: The Left tells us that all girls are equal, so all girls should be treated as princesses. If therefore, all girls are princesses, then in reality no girl is a princess because by the very definition of being a princess, princesses are somehow above common. If all girls are above common then all girls become common. The term princess becomes meaningless in a Leftist Utopia.

The Left, as does their initiator Lucifer, relies on confusing the audience using "circular reasoning" which of course is an emotion based Re-Name game of confusion and *not* reasoning at all. Circular Reasoning appears at first blush to be logical but is exposed as a *Lie* of manipulation on closer examination. Here is how Lucifer uses confusion, or subtilty: But I fear, lest by any means, as the serpent beguiled Eve through his subtilty, so your minds should be corrupted from the simplicity that is in Christ[264]. Circular Reasoning starts with a statement, then tells us that that first statement is valid because a second statement is valid, and then a third and fourth statements are valid because the original statement is valid. The basic premise of Circular Reasoning is that the initial statement is true because... I told

---

[263] Rossiter, Lyle H., Jr., M.D.; *The Liberal Mind: The Psychological Causes of Political Madness*; 2011; pgs. 329-330.
[264] The Holy *Bible*: 2 Corinthians 11:3

you the first statement is true! It's like the parent who tells the child it's true because I told you so!

As a second example, if weight does not matter and all women are "beautiful", then even anorexic waif-models are beautiful. But of course this contradicts the Left's preaching that anorexic waif-models are not beautiful and bad examples to women! The Left's "reasoning" is always circular, and by the laws of logic, self-defeating and devoid of reasoning. No wonder that the Left will never have a reasoned conversation but will always resort to emotional and usually incoherent shouting and name-calling! The Left's clichés never make sense outside of the 15 second sound-bite. The Left lives in the imagination of their own totally self-deluded mind entirely disconnected from the real world. This is by definition... insanity![265]

Let the insane, ugly, and hideous Leftist women "build a wall around their vaginas"! It is self-imposed birth control that will greatly aid in reducing the like-minded demented and *insane* spawn of evil! The world would be a better place without the likes of cloned Whoop-tido Goldbergs and Joyless Behars!

Everyone cannot be equal and special and unique at the same time! Does this sound crude from your P.C. perspective? You want to stand on the Left's position that all people are inherently equal? Okay, let's personalize it. If your child, or yourself, are in dire need of immediate life-saving brain surgery, would you consider your high-school dropout, pot smoking, ADHD neighbor as an equal substitute for a fully trained, certified, and experienced brain surgeon? Of course not. (Unless you are brain-dead, mentally retarded, or brainwashed!) That's reality!

We as Conservatives *must* learn to recognize the unique dynamics of modern Emotion Based Politics. Here is a fact that the Left will tell you is bigoted and sexist, but a fact nonetheless... in general women are *more emotional* than rational. Now let's wait for the screams of the militant Leftists to quiet down... Ok let's continue. As such the

---

[265] See the broader discussion of insanity in the chapter *The Left Is a RELIGION!*.

Right must learn to communicate their arguments both reasonably *and emotionally*. While it might seem obvious, we on the Right must remember that 50% of the registered voters are women who are more easily swayed by *emotion* than reason! Now let's wait again for the screams of the militant Leftists to quiet down... Ok let's continue. This is the primary reason that the Left has sought to corner and control Emotion Based Politics since women were granted the right to vote.

This is not in any way a call to return to a pre-suffrage era, as the Left would have everyone to believe, but a recognition of the complexities of reaching an ***emotionally*** based constituency. Women's suffrage brought a dramatic shift from men's reasoned politics to Emotion Based Politics. Yes there are some reading this who have been so pre-programmed, by the Politically Correct Thought Police of the Left, that they automatically reacted negatively to this statement. However, history and human nature bear this out. There are innumerable scientific studies that come to the same conclusion that *women are different than men*. (Imagine that, duh. Right?) Studies of the counter-conclusion have all been manipulated out of the realm of science to falsely force a Politically Correct conclusion. Anyone who has both a son and a daughter can attest to this from practical experience. Again we use Emotionally Based Politics as the Pavlovian example here of how we have been pre-programmed to accept or reject a statement based solely on an emotionally charged response and in total disregard for what we know to be right, the truth, and factual. Pandora's Box has been opened but as Pandora commented, and the Right continues to hold onto, "there is still hope in the bottom of the box".

Let's consider the Left's most effective use of Emotion Based Politics and the Left's maneuvering to prevent the Right from following suit. The issue is abortion. The Left uses an array of Emotion pandering to convince women that abortion is "a woman's right to choose" and that the Right wants to "take away their right to birth control". The Left tells women that the Right wants them "in back alleys with coat hangers". When the Right uses Emotional arguments against abortion the Left comes unglued. When the pro-life group the Center for Medical Progress released its anti-abortion videos the Left in shrieking chorus went *crazy*. Why? Because these videos were overwhelmingly emotional for women in exposing the horrors of baby killing! The videos expose the Left's narrative of abortion as simply being a case for "a women's right to choose". The videos clearly show that an "unborn fetus" is clearly "a real baby". That moves the issue beyond a simple choice of a women's "right to choose", to the taking of a life of a baby. This is Emotion Based Politics with real-world reasoning using the Truth! No wonder that the Left is in an uproar! The Leftist animals like Nancy Pelosi even called for an investigation of the Center for Medical Progress' staff in order to recapture the Emotional Political Game! The Left cannot stand against their own tactics when the Truth is the basis of the *emotional* appeal.

It is important to note here that women's suffrage was fundamental in the Italian Fascists plan in implementing their takeover Italy[266]. Why? Because suffrage was the door to Emotion Based Politics and the takeover of Italy by the Leftist Fascists. The Left's Emotion Based Politics has always been the entry point of Evil into the affairs of men. Satan in the Garden of Eden did not use his emotional appeal to Evil upon Adam, the man, but against Eve, the woman! Evil knows how and where to strike against humanity and Emotion Based persuasion devoid of reason is the calling-card of Evil.

The Left has been entirely effective in their manipulation of Emotion Based Politics. Their success comes partly from sagacious political maneuvering, but more that emotions drive an *un*reasonable ideology. The Right who is by nature reasonable *must* adapt to the modern nature of politics. The principle reason that Republicans have lost almost every major election was their inability to connect with the American voters at a gut *emotional* level. It is not enough simply to be right. We must be right and make the voter *feel* it! As the old adage goes: A person may not remember what you have said, but they will never forget how you made them feel!

---

[266] Goldberg, Jonah; *Liberal FASCISM: The Secret History of the American Left From Mussolini to the Politics of Meaning*; 2007; pg. 46.

Using emotion is necessary in today's political reality, but in addition the emotional argument must be tied to real world experiences that the audience can easily relate to through their own real-life experiences. One of the unrecognized reasons for Ronald Reagan's celebrated success was Reagan's natural ability to connect with the electorate on an emotional level. Reagan used real-life examples that touched the hearts of Americans. Reagan used props more effectively than any other Conservative politician in modern history, props which tied gut level emotion politics to the reality of the issues of the day. For those old enough to remember, who could forget Reagan's speech standing at the Brandenburg Gate of the Berlin Wall in West Berlin, Germany and saying, "Mr. Gorbachev tear down this wall!"? Reagan also used props that allowed Americans to visualize the logical conclusion of the Left's agenda. On the National debt "…if you had a stack of thousand-dollar bills in your hand only 4 inches high, you'd be a millionaire.", Reagan told Americans in front of a joint session of Congress, "A trillion dollars would be a stack of thousand-dollar bills 67 miles high!". Reagan related to Americans on a base emotional level and won many national debates using emotional pleas based in the Truth. The Right must regain the mastery of emotion-based politics and anchor it in Truth.

For the connection between *emotion* and the Big Lie we return again to Adolf Hitler's memoirs in *Mein Kampf* (*My Struggle*):

> "All this was inspired by the principle—which is quite true within itself—that in the big lie there is always a certain force of credibility; because the broad masses of a nation are always more easily corrupted in the deeper strata of their **emotional** nature than consciously or voluntarily; and **thus in the primitive simplicity of their minds they more readily fall victims to the big lie** than the small lie, since they themselves often tell small lies in little matters but would be ashamed to resort to large-scale falsehoods. It would never come into their heads to fabricate colossal untruths, and they would not believe that others could have the impudence to distort the truth so infamously. Even though the facts which prove this to be so may be brought clearly to their minds, they will still

doubt and waver and will continue to think that there may be some other explanation. For the grossly impudent lie always leaves traces behind it, even after it has been nailed down, a fact which is known to all expert liars in this world and to all who conspire together in the art of lying.[267]". (emphasis added)

Here is the Left's template today for their Big Lies:

> 1) Use a tragedy as a crisis, or create a crisis where none exists.
>
> 2) Paint the crisis with as much **emotion** as possible, and throw logical analysis out the window.

This is not about winning a reasoned, or logical, or intellectual debate:

> Hitler mocked those who believed that arguments and reason should trump the naked power of the people. When four renowned economists sent Hitler a letter disputing his socialist schemes, Hitler responded, "Where are your stormtroopers? Go on the street, go into folk meetings and try to see your standpoint through. Then we'll see who is right--we or you.[268]".

When emotion *alone* rules all sense of reality dies. Because Leftism is almost exclusively based and perpetuated on irrational and frenzied emotions, "… in order to govern *liberalism* [Leftism] *is forced to tyrannize and Lie*. Lack of moderating principles means that it cannot help but overreach, eventually catastrophically"[269].

Leftism is a form of mental insanity! Think that is harsh? Webster's Dictionary tells us that mental insanity is the inability to reason, literally a person who is "*un*reasonable". There is nothing reasonable about the Left. As we have seen all Leftist doctrine is based on

---

[267] Adolf Hitler, *Mein Kampf*, vol. I, ch. X.
[268] Goldberg, Jonah; *Liberal FASCISM: The Secret History of the American Left From Mussolini to the Politics of Meaning*; 2007; pg. 178.
[269] Kalb, James; Modern Age Quarterly; *The Tyranny of Liberalism: The Iron Heel of Freedom*; Summer 2000.

destruction, chaos, unrestrained emotion, hatred for GOD and GOD's people, or opposition to GOD's laws in restraint of the individual's pet sins. This set of behaviors can only be described as *insanity*. [270]

Conservatives must learn to argue with *emotion*. This does not mean that the Right must abandon its principles, but we must not necessarily make the principles the lone public argument. We must turn Alinskyism[271] on its head and live by "The issue is never the issue. The issue is always the *counter*-revolution"! We can argue our case using Emotion Based Politics to drive people to the *right* decision. We do not need to argue the issue only logically, but always argue the issue *emotionally*. We use the Left's tactics against them. The Right then would have momentum and Truth on our side! This is imperative to winning the Battle for the hearts and minds of America.

The Right must use all facets of Emotion Based Politics. Emotion is not just fear as the Left uses it, but Emotions are also based in love, happiness, a sense of "fairness", and, among others, humor. Humor is a persuasive weapon of emotion in arguing especially when aimed at the real-life absurdity of the Left's positions. The old adage "it feels so good, it must be right" is a *Lie* of the Devil! But we on the Right can take what is Right and make it emotionally charged and feel good!

What the Right needs desperately to understand is that the truth means *nothing* to the Left, so reasoned and logical debates are an anathema to the Left. Ann Coulter's pithy analysis sums up the situation nicely:

> "If it were true that conservatives were racist, sexist, homophobic, fascist, stupid, inflexible, angry, and self-righteous, shouldn't their arguments be easy to deconstruct? Someone who is making a point out of anger, ideology, inflexibility, or resentment would presumably construct a flimsy argument. So why can't the argument itself be

---

[270] See the broader discussion of insanity in the chapter *The Left Is a RELIGION!*.
[271] For Alinskyism's Leftist doctrines see Saul Alinsky in the Index.

dismembered rather than the speaker's personal style or hidden motives? Why the evasions?"[272].

The Left's Emotion Based Political idea of the false dichotomy that Conservatism is mutually exclusive from desirability can be epitomized in the retort, which is usually spit out like a mouth full of wasps, "They want to take us back to the 1950's!". Let's dissect that *emotional* catch-phrase for a moment which is meant to epitomize the supposed horrors of Conservativism. What exactly about the 1950's was so unspeakably horrifying? The 1950's was an economically prosperous period, families generally stayed together, AIDS did not exist, teen pregnancy was virtually non-existent, and we had relative peace[273]. So, what could leave the Left so aghast about the 1950's? With the one exception that the 1950's predates black civil rights legislation, what possible negative connotation could be so hopelessly attached to this decade? The honest answer is that it predates the Left's cultural victories such as the legalization of abortion, acceptance of the homosexual lifestyle following the overturning of sodomy laws, the onslaught of the women's liberation movement, the Leftist takeover of our schools, legalization of homosexual marriage, the time before the glorification of the black liberation thug cult, and the time before the glorification and the general acceptance of the Leftist ideology! The thought of living in a time without these Leftist doctrines is simply unimaginable to the Left in the same sense as living in a 1940's Nazi concentration camp is unimaginable to any otherwise rational thinker. Unfortunately, the Right has let this "1950's" Leftist conceived euphemism go unchallenged and it has become an American colloquialism automatically associated as something unimaginably horrific without even a rational thought as to what is really being said. The phrase "They want to take us back to the 1950's!" has literally become a Leftist Pavlovian reaction at which the Left's own mouths salivate. These types of deceptive catchphrases must be challenged. The Right must force Americans to use critical

---

[272] Coulter, Ann; *Slander: Liberal Lies About the American Right*; 2003; pg. 10.
[273] The United States was involved in the Korean War from 1950-53 begun under Democrat president Truman and had minimal involvement in the Vietnam War prior to the escalations in the 1960's by Democrat presidents Kennedy and Johnson.

and reasoned thinking instead of the mindless, reactionary, and knee-jerk *emotionalism*.

Arguments must show the natural consequence or logical conclusion of that path offered by the Left. Public school sex-ed programs result in mass teen pregnancy. Condoms handed out in school results in teen sex. Abortion results in the murder of an unborn child. Homosexuality results in a complete abandonment of GOD and a horrifying death from AIDS. Actions have consequences. Emotion Based Politics devoid of Truth and reasonability is simply another weapon in the arsenal of the Left to bludgeon non-conformists into submission. There is a reason that the Left screams against the Right's sporadic attempts to utilize emotion in its Battle Against Evil and the Left... *emotion works*! Again, a person may not remember what you have said, but they will never forget how you made them feel!

It is far past time that the Right take up the weapon of Emotion Based Politics and wield it with the Sword of Truth in our Epic Battle Against the Left and Evil! Emotion and Truth together will always defeat Evil and the Left!

14. TOLERANCE

Chapter 14

Tolerance can be defined as the Left's insistence that we put up with what we know is *Wrong* until we are forced to accept Evil as right. In other words, tolerance is a demand by the Left for all those with opposing views to shut up until the Left has seized control because the right has been effectively silenced and disarmed! Here is how James Kalb succinctly puts it:

> "The actual function of the liberal [Leftist] insistence on neutrality is to stifle debate. To the extent they have concrete implications, moral objections to liberalism [Leftism] are rejected out of hand as intolerant and divisive, so resistance becomes impossible. Distortion of language complements suppression of speech. Hatred and intolerance now include all serious opposition to liberalism [Leftism]. Inclusiveness insists that others be tolerant to the point of abandoning their principles and even identity while rejecting accommodation in its own case. Diversity and tolerance mean *thought control*"[274]. (emphasis and clarifications added)

The Left's Politically Correctness is *intoleration* of speaking the Truth! Intolerance is at the core of who the Left is and employs Orwellian DOUBLESPEAK in an attempt to cloak its own glaring hypocrisy. The Left takes away opportunity and claims to be the party of opportunity. The Left takes away freedom and claims to be the party of freedom. The Left demands inclusion but excludes anyone who does not go along with their Fascist agenda. The Left demands tolerance and is absolutely and militantly intolerant.

Only Christianity teaches and practices true tolerance. The Left pays lip service while using "tolerance" as a billy-club to force conformity

---

[274] Kalb, James; Modern Age Quarterly; *The Tyranny of Liberalism: The Iron Heel of Freedom*; Summer 2000.

to its Evil agenda. It is a self-contradiction for a government to demand tolerance and simultaneously practice absolute non-tolerance of anyone who ideologically opposes them. This is in reality not tolerance, but the practice of the Left's Totalitarianism!:

> [I]t is less a government's conception of the good that makes it tolerant than its willingness to put up with other conceptions. In that regard there is nothing intrinsically tolerant about liberalism [Leftism]. To the contrary, liberalism [Leftism] is an evolving outlook based on abstractions whose demands expand without limit. In practice it tries to root out one illiberal [anti-Left] arrangement after another, and becomes more and more intolerant of competing views and practices. A non-liberal [non-Leftist] government that views, say, Christian virtue as the ultimate goal of social order will try to facilitate it in various ways, but it is also likely to accept that virtue cannot be coerced, and so adopt a laissez-faire attitude in many respects (Tolerance by definition). A liberal government that aims at equal preference satisfaction and that takes a technological approach to the social order is likely to notice that people inconvenience each other in ways that are unjust by its standards and conclude that a comprehensive system of ***politically correct*** supervision, indoctrination, and control is needed to keep them from doing so (***Intolerance*** by definition). Which government will be more tolerant in practice?[275] (emphasis, comments, and clarifications added)

In another glaring contradiction, how can the Left demand total "tolerance" from its subjects while also demanding certain policies of "zero tolerance"? The obvious answer is that the Left in fact does not believe in tolerance, but tolerance only from those who disagree with the Left's policies, decrees, and practices:

> The great issues of the "culture war" – political correctness; multiculturalism; the struggle over sex and family life; the

---

[275] Kalb, James; Intercollegiate Review; *After Liberalism: Notes Toward Reconstruction*; Spring 2012, Volume: 47 Number: 1.

aggressiveness, intolerance, and growing dominance of the radical secularist Left – are all aspects of the campaign by [Leftist] institutions to make their power absolute by destroying, as manifestations of bigotry, other forms of social organization[276].

The "social organization" which the Left so abhors is any organization which is intrinsically tied to Judeo-Christian moorings. The word behind the Left's accusatory finger pointing at the Right is various forms of imagined "bigotry": racist, homophobe, hater, intolerant, discrimination, right-wing extremist, fundamentalist... *ad absurdum*. These are politically contrived accusations designed to bludgeon the opposition of the Right into submission, or at least non-resistance, to the Left's quest to *transform America*. Again, make no mistake the Left's attempt to "transform" America is a P.C. doublespeak for destroying America as we know it! So much for the Left's demand for "tolerance"! In truth it is the Left who is absolutely guilty of every one of the accusations to which they accuse the Right

The Left's definition of "tolerance" has expanded to include the bywords of "non-discrimination" and "equality". The term "Non-Discrimination" has become a buzzword of the Left. Non-Discrimination would, at least in Leftist theory, make everyone and everything "equal". In reality absolute non-discrimination only makes everyone and everything simply a replaceable cog in a large Leftist State machine, which is commonly called *Collectivism*, or by any other name: Progressivism, Fascism, Communism, Socialism, Liberalism, which is all collectively *LEFTISM*!

The result of the Left's making everyone and everything "equal" is that nothing has any significance, no person can have any individual value or distinction because every person becomes indistinguishable from any other. There can be no distinguished achievements and no heroes. Individual achievements would distinguish achievers from non-achievers and underachievers and heroes from cowards.

---

[276] Kalb, James; *The Tyranny of Liberalism: Understanding and Overcoming Administered Freedom, Inquisitorial Tolerance, and Equality by Command*; 2008; pg. 28.

Have you *ever* heard of a child being disciplined, sent home, suspended, or expelled for bringing a Koran, Bhagavad-Gita, or Satanic "bible" to school? Ever? The answer is *never*! This type of attack is exclusive to the Left's secondhand *War Against* Christianity in *The Left's War Against GOD!* Christian students routinely get disciplined, sent home, suspended, or expelled for bringing a Bible to school, reading the Bible, praying, having a Christian Cross, and yes even saying "bless you" when someone sneezes! Don't believe it? Not in America? Google it and you will be horrified and mortified at the extremist extent to which the Left has been allowed to go in its *War Against GOD*! Students have been ordered to not discuss Christianity in public schools! What ever happened to "free speech"? The Left only "tolerates" free speech when it benefits them and their agenda. In fact, the Left does not believe in free speech at all but only pays lip service to the concept when in benefits their political agenda.

For the Left even America must become indistinguishable from any other nation, or as Barack Hussein Obama in a speech in Strasbourg, France in 2009 said, "I believe in American exceptionalism, just as I suspect that the Brits believe in British exceptionalism and the Greeks believe in Greek exceptionalism". This is psychobabble basically saying that everyone is exceptional, which is impossible because for exceptionalism to exist it must be rare or the "exception" to the norm! You cannot have exceptionalism in a group of one. This is tantamount to the Left's insistence to give every child who plays in a sporting event a trophy. The end result is not boosting a child's self-esteem, but making all child sports trophies meaningless, and the child's experience meaningless as well. So much for self-esteem[277]!

Major Garret's question to Obama on the four American hostages being held by Iran who were intentionally left out of the nuke negotiations is a telltale admission by Obama's response. Obama acts as though America is not a Superpower, but simply an unexceptional equal with Iran. Obama's negotiator, and American traitor, John Kerry

---

[277] As previously discussed, "self-esteem" is a guise of the Left as emphasized in Maslow's Anti-GOD teachings to push children to collectivism.

was not negotiating from a position of power, but from one who needs to grovel at the feet of a long-suppressed country. Obama abandoned all "notions" that America was a Superpower in the negotiations and acted as though America had nothing to hold over Iran. Obama wants as his legacy to lay the foundation for a Muslim caliphate in the Middle East and the elimination of Israel, the only Middle East democracy! Why does Obama not care, and even have hostility matched only by Iran's, against the four American hostages? Each of these four Americans is the very embodiment of American Exceptionalism! It's like a finger poking Obama in the eye.

The net result of the Left's campaign of "equality" and "tolerance" is that no nation can be distinguished as exceptional as that would be discrimination. There is a hidden agenda for the Left's obsession with equality and tolerance, which is that it is a below the radar attack on the unique Judeo-Christian worldview. In the Left's eyes for anyone to really believe in American exceptionalism is to believe that GOD has specifically blessed America and made it exceptional precisely because of America's Judeo-Christian worldview. Ronald Reagan once wisely pointed out, "The frustrating thing is that those who are attacking religion claim that they are doing it in the name of tolerance - Question: Isn't the real truth that they are intolerant of religion?".

The Left's campaign of "tolerance", "equality", and "non-discrimination" is nothing more than a guise for the justification to eliminate the competing world view of the Judeo-Christian influences on which America was founded. After all, if two people's opinions conflict on fundamental issues, as they nearly always will, and the government steps in to make all things "equal", then the only solution is to disallow both beliefs making them equal believers in *nothing*. In effect the government becomes the enforcer of *nihilism*. Nihilism gives the individual *nothing* to live for. The State then is free to step in and supply an individual's only sense of worth as part of a "greater" State Village. Every life "choice" being predesignated as "equal" has the effect that no choice matters, or can matter!

In the epitome of Elitism, the same Leftist leaders who decry exceptionalism also consider themselves exceptionally exceptional.

Name the Leftist leader and you will see an arrogant elitist who looks down their nose at the "common" man: the Obamas, Nancy Pelosi, Harry Reid, Jonathan Gruber, any Leftist media personality, Rahm Emmanuel, *et al, ad absurdum*. If others are allowed to achieve then the elite are exposed for what they really are... imposters and *unexceptional*. When no one is allowed to stand as an exceptional individual next to the elitist then even an unexceptional Leftist can by deception appear exceptional! A 5'5" man in China may appear tall until he comes to America!

As Paul Thomas Mann reminds us, "Tolerance becomes a crime when applied to Evil". Paul Thomas Mann was a Nobel Prize laureate who escaped Germany in 1939 at the rise of the Nazi takeover. When Hitler came to power in 1933, Mann fled to Switzerland. When World War II broke out in 1939, he moved to the United States, returning to Switzerland in 1952.

As a warning to America after the defeat of European Fascism by historian Friedrich Hayek about the *Road to Serfdom* that America was then beginning its own march down to its own brand of Liberal Fascism, Hayek stated of the Left's Fascist doctrine of tolerance:

> No doubt an American or English 'fascist' system would greatly differ from the Italian or German models; no doubt, if the transition were effected without violence, we might expect to get a better type of leader. Yet this does not mean that our fascist system would in the end prove very different or much less **intolerable** than its prototypes. There are strong reasons for believing that the worst features of the totalitarian systems are phenomena which totalitarianism is certain sooner or later to produce[278].

Leftist "tolerance" is nothing more than a means to the rejection of the Judeo-Christian traditions and for the total control of the people by

---

[278] Hayek, Friedrich A.; *The Road to Serfdom with The Intellectuals and Socialism* (Readers Digest Condensed version); 1945; pg. 51.

Evil. James Kalb is right in his assessment of what he has called the "Inquisitional Tolerance" of which the Left demands and enforces:

> "To all *appearances*, liberalism [Leftism] empowers the individual by letting him choose what he wants and getting what he chooses. However choice is useless unless distinctions make a difference, and "diversity" and "tolerance" mean that distinctions must be treated as interchangeable matters of purely private taste. As a result, advanced liberalism [Leftism] becomes freedom to make the choices that are not permitted to matter. The glitter of unlimited choice dissipates when we find that nothing significant has changed because **equality** has deprived all changes of meaning. Cheap and easy travel seems wonderful until television, world markets, mass tourism, and immigration make all places alike. The same principle applies when other objects of desire lose their distinctiveness. The consequences of such experiences, repeated in all the affairs of life, are boredom, depression, and addiction to intoxicants that distract us from a featureless here and now. Not only the objects of our choice but we ourselves lose our identities in a liberal [Leftist] society"[279]. (emphasis and clarifications added)

Those illegals who come illegally to the United States and seek to change our culture to the culture from which they came are either *idiots* or *hoodlums*! Idiots don't know better and hoodlums want to corrupt us for their nefarious benefit. Either way to yield to them is insane! The very reason to come to America is to escape a culture which *does not work*! To wish to then attempt to change our culture to theirs is insane! The Left supports all things illegal under a Christian America in order to illegally graft votes to support their takeover of America! Legalizing illegals buys votes from those illegals.

---

[279] Kalb, James; *The Tyranny of Liberalism: Understanding and Overcoming Administered Freedom, Inquisitorial Tolerance, and Equality by Command*; 2008; pg. 98.

The Left demands tolerance from others while the Left itself harbors and spews the most extreme forms bigotry, vileness, and hate mongering known to man. Nancy Pelosi spews vile sexual insults against Tea Party activists as "tea baggers" and the Left is silent. Obama spews bigotry and racial hatred and again the Leftists and their media propaganda machine is silent only nodding their approval. Tolerance as defined by the Left is: Shut up and comply!

Even some on the Über-Left are acknowledging the move of the Left to silence all debate on issues by screaming epithets like racist, homophobe, sexist, *ad infinitum*. Über-Leftist Kirsten Powers in her new book *The Silencing: How the Left Is Killing Free Speech* speaks of just a movement on the Left:

> "It's a systematic silencing that is going on," Powers said. "And they use the same tactics. I also am not talking about disagreement. I'm not talking about people being civil. I'm talking about these are people who will not have a debate. They will attack you: 'You are racist. You are misogynist.' It's never about what the actual issue is…And it's really impinging people's ability to debate issues, because there is no debate. They tell you there is no debate because you're a racist"[280].

As an author's side rant, When in the Hell did it become legal and "Constitutionally protected" to advocate, preach, and riot to destroy the very foundations of Free Speech!? That in-itself is insane! When is it protected "free speech" to scream to take away someone else's Free Speech!? This was a foundational ploy of the Left to preach that calling for the end of free speech on the Right is *Constitutionally* protected! The assault of protections against calling for the demise of America as we knew it began by two dissenting opinions of the US Supreme Court in 1919 by Leftist Anti-GoD Justices Oliver Wendell Holmes and Louis D. Brandeis. These two self-avowed "Progressives" or Leftists wrote two dissenting opinions in Abrams vs. U.S. arguing that speech could only be punished if it presented "a

---

[280] Kirsten Powers; *The Silencing: How the Left Is Killing Free Speech;* "The O'Reilly Factor"; 'A Systematic Silencing': Powers on the Left's War on Free Speech; May 12, 2015.

clear and present danger" of imminent harm. Ultimately these two Leftists were able to convince a majority of other Justices to adopt a "clear and present danger test". If there is no "immediate" violent reaction to speech then according to the Left, all calls to destroy America are "Constitutionally protected Free Speech"! This is lunacy! We need to fight back and reclaim our GOD-given right of protection against those who aim to destroy us!

If you oppose the Left's doctrine they will force your compliance or if they cannot force compliance, they will make every attempt to destroy you. They will attack you personally, financially, in your employment, your family, and make false accusations privately and especially publically. The Left attacks the person and always avoids discussing the truth of what the opponent of the Left says. The Left virtually never engages in reasoned debate but will always resort to name calling and made-up accusations. Do you remember when the phrase "discriminating taste" was considered good and prudent?

The constitution of the United Nations (UNESCO) in its *Declaration of Principles on Tolerance* states, "Tolerance . . . involves the rejection of dogmatism and absolutism." The natural question against this type of nonsense is, "Are they absolutely sure they absolutely reject absolutism?"[281]. In logic this self-contradiction is called a self-defeating statement. However with the Left neither defiance of logic nor the lack of truth deters them in their quest.

The Left's definition of tolerance has evolved from simply allowing others to hold and articulate their opposing views to mandating that we accept their views as equally valid. The evolution has progressed from demanding free expression of their thoughts to demanding that we think that their thoughts are as much truth as any other thought. It is a backdoor tactic to require acceptance of an Anti-GOD culture at every level in America. American's are no longer allowed to even think that the positions of the Left are wrong as that constitutes a hate crime! (Think this is an exaggeration? Stay tuned!) Tolerance has now

---

[281] United Nations, UNESCO; constitution; Declaration of Principles on Tolerance; Article 1 - Meaning of tolerance, subsection 1.3; 16 November 1995.

come full circle, from tolerating Leftist views to forcibly mandating our acceptance of their views. This is what James Kalb referred to as **Inquisitional Tolerance**. The Left simply will not tolerate any dissent!

> "The result is that the [Left's] new tolerance holds the obvious moral high ground while dissent is considered irrational and presumptively violent. [The Left's new tolerance] demands are treated as uniquely neutral, and for that reason it carries the rights but not the responsibilities of truth: it has the right to prevail, but no obligation to explain itself. To add to the confusion, both the new and old approaches to tolerance remain in circulation and discussions [from the Left] shift opportunistically from one to the other. It thus becomes all the more difficult to discuss basic issues in a rational way"[282].

A prominent example of tolerance turned to mandated acceptance of the Leftist agenda would be the Left's strident anti-bullying campaign. On the surface who could be against an "anti-bullying campaign"?! Everyone at one time or another has been the victim of bullying. We can all relate to the helplessness of that situation. The Left, however, takes a bad moment and *politicizes* it, not to the advantage of the victim, but to the advantage of the Leftist agenda! Under the guise of universal toleration and "student safety", the Left mandates acceptance of homosexuality. Yes, the Left's "anti-bullying campaign" is a cloak for the homosexual agenda! Do you think this another exaggeration? Let's consider the words of Kevin Jennings, the *founder* of the national anti-bullying campaign and later Obama's "Safe Schools Czar" from 2009 to 2011, from a speech Jennings gave to fellow homosexual activists in 1995 titled *Template for Homosexual and Transgender Activism in Schools across the U.S.*:

Already in 1993, Jennings was employing the "bullying" accusation as an intimidation tool... Jennings admitted his manipulative approach in a 1995 speech to fellow GLBT (Gay, Lesbian, Bi-sexual, Transgender) activists, explaining that he and the Governor's

---

[282] Kalb, James; Crisis Magazine; *The Intolerance of Liberal Toleration*; June 5, 2013.

Commission "**framed the issue**" as one of "**student safety**". That way, no one could object to the homosexual and transgender indoctrination the activists planned to push in the schools. Whoever opposed their efforts could be accused of heartless disregard for students! Jennings said in that speech:

> "If the Radical Right can succeed in portraying us as preying on children, we will lose. Their language – '**promoting homosexuality**' – is laced with subtle and not-so-subtle innuendo that we are '**after their kids**'. We must learn from the abortion struggle, where the clever claiming of the term 'pro-life' allowed those who opposed abortion on demand to frame the issue to their advantage, to make sure that we do not allow ourselves to be painted into a corner before the debate even begins.

> In Massachusetts **the effective _reframing_ of this issue was the key to the success** of the Governor's Commission on **Gay and Lesbian Youth**. We immediately seized upon the opponent's calling card – safety -- and explained how **homophobia represents a threat to students' safety** by creating a climate where violence, name-calling, health problems, and suicide are common. **Titling** (read: lying by using misleading title!) our report '**Making Schools Safe for Gay and Lesbian Youth**', we automatically threw our opponents onto the defensive and **stole their best line of attack**. This **framing** (again: lying by using misleading title!) short-circuited their arguments and left them back-pedaling from day one.

> Finding the effective **frame** (again: lying by using misleading title!) for your community is the key to victory. It must be linked to universal values that everyone in the community has in common. In Massachusetts, no one could speak up against our **frame** and say, 'Why, yes, I do think students should kill

themselves': this allowed us to set the terms for debate"[283]. (emphasis and clarifications added)

Still think this is coincidence? An exaggeration? Are they really after our children? Let's get the truth from gay rights activist Daniel Villarreal, cohort of Kevin Jennings, as quoted in Villarreal's own words on the website Queerty.com, which promotes the homosexual agenda:

> While gay activists usually deny that they want to indoctrinate children, said Villarreal, **"let's face it—that's a lie"**. "We want educators to teach future generations of children to accept queer sexuality. In fact, **our very future depends on it**," he wrote. **"Recruiting children? You bet we are**," he said. "Why would we push anti-bullying programs or social studies classes that teach kids about the historical contributions of famous queers unless we wanted to deliberately educate children to accept queer sexuality as normal?"

> In fact, Villarreal said that his dream of increasing not only the acceptance, but the future practice of homosexuality among youngsters was common among those in the gay lobby, **"I and a lot of other people want to indoctrinate, *recruit*, teach, and expose children to queer sexuality AND THERE'S NOTHING WRONG WITH THAT**"[284]. (emphasis and clarifications added)

Again, the Left always begins with seemingly benevolent guidelines, which quickly morph into State-enforced "mandates". Do you think this an exaggeration? Let's look at one example that shows this as a gross understatement. In the California Alameda school district an

---

[283] Contrada, Amy; MassResistance Special Report; Kevin Jennings – Author of 1993 Education Report to the Massachusetts Governor's Commission on Gay and Lesbian Youth: Template for Homosexual and Transgender Activism in Schools across the U.S.; May 2011.
[284] Baklinski, Peter; lifesitenews.com; *The real agenda behind gay anti-bullying clubs in your school*; Tue Sep 6, 2011 - 5:37 pm EST.

"anti-bullying" curriculum was adopted which mandated "safe schools" policies that specifically protected "sexual orientation", "gender identity", and "gender expression". Many families objected to their children being taught this curriculum and these families sought to opt out based on Constitutionally protected religious beliefs and faith issues. The school district refused to allow the children to be excused from what the parents considered homosexual indoctrination. The parents filed suit. However in December 2009, Judge Frank Roesch of the Superior Court of California in Alameda County determined that any "opt-out right" is "outweighed by the policies against discrimination and harassment of students from LGBT (lesbian, gay, bi-sexual and transgender) families". The benevolent "guidelines" thus became what they were always intended to become, a State mandated indoctrination of the homosexual lifestyle!

Here is another real-life example of the Left's deceit behind their rhetoric:

> "The [Minnesota] governor's task force gives the green light to activist groups like OutFront to move into public and private schools. It calls for "actively enlisting ... community-based advocacy groups" to "chang[e] peer and community norms" and develop bullying-intervention strategies.
>
> Not surprisingly, the task force's proposed new antibullying regime would not treat all children equally, despite lip service to this goal. Instead, it focuses on students in "protected classes," including sexual orientation and "gender identity or expression."
>
> Under the task force's vague and overbroad definitions of bullying and harassment, **students could be punished for "direct or indirect interactions" that other students -- especially those in protected groups -- claim to find "humiliating" or "offensive," that have a "detrimental effect" on their "social or emotional health," or even that promote a "perceived imbalance of power."**

By this standard, a student who voices reservations about same-sex marriage could be accused of bullying LGBT students.

We get a sense of what may be on the horizon from "Welcoming Schools" -- a K-5 "antibullying" program developed by the Human Rights Campaign, a gay and transgender advocacy group. The program was scheduled to be piloted at Hale Community School in Minneapolis in 2008.

"Welcoming Schools" had little to do with bullying, and much to do with ensuring that kids as young as age 5 submit to the group's orthodoxy on sexuality and family structure.

The curriculum advised teachers not to call students "boys and girls," on grounds this can create "internal dissonance" in some children. It called for students to read books like "Sissy Duckling," and to be evaluated on "whether or not [they] feel comfortable making choices outside gender expectations." Kids in grades three to five "acted out" being members of nontraditional families, including same-sex-headed families.

In lesson after lesson, teachers were instructed to urge their students -- ages 5 to 11 -- to **reject traditional views on sexuality and family structure** as hurtful "stereotypes," and to use group exercises and **classic indoctrination techniques** to pressure them to adopt the curriculum designers' attitudes and beliefs.

The governor's task force recommendations could entail serious consequences for dissenting students. The report includes language suggesting that **students who express views that others consider offensive could be referred for "counseling"** or **"mental health needs"**[285]. (emphasis added)

---

[285] Kersten, Katherine; Minneapolis Star Tribune; *The real agenda behind antibullying campaign*; January 12, 2013.

Notice again the threat of deeming anyone that disagrees with the homosexual agenda or who express views that others consider "offensive" could be referred for "counseling" or have "mental health needs" which need to be dealt with by the State! Afraid yet? You should be terrified! This is a government mandate to declare Christians, and many others on the Right, mentally incompetent, which was exactly what the Nazis did under Hitler as a pretext for imprisonment and eventually extermination! If you still think that history does not repeat itself, then you are living in a make-believe world that will be shattered like the Nazi *Kristallnacht* (the Night of Broken Glass), the opening salvo of the *Holocaust*!

Keep in mind that the DOJ statistics show that the percentage of 12 to 18-year old students that reported being targets of "hate-related" words based on their sexual orientation declined from 1.0 percent in 2007 to 0.6 percent in 2009. Not only has this issue been in steep decline, but the numbers do not represent a crisis nor warrant any knee-jerk hysterical reaction. It is simply a self-created "crisis" for the Left to implement one of the largest and final steps in its Religious *War Against GOD* in America!

Do you think any of these conclusions a bit melodramatic or overstated? Let's let the Left definitively state the nature of their brand of *violent* extremism. In his first book, *Reveille for Radicals* Saul Alinsky, the godfather of the Left in America wrote:

> "While liberals are most adept at breaking their own necks with their tongues, radicals are most adept at breaking the necks of conservatives"[286].

Now there is Leftist "tolerance" for you!

Here is yet another poignant example of the Left's total intolerance of the right, when Hillary Rodham Clinton on October 13, 2015 was asked "Which enemy that you made during your political career are you most proud of?", she replied "Well, in addition to the NRA, the

---

[286] Alinsky, Saul; *Reveille for Radicals*; 1946; pg. 29.

health insurance companies, the drug companies, the Iranians ... *probably the Republicans*"!

The Left never operates under the rules that they impose on everyone else. The Left demands "tolerance", but the Left has no tolerance for any dissent from the Left's Party-line in general, and all things Christian in particular. A few glaring hypocrisies come immediately to mind. Gore flies on a private jet and wants others to give up large "gas-guzzling" vehicles. Homosexuals demand tolerance but are the most militantly intolerant. Michelle Obama demands weight control for children through her public school lunch initiatives, while she herself is noticeably overweight. Hillary Rodham-Clinton as Secretary of State instructs underlings at the State Department to never use private servers to conduct State business, while she installs her own private server by which she conducts all of her official State business. The lists go on *ad absurdum*. Tolerance for the Left is a blind-man's-bluff in which Americans are blindfolded and shoved around until the blindfold is removed only when America has been fully bullied into compliance!

TOLERANCE TO ACCEPTANCE:

Before we close our discussion on "tolerance" I must add that: "Tolerance" is not the Left's and Evil's endgame, but simply a Politically Correct foot-in-the-door to the perversion of the individual. "Tolerance" is a transition to "acceptance", which is a transition to the endgame of the total subjugation of all individuals to the Left's agenda. "Tolerance" is a broad *societal* control, and "acceptance" is the control of the *individual*!

The Left's use of the word "accept" is intentional when it discusses the Right's *obligation* to be "accepting" of the perversions of the Left. To "accept" is a bridge too far and transitions the individual from "tolerance" to "acceptance". "Tolerance" allows a perversion to grow and fester *around* us, whereas "acceptance" allows a perversion to grow and fester *inside* of each of us! The things that GOD calls perversions the Right should *never* accept! (Most Leftist, Anti-GOD perversions should never be tolerated! There are some exceptions, but very few.)

The Right should not, and by definition cannot, "accept" wrong. For the Right to "accept" wrong makes the Right now Wrong or Left! Acceptance of Evil is the self-destruction of Right. The Left is in fact seeking to remake the Right into its own image one compromise at a time! The Right should not accept homosexual marriage, mandated atheism, or abortion, any more than the Right should learn to accept murder. Do you think that this analysis is a bit exaggerated? Let's see what *Webster's Dictionary* defines the word "accept" as:

Full Definition of *Accept*[287]

transitive verb

1 a : to **receive willingly** <accept a gift>
　 b : to be able or **designed** to take or **hold** [to embrace] (something applied or added)
2 : **to give admittance or approval to**
3 a : **to endure without protest or reaction**
　 b : **to regard as proper, normal, or inevitable**
　 c : **to recognize as true : believe**
4 a : to make a **favorable response to**
　 b : **to agree to undertake** (a **responsibility**)
5 : **to assume an obligation** to pay; also : to take in payment
6 : **to receive** (a legislative report) **officially**

It is also important to note that the *"transitive"* nature *Webster's* defines as:

3 : of, relating to, or characterized by *transition.*

To "accept" is to transition, or move, one to a new place. To go from "tolerating" to "embracing" or "accepting" the perversion! Tolerance

---

[287] Emphasis and brackets added.

is not the Left's and Evil's endgame. Evil is not stupid, ignorant, naïve, or unprepared. Evil has millennia of practice, adjusting, and improving the process of infiltration and conquering the minds of mankind. *Tolerance* was never the final step in implementing the Left's agenda, but a first foot-in-the-door, which then necessarily follows to "accepting" Evil as "proper, normal, or inevitable"! The Left's "tolerance" is the path to the "acceptance" and the surrender of the Right... to Evil!

15. THE LEFT IS A RELIGION!

Chapter 15

Political Correctness is *political enforcement* of the Left's Religion!

America is *not* under siege by the "forces of secularism", but from the "forces of Evil" from the Left's "Religion of Evil"! This is ***not*** a "secular" religion in the sense of "irreligion", but as Alinsky admits is a Leftist Religion founded on the most ancient form of *Evil* begun by *Lucifer* himself! "Secularism" is the Trojan Horse of the Left. Now that the Left has torn down the gates of GOD which once protected America and the Trojan Horse has been dragged into our once Shinning City on the Hill, the true Evil *religious* nature which lurked inside the hollow shell has been set free to destroy and plunder our once great Republic. Assaults on America's traditional Christian values, which characterized this Country and which was the bond which held America together, are *NOT* assaults from irreligious "secularists", but assaults of Leftist Religious zealots!

By the way… The worship of Lucifer qualifies as a *Religion*! That is whether the worship is indirectly or directly.

The Left wants to "fundamentally transform America", but have you ever asked yourself: Why? America is the freest and most prosperous Nation in the history of the world with more opportunity for all of its citizens than any nation. Who would want to "transform" that? The reason is that America was built on the Judeo-Christian principles and ideals. The same principles and ideals that made America the greatest Nation in history. The Left wants to destroy all existing vestiges of this Christian Faith still remaining in America today. There is nothing else to "transform"! American Christian foundations fundamentally oppose the Left's core philosophies and acting goals. America's Christian heritage and the Left's manifestation of Evil are fundamentally irreconcilable. This conflict is at its core two Religions at War. The Left's only option, then, is to destroy all Christian associations and all those who still "cling" to them! (As Barack Hussein Obama, Jr. not so candidly phrased it!) This is history repeating itself in the Left's age-old *War Against GOD*! Christianity and the Religion of the Left are two religious philosophies at War!

James Hitchcock writing for *Crisis Magazine* in an article fittingly titled *The Religion of Liberalism & the New Heretics* makes several poignant observations:

> ... liberalism [Leftism] is now not merely a political philosophy compatible with many kinds of religion but has itself become a religion[288].

> Liberalism [Leftism] is a religion because, for liberals, ultimate meaning lies in a commitment both to the ever-expanding welfare state, which is the fulfillment of the ideal of justice, and to the continuing liberation of individuals from all binding authority [GOD], which is the key to personal happiness. Liberal [Leftist] ideology ultimately rests on an act of faith[289].

The "New Heretics" which Hitchcock alludes to are the traditional Christian denominations which still oppose the Religion of Evil of the Left. What was once the *Biblical* and doctrinal term of Christianity for opposition to Christianity, "Heretics", has been usurped by the Left *Against GOD* and His people. The Left has indeed turned truth upside-down and into a *Convenient Lie*! Do you doubt this? Here is a description of "Religious Liberalism" in the "secular" and Left slanted online publication Wikipedia:

> Religious liberalism [Leftism] is a form of approach to religion which is critical, rationalistic or humanistic. It is an attitude towards one's own religion (as opposed to criticism of

---

[288] James Hitchcock; Crisis Magazine; *The Religion of Liberalism & the New Heretics*; May 21, 2013.
[289] James Hitchcock; *Crisis Magazine*; *The Religion of Liberalism & the New Heretics*; May 21, 2013.

religion from a secular position, or criticism of a religion other than one's own) which contrasts with a traditionalist or orthodox approach, and it is directly opposed by trends of religious fundamentalism.[290]

"Religious liberalism" is "critical" of "traditionalist or orthodox" religion which can only describe Christianity; "rationalistic" which is non-rational, or characteristic of being emotional, unreasonable, and self-centered; and "humanistic", man-centered and Pagan in nature. "Secular" as we have seen is *not* "non-religious", but based in the Pagan religion of Evil and the Left. The Left's angst is particularly vicious towards Christian "fundamentalism" which strives to preserve the unadulterated Word of GOD, the *Bible*, and preaches Jesus as the only Way to salvation and ultimately Heaven. Fundamentalists are also particularly characterized for not being afraid to mix "religion and politics" as Jesus in the *Bible* teaches[291], a particularly heinous crime from the Left's perspective!

Religion and politics are inseparable and have been even before the Tower of Babel at the beginning of history. The discussion of religion must therefore include politics. Political Correctness is *political enforcement* of the Left's Religion! Evil is always on a Crusade to destroy the Right, as the Right is the only threat against the Left's Evil agenda. Religion and politics are two sides of the same coin. The spiritual and physical sides always co-exist together side by side. The Left is not actually opposed to the sanctioning of religion and state's joint function together as they would have us believe. It is the separation of the Christian "Church and State" which the Left so vehemently demands. The Left is only opposed to Christian influence upon the State. The State in its current Leftist manifestation, will endorse and promote virtually *any* religion *except* Christianity. To paraphrase C. S. Lewis, when it comes down to it, there are only two religions in the world, Christianity and Hinduism as it manifests in all other religions whose common theme is their opposition to Christianity! The uniting force of every other religion is their common

---

[290] Wikipedia, *Religious liberalism*; accessed 7/5/2015.
[291] See the chapter: *Jesus, Christians, and Political Activism: Debunking the Lie of the Left.*

219

opposition to the *Bible*'s One true GOD. In this sense Hinduism, as carried over as all forms of Paganism, can be defined as "any religious manifestation other than that of JEHOVAH GOD of the *Bible*".

False religions have always strived to control the State as the mechanism of control and enforcement as a means to force compliance to the false religion. This is the Left's backdoor approach to accomplishing its ends in usurpation of total power. Religion and politics are the inseparable halves of a symbiotic relationship of which one cannot survive without the other. A physical, or political, system requires empowerment from a spiritual or religious kingdom.

There are only two spiritual power sources in the Universe, GOD and Evil. Only Christianity, and by extension Judaism, even claim empowerment from the One true GOD OF the *Bible*. Other religions are at least by default empowered by Evil. The Religion of the Left, as even they confess, is empowered by Evil! This is the motivation of the Left's insistence that there be no public discussion of religion and politics. If people discuss a subject long enough they will eventually get to the truth of the matter, so the Left strives to keep the truth of their deceptions from being discussed and thereby discovered. Out of sight out of mind!

The Left's actions are nothing less than religiously missionary in nature. Their zeal, focus, and intensity can only be explained in a religious missionary context. This missionary zeal drives Leftists at their core and provides them with their very meaning for existence. When an earthly Utopia is their highest imaginable attainment, a sense of dire emergency under the constraints of a lifetime, and the presumed oblivion to follow, excuses any action to bring about their imagined earth-bound Paradise. This explains the radical's overwhelming need for *action, action, action* in the here and now. Christians' missionary mindedness in the here and now is not intent on creating an earthly paradise by our own works, but in anticipation of GOD delivering His people into the coming Heavenly Paradise.

This also explains the Left's incessant action by, as Alinsky put it, success *by any means necessary*. The Left usurps its power by force in destroying everyone and everything that stands in its way, while Christians advance their Kingdom not by force, but by demonstrating the love of GOD. How is it that the GOD of love is the target of so much hate? This is the only true extant "hate crime"! The GOD of the *Bible* is the only GOD who defines Himself as literally, "GOD is love"[292]. The Left's Religion is mandated and forced, while Christianity must be accepted as a matter of personal choice. The Left's Religion is a matter of forced compliance; Christianity is a matter of the heart. These are the two Religions at *War*!

It is interesting to see the overview of the word "religion" in the *Webster's Dictionary*. It shows a clear degradation of the connotation of the word "religion" and a conforming to the Leftist Politically Correct machine which now permeates and determines modern America culture. Here is the Webster's overview:

> : the belief in a god or in a group of gods
> : an organized system of beliefs, ceremonies, and rules used to worship a god or a
>   group of gods
> : an interest, a belief, or an activity that is very important to a person or group[293]

The last definition belies the modern influence of the Leftist Religion in language and the Left's attempt to hide itself as *not* a religion, when in fact the Left, as will be shown here, *absolutely* is a Religion. It is also significant to note that the *Webster's Dictionary 1828 Edition* makes the distinction between Christianity as the "true religion" and all others as "false religion" as:

> Any system of faith and worship. In this sense, *religion* comprehends the belief and worship of pagans and Mohammedans, as well as of Christians; any *religion* consisting in the belief of a superior power or powers

---

[292] The *Holy Bible*; 1 John 4:8, 16.
[293] Webster's Dictionary Online; http://www.merriam-webster.com/dictionary/religion. Accessed 6/21/2015.

governing the world, and in the worship of such power or powers. Thus we speak of the *religion* of the Turks, of the Hindoos (Hindus), of the Indians, etc. as well as of the Christian *religion*. We speak of false *religion* as well as of true *religion*.

The very definition of religion makes the Left a *Religion* of its own. The Left's goal is to destroy the only true Religion, the Christian Religion, which by its very exclusive nature of GOOD, opposes the Left's Religion of Evil:

> "Government must take a position on questions that depend on the nature of man and the moral world and **are therefore religious**. [Government] must try to get people to agree with its answers. Every government inculcates and enforces the understanding on which it is based, **including the religious ones**, in a variety of ways. At present a favorite method of enforcing the official view is stealth: **excluding other religious views from public affairs while claiming that the official view is not religious**. The exclusion is passed off as necessary for political freedom, but it destroys [freedom]. Politics is the interplay between the traditions of a community, which establish the general order of its life, and **public decisions backed by force**. To suppress the religious aspects of community tradition in public affairs is to make it impossible for the community to carry on its business in the way it finds natural and comprehensible. It is to cripple popular participation in the government"[294]. (emphasis and clarifications added)

C. S. Lewis made the profound observation in 1945 as WWII was winding down that there are actually only two Religions in the world, Christianity and Hinduism. As a quick religious study, the core of the Hindu Religion is devil, or demon, worship, which is by definition the worship of Evil. If you even take a moment to observe the appearance

---

[294] Kalb, James; *The Tyranny of Liberalism: Understanding and Overcoming Administered Freedom, Inquisitorial Tolerance, and Equality by Command*; 2008; pg. 98.

of the Hindu "gods" each has its own distinct Evil appearance. The Sanskrit (Hindu language) word for demon is the female *devi* and the male *deva* which shares the common root word in English for *devil* (often referred to as demon). Not coincidentally, as will be more fully discussed later[295], the Leftist Nazi swastika is a symbol of the Hindu god *Skandanava*, also called *Ganesha*. This same swastika was carried down through many religious reincarnations by subsequent Pagan Hindu manifestations including the Pagan Norse god *Thor* and plays a central role in Blavatsky's Worship of Lucifer which was later specifically picked up by Hitler himself, and subsequently the Nazis of the Fascist Left. Truly in the Leftist Religion of Evil the names change, but the devils stay the same!

Kalb profoundly reminds us:

> "A system of transcendent [morals] grounding a way of life is in effect *a religion*; the choice, therefore, is between the [Left's] reign of force and fraud (perhaps disguised and perhaps not), and the recognition of the [Right's] religious basis of society and government. ***The fundamental question of politics is which religion shall be established***"[296]. (emphasis and clarifications added)

Force is the hallmark of the Leftist movement "*...the religion of liberalism [Leftism]* **considers itself the one true faith** that has the obligation (and the power) to impose its beliefs [by force][297]". Again, the Left's Religion is a matter of forced compliance; Christianity is a matter of the heart. Freedom to the Left consists only of freedom *from* Christian traditions. Further:

> The religion of liberalism [Leftism] holds that the media and the educational system should enshrine liberal [Leftist] beliefs and discredit conservative ones, that government should

---

[295] See the later chapter *Fascism and the Left in America: Kindred Spirits and Familiar Bedfellows*.
[296] Kalb, James; Modern Age Quarterly; *The Tyranny of Liberalism*; 2000; pg. 251.
[297] James Hitchcock; Crisis Magazine; *The Religion of Liberalism & the New Heretics*; May 21, 2013; (emphasis and clarifications added).

223

enforce liberal [Leftist] programs by law, and that it is an open question how far heretics should even enjoy freedom of expression.[298]

As previously noted, philosopher Blaise Pascal observed: *Men never do **evil** so completely and cheerfully as when they do it from religious conviction.*

Maslow recognized the Left as a *Religion* or a "Common Faith"[299].Maslow's concept of "self-actualization", as discussed in the opening chapter *Defining The War: Evil Against GOD, Left Against Right*, is borrowed directly from the Hindu-Buddhist religious teachings. In Buddhist teaching the highest level of attainment is full-conscious Enlightenment, or "self-actualization"! According to Hindu-Buddhist religious teachings Enlightenment (or self-actualization) transforms or "actualizes" one to "pure spirit" and the spirit is re-assimilated into the cosmic consciousness or *Nirvana*. "Self-actualization" is in fact a *religious* term. Your children are being indoctrinated into Hinduism, the Evil Religion of the Left, in our public schools and most parents are completely unaware of this missionary endeavor of the Left! Meditation (Transcendental Meditation or TM) and Yoga as taught in many American public schools is a Hindu religious practice used to attain Enlightenment and self-actualization! Wait before you roll your eyes, even the Russian government recognizes the *religious* Hindu roots of yoga. The Russian government has taken steps to remove all forms of yoga in central Russia because in order to "to Stifle the Spread of Occultism"[300]. The Left goes to great lengths to disguise its *religious* underpinnings, but the Left is totally and absolutely founded on the *religious* concepts of Hinduism, the Religion that Wars *Against GOD*!

The Religion of the Left can best be described as *occultism* or revived *Paganism*, with roots that are embedded in what the *Bible* calls the

---

[298] James Hitchcock; Crisis Magazine; *The Religion of Liberalism & the New Heretics*; May 21, 2013.
[299] Maslow; *Religions, Values, and Peak Experiences*, p. 39.
[300] The Moscow Times; *Central Russian Officials Crack Down on Yoga in Bid to Stifle Spread of Occultism*; Jun. 28 2015 21:29.

ancient *Religion of Babylon*[301]. This Religion of the Left was organized at the beginning of Pagan an civilization at the Tower of Babel in a land that would become known as Babylon. The Religion of Babylon is eclectic in nature as it encompasses all non-Christian religious theologies. The Religion of the Left is the Theocratic, Fascistic, and Totalitarian Religion of Babylon! The Religion of Babylon has always acknowledged its allegiance to the Force of Darkness and Evil itself, named variously through the ages as Molech, Baal, Ra, Gaia, Zeus, Jupiter, Allah, which are all different manifestations of the same Evil entity... *Lucifer*!

This is a good place to briefly discuss the association of Islam or "Muhammadism" to Hindu pa Paganism and as such is wholly at *War Against* Christianity. This brief explanation will go a long way in understanding why with one voice Islam cries for the destruction of Christianity and daily executes Christians worldwide for no other crime but for rejecting Islam for their faith of Christianity. "Allah" is *not*, contrary to what the Muslims would have us deceptively believe, equivalent to the Christian GOD JEHOVAH. Allah was a carryover from the official Pagan "Moon god" of Muhammad's tribal Religion. Notice the symbol of Islam, found on *all* Muslim flags and symbols, is the Crescent Moon. The Muslim calendar is constructed around the lunar (Moon) cycle. The Muslim year begins with the first appearance of the "crescent Moon", the 'hilal' in Arabic, heralding the beginning of Ramadan and ends with the Muslim holy day celebration of *Eid ul Fitr*, the "day of the full moon". The most sacred site of all Islam is Mecca to which all Muslims are *required* to make a pilgrimage at least once in a lifetime. The center of this worship in Mecca, which all Muslims gather around to worship Allah, is a building which houses a "sacred rock", taught by Islam to be a piece of the Moon! Islam is nothing more than a degenerated form of Hindu Paganism! (See also the larger discussion of the dangers of Islam in America in the chapter *The Obamas: The Epitome of the Left*)

---

[301] Revelation 17:1-5, 18:1-3

It should also be noted again here that: The enforcement of Muslim of Blasphemy Laws is the equivalent Leftist enforcement of Politically Correctness!

In man's rejection of GOD, man has always tried to make themselves a god and counterfeit their own Religion. As has been aptly said: **"What has always made the state a hell on earth has been precisely that man has tried to make it his heaven"**[302].

David Horowitz profoundly notes, "Because progressives [Leftists] see themselves as social redeemers and their goal as saving the world, they regard politics as a **religious war**..."[303]. Horowitz understands the mechanics of the fight but not the reality nor extent of the nature of the *absolute* Evil behind the Left. Horowitz acknowledges the association of the Left to evil in general and Lucifer in particular, however Horowitz fails to see the reality of the Evil, and Evil's hand upon every Evil deed of the Left.

The Left's faithful instinctively recognize the Left as a Religion. David Axelrod's autobiographical book titled *Believer: My Forty Years in Politics* admits his status as a "Believer". This is unquestionably a religious term and intentionally used by Axelrod to describe his evangelistic crusade using politics to promote the Religion of the Left. Of course the term is stolen from Christianity and Christian "believers" in Jesus the Christ. This is a common practice of the Left who use Christian terminology as a cloak to camouflage their true intentions in the same way that Jesus in the *Bible* warns of the ravenous wolves who disguise themselves beneath sheep's clothing in order to devour Jesus' sheep... Christians![304]

The Left's Religion is irrational, unbelievable for the sane person, and deceptive:

---

[302] Hayek, Friedrich A.; *The Road to Serfdom with The Intellectuals and Socialism*, quoted from German poet Friedrich Hölderlin; 1944; pg. 24.
[303] David Horowitz; *Take No Prisoners: The Battle Plan For Defeating The Left*; pg. 44.
[304] The *Holy Bible*; Matthew 7:15.

"Man needs a life in common with his fellows, and common life requires a common understanding of the nature of the world and man's place in it. Our public life, to the extent that it exists, is now based on a [Leftist] religion that is hard to make sense of, harder to believe, and in the end relies on deceiving self and others"[305].

As will become abundantly clear in the chapter *Fascism and the Left in America: Kindred Spirits and Familiar Bedfellows*, the Fascism of Italy and Nazi Germany is exactly the same movement as that of modern Leftism in America today. Mussolini repeatedly proclaimed that "Fascism is a *religion!*[306]". He saw the implementation of the State religion as, "It is the State which educates its citizens in civic virtue, gives them a consciousness of their mission, and welds them into unity". Is this not the very identity which the New Left in American has given itself today?! Even more disturbing is Mussolini's admission that: "Two *religions* are today contending with each other for sway over the world - the black and the red. We declare ourselves the heretics of these two expressions"[307]. The "black" referenced Christianity and the "red" the State Religion expressed in Communism. Mussolini even referred to these Fascist ideas using the religious term "doctrine" in the title of his autobiography *"My Autobiography: With The Political and Social Doctrine of Fascism"*. Mussolini saw Fascism as a third and competing "religion" for world domination as is today "expressed" through the New Left in America!

According to the Diaries of Joseph Goebbels, one of Hitler's most ardent followers and Nazi Reich Minister of Propaganda in Nazi Germany from 1933 to 1945: "The Fuhrer is deeply religious, though completely anti-Christian"[308]. Goebbels wrote in an 8 April 1941 diary entry, "He hates Christianity, because it has crippled all that is

---

[305] Kalb, James; Modern Age Quarterly; *The Tyranny of Liberalism*; 2000; pg. 252.
[306] brainyquote.com.
[307] Mussolini, Benito; *My Autobiography: With The Political and Social Doctrine of Fascism*; Dover Books on History, Political and Social Science; Mar 6, 2012; pg. 74.
[308] Bonney, Richard; *Confronting the Nazi War on Christianity: The Kulturkampf Newsletters, 1936–1939*; Bern, Switzerland; Peter Lang Publications; 2009; pg. 20.

noble in humanity"[309]. Hitler himself comments on Christianity: "You see, it's been our misfortune to have the wrong religion"[310]. The Left is, and always has been a "religion" of Evil set specifically on eliminating its one and only true enemy… Christianity![311]

This is not to say that the Left does not occasionally invoke the name of "God" as they find convenient as a means to manipulate the masses. However, they invoke the word "God" like a witch employs an incantation. The Left's attempt at an association with GOD is purely a blasphemous one invoked as a matter of expediency and convenience in deception to further the Leftist cause.

The *Bible's* use of the specific terms of "right" and "left" is no accident. The Holy Bible says, A wise man's heart is at his right hand; but a fool's heart at his left[312]. Jesus said, "And [I, Jesus] shall set the sheep on his right hand, but the goats on the left. Then shall the King say unto them on his right hand, Come, ye blessed of my Father, inherit the kingdom prepared for you from the foundation of the world. Then shall he say also unto them on the left hand, Depart from me, ye cursed, into everlasting fire, prepared for the devil and his angels.[313] The "right" is GOOD is always associated with GOD, and the "left" with Evil. This is easily evidenced by Leftist books such as *The Left Hand of God: Taking Back Our Country from the Religious Right*, written in 2006 by the radical Leftist Rabbi Michael Lerner, a spiritual advisor to the then Governor Bill and Hillary Clinton, betrays the true Anti-GOD religious nature of their Religion of the Left and the leadership of the Left.

As demonstrated, "the left hand of GOD" is designated by Jesus Himself as the place of the damned when they stand before Jesus as GOD in judgement. Lerner uses this Biblical term of condemnation to

---

[309] Taylor, Irene, and Alan; *The Assassin's Cloak: An Anthology of the World's Greatest Diarists*; 2002; pg. 184.

[310] Speer, Albert; *Inside The Third Reich Memoirs By Albert Speer*; Translated from the German by

Richard and Clara Winston; The Macmillan Company; 1969.

[311] For more see: *Fascism and the Left in America: Kindred Spirits and Familiar Bedfellows*.

[312] Ecclesiastes 10:2.

[313] The *Holy Bible*; Matthew 25:33, 34, 41.

Hell as a badge of honor in the Leftist Religion reminiscent of Alinsky's open association of the Left to their icon Lucifer. Again, Alinsky, as well as Lerner, was also a mentor to Hillary Clinton. The Clinton's are entrenched in this Evil association to *Lucifer*. Remember these associations of Evil to the leadership of the Left are firsthand associations not some far removed or indirect association. More unbelievably, much of the Left no longer strives to hide their direct self-avowed association to Evil! Luciferians also embrace this association to the association of the Left to Evil and use the "goat" in their religious rites as a symbol of their fellowship with Lucifer. The Left will scream and Hillary will mock behind her pompous, condescending grin, but as the facts attest, the truth is that these Leftists willfully and intentionally choose their association with Evil and to Lucifer himself. This is the Religion of the Left!

Even Richard Neuhaus, a Leftist Catholic Priest, acknowledges that what was begun by the Leftist fellow-traveler John Dewey and his Leftist compatriots in the 1930's, initiated the public establishment of what is now the Religion of the Left:

> "...John Dewey in 1934. It sounds strange to us now, but it was less than 70 years ago, who wrote *A Common Faith*, and very seriously along with some of the most prestigious, influential [Leftist] intellectuals in America proposed a new version of essentially Jean-Jacques Rousseau's notion of the civil religion except attuned to the American democratic experiment"[314].

Recall that "Rousseau's notion of the civil religion" involved the liberal use of the guillotine and the mass execution of all Christians as the number one enemy of the Leftist State! It was in 1934 that Dewey, author of the Leftist tome *A Common Faith*, who referred to the characteristic of the battle that the Left waged against the Right as having a "religious quality". In 1935 John Dewey would write in *Liberalism and Social Action* that activist government in the name of

---

[314] Neuhaus; Richard John; *God Bless America: Reflections on Civil Religion After September 11*; Pew Research: Religion and Public Life Project; February 6, 2002; PewForum.org.

the economically disadvantaged and social reconstruction had "virtually come to define the meaning of **liberal faith**"[315]. In private the Left acknowledges the "religious quality" of their *War Against GOD*. In public the Left uses missionary-like language in their call to War *Against* the Right. In reality the Left's Anti-GOD Religion is its spiritual empowerment in its War *Against* the Right.

Leftism today is a Religion that is anti-rational, Anti-GOOD, Anti-GOD, and even by secular definition… Evil:

> "The liberal [Leftist] cure for this endless malaise is a very large authoritarian government that regulates and manages society through a cradle to grave agenda of redistributive caretaking. It is a government everywhere doing everything for everyone. The liberal [Leftist] motto is "In Government We Trust." To rescue the people from their troubled lives, the agenda recommends denial of personal responsibility, encourages self-pity and other-pity, fosters government dependency, promotes sexual indulgence, rationalizes violence, excuses financial obligation, justifies theft, ignores rudeness, prescribes complaining and blaming, denigrates marriage and the family, legalizes all abortion, defies religious and social tradition, declares inequality unjust, and rebels against the duties of citizenship. Through multiple entitlements to unearned goods, services and social status, the liberal [Leftist] politician promises to ensure everyone's material welfare, provide for everyone's healthcare, protect everyone's self-esteem, correct everyone's social and political disadvantage, educate every citizen, and eliminate all class distinctions. With liberal [Leftist] intellectuals sharing the glory, the liberal [Leftist] politician is the hero in this melodrama. He takes credit for providing his constituents with whatever they want or need even though he has not produced by his own effort any of the goods, services or status

---

[315] Dewey, John; *Liberalism and Social Action;* Prometheus Books, 2000; p. 30.

transferred to them but has instead taken them from others by force[316].

Radical liberalism [Leftism] thus assaults the foundations of civilized freedom, and for that reason it **is a genuine evil**. Further, given its irrational goals, coercive methods and historical failures, and given its perverse effects on human development, there can be no question of the radical agenda's madness. Only an irrational agenda would advocate a systematic destruction of the foundations on which ordered liberty depends. Only an irrational man would want the state to run his life for him rather than create secure conditions in which he can run his own life. Only an irrational agenda would deliberately undermine the citizen's growth to competence by having the state adopt him. Only irrational thinking would trade individual liberty for government coercion, then sacrifice the pride of self-reliance for welfare dependency. Only an irrational man would look at a community of free people cooperating by choice and see a society of victims exploited by villains.[317]"

Welfare creates dependence and enslavement. When you take away someone's incentive to work you hollow out the man into a shell of his former self, he or she becomes a ghost. Welfare as we know it today is designed by the Left to create a dependent class, dependent on the Left for even the most basic necessities, especially food. There is no coincidence that in Obama's administration he fostered an increase of over 13,000,000 food stamp recipients. That is an additional 13,000,000 million Americans depending on Big Brother for their very *survival*. Obama and the Left are not interested in creating jobs, but creating dependency on the Left. The *Bible* only allows "welfare" under extreme circumstance where the family or extended relatives are not available.

---

[316] Rossiter, Lyle H., Jr., M.D.; *The Liberal Mind: The Psychological Causes of Political Madness*; 2011; pgs. 329-330.

[317] Rossiter, Lyle H., Jr., M.D.; *The Liberal Mind: The Psychological Causes of Political Madness*; 2011.

For those of you who are admirers of, or at least familiar with Dostoevsky, here is a quote that illustrates the point in the subtle substitution of the Religion of the Left for Christianity:

> "This undertaking took courage, for the Russian novelist's 'Grand Inquisitor' parable is a favorite of good people who agree with Horowitz on most of the practical issues. Dostoevsky's discursion at the end of *The Brothers Karamazov* is everywhere cited as an exemplary defense of faith against materialism, by reduction ad absurdum. The Inquisitor famously denounces the returning Christ for refusing Satan's dare to make bread from stones, admonishing him that the religion of bread - communism - will displace the religion   of   eternal   life.

It is easy to attack the fallacies of one's enemies, but much harder to take on one's friends. Dostoevsky is a hero of faith to many good people; Horowitz exposes the great writer's faith as inadequate, even twisted. The author of *The Brothers Karamazov* gave lip service to life after death, but poured his passion into an earthly paradise. Although Dostoevsky exposed the horror behind the socialist utopia, he conjured another earthly dystopia. As Horowitz writes:

> Dostoevsky had written in his notebooks: 'I want the full kingdom of Christ.' He had then crossed out the words 'I want' and put in their place: 'I *believe* in the full kingdom of Christ.' And then: 'I believe that this kingdom will be accomplished, and it will be with us in Russia.' Other nations lived only for themselves but Russia was different, he believed; it was a nation that lived for Christ. 'Now that the time has come,' Russia would take the lead in establishing the kingdom of God, 'becoming the servant of all for the sake of universal reconciliation ... [and] ... the ultimate unifying of humanity.' Dostoevsky, Horowitz concludes, 'had become his own Inquisitor incarnate,' a nominal Christian who eschews the Kingdom of Heaven for earthly rewards. It turns out that the writer did not find the prospect of contemplating the Godhead

through eternity especially satisfying, and preferred to bring heaven down to Earth[318]".

The Left manifests itself as a feigned "moral indignation" (usually as "moral outrage"). It's the almost inexplicable look and tone of the Left's mouth pieces. When you watch the Left's leadership like Nancy Pelosi spit and spew her vitriol you can actually see the "moral indignation" in their expressions. As is with the Left's talking heads on the Left-Stream Media. The "morals" and "ethics" of the Left are evil. Yes, you can have evil "morals" and "ethics"! The Nazi's also had these identical "morals" and "ethics". Notice the intentional use of "moral indignation", this the Left uses to imitate the "righteous indignation" that can only come from GOD! Evil always uses language that imitates GOOD.

David Goldman concludes with a profound and frightening observation in his review of David Horowitz's book analyzing Dostoevsky's literary work *The Brothers Karamazov*:

> There are some things we cannot think about without projecting our own limitations. **That is true of the vision of an eternity in static contemplation, as well as the displacement of messianic hopes onto a supposed earthly paradise... And we cannot build a paradise on earth without magnifying our own imperfections**, as Dostoevsky's example illustrates. We cannot live in the World to Come because we do not know what it is like. **And if we try to force fallible humans to live in an earthly paradise, ultimately we shall have to kill them all for their failings**". (emphasis added)

This analysis certainly explains the Left's murder of hundreds of millions of people in the name of creating the Leftist Utopian "Earthy Paradise". The struggle against the Left's coopting of religion today

---

[318] David Goldman; Book Review of *Angels and Inquisitors: A Point in Time*, by David Horowitz; Asia Times Online; Dec 22, 2011.

is no less dangerous as they continue to justify any means to their ends of their continued fantasy in striving to build an Earthly Paradise.

Every Leftist manifestation in history has presented itself as a *religious* substitute to the Religion of Christianity. Robespierre used his contrived "Goddess of Reason". Communism has always presented itself as a Religion as Dostoevsky acknowledged "the religion of bread - communism - will displace the religion of [GOD's] eternal life". Nazism as Paganism with Hitler as its messiah. The modern Left with its mix of New Age, Paganism, and spirit worship.

It should be fearfully noted that Robespierre did not start out the French Revolution, *at least in public*, by saying, "join the Revolution and we will murder hundreds of thousands of Christians and dissenters of the state!". But that was exactly what happened! Darwin did not start out the scientific Revolution, *at least in public*, by saying, "join the Revolution and we will murder all the scientifically unfit, millions of babies, and skeptics!". But that was exactly what happened! Lenin did not start out the Russian Revolution, *at least in public*, by saying, "join the Revolution and we will murder all the Christians, Jews, and dissenters!". But that was exactly what happened! Hitler did not start out the Nazi Revolution, *at least in public*, by saying, "join the Reich and we will murder all the Christians, Jews, and *Lebensunwertes Leben* ("life unworthy of life")!". But that was exactly what happened! Mao did not start out Chinese Cultural Revolution, *at least in public*, by saying, "join the Revolution and we will murder all the Christians, Republicans, and all other "undesirables"!". But that was exactly what happened! Pol Pot did not start out the Khmer People's Revolution, *at least in public*, by saying, "join the Revolution and we will murder all the Christians, and "intellectuals"!". But that was exactly what happened! Abortionists did not start out the Sexual Revolution, *at least in public*, by saying, "join the Revolution and we will murder millions of babies!". But that was exactly what happened! Hundreds of millions have been sacrificed upon the altar from which the Left worships and in the name of instating the Left's Utopian Religion. The Left's Evil Utopian ideologies have Evil and murderous consequences.

Notice that the truth is rarely spoken out loud by the Left in front of bright lights and a teleprompter, but aside from an occasional slip-of-the-tongue, the ugly truth is spoken only when hidden away behind closed doors in dark rooms where the Leftist faithful are cloistered in secret.

To the Leftist radical, consequences are meaningless and *action* is the only objective. The radical needs to be *doing* something, anything to destroy the old *status quo* of American society. *Especially* action against America's Christian foundations and institutions. *Lack of action is death to the radical and his cause.* The Left ultimately is defined by their *actions* in opposition to GOD. Actions do speak louder than words!

You know a Leftist by his *actions*, by his works, by his deeds and *not* by his words or rhetoric. Obama can *say* that he is a Christian, for example, but his actions absolutely demonstrate that Obama is *not* a Christian[319]. Moreover, as the Christian evangelist James Dobson reminded us back in 2008, Senator Obama had delivered a speech mocking the Bible a couple of years earlier:

> "I think he's *deliberately* distorting the traditional understanding of the Bible to fit his own world view, his own confused theology," Dobson said, adding that Obama is "dragging biblical understanding through the gutter".

Leftists *say* that they are "for the people", but their actions of murder and enslavement of hundreds of millions show that they are *not* "for the people", but for Evil. The age-old proverb *actions speak louder than words* has never been more striking in its wisdom than when it is applied to the Left. In fact the Left's mantra is literally *words speak louder than actions*! The truth turned upside down. An illustrative and illuminating example is the Wizard of Oz who yells at Dorothy "pay no attention to the man behind the curtain", which belies the Left's hidden agenda deftly tucked away "behind the curtain" veiling its

---

[319] For a wider discussion see the chapter: *The Obamas: The Epitome of the Left* and the sub-section: *Obama as a Muslim or Muslim Sympathizer.*

subversive *actions* hidden behind its words. The Wizard was admonishing Dorothy to just *listen to what he said* and ignore any *actions* that may inadvertently come into her peripheral vision. The Left's words and actions demonstrably contradict each other. When words and actions contradict each other, this is the definitive characteristic of a Lie!

So it is with the Left in America today and through all of history, the Left *Lies* to us as it admonishes us to pay no attention to its own same actions. The Left even goes as far as to falsely paraphrase the *Bible* in admonishing us that "only God knows what's in the heart". What does GOD *actually* have to say about that? Nothing like the Left would have us believe. GOD says a man can in fact be "known by his *fruit* [actions]"[320], "Now the *works* of the flesh are manifest"[321], "They profess that they know God; but in *works* they deny him, being abominable, and disobedient, and unto every good work reprobate."[322], "What doth it profit, my brethren, though a man say he hath faith, and have *not works*? can faith save him?[323]", "Even so faith, if it hath *not works*, is dead, being alone.[324]", "Yea, a man may say, Thou hast faith, and I have *works*: shew me thy faith *without thy works*, and I will shew thee my faith *by my works*"[325], "But wilt thou know, O vain man, that faith *without works* is dead?[326]", "For as the body without the spirit is dead, so faith *without works* is dead also[327]", "and the dead were judged out of those things which were written in the books, according to their *works*[328]", and "And the sea gave up the dead which were in it; and death and hell delivered up the dead which were in them: and they were judged every man according to their *works*"[329]. Can GOD and His *Bible* be any more clear? We are to judge

---

[320] The *Holy Bible*: Matthew 12:33.
[321] The *Holy Bible*: Galatians 5:19.
[322] The *Holy Bible*: Titus 1:16.
[323] The *Holy Bible*: James 2:14.
[324] The *Holy Bible*: James 2:17.
[325] The *Holy Bible*: James 2:18.
[326] The *Holy Bible*: James 2:20.
[327] The *Holy Bible*: James 2:26.
[328] The *Holy Bible*: Revelation 20:12.
[329] The *Holy Bible*: Revelation 20:13.

a man by his *works*! The Left Lies, even about GOD! We can and must judge men by their *works* and not merely by their words!

The Left in the West has itself fallen victim to the Evil which it battled two catastrophic World Wars to defeat:

> As the supreme guide to a just social order, that principle of maximum equal satisfaction is considered worthy of a loyalty that trumps all others. For that reason it naturally receives a quasi-*religious* interpretation, one that sanctifies individual feelings and purposes as the source and goal of all value. Such an outlook has become the criterion for what amounts to a public religious orthodoxy: **liberal [Leftist] religion**, which affirms the equal dignity of values, is good and beneficial; anti-liberal [anti-Leftist] religion, which proposes a substantive higher standard, is dangerous and oppressive.
>
> Despite claims to the contrary, it thus turns out that contemporary Western government *can* be identified with a particular view of ultimate and even **religious** issues. There is nothing surprising in that result. As Kenneth Craycraft and others have noted, **religious neutrality is a myth**. Basic social institutions inevitably claim the right to make decisions on matters of life and death, and to demand sacrifice—even extreme sacrifice—of personal interests. To do so, they must be seen as grounded in ultimate realities regarding the meaning and value of life, and thus correspond to an **authoritative religious outlook**[330]. (emphasis added)

The Right believes in self-restraint under the laws of GOD, whereas the Left believes in State-restraint as it plays god and enforces its self-serving laws by external force and coercion. In elevating itself to god status, the Left has created its own Religion of self-worship. This is exactly the Religion begun by Lucifer himself when in the Garden of

---

[330] Kalb, James; Intercollegiate Review; *After Liberalism: Notes Toward Reconstruction*; Spring 2012, Volume: 47 Number: 1.

Eden Lucifer Lied to Eve and said that if they would follow Lucifer, "Ye shall be as gods"[331]!

Some things are worth repeating, and at the risk of sounding redundant I will restate here what I said in the chapter *Understanding The Battle*:

> "The Left told the Right to stay out of the bedroom, but the Left brought the bedroom out into the public by sanctioning sexual perversion, and politicized it! To the Left everything is politics: sex, gender, religion, *Bibles*, speech (which is no longer free), motives (hate crimes assume motives not just actions), race (some protected for political advantage), what you eat (trans-fat), what you drink (criminalizing 32 oz. sodas), wearing a seatbelt, putting your child in a car seat, health insurance, even thinking! Yes you can be arrested for *thinking* about committing an act of violence and for even disagreeing with the Left's doctrines. Nothing is sacred in the traditional Christian sense in a Leftist Utopian America, yet in an Orwellian self-contradiction of the Left's new Religion, everything is sacred and therefore needs to be controlled by the State! We need to be controlled by the State for our own good, of course, which the Left in another Orwellian twist re-defines as the "greater good".

The Left by using their concept of "greater good" and thereby replacing GOD as the ultimate "GREATER GOOD", have by smoke and mirrors illusion made themselves in the incarnation of the Leftist State to become... god! In Christianity the emphasis is on the "GREATER GOOD" of the individual. Once GOD changes the heart of the individual, then, and only then, can GOD work through that individual for GOOD. The "GREATER GOOD cannot be accomplished except through the mass conversion of the populace one-by-one to the ideals of the Right by an act of GOD. The "GREATER GOOD" of GOD then is an individual concept not as the Left would have us believe, a Socialistic group endeavor. A societal change to a *greater societal good* happens only when many as individuals are converted to the

---

[331] The *Holy Bible*: Genesis 3:5.

"GREATER GOOD" by GOD. Thus the "GREATER GOOD" of GOD stands in absolute obstruction to the Left's socialist group endeavor. The Left's agenda of its "greater good", because it excludes GOD Who is the only one from which "GREATER GOOD" can occur, then leads exactly the opposite direction from a "GREATER GOOD" to a *greater Evil*!

The Left's employment of the "greater good" is nothing short of a contrived *political* mandate to enforce the Left's Religion of Evil. It is through the Left's "Politically Correct" P.C. *pogrom* by which the Left seeks to dominate and control the American population and force compliance with the Left's Religion. Leftist P.C. mandates began as intellectual Utopian ideals, progressed to pier-pressure guidelines as indoctrinated through the media and public education, then to government enforced Leftist absolutes! As discussed briefly in the opening chapter *Defining The War: Evil Against GOD, Left Against Right*, it is impossible to separate religion and politics. Religious decisions are inescapable in politics. The Left pretends to not make "religious" decisions by writing them off as "moral" or "ethical" decisions, but it is nothing more than another cleverly disguised *Lie* of the Left! A horse is still a horse no matter what color it is painted. Moral imperatives by which all governments must act and rule are by their very nature *religious*. They are either based on *religious* Christian or *religious* Pagan beliefs. All Pagan Religion can be traced back even past Hinduism to the ancient Tower of Babel, and ultimately to the Religion of Babylon. These Babylonian religious manifestations of Evil are by nature opposed to GOD. This Law of the inseparability of religion and politics, by its very definition, is as inescapable as gravity, breathing, and death! Moral decisions are inescapable and inherently *religious*.

Louis Michel Le Peletier, a Jacobean and co-conspirator with the murderous Robespierre, in the French Revolution's *Reign of Terror* philosophized:

"Considering the extent of human degradation, I am convinced that it is necessary to effect a total regeneration and, if I may so express myself, **of creating a new people**"[332].

This is the universal goal of Leftists from the *Reign of Terror* to the Left in America today, to not simply recreate society, but as Obama promised to "fundamentally transform America" in the goal of using this new society in the "creating of a new people". This is what "Saint" Hillary Rodham-Clinton meant when she said **"Let us be willing to remold society by <u>redefining what it means to be a human being</u>**"[333]. You caught that, right? It bears repeating: "…**by redefining what it means to be a human being**"! Again *the Left wants to redefine what it means to be a human being*! This is not a Utopian fantasy but a Frankensteinian nightmare in attempting to recreate what we are as human beings! This makes the *Reign of Terror* look like a Sunday-School picnic! The one thing that remains consistent in the Left's ongoing *Reign of Terror* is that the only alternative for those who refuse to have their nature and minds "recreated", in the image of the superhuman Utopian ideal, the Nazi *Übermensch* or Superman, is genocidal extermination! Here we recall again, with little risk of over-emphasis, the haunting warning of David Goldman: **"And if we try to force fallible humans to live in an earthly paradise, ultimately we shall have to kill them all for their failings"**!

The very concept of *transforming human nature* is a fundamental concept in defining a *religion*. Most would ascribe this ability only as an act ascribed to GOD and as a divine miracle! The arrogance of the Left in even imagining to undertake an attempt to create a Utopia is to literally attempt to play GOD, as history clearly demonstrates mortals are not equipped for it. It would be comical, if it were not so tragically destructive and genocidally catastrophic!

As if this were not enough to try and convict Hillary Rodham-Clinton for crimes against humanity, she further elaborates:

---

[332] Bastiat, Frédéric; *The Law*; 1850; translated by Dean Russell 1950.
[333] Kelly, Michael; New York Times; *Saint Hillary*; May 23, 1993.

"Laws have to be backed up with resources and political will, and deep-seated cultural codes, ***religious beliefs*** and structural biases ***have to be changed***"[334].

It is Christianity which alone stands in the way of the Left's realization of its Draconian Utopia! Here Hillary Rodham-Clinton is using the threat of force of *physical violence* as the then would-be President of the United States against Christians whose "deep-seated... religious beliefs" stand in the way of the Left's agenda! Ms. Clinton gave us a hint of how far she is willing to go as President when she said in 2015 that jail was the "right thing" for the Kentucky clerk who refused to issue marriage licenses to homosexual couples. If Hillary Rodham-Clinton had been elected to the Presidency she would have used her office to ensure that any Christian either denies their Biblical beliefs when they conflict with the Left's agenda, or they will go to prison!

Louis Antoine Léon de Saint-Just, another Leftist collaborator of the murderous Robespierre and *The Reign of Terror*, was a foundationalist of the modern Leftist juggernaut:

"The legislator commands the future. It is for him to will the good of mankind. It is for him to make men what he wills them to be".

This is the goal of the modern Left in America today, to inextricably alter not only the foundations of America, but *to alter who we are as human beings*! This is more terrifying than any Frankensteinian monster ever imagined by horror writers. The Left wants to play God! That *is* a Religion! Real lives will be sacrificed again by the millions in the Left's quest to create a new concept of the Nazi *Übermensch* or Leftist engineered "Superman"!

Again, don't be fooled by the Left's rhetoric concerning the Left and Right of "we all have the same good goals at heart, just different methods of reaching those goals". This is a self-admission that the

[334] Hillary Rodham-Clinton speech to Women in The World Summit in New York; April 23, 2015.

Left's "good goals" are a *religious* endeavor. The Left cannot afford to be exposed for its true *religious* nature of Evil in opposing GOD, so the Left creates its own *religious* dogma camouflaged as secular language of the "greater good".

Abortion as an Historical Satanic Religious Rite:

Abortion is without question one of the primary pillars supporting the Left's ideological cathedral in holding up their *belief* and *Faith system*. Do you doubt this? Barack Hussein Obama, who is at present the titular head of the Leftist juggernaut, says abortion is "a matter of *faith*"... "is a difficult *moral* issue" ... "different people have different views [on abortion] depending on their *faith* and their *beliefs*" ... "it's up to her conscience in consultation with her doctor and her *minister*"[335]. Faith, as *Webster's* tells us, is by definition "*a system of religious beliefs*"[336]. The Left's *Faith* in its ideological *beliefs* are the foundation for the Left's *Religion*!

Any reasonable and thinking man would be convinced that abortion is viewed by the Left as a *religious* rite in the Left's *Religion of Evil*. This is obvious just based on the above stated imperative words of Barack Hussein Obama. Obama who is the quintessential Leftist. Remember Obama's wholehearted support for partial-birth abortion?[337] But for those who need more convincing, hold on because we are about to go from horrifying... to terrifying!

The passing of New York Senate Bill *S00240* legalizing abortion up to birth passed January 2019 to a *standing ovation* by New York Democrat lawmakers. The New York Leftist Democrat Governor Cuomo lit up WTC spiral pink in celebration! A Democrat sponsored bill in Virginia which would have allowed for abortion even during labor was defeated in committee. In a competition to see which Democrat controlled state can violate GOD's Law more grotesquely, über Leftist Illinois Governor J.B. Pritzker signed into law in January

---

[335] CSPAN; Obama as a Democrat U.S. Senate candidate; Chicago; 9/29/2004.
[336] www.merriam-webster.com/dictionary/faith
[337] For details see the chapter: *The Obamas: The Epitome of the Left.*

2019 a bill that has been called worse than NY's Reproductive Health Act. Remember when the Left said that abortion should be legal but rare?! The Left in America is lurching down the road to total Paganism!

Ancient Evil through time has always incorporated abortion into their *Religion of Evil*, in one manifestation or another, as a "sacrificial rite" in a myriad of sacrificial ceremonies dedicated to *Lucifer*. If at first glance this seems a bit exaggerated, hold on it gets worse... much worse. As we have discussed, Evil has changed his name through history: *The Serpent, Molech, Baal, Ra, Isis, Zeus, Aphrodite, Jupiter, Allah, Gaia,* and hundreds of other names which are more or less recognizable than these, but the Evil behind each manifestation remains an incarnation *Lucifer*. The *Bible* identifies Lucifer as "the dragon, that old serpent, which is the Devil, and Satan"[338]. Remember also that Lucifer was Saul Alinsky's "over the shoulder acknowledgement" as the Left's first Leftist Radical in history. The *Bible* tells us that the ancient Pagan Religions of *Molech* and *Baal* centered around unborn and newborn baby-sacrifice to their "gods" Molech[339] and Baal[340]. The *Bible* also identifies Molech and Baal as Satan! The births of babies in the sacrificial rites of these ancient religions were often chemically or physically induced to cause premature births very similar to today's "modern" abortion procedures. Amos, an ancient Biblical historian, tells us that it was not uncommon for Pagans to rip out, literally to brutally cut out, unborn babies from their mother's wombs specifically for religious sacrifice to Molech[341]!

Many of these pregnancies were intentionally conceived through the religious sexual rituals involving the numerous temple prostitutes as a central tenant of their Evil *Religion*. The premature and newborn babies would then be murdered in sacrifice to Satan. Let me explain the method for you. The Evil Religion of Molech erected tall iron statues of their god Molech. These idols were forged from iron with

---

[338] The *Holy Bible*: Revelation 20:2.
[339] The *Holy Bible*: Leviticus 20:2.
[340] The *Holy Bible*: Jerimiah 19:5.
[341] The *Holy Bible*: Amos 1:13.

Molech's arms outstretched with a large bowl-shaped saucer that rested upon its forearms. A raging fire was kindled under the saucer until the saucer was glowing red from the extreme heat. Then the babies to be sacrificed to Molech were then thrown on the saucer and fried to death while their screaming shrieks of terror echoed into the sky until the infant was finally consumed by the fires! This is what the *Bible* describes as the parents having their babies sacrificed to devils by burning them to death which is "to cause them to pass through the fire"[342]!

Archeologists and anthropologists tell us that Molech and Baal represent the same Pagan god in different cultural manifestations. The wife of Baal was *Asherah* and the wife of Molech was *Ashteroth*. *Asherah* and *Ashteroth* in fact represented the same *"fertility goddess"*. This same Devil was also incarnated to the Egyptians as *Isis*, to the Greeks as *Aphrodite*, to the Phoenicians as *Tanet*, and to us today as *Gaia* and *Mother Earth*. All of these manifestations of the same Evil by a different name which involved then, and involves now, the human sacrifice of babies to the source of all Evil... the Devil!

The Devil stays the same but his names change to remain Politically Correct and "relevant" to Evil's contemporary audience. The name change is also necessary for Evil to hide, so that each successive generation does not associate the Evil of the prior generations to their own "modern" manifestation of Evil. The *Bible* calls Molech "the detestable idol of the Ammonites[343]". The name "Molech" means "to ascend to the throne", or as Lucifer is described in his attempt to take GOD's Throne in Evil's first salvo of *the Left's War Against GOD*, for which Satan boasted: "I will be like the most High"[344]! Satan, Lucifer, or the Devil, and the subsequent humans consumed with Evil, want to make themselves "like GOD" in rejection of, and in total rebellion *Against*, the One True GOD. It is the oldest form of Evil. It is *The Left's War Against GOD!*

---

[342] The *Holy Bible*: Ezekiel 16:2.
[343] The *Holy Bible*: 1 Kings 11:7.
[344] The *Holy Bible*: Isaiah 14:12-14.

Today the babies sacrificed to Satan at the Left's "modern" Sacrificial Temples, euphemistically named abortion "clinics", are no less tortured to death while they are ripped apart limb-by-limb, or born alive to be dissected while still alive for their body parts by the no less Evil priests and priestesses of the newest manifestation of the *Religion of the Left*! A stretch you say? Here are just a couple modern examples of Satan worship that occurs every day in the abortion Temples of the Left's *Evil Religion* like Planned Parenthood who sacrifice our babies to Satan.

Manifestations of the Left's Evil Religion include, but are certainly not limited to, Paganism, Neo-Paganism, Wicca[345], Witchcraft, New Age Eastern mysticism, Gaia/Mother Earth/goddess worship, Church of Satan, the Luciferian Society, the Lucis Trust, Feminism, and many, many others, including even some sham "Christian" organizations and denominations.

Abigail Seidman tells us of her firsthand experience from childhood into adulthood of abortion clinics that were wholly centered around Wiccan witchcraft and the sacramental sacrifice of the unborn babies to the female goddess commonly referred to as "The Goddess". "The Goddess" was represented around the abortion clinic by religious figurines from various religious traditions including Hindu, Greek, Roman, Babylonian, Egyptian, and other manifestations. The Goddess was also known to the staff as the "Great Dragon" which was said to be The Goddess' "truest form". (Remember that GOD's *Bible* identifies the Great Dragon as Lucifer, Satan, and the Devil!) In her descriptions Seidman details how all of the female workers in a Toledo, Ohio abortion clinic, where her mother was a nurse, wore clothes and jewelry that represented the Wiccan witchcraft and Satanic symbolism. When asked about abortion as religious worship in the clinic Seidman responded, "It is very real," she explained. "It

---

[345] The term "Wicca" first appeared in the Early English of an Anglo-Saxon scribe written as "Wyccan" which was the Old English spelling of "Witch". Wiccans today will try to convince you that it means "Wise One", however, remember "Wise One" is also a euphemism for Lucifer and the Gnostics who seek after "secret knowledge", the same "knowledge of good and evil" that Satan offered Eve in the Garden of Eden which Lucifer promised would make her "to be like GOD". This "secret knowledge" also put every human being on earth on the path to Hell.

can sound fantastical, but some go so far as to worship death goddesses like *Kali* and *Hecate* (manifestations of The Goddess) and consider abortion to be a form of *sacrifice*". "Sacrifice" *is a religious* ritual.

Ex-Satanist Zachary King was a high wizard in the World Church of Satan. King personally performed 146 abortions murdering unborn babies as part of a Satanic ritual. King explains:

> Now, I don't think I would have been okay with killing a baby outside of a woman's body, but knowing that I could kill as much as I wanted to if someone was inside the body … in Satanism, killing something or the death of something is the most effective way of getting your spell accomplished. As far as trying to get Satan's approval, to give you something that you want, killing something is the best way to go. Killing something is the ultimate offering to Satan, and *if you can kill an unborn, that is his ultimate goal.*[346]

King describes the first satanic abortion ritual in which he was involved:

> The first one I did was about 3 months before turning 15. It took place in a farm house that was surprisingly more sterile than many of the other abortion clinics I had done abortions in. There was an abortion doctor and an abortion nurse. There was a woman in stirrups about to have a baby who was surrounded by 13 top members of our coven, which were all high priests and priestesses. I was inside the circle with the woman and the abortion doctor. All the adult members of my coven were there. There were several women kneeling on the floor, swaying back and forth chanting "our body and ourselves" over and over again. Off to the side were several male members of our coven all chanting and praying. The ritual started at 11:45 at night, and the spell began at midnight,

---

[346] Hichborn, Michael; Lepanto Institute; *Former Satanist: "I Performed Satanic Rituals Inside Abortion Clinics"*; 2015-08-18.

which is the witching hour, and the actual death of the child happened at 3:00 am, which is called the devil's hour.

My whole role in all of this was to insert the scalpel. I didn't necessarily have to do the actual killing ... what was important was that I get blood on my hands. So, I had to get somebody's blood on my hands, whether the woman's or the baby's, and then the doctor finishes out the procedure. In that particular one, which was probably one of the more heinous abortions I had ever done, the doctor reached in, ripped the baby out and threw it onto the floor where these women were swaying. The women looked like they were possessed, and when the doctor threw the baby out to them, they cannibalized the baby.[347]

Do you feel the terror of Evil yet? If this description does not make your blood run cold and prompt you to *action* against abortion you are inhuman and already in full possession of Evil!

King estimates that he performed over 20 similar Satanic ritual abortions in a "high profile abortion facility". The term "high profile abortion facility" was used to substitute for "Planned Parenthood abortion facility". The redaction was done in its printed form out of fear of lawsuits by the abortion giant.

When King was asked the question: "Would you say that [high profile abortion facilities] attract members of the occult because of the opportunity to perform ritual abortions?" King responded:

I would say that yes, that is absolutely a true statement. You know, you've got the people that belong to NOW [the National Organization of Women], and a lot of those people are *wiccan*, and the wiccans, though they profess to have a stance for the preservation of life, they're allowed to "smite" or "smote" anyone who goes against them in any way, which is to say that they're allowed to destroy them by any means necessary,

---

[347] Hichborn, Michael; Lepanto Institute; *Former Satanist: "I Performed Satanic Rituals Inside Abortion Clinics"*; 2015-08-18.

which is through magick (sic) for them. For instance, as Christians, we pray for their conversion. Well, they see that as open season on Christians. They as well see the female figure, the woman, like *Mother Earth*, or *Gaia*. So, they have this womanly figure that they worship and they imagine that she as she is *the goddess*, a child takes away from that, and so *abortion is a satanic sacrament* so to speak.[348] (emphasis added)

Another interviewer of King notes:

[King] said he would show up and change into his wizard's robe to perform the incantations. King explained that he wore the same type of wizard's garb seen in a music video by female rocker Pink for her song, "Just Like a Pill." The video shows a wizard, dressed in black, his face painted pale and wearing a black top hat, reciting a spell behind the singer, as the scene then flips to simulated group sex. He said the women whose abortions he attended would get pregnant with the intent of killing their unborn baby as a *sacrifice to Satan*. "So the women knew why I was there," King said. "*They know there's a satanic ritual going on.*[349]

King is not alone in his outing of the Satanic *religious* nature of abortion, but King certainly stands as a prime case-in-point that abortion is a *religious* ritual of Evil. There are literally dozens of witnesses who have come out of the shadows to shine a light on the Evil that lurks behind abortion. While not every abortionist knows of the specific Satanic *religious* nature of abortions, every abortionist certainly knows the Evil nature involved in abortion. It is *impossible* to murder babies, born or unborn, and not see the Evil nature of abortion! Impossible! In GOD's eyes there is no excuse for ignorance

---

[348] Hichborn, Michael; Lepanto Institute; *Former Satanist: "I Performed Satanic Rituals Inside Abortion Clinics"*; 2015-08-18.
[349] Hohmann, Leo; WND.com; *Ex-Satanist: Babies Ritually Aborted for Devil*; August 24th, 2015.

of Evil, and no excuse before GOD for that ignorance when Evil is done[350], especially to innocent babies[351]!

A newsletter published by the National Abortion Federation lets us see into the heart of false "Christianity" and its sheep's clothing imitation and infiltration of true Christianity. The National Abortion Federation newsletter provides an account of their 1985 national convention. One of the featured speakers was Carter Heyward, an ordained Episcopal "priest", who had been active for years in the Feminist Movement. Heyward is quoted: "If women were in charge, abortion would be a *sacrament*, an occasion of deep and serious and *sacred* meaning". These bastard Feminist "Christian" pretenders are preaching that murdering babies is a *religious* "sacrament" and "sacred", but as we have seen this fundamentally contradicts GOD and is attributable only to Satanic worship rites! Heard enough yet? There's more… much more.

Steve Beard of *World Magazine* exposes the connection between false "Christian" religious organizations and the Evil of abortion:

> "One of the **Religious Left's** premier organizations is the **Religious Coalition for Abortion Rights**. RCAR is a hardline supporter of federally funded abortions and the Freedom of Choice Act. RCAR represents groups of *liberal* [Leftist Anti-GOD] Presbyterians, Episcopalians, Lutherans, Brethren, Moravians, Jews, Humanists, and Unitarians".[352] (emphasis and clarifications added)

Here is a quote from a now defunct Feminist/Leftist *Ms. Magazine* that describes the Satanic Leftist Religion relationship between the Feminism Movement, the occult, and abortion:

> "The feminist *spirituality* movement began to emerge in the mid-1970s and has become one of the largest submovements

---

[350] The *Holy Bible*: Leviticus 4:13; 5:17-18; Luke 12:48.
[351] The *Holy Bible*: Ezekiel 16:36-38, 23:45.
[352] Beard, Steve; World Magazine; May 22, 1993.

(sic) within feminism. It's amorphous, blending in a surprisingly smooth amalgam *radical feminism, pacifism, witchcraft, Eastern mysticism, goddess worship, animism, psychic healing, and a variety of practices normally associated with 'fortune-telling'.* It exists nationwide and takes the form of large, daylong workshops, small *meditation* groups, and even [witches] *covens* that meet to work *spells* and do [religious] *rituals* under the full moon. But to the women in *feminist spirituality*, *witchcraft* had even a more fundamental meaning. It is a woman's *religion*, *vilified by patriarchal Christianity*, and now, finally, reclaimed"[353]. (emphasis added)

In this same issue of *Ms. Magazine* there was "much space" devoted to the devil gods *Isis* and *Aphrodite* who are specifically associated with abortion and the infant sacrificial rites of Satan worship! GOD passed judgement on His own people Israel and subsequently destroyed Israel as a nation in large part because of abortion and its inseparable aspect of sacrifice to Satan. GOD said:

"Moreover thou hast taken thy sons and thy daughters, **whom thou hast borne unto me**, and these hast thou *sacrificed* unto them to be devoured. Is this of thy whoredoms a small matter, That thou hast *slain* **my children**, and *delivered them to cause them to pass through the fire* for them? And in all thine abominations and thy whoredoms thou hast not remembered the days of thy youth, when thou wast naked and bare, and wast **polluted in thy blood**. And it came to pass after all thy wickedness, (**woe, woe unto thee! saith the LORD GOD;**)"[354]

GOD considers *all* children His own, "my children", and it is the parents' absolute duty before GOD Almighty to raise and protect them as such. In the *Bible* "abominations" are specifically *devil* (Greek: demon) associated sins *Against GOD*. The judgement for parents who violate this sacred responsibility that GOD Himself pronounces to be:

---

[353] Lindsey, Karen; *Ms. Magazine*, December 1985, p.38.
[354] The *Holy Bible*: Ezekiel 16:20.

"**woe, woe unto thee! saith the LORD GOD**"! Abortion Cathedrals are the Temples of the Left in America today devoted and ordained to the Left's *Evil Religion* with their infant sacrifices with all of Abortion's historically associated horrors! America if it does not repent of the Evil of abortion will, like Israel, GOD's chosen people, pay the ultimate price of judgement and destruction from GOD! How's "a woman's right to choose" sounding now?

On March 7, 2015 in Selma, Alabama Obama admiringly quoted Langston Hughes: "We are the people Langston Hughes wrote of, who 'build our **temples** for tomorrow, strong as we know how.'" This phrase by Hughes in 1926, "We build our temples for tomorrow, strong as we know how", was offensive to many in the black community and particularly the black Christian ministers who recognized the anti-Christian bigotry[355]. The scholar Anthony Pinn has noted that Hughes was a humanist "**critical of belief in God**". Not coincidently, in 1961 the United States Supreme Court ruled in *Torcaso v. Watkins* that secular *Humanism is a Religion*! Pinn has found that such writers are sometimes ignored in the narrative of American history that chiefly credits the civil rights movement to the work of affiliated Christian people[356]. Hughes was a self-declared "radical Socialist". Hughes, like many black writers and artists of his time, was drawn to the promise of Communism and Hughes's poetry was frequently published in the CPUSA (Communist Party of America) newspaper[357]. By associating himself with Hughes, Obama clearly demonstrates that he is an avowed "anti-Christian" as well as a "radical Socialist".

Hughes signed a 1938 statement supporting Joseph Stalin's purges[358] by which Stalin, the Communist leader of the Soviet Union, murdered all those who opposed his tyrannical dictatorship. Stalin's purges, reminiscent of David Goldman's quote "And if we try to force fallible humans to live in an earthly paradise, ultimately we shall have to kill

---

[355] Roessel, David and Rampersad, Arnold; *Poetry for Young People: Langston Hughes*; 2006; pg. 6.
[356] Wikipedia; Langston Hughes; accessed 3/8/2015.
[357] Wikipedia; Langston Hughes; accessed 3/8/2015.
[358] Wikipedia; Langston Hughes; accessed 3/8/2015.

them all for their failings", was the subject of Robert Conquest's 1968 book *The Great Terror*, whose title was inspired by the French Revolution's *Reign of Terror*, the *Terror* which targeted every Christian in France for extermination. Again Obama intentionally associates himself with Hughes who was in total support of Stalin's campaign of mass murder against all who opposed his Leftist designs. Obama as well as the Left do have their own *Religion*, the *Religion of the Left*, with their own "temples", the *Religion* which is homicidally anti-Christian! This is the Hughes who Obama pays homage to!

Margaret Sanger, founder of Planned Parenthood, promoted what she termed "the ***religion*** of birth control"[359].

As Igra explains in *Germany's National Vice*, "the criminals who wreaked such astounding horrors on innocent civilian populations were not acting as soldiers drunk with the fury of battle, nor as patriotic fanatics, but as chosen instruments of a ***satanic religion*** to the service of which they had been dedicated by the systematic teaching and practice of unnatural vice [homosexuality]" (Igra: 94)[360].

The emasculation of America is intrinsically tied to the homosexual and the Feminist agenda. The *Bible* is innately a patristic oriented document. That is a male/masculine headed hierarchy where men bear the responsibility before GOD for the family and society. GOD refers to Himself as a *male* Person hundreds of times in His Word the *Holy Bible*. The Feminist, and Feminist-influenced, have even gone as far as rewriting blasphemous "new versions" of the "bible" to remove all references to GOD as a *male* Person and all mandates in the Scriptures that specifically identify "the head of the woman is the man"[361]. The Feminist movement began in the Garden of Eden when Eve rebelled *Against GOD*, and specifically Eve rebelled against Adam her husband as her GOD-ordained head. The Feminist Movement is a direct contradiction to, and Attack upon GOD!

---

[359] Goldberg, Jonah; nationalreview.com/article/224136; June 24, 2008.
[360] Lively, Scott and Abrams, Kevin; *The Pink Swastika: Homosexuality in the Nazi Party*; pg. 11.
[361] The *Holy Bible*: 1 Corinthians 11:3.

The problem for the Left is that the vast majority of Americans instinctually understand and believe the patriarchal necessity of a free and working family and society. This is why the Left must rely on iron fisted implementations of the homosexual and Feminist Movement agendas. It is the craft of the Leftist institutions to force compliance to the Leftist Utopian nightmare and overturn the will and votes of the people, overturn the US Constitution, and spit in the face of GOD! The Leftist public education machine is the frontline in indoctrinating the youth to accept what their parents were first forced to accept through imperialistic fiat. Remember that it is a form of insanity to attempt to force the mind to accept what it knows to be fundamentally wrong![362]

Feminism is another form of Pagan *religion* whose manifestations include Wicca (Witchcraft as devil worship) and Mother Earth worship, among many others. In Feminism the sects of Wicca and *Gaia*, or Mother Earth, worship are inextricably linked with a common foundation in ancient Hinduism. Feminism is an ancient Pagan Religion whose roots are firmly planted in Hinduism and whose primary female "god" is the six armed *Kāli*, not coincidently also worshipped in Hinduism as the "mother goddess"[363]. *Gaia* is in fact the later Greek manifestation of *Kāli*, the "mother goddess". As such Feminism in its many manifestations is a form of *Gaia* worship which is diametrically opposed to Christianity:

> "God is going to change, We women...will change the world so much that He won't fit anymore." -Naomi Goldenberg in *Changing of the Gods: Feminism and the End of Traditional Religions*[364]

Notice that Feminists are not opposed to "religion" *per se*, but to "traditional religions" referring primarily to the different Christian denominations.

---

[362] See the chapter: *The Left Is a RELIGION!* and the discussion on neurosis and insanity.
[363] Different sects of Hinduism call this goddess by different names including *Parvati* and *Durga*.
[364] Huff, Jim; WRS Journal 8/1; *Environmentalism & The Worship Of "Mother Earth"*; February 2001; pgs. 24-26.

Über-Leftist Al Gore agrees with the militant Feminist leadership and blames the falling away from this Pagan god *Gaia* on the religiously intolerant Christians:

> "The last vestige of organized goddess worship was eliminated by Christianity…"[365].

In his book *Earth In The Balance*, Gore makes some interesting admissions and deifies "Mother Earth" whom Gore names as the ancient Pagan Greek goddess *"Gaia"*:

> **"*Our religious* heritage** is based on a single earth goddess (Mother Gaia) who is assumed to be the fountain of all life. . . All men have a god within. Each man has a god within because creation is god. Nature in its fullness is god." (emphasis and clarification added)

Gore suggests that in the name of the Left's *Religion* of Evil much of the earth's human population would need to be sacrificed (Read Genocide on a global level!) in order to "cleanse" the earth for thousands of years of offense against Mother Earth, or *Gaia*:

> "[*Gaia*] has been seriously 'wounded' by the expansion of human civilization, and now there must come a universal atonement for these many millennia of grief on 'her' part" through an event or process they call 'cleansing'.

How horrifying is that?! Gore is calling for the outright murder of hundreds of millions of people in the name of the *Religion of the Left*!!!

Gore further identifies the Left's Pagan worship as the *Religion* on which the fate of mankind rests:

---

[365] Gore, Al; *Earth in the Balance: Forging a New Common Purpose*; Routledge, Sep 13, 2013; pg. 260.

"The fate of mankind, as well as *religion*, depends on the emergence of *a new faith* in the future. *__Armed__ with such a faith*, we might find it possible to resanctify the earth". (emphasis added)

You caught that right?! The term "armed" is specific to a use of force!

In the name of the Left's Religion and as an excuse to suspend freedom in the West, James Lovelock, known as founder of "'Gaia' concept" suggests:

"I have a feeling that **climate change may be an issue as severe as a __war__**. It may be necessary to put democracy on hold for a while". (emphasis added)

Everything ultimately is either sanctioned by the *Religion of the Left* or is held accountable or in contempt according to the mandates of the *Religion of the Left*. Political Correctness is *political enforcement* of the Left's *Religion*! This is the Fight in *The Left's War Against GOD* and the Right!

For instance, the Left sees taxes as "charitable contributions" to the *Religion* of the Left in its effort to build its imagined Leftist Utopian Paradise. All other charitable contributions, especially to Christianity, are viewed as an anathema and in competition to funding the *Left's Religion*!

All manifestations of the Leftist *religious* agenda are mobilized through political agendas which the Left steps in to impose by overwhelming force! Global Warming is but another prime example. (Just by the mere fact that Global Warming was just capitalized and few reading it noticed its significance as an accepted Leftist concept shows how far the Left has gone in forcing acceptance of their *religious* views.) Dr. Richard Lindzen, an American atmospheric physicist, of the Massachusetts Institute of Technology is a leading international expert on "Climate Change", the new *Bait and Switch* name for "Global Warming":

> *"Global Warming has become a **religion**…* A surprisingly large number of people seem to have concluded that all that gives meaning to their lives is the belief that they are saving the planet by paying attention to their carbon footprint[366]" (emphasis added)

To tie even the seemingly unrelated Leftist *Religious* concepts of Global Warming/Climate Change and Taxation together let's refer again to the Leftist and secular scientist Dr. Richard Lindzen:

> "Global warming, climate change, all these things are just a dream come true for politicians. The opportunities for taxation, for policies, for control, for crony capitalism are just immense, you can see their eyes bulge[367]"

In an April 30, 2012 *New York Times* article in response to Lindzen's stand against the existence of "manmade climate change" fellow MIT scientist Kerry A. Emanuel argued that the whole issue of Global Warming/Climate Change for the Left was based on "political implications". Politics and religion cannot be separated and the Left understands and acts upon it with missional zealotry. The Left wants to keep Americans ignorant of the fact of this inseparability as a means to implement the Left's *Religion* through its politically mandated iron fisted domination!

John Howard, former prime minister of Australia, used a lecture in London recently to denounce people who in his view exaggerate the certainty of global warming and demand urgent efforts to mitigate it. His talk was called "*One **Religion** is Enough*" and he explained that:

> *I chose the…title largely in reaction to the sanctimonious tone employed by so many of those who advocate substantial and costly responses to what they see as irrefutable evidence that*

---

[366] Bastasch, Michael; dailycaller.com; *MIT professor: global warming is a 'religion'*; 08/29/2013.
[367] CBS News Boston; *MIT Professor Urging Climate Change Activists To 'Slow Down'*; January 14, 2014.

> *the world's climate faces catastrophe...To them the cause has become **a substitute religion**.[368]* (emphasis added)

Mr. Howard was, in a sense, preaching to the converted. He was addressing the Global Warming Policy Foundation, a think-tank whose founder Nigel Lawson—a former British chancellor—has made an equally negative correlation between Climate Change concern and faith. "Global warming is a **new religion** and blasphemy against that **religion** is not a laughing matter," Lord Lawson has said, adding that "there is a great gap in Europe with the decline of any real belief in Marxism and any real belief in Christianity. This has filled the [religious] vacuum".[369] (emphasis added)

Even a secularist like Evan Sayet can recognize the inherent problem of Evil in the Left's agenda and thought pattern. Sayet author of *KinderGarden Of Eden: How the Modern Liberal Thinks*[370] asks the inevitable question, "Why... The Modern Liberal will invariably side with **evil over good**, **wrong over right**, and the behaviors that lead to failure over those that lead to success"[371]? (Emphasis added)

Commenting in January 2017 on Obama's farewell speech George Stephanopoulos said the speech was a "***sermon** on democracy*"! Not to be outdone and a little over two months after she cried on Election Night, Martha Raddatz added "He was ***preaching*** to the choir in that room".

Unfortunately not every Conservative understands the connection between Evil and an absolute historical *Evil Religion*. The same is true of the Left's redefinition of "secular" in advancing their age-old *Religion of Evil*:

---

[368] B.C.; The Economist online; Global Warming and Religion, Faith Upon the Earth; November 6, 2013.
[369] B.C.; The Economist online; *Global Warming and Religion, Faith Upon the Earth*; November 6, 2013.
[370] Sayet, Evan; *KinderGarden Of Eden*: How the Modern Liberal Thinks; 2012.
[371] Sayet, Evan; *Regurgitating the Apple: How Modern Liberals "Think"*; Lecture #1020 on Political Thought, The Heritage Foundation; May 10, 2007.

"**Leftism**, though secular, **must be understood as a** *religion* (which is why I have begun capitalizing it). The Leftist value system's hold on its adherents is as strong as the hold Christianity, Judaism, and Islam have on theirs.[372]" (emphasis added)

Dennis Prager here understands the religious nature but not the fact that *The Religion of the Left IS* the *Religion of Evil* as practiced through the varied Pagan manifestations of Evil throughout history.

Not everyone is initiated, however, into the Evil aspects of the Left's *Religion*. These are the Left's and Evil's "useful idiots" to which Leftist, murderous Soviet dictator Vladimir Lenin referred. The "useful idiots" of the Left who work for the Leftist Revolution, but are clueless as to the empowerment of Evil behind the scenes. Let's look at it from a strictly secular right point of view:

"...the Modern Liberal looks back on 50,000 years, 100,000 years of human civilization, and knows only one thing for sure: that none of the ideas that mankind has come up with--none of the religions, none of the philosophies, none of the ideologies, none of the forms of government--have succeeded in creating a world devoid of war, poverty, crime, and injustice. So they're convinced that since all of these ideas of man have proved to be wrong, the real cause of war, poverty, crime, and injustice must be found--can only be found--in **the attempt to be right**.

If nobody ever thought they were right, what would we disagree about? If we didn't disagree, surely we wouldn't fight. If we didn't fight, of course we wouldn't go to war. Without war, there would be no poverty; without poverty, there would be no crime; without crime, there would be no injustice. **It's a utopian vision, and all that's required to usher in this utopia is the rejection of all fact, reason, evidence, logic, truth, morality, and decency**--all the tools that

---

[372] Prager, Dennis; National Review online; *Leftism, The Religion*; March 30, 2010.

you and I use in our attempts to be better people, to make the world more right by trying to be right, by siding with right, by recognizing what is right and moving toward it.

What you have is people who think that the best way to eliminate rational thought, the best way to eliminate the attempt to be right, is to work always to prove that right isn't right and to prove that wrong isn't wrong. You see this in John Lennon's song "Imagine": "Imagine there's no countries." Not "imagine" great countries, not "imagine" defeat the Nazis, but "imagine no religions", and the key line is imagine a time when anything and everything that mankind values is devalued to the point where there's nothing left to kill or die for.

In the meantime, everything that they teach in our schools, everything they make into movies, the messages of the movies, the TV shows, the newspaper stories that they pick and how they spin them have but one criterion for truth, beauty, honesty, etc., and that is: Does it tear down what is good and elevate what is evil? Does it tear down what is right and elevate what is wrong? Does it tear down the behaviors that lead to success and elevate the ones that lead to failure so that there is nothing left to believe in?"·

So the mindless foot soldier, which is what I call the non-elite, will support the elite's blueprint for utopia, will side with evil over good, wrong over right, and the behaviors that lead to failure over those that lead to success, out of a sense of justice. As I said at the beginning, they're not evil. It's just a mindless acceptance without any true Socratic desire to talk about the real consequences. It's meaningless to them, and it's why John Lennon said utopia was all the people living for today[373]. (emphasis added)

---

[373] Sayet, Evan; *Regurgitating the Apple: How Modern Liberals "Think"*; Lecture #1020 on Political Thought, The Heritage Foundation; May 10, 2007.

The ranks of the "mindless foot soldier" is the "useful idiots" to which Vladimir Lenin referred. If the Left could just persuade or coerce all people to just not think, then all would be possible! This is what Hillary Rodham-Clinton referred to as **"Let us be willing to remold society by <u>redefining what it means to be a human being</u>"**!

James Kalb makes this astute statement about the Left's deception of *Bait and Switch* concerning the supposed "separation of Church and State" *Lie* and the Left's replacement of Christianity with the Left's own *Religion*:

> Where absolute separation between government and religion is demanded, the demand should be recognized as a screen *for the suppression of one [religion] in favor of another that also functions as a **religion***[374]. (emphasis added)

The politics of all nations must have some moral, that is *religious*, fixture on which to determine and guide the laws of that nation. These guiding forces are by definition a *"religion"*. Traditionally America's moral lynchpin has always been directly tied to the *Bible* of Christianity and Judaism. All other governments have either used the same foundations or some form of man-made religion. Kalb goes on to elaborate:

> **"The fundamental question of politics is which *religion* shall be established.** Authority must be based on a common understanding of principles superior to the human will that are rooted in the nature of things. To the extent it tries to be principled [Leftism] itself cannot help but answer such questions. In spite of claims of neutrality, American law today embodies a **religious** understanding. It excludes from public life views that take transcendent religion seriously, in substance treating them as false. It cannot get by without a conception of the world and the source of moral obligation, however, and it finds both in man the measure. It makes

---

[374] Kalb, James; *The Tyranny of Liberalism: Understanding and Overcoming Administered Freedom, Inquisitorial Tolerance, and Equality by Command*; 2008; pg. 98.

human genius the principle of creation and individual will the source of value. **Such a [Leftist] outlook is *religious*, the *religion* of man as creator and judge of all things.** As the response to ultimate concerns that silently motivates our public order it is our **established religion**"[375]. (emphasis and clarification added)

There are three kinds of unintelligent people: the ignorant, the stupid, and the insane. The ignorant are those who have either chosen to be uninformed or have lacked the opportunity for specific knowledge, the stupid are those who lack the ability to be informed (e.g. mentally retarded, commonly called "idiots"), and the insane are those whose mind has been taken over by an extraterrestrial being, which is Biblically[376] more accurately referred to as "demonic insanity"[377]. Insanity is a surrender of the mind to Evil. (P.S. In the very least sense: ***Evil makes you stupid!***[378])

The *Religion of the Left* can only be described as *INSANE!*[379] Their *Religion* is unreasonable, based totally on *Lies!*, founded in hatred, and is self-deceptive. That *is* the very definition of *insanity!* Recall our earlier discussion of the Left's insanity: "Leftism is a form of mental insanity! Think that is harsh? Webster's Dictionary tells us that mental insanity is the inability to reason, literally a person who is "unreasonable". There is nothing reasonable about the Left. As we have seen all Leftist doctrine is based on destruction, chaos, unrestrained emotion, hatred for GOD and GOD's people, or opposition

---

[375] Kalb, James; Modern Age Quarterly; *The Tyranny of Liberalism: The Iron Heel of Freedom*; Summer 2000.

[376] E.g. *The Holy Bible*: Lk 8:35; Rom 1:28; 2 Tim 1:7.

[377] The insane have surrendered their mind to an otherworldly being. The surrender can be involuntarily through the parents in youth or even in the womb. The surrender can be unintentional by actions which the *Bible* warns against but which the offender may be unaware. The Left would have us *believe*, a religious term, that varying degrees of insanity are nothing more than chemical imbalances in the brain and can be treated with chemicals prescribed through Leftist psychiatrists. However the best that can be hoped for in this scenario is for a covering over of symptoms, and at worst a slobbering unresponsive patient. Medication cannot deal with the underlying demonic influence. Only the Biblically prescribed countermeasures and precautions can effectively deal with and prevent insanity.

[378] *The Holy Bible*: Psalms 107:17

[379] For the discussion of Insanity and the Left see also the chapter: *Emotion Based Politics.*

to GOD's laws in restraint of the individual's pet sins". This set of behaviors can only be described as *insanity*.

A claim of Atheism, a favorite position of many Leftists in avoiding any appearance of "religion", can lead to self-delusion and/or *neurosis*. Acclaimed *secular* psychologist and psychotherapist Rollo May describes the neurotic effects of Atheism this way:

> I have been startled by the fact that practically every genuine atheist with whom I have dealt has exhibited unmistakable **neurotic** tendencies.[380] (emphasis added)

You simply cannot tell your mind to believe something that the mind instinctively knows is not true. The natural result of a successful self-deception is *neurosis*. Neurosis is a form of *insanity*! A point that author Michael Savage so astutely points out by the title of his book *Liberalism is a Mental Disorder*!

Ann Coulter in her book *Liberal Lies About the American Right* also hits the nail on the head:

> "Much of the left's hate speech bears greater similarity to a **psychological disorder** than to standard political discourse. The hatred is blinding, producing logical contradictions that would be impossible to sustain were it not for the central element faith plays in the left's new religion. The basic tenet of their faith is this: Maybe they were wrong on facts and policies, but they are good and conservatives are evil"[381]. (emphasis added)

Nelson Price in his book *The Emmanuel Factor*[382] tells of how Brown Trucking Company in Atlanta, Georgia conducted lie detector tests on every employee over the course of years and asked every applicant, over 15,000 in total, "Do you believe in God?". Without exception

---

[380] May, Rollo, *The Art of Counseling*; NY: Abingdon, 1967; p. 215.
[381] Coulter, Ann; *Slander: Liberal Lies About the American Right*; 2003; pg. 199.
[382] Price, Nelson L.; *The Emmanuel Factor*; Broadman Press, 1987.

EVERY one of those who answered that "No" they did not believe in God were shown by the polygraph results to be lying on that question! *The truth is that there literally is no such thing as an Atheist!* The self-claimed "Atheist" simply wants to dismiss in his mind any responsibility from sin *Against GOD* and continue to commit offenses that would otherwise make him feel responsible before GOD. This is self-delusion and an ironic turnabout on the self-avowed, and self-deluded, Atheist Richard Dawkins's *The God Delusion.* Self-delusion is a form of insanity!

Remember Maslow's warning that those people not properly prepared for the Leftist religious "transcendence", the highest point of self-actualization of which Maslow preached, risked that "a peak experience could, he warned, lead to *insanity*"! The Left's *Religion* should be required to come with warning labels!

Saul Alinsky, the godfather of the Left, admits that the Leftist radical is himself by definition *insane...* a schizophrenic:

> "For the real radical, doing 'his thing' is to do the social thing, for and with people. In a world where everything is so interrelated that one feels helpless to know where or how to grab hold and act, defeat sets in; for years there have been people who've found society too overwhelming and have withdrawn, concentrated on 'doing their own thing.' Generally we have **put them into mental hospitals** and diagnosed them as *schizophrenics*. If the real radical finds that having long hair sets up *psychological* barriers to communication and organization, he cuts his hair".[383] (emphasis added)

Schizophrenia is a form of mental insanity.[384] Schizophrenia is not generally a disease of the physical mind, but an abnormal *spiritual* condition of which the brain function is controlled in some part by internal demonic voices that often manifest as "alternate

---

[383] *Rules For Radicals*; Prologue.
[384] Mayo Clinic defines *schizophrenia* as: A brain disorder in which people interpret reality abnormally.

personalities". There may be some exception to this rule but, with my experience with hundreds of individuals, I have yet to encounter an exception in real life. This also explains those who have false memories of a "previous life". They are simply seeing falsely implanted "memories" from an Evil source leading the victim to conclude that from "personal experience" that reincarnation is real and the GOD of the *Bible* therefore cannot be true. The Devil goes to great lengths to obscure his existence and himself as the source of Evil and especially Evil's inevitable *insane* consequences upon mankind both in this world and Eternity to follow.

Evil ties together all of the questions that seem to be without answers in our War of GOOD Against the Left, and *The Left's War Against GOD*. Our recognition of the Left's *Religion of Evil* pulls back the veil and answers *all* the questions. For this reason I will, repeat here the three opening paragraphs from the chapter *Understanding The Two Faces of The Enemy*:

> The Right in America has been baffled by the unmitigated success of the Left's *War* Against the Right. Innumerable explanations have been posited for the Left's seemingly unexplainable success, but none have adequately, nor nearly, explained nor accounted for this phenomena of the Left's success. An honest and all-encompassing assessment of the *War* is *absolutely* necessary in order to confront and overcome the unseen assaults of the Left Against the Right. The Right has been continually blindsided by the bludgeoning blows from an unseen fist. The Right staggers around stupefied and has no idea what has hit them. The blows of the Left are relentless and without mercy. The Left, whether the Right realizes it or not, is simply waging a two-front *War*. One front is visible and the other front is invisible. Defeat is guaranteed when one faces two enemies, of which only one is seen and recognized, because the unseen source of the assaults cannot be actively defended against nor can the *War* even be waged on that front! This is where the Right stands today, completely undefended on one front of a two-front *War*!

It has never been so clear that this *War* cannot be understood by the surface definitions of simply "Left Against Right" or "Liberal Against Conservative", but must also be seen as "Evil *Against GOD*"! The Left's unseen spiritual presence of Evil is the power behind the Left and its second front in this *War*. This second front is the hidden "religious" aspect of the Left's wildly successful *War* strategies against the Right. Again we are reminded again of the line of the French poet Charles Baudelaire "the finest trick of the devil is to persuade you that he does not exist". If we cannot see the invisible Enemy, Evil incarnate, the Devil, behind our visible enemy for who and what he really is, then we are powerless to resist and defend against Evil's strategies. The Right has attempted to Fight this *War* as if Evil "does not really exist". This has been the deadliest of mistakes and miscalculations of the Right in Battling Against *The Left's War Against GOD!*

The *Bible* tells us that "though we walk in the flesh, we do not *war* after the flesh"[385], but the *War* is against demonic "powers, against the rulers of the darkness of this world, *against **spiritual** wickedness* in high places". The true *War* is on the "religious", *spiritual* level and spills over into the second arena of the physical world of *politics*. The Left has been Fighting the spiritual prong of this *War* all along, while the Right has been humiliated into surrender on this front. After all, the Left reminds us, what idiot believes in an *unseen* Evil power; only the dim-witted and superstitious imbecile believes in the Devil. We *must* carry on the Fight on both the *physical* and *spiritual*, the *seen* and the *unseen* fronts, ever considering that the true *power* of Evil comes from the *unseen*, *spiritual* realm. If we neglect, or deny, the *spiritual* side of the *War*, the Battle for America will be lost.

As a final thought, we must remember that *Evil is,* in and of itself, *a Religion!* Not many people stop to fully consider this. Following the Evil of the Left, is the worship of Evil. The *Religion of Evil* worships

---

[385] The *Holy Bible:* 2 Corinthians 10:3 (emphasis added).

Evil itself through a nearly endless variety of methods and icons. While Right has but one GOD, Evil has myriad gods, which the *Bible* calls devils, to worship: lust (take from those that have and give to those who don't), *Lies* (the trade of the Left), adultery (free love), gluttony, self-indulgence (me first), stealing (redistribution of wealth), murder (abortion and assisted suicide), *ad nauseam*. Jesus says "I am the only way". Evil says you can go any way with their *Religion of Evil* with thousands of possibilities... except of course that Way of Jesus.

Leftism is an inherently Evil **Religious** system. The choice then becomes which religious system will each of us choose... GOD or the Left!

16. LEGISLATING MORALITY

Chapter 16

(Ps 94:20)   "The throne of iniquity...which frameth mischief by a law"

The Left who for years has been screaming at the top of their lungs that it is unconscionable to attempt to "legislate morality" has in fact been behind the scenes doing just that! The Left uses cleverly disguised sayings under the guise of "rights" to appear to offer what is presented as good when in fact they are delivering enslavement! (Tolerance; special rights; workers' rights; women's rights/equal rights; gay rights; abortion rights; the right to universal healthcare; human rights; minority rights; even animal rights!) Rights are not given by man, but by GOD alone as testified to in the American Declaration of Independence:

> "We hold these truths to be self-evident, that all men are created equal, that *they are **endowed by their Creator** with **certain unalienable Rights***, that among these are Life, Liberty and the pursuit of Happiness.--That to secure ***these rights***, Governments are instituted among Men, deriving their just powers from the consent of the governed"

The very core beliefs which led America to the *Declaration of Independence* was that a tyrannical dictator King George III of England had deprived the Americans of their GOD given Rights and substituting them with his manmade corruptions posing as rights. The Left's *War Against GOD* is a substitution of GOD's inalienable Rights for man's evil counterfeit "rights" of the subjugated.

America was founded as a *Christian* Nation:

Offenses against religion and morality strikes at the root of moral obligation, and weakens the security of the social ties that bind America together. This First Amendment declaration never meant to withdraw religion. And with it the sanctions of moral and social obligation from all consideration and notice of the law. *People v. Ruggles* 8 Johns. R. 290 N.Y. 1811

Whatever strikes at the root of Christianity tends manifestly to the dissolution of civil government, because it tends to corrupt the morals of the people, and to destroy good order. *People v. Ruggles* 8 Johns. R. 290 N.Y. 1811

The destruction of morality renders the power of the government invalid. *The Commonwealth v Sharpless*, 2 Serg & R. 91 (Sup. Ct. Penn. 1815)

A malicious intention, to vilify the Christian religion and the scriptures, would prove a nursery of vice, a school of preparation to qualify young men for the gallows, and young women for the brothel, and there is not a skeptic of decent manners and good morals, who would not consider such a common nuisance and disgrace. *Updegraph v. Commonwealth*, 11 Serg. & Rawle 394 Pa. 1824

No free government now exists in the world, unless where Christianity is acknowledged, and is the religion of the country. Christianity is part of the common law. Its foundations are broad and strong and deep. It is the purest system of morality and only stable support of all human laws. *Updegraph v. Commonwealth*, 11 Serg. & Rawle 394 Pa. 1824

Christianity has reference to the principles of right and wrong; It is the foundation of those morals and manners upon which our society is formed; it is their basis. Remove this and they would fall. Morality has grown upon the basis of Christianity. *Charleston v. Benjamin*, 2 Strob. 508 (Sup.Ct. SC 1846)

What constitutes the standard of "good morals"? Is it not Christianity? There Certainly is none other. Say that cannot be appealed to, and what would be good morals? The day of moral virtue in which we live would, in an instant, if that standard were abolished, lapse into the dark and murky night of pagan immorality. *Charleston v. Benjamin, 2 Strob. 508 (Sup.Ct. SC 1846)*

As we have already discussed in the last chapter *The Left Is A RELIGION*, the Left wants us to believe that they oppose *all* religion, but in fact the Left is merely substituting Evil for GOD and imposing their own *Religion* of Evil. The Left wants to be the one to impose its belief system, their *Religion of Evil*, on every person that they can subject under their control. Their rationalization is convoluted, deceiving, and self-serving.

The nature of the Left's *Religion* was personified on the May 22, 2008 *Ellen DeGeneres Show* where DeGeneres proceeded to lecture Senator John McCain as the Republican Presidential candidate how her beliefs on gay "marriage" were morally superior while offering no foundation whatsoever, other than because "she said so". Because McCain was not himself a Christian, nor a Conservative, McCain had no response other than "we will have to agree to disagree". McCain also had no Court of Higher Authority upon which to appeal other than his opinion which he felt, at best, was morally superior. The Left's moral battle is simply a battle of wills.

I watched in horror as McCain blew his opportunity to show DeGeneres that she had no "moral ground" to stand on and could only say that "gay marriage" was the "right thing to do". I wanted to scream: "By whose standards!?". McCain blew his opportunity. As an emotionally based point, McCain could have simply told DeGeneres that he was going to introduce legislation into the United States Senate that would legalize "marriage" of 12-year-old girls to older men. Of course DeGeneres would have come unglued! (and rightfully so) However, this conversation would have created a teachable moment. (Perhaps not for DeGeneres who by all appearances is lost and sold out to Evil, but certainly for the persuadable in her studio and TV audiences.) McCain could have then asked DeGeneres: "By what authority would you oppose legislation for forced marriage for 12-year-old girls?". The only response that DeGeneres could ever hope to respond would be some form of "it's just not right". To which

McCain could again pose the question: "By what authority would you oppose legislation for forced marriage for 12-year-old girls?".

Eventually McCain could have made the point that the question of "marriage" in DeGeneres' eyes, as well as that of *all* of the Left, was simply a matter of imposing their own *force*-of-will over that of the Right and all who opposed them. DeGeneres simply wanted to impose her own views on America to re-define "marriage" and *legislate* her own "morality". The Left always forces the Right through its *legislated morality* to accept the perversions of the Left. It is an implementation of an unmoored *Evil Religion* that has no set morals taking control over existing Christianity in America.

(This teachable moment could have been extended through a series of questions referring to eminent legislation, beginning subtly and progressing to the more seemingly absurd, allowing forced marriage to multiple men, all men through temple prostitution, etc., but the absurdity of DeGeneres's, and the Left's, point remains the same… with no fixed moral point of reference, there simply are no constraints to which the Left will not eventually count as "morally" out-of-bounds or "wrong". For example, after the "legalization" of homosexual "marriage" the Left is now in fact seeking to further re-define marriage as extending to polygamy and bestiality, and a renewed effort to legalize prostitution! The Left's perversion of GOD's morals has no "moral boundaries" except death and destruction as Evil seeks but to steal, kill, and destroy[386]. As Pandora's Box lid is pulled open further-and-further, the larger-and-larger the demons are which escape its restraint.)

Christianity has an eternal and unmovable standard anchored in GOD Himself. DeGeneres just wanted to implement her own invented, perverted, convoluted, deceiving, and self-serving "morals", subjugating those of the Right, Christianity, and GOD Himself. The hubris is glaring when watching from the outside. DeGeneres has no "moral ground" on which to stand. *Morals by definition are derived from GOD*, eternal and unalterable by men's selfish whims. It is only

---

[386] The *Holy Bible*: John 10:10.

from a "because I said so" ***force***-of-will which DeGeneres and the Left conspire to use the age-old Evil trick of the *Bait and Switch/Re-Name-Game* to substitute the Left's "morals" for America's foundational Christian morals. GOD Himself created, defined, and instituted marriage[387]. However, the Left, as empowered by Evil, wants to play "God" and redefine marriage to fit an Evil agenda! If you "re-define" marriage… then marriage is meaningless. When marriage can be re-defined at will… marriage is no longer marriage! Marriage effectively no longer exists for anyone! That of course is the underlying objective of the Left, to change the GOD-ordained definition of marriage to suit its own Evil desires in *the Left's War Against GOD!*

McCain blew his opportunity. At least that was my initial reaction. However later I realized that McCain had not blown his opportunity, but as a non-Christian, McCain had had no opportunity to begin with. McCain, as much as DeGeneres, was morally untethered from Christian values of Right and Wrong and therefore had no sense of absolute and unmovable moral laws. McCain simply had no foundation from which to argue because he had no unmovable religious convictions from which to be Right. He was simply bobbing in the water without any tethered religious mooring-lines to secure him! This is the dilemma in which so many who claim to be Right find themselves today.

This can be further exemplified in McCain's stand on abortion. McCain said that he was "Pro-Life". However, McCain in a 2012 Fox News *post-election* interview showed that his views on abortion, because they were *not* based in an unshakable set of Right morals, were not in his own mind worth fighting for, and certainly not worth possibly losing elections over:

> "As far as young women are concerned, absolutely, I don't think anybody like me — **I can state my position on abortion but, other than that, leave the issue alone**, when we are in the kind of economic situation and, frankly, national-security

---

[387] The *Holy Bible*: Genesis 2:20-24, Matthew 19:3–6, Ephesians 5:31.

situation that we're in… I would allow people to have those opinions and respect those opinions. **I'm proud of my pro-life position and record. But if someone disagrees with me, I respect your views**."

This statement certainly unmasks the convoluted, deceiving, self-serving, and dangerous nature of McCain's own "moderate"[388] views on abortion. If abortion is Evil, as McCain has advocated, how can anyone "respect" someone's Evil views and subsequent Evil consequences?! That is self-delusion! As we have seen previously… *self-delusion is insanity*! If as the *Bible* teaches life begins at conception, a view that McCain himself has stated, how can you simply state your view and then shut up so that no one is offended? If the life of the unborn child is at stake, to shut up would be complicit in infanticide… the murder of a baby! Because McCain's views, like most "moderates" and RINOs[389], are unfounded in an eternal and absolute sense of Right and Wrong, they bob listlessly on the sea of uncertainty. We must throw off the untethered "moderates" and replace them with a new generation of people with an unshakable and innate sense of Right.

The Left demands that the Right has no "right" to "force" their morality on anyone, yet this is exactly what the Left is doing in *legislating their morality* and *forcing* their *morality* on *everyone*! The Left is legislating their morality every day as they substitute the Left's corrupt morality for the established Christian morality. If you disagree with their morality they attack, humiliate, imprison, and bankrupt you, in an attempt to destroy anyone daring to oppose their agenda. If you do not want to photograph their homosexual "wedding" because of your Christian beliefs, they sue you in court in New Mexico and impose their moral beliefs on you by Leftist judicial fiat.

A nation's belief system and morals, by its very definition, a nation's *Religion*, must be codified into law as the guiding principles on which

---

[388] For the dangers of so-called "moderates see especially the chapter: *Fighting To WIN!: How Do We Fight The War? The Right's RULES FOR ANTI-RADICALS! A Call To ACTION!*.
[389] "Republicans In Name Only", that is Leftists parading as Conservatives for political expediency.

America will be governed. Otherwise there would be only anarchy and chaos. The question is then, which set of religious beliefs will be legislated and govern America, those of GOD or those of Evil? The Left is demanding that the Right cannot "Legislate Morality" while *the Left is itself legislating its own substitute Evil form of "morality"*. The question for us is not "if" morality will be legislated, but *WHOSE* morality will be legislated!

17. P. C. POLICE:

Chapter 17

This will be a short chapter. Much of the discussion of the Left's Political Correctness (P.C.) is adequately covered in other chapters. Here I will highlight some of the more obvious aspects of Political Correctness.

Political Correctness is political enforcement of the Leftist *Religion*! This is the reason that the enforcement of Political Correctness is so obsessively demanded by the Left and its minions. You go to jail if you refuse to issue homosexuals marriage licenses. You get fined tens of thousands of dollars if you refuse to make a wedding cake for a "gay wedding". You lose your business if you make what the Left considers an "intolerant" comment about homosexuals. Yet children get suspended for bringing a *Bible* to school. With no chance of overemphasis:

Political Correctness is political enforcement of the Leftist *Religion*!

Akin to tolerance, Politically Correct is the natural outcome through strict enforcement of "tolerance" as defined by the Left. The most frighteningly humorous and perhaps the most accurate definition of Political Correctness is in this symbolism:

POLITICAL CORRECTNESS IS

FASCISM
PRETENDING TO BE MANNERS

Freedom of speech is taught as a doctrine of the Left but they do not tell you that they only qualify "free speech" as covered under the confines of the Left's P.C. policy. This of course is a self-contradiction and a self-defeating statement which defies all rules of Logic and Reason. Remember that those who cannot reason by Webster's definition are *insane*! These are the *Kookaphants* of the Left today! You simply cannot have "freedom of speech" in which you may only recite the positions of the Left by rote robotics. Even Über-Leftist Bill Maher calls Leftists who once championed "free speech" and who now champion the Politically Correct altered version "regressive Leftists"[390]. Sometimes even Leftists who cannot swallow the Leftist Kool-Aid occasionally wander from the plantation.

The term "useful idiot" of the Left was exemplified in Bill Maher's Leftist oriented television show *Politically Incorrect*[391]. Maher describes himself as a "liberal about everything". *Politically Incorrect* was a spoof against those who find themselves, in the Left's view, in the untenable position of opposing Political Correctness. Maher and his Leftist colleagues basically mocked the one Conservative guest and all that is Right about America. There was no proffered rational discussion, basically just a "Conservatives are stupid" discussion void of any real-world evidence followed by sneering and fits of laughter bolstered by inserted laugh-tracks. Religion, Maher says, is "easy to make fun of"[392]. Maher has also defined Jesus as a Socialist! I wonder if as Maher is burning in hell if his "jokes" will seem as levitatingly funny to him in retrospect? I doubt that Maher's audience will seem as amused in Hell as they do today.

Kimberly Guilfoyle on Fox News Channel said that "Americans have become so Politically Correct that we have become suicidal!".[393] That of course is the objective of the Left, to cause Traditional American values and the expression of the Right to cease to exist. To effectively kill the last vestiges of Conservatism as expressed through the Right.

---

[390] *Real Time with Bill Maher*: Richard Dawkins; October 2, 2015.
[391] In 2002 *Politically Incorrect* was cancelled and Maher now hosts an hour-long program on HBO called *Real Time with Bill Maher*, which follows a similar Leftist format.
[392] *Real Time with Bill Maher*: Richard Dawkins; October 2, 2015.
[393] *Fox News*; The Five; 1/8/2015.

Through the Right's acquiescence to the Left's Political Correctness, the Right is effectively committing suicide! To quote Jesus in the Apostle Paul's (formerly Saul) acquiescence to Evil before Paul's conversion to Christianity Paul recounts "I heard a voice speaking unto me, and saying in the Hebrew tongue, Saul, Saul, why persecutest thou me? it is hard for thee to kick against the pricks"[394]. Equally today the Right has difficulty in standing up against the Left and Evil in "kicking against the" unGODly Leftist "pricks"!

Political Correctness is directly in contradiction to all Judeo-Christian religious imperatives and are aimed at eliminating GOD's imperatives from public and private concern:

> Political correctness shows that it is now possible to establish as authoritative moral [religious] views that are profoundly at odds with long-established [Christian religious] understandings, as long as those who dominate public discussion are committed to them [Leftist ideals][395]. (clarification added)

The Left sits around waiting and hoping to catch someone on the Right in an imagined P.C. offense, in Leftist urban lingo it is to "dis" someone on the Left. Those of us who have a vocabulary above a Neanderthal and can actually speak English, it is to "disrespect" someone. The Left applauds ignorance because only the ignorant (or mentally insane[396]) can be fooled into believing the fantastic *Lies* of the Left. These are Lenin's "useful idiots".

(Here is a suggestion: Christmas is OUR "HOLIDAY"!!! Put *Christ* Back in *Christ*mas! Start saying "Merry Christmas!" everywhere you go. Why is the Left so horrified and "offended" by the use of "Merry Christmas"? Because its root is "Christ", GOD in the flesh! If the Left doesn't like it, then they can kiss our collective asses!!!! Another

---

[394] The *Holy Bible*: Acts 26:14.
[395] Kalb, James; Modern Age Quarterly; *The Tyranny of Liberalism*; 2000; pg. 242.
[396] See the broader discussion of insanity in the chapter *The Left Is a RELIGION!*.

thought: Marriage does not include "homosexual marriage" and Christmas does not include a Pagan or atheist "holiday"!)

Leftist Politically Correct enforcement is the Muslim equivalent of Blasphemy Laws! As the Left's Politically Correct evolves it becomes almost indistinguishable from Islam's Blasphemy Laws. The end-game for both is *political* and *religious* domination and absolute control over the lives of every American! As we have seen in previous chapters, the Left want's to *fundamentally transform* every aspect of what it means to be a human being down to the very thoughts that we are forced to have. Compliance to the Left's demands is forced, and anomalies are *eradicated*. The Left fully intends to march us into the gas chambers, the guillotine blade, and psychiatric wards with a smile on their collective faces. This is the agenda of the Left's Political Correctness. This is *the Left's War Against God!*

18. EVIL IN OUR SCHOOLS

Chapter 18

The problem of Evil in our public schools is so bad that it warrants its own chapter. This discussion will also be touched upon in several other chapters as they relate specifically to individual chapter subjects.

The Evil and corrupted head of SHIELD in the movie *Captain America* noted: "That to build a really better world that sometimes means that you have to tear the old one down". Leftist rhetoric has found its way into every facet of our lives so much so that we have a hard time even recognizing it for what it is... Leftist propaganda. Leftist propaganda designed to infiltrate the minds of America, especially targeting our youth who lack the maturity to recognize the programming. It is no coincidence that Leftist ideologies of history have depended upon the youth to carry the Battle to the streets. As Thomas Jefferson so astutely observed "An educated citizenry is a vital requisite for our survival as a free people".

American education has been intentionally dummied-down by the Left to remove all vestiges of historical fact. The fact that the Left's ideology always leads to chaos and destruction to be reincarnated as a Leftist power state and enslavement of the people! It is no coincidence that the first target of the Left was the American education system. Allan Bloom warned us of this imminent danger almost 40 years ago in *The Closing of the American Mind*, but few took notice. It could not happen here went the reasoning. There is a reason that the Left and the educational establishment fights tooth-and-nail like a savage beast against any legitimate attempt to reform the American educational system. As Hitler said they that control the minds of the youth control the future of the country! Most on the Right do not understand the ultimate goals of the Leftist educational movement, which is not simply a differing of opinion on how to better educate our children. The Left is not concerned with the intellectual education of our children, but the indoctrination of Leftist ideals and activation to the Leftist revolution!

The Left's obsession with controlling the youth through education and government mirrors that of Nazi Germany. Historian William Shirer, an unchallenged authority on Nazi Germany, in *The Rise and Fall of the Third Reich*, documents that upon Hitler's ascendance in Germany "The German schools, from first grade through the universities, were quickly Nazified"[397]. In America the Left is Nazifying our schools as a means of takeover! Hitler scoffed:

> "When an opponent declares 'I will not come over to your side,'" Hitler's response was, 'Your child belongs to us already'. On May 1, 1937, [Hitler] declared 'This new Reich will give its youth to no one, but will itself take the youth and give to youth its own [Nazi] education and its own [Nazi] upbringing'. It was not an idle boast that was precisely what was happening."[398]. (clarifications added)

The Left is not opposed to religion *per se*, but is just opposed to the Christian Religion. The Left does promote *Religion* in schools. The Left promotes *any* religion… *any* religion except Christianity! On any given day in America you can find classes on yoga, transcendental meditation, channeling, and familiarization with "spirit guides". These are *all* manifestations of Hinduism and "spirit worship", which the *Bible* calls demon worship! The University of Michigan in 2007 installed Muslim feet washing stations in bathrooms to cater to Islamic students. Entire curriculums have been altered in an effort to try to shed a better light on Islam. These curriculums go as far as to outright *Lie* about the Evil nature of Islam.

The Left's modern public school curriculum is based, in large part on the self-esteem project developed by Abraham Maslow as discussed

---

[397] Shirer, William L.; *The Rise and Fall of the Third Reich: A History of Nazi Germany*; Simon & Schuster; Reissue edition (October 11, 2011); pg. 249.
[398] Shirer, William L.; *The Rise and Fall of the Third Reich: A History of Nazi Germany*; Simon & Schuster; Reissue edition (October 11, 2011); pg. 249.

in the opening chapter *Defining The War: Evil Against GOD, Left Against Right*. The core of that discussion will be repeated below.

It is no coincidence that the Left envisions Christianity as the Left's only true enemy. For instance, children are punished and even suspended for bringing a *Bible* to a Leftist dominated public school, even while our children are being preached to by the Left that the children are gods and that there is no absolute criteria by which to judge right or wrong. As a "god" our children are free to determine each for themselves what is "right" and what is "wrong". Even Abraham Maslow, the Left's preacher of schoolchildren's self-esteem and "godhood", discovered that his theory of "self-actualization", or full attainment of one's own "godhood", only leads to chaos and self-destruction. When Maslow tried to implement his theory in an actual classroom setting, all sense of order abruptly vanished as the children realized that, if they were in fact "gods", then there was no "right" or "wrong" by which they could be held accountable. Chaos inevitably ensued as each child chose his own set of self-created and self-centered "morals". Maslow was forced to abandon his experiment and conclude that self-actualization was neither a realistic nor a workable model. In the late 1960's Maslow even worried over the fact that his speculations were being too eagerly accepted as literally "gospel" rather than as scientific theory[399].

However the Left continues today to foist Maslow's principles upon our children. Why? Because it is the goal of the Left to create chaos and destruction by creating a vacuum of moral standards into which the Left can appear as the "savior" and implement its own Evil "morals" and "rescue" society from the very situation which *the Left itself has created* specifically for this Evil ends (See later discussion of Rahm Emanuel and *'You never want a serious crisis to go to waste'*). We see this tactic being used by the Left today in virtually every area of American society. For example, the Left's answer to teen pregnancy in the 1960's was sex education in schools, which led to

---

[399] Maslow, Abraham H.; *Critique of Self-Actualization Theory*; edited by Edward Hoffman; The Journal of Humanistic Education and Development; Volume 29, Issue 3; pgs. 103-108, March 1991.

more sexual promiscuity and more teen pregnancy[400]. The Left's "answer" to this new rise in teen pregnancy was... more sex education, which of course led to higher teen pregnancy! They have added to this cycle birth control pills, then condoms handed out in our schools, then abortion coaching couched as "advice", then promoting the homosexual agenda disguised as "counseling" and more recently as "anti-bullying"[401] campaigns (The list of course is much longer, but these examples are sufficient to make the point). The cycle of "fixing" evil with more evil is a doxology of the *Religion* of the Left.

Maslow himself admitted that his beliefs that he peddled were in fact a "religion" which Maslow identified as a "common faith"[402] saying, "...all religions are the same in their essence and have always been the same"[403]. This is a direct contradiction of the Christian Faith in which Jesus clearly says "I am the [only] way"[404] and that "no man cometh unto the Father, but by me". Maslow believed in a "Taoistic" religious transcendence based in a Hindu religious system which he believed could be achieved by a psychotherapy short-cut using LSD[405]. According to Maslow, those people not properly prepared for this "religious transcendence", the highest point of self-actualization of which Maslow preached, risked that "a peak experience could... lead to *insanity*[406]"! Our public schools are controlled by the priests and priestesses of the Left's totalitarian regime and have been turned into temples of Leftist ideology[407]. The Left promotes is own *Religion of Evil* under the guise of non-religion.

John Dewey by whom our educational library cataloging system was built and who is considered by the Left the father of modern education,

---

[400] For further discussion see the chapter: *The Progressive Face of The Left*.

[401] See the full discussion in the chapter: *Tolerance*.

[402] Maslow: *Religions, Values, and Peak Experiences*; pg. 39.

[403] Maslow: *Religions, Values, and Peak Experiences*; pg. 20.

[404] The *Holy Bible*: John 14:6.

[405] Wisniewski, Theodore; Experimenting with Power: *Liberal Psychologists and the Challenge of Social Reform: 1945-1975*; 2008; pgs. 136-137.

[406] Wisniewski, Theodore; Experimenting with Power: *Liberal Psychologists and the Challenge of Social Reform: 1945-1975*; 2008; pg. 137. See the broader discussion of insanity in the chapter *The Left Is a RELIGION!*.

[407] This effort to subvert the schools and thereby our children, was hallmarked by Dewey an icon of the Left.

was a foundational Leftist in America. Remember this: Dewey and his Leftist compatriots in the 1930's, initiated the public establishment of what is now the Religion of the Left:

> "...John Dewey in 1934. It sounds strange to us now, but it was less than 70 years ago, who wrote *A Common Faith*, and very seriously along with some of the most prestigious, influential [Leftist] intellectuals in America proposed a new version of essentially Jean-Jacques Rousseau's notion of the civil religion except attuned to the American democratic experiment"[408].

Recall that "Rousseau's notion of the civil religion" involved the liberal use of the guillotine and the mass execution of all Christians as the number one enemy of the Leftist State! It was in 1934 that Dewey, author of the Leftist tome *A Common Faith*, who referred to the characteristic of the *War* that the Left waged against the Right as having a "religious quality". In 1935 John Dewey would write in *Liberalism and Social Action* that activist government in the name of the economically disadvantaged and social reconstruction had "virtually come to define the meaning of **liberal faith**"[409]. The Left today very much teaches and supports the *Religion* of the Left and is only opposed to the inclusion of the religion of Christianity!

First the Left convinced us that it was the obligation of American "institutes of higher learning" that they were the places of "speaking out". Now the Left is convincing us that the Universities are the places of "acting out". A Leftist said on Fox News that Universities are a place to protest. The commentator, supposedly representing the Right's view, did not even do as much as question the statement, let alone confront the Leftist on the issue! Newsflash, Universities are a "place for learning"! Whatever happened to the Universities being the bastion of free speech... oh that's right, it's only free speech for the

---

[408] Neuhaus; Richard John; *God Bless America: Reflections on Civil Religion After September 11*; Pew Research: Religion and Public Life Project; February 6, 2002; PewForum.org
[409] Dewey, John; *Liberalism and Social Action;* Prometheus Books, 2000; p. 30.

Left to spew its evil! When the Right tries to speak it's considered "hate speech" to be shut down with whatever *force* is necessary!

The Left can only usurp power with an illiterate and therefore ignorant population. The history of America has been rewritten to accommodate the Left's revisionist history. Think this is an exaggeration? Remember Michelle Obama's words, "Barack knows that we are going to have to ... change ... our history"[410]!

Here is the hidden agenda of the Left for our children exposed through the national school teachers union:

> "For the past several months, the NEA (National Education Association) website has recommended that its members read books by *Communist sympathizer Saul Alinsky*. And, for a time, the website listed October 1 as *a day for teachers and students to celebrate the anniversary of the Communist takeover of China by Mao Zedong*. Saul Alinsky, who has been described by his biographer Sanford Horwitt as a "Communist fellow-traveler, wanted to transfer power from the so-called *Haves* to the so-called *Have-nots* and *transform* the U.S. into a communist state." Saul Alinsky's primary goal of revolution was to establish *"the political paradise of communism"*[411]. (*emphasis* added)
>
> In his book, *Rules for Radicals*, Alinsky states, "A Marxist begins with his prime truth that all evils are caused by the exploitation of the proletariat by the capitalists. From this he logically proceeds to the revolution to end capitalism, then into the third stage of reorganization into a new social order of the dictatorship of the proletariat, and finally the last stage-*the political paradise of communism.*"[412] (*emphasis* added)

---

[410] See further discussion in the chapter: *The Obamas: The Epitome of the Left*.
[411] Alinsky, Saul; *Rules For Radicals*; pg. 10.
[412] Costello, Bill; *National Education Association Selling Its Saul*; August 21, 2010; AmericanThinker.com.

This is the direction the Leftist juggernaut of the teachers' movement in America is ramming down our children's collective throats! Public school teachers are the frontline of the Left's push to "transform" America into a Leftist State. Schools not only teach but demand compliance to its "tolerance" police in accepting every form of Evil: relativism (no absolute Wrong), gender neutrality, homosexual agenda, "anti-bullying" campaign, Common Core indoctrination and non-sense, "gay" marriage, transgender studies, Mao worship, Leftist radicalization (Alinsky above), *Bible* and Jesus-free zones, guns are evil, cradle-to-grave indoctrination, every form of Leftism (Socialism, Communism, et al), Environmentalism, Hinduism (by transcendental meditation, Yoga, spirit (devil/demon guides), revisionist history. The Left lifts its icons for worship: Fidel Castro, Chairman Mao, Ché Guevara, Saul Alinsky, Malcom X, Cesar Chavez, Barack Hussein Obama (remember the school children taught Mao-like songs to sing in praise of Herr Obama? One such dirge set loosely to the tune *Jesus Loves the Little Children!*[413]), Al Gore, Dewey, FDR (Franklin Delano Roosevelt, Obama's personal icon), Jesse Jackson, Manuel Noriega, Rahm Emanuel, Hillary Rodham-Clinton, Bill Clinton, Bernie Sanders, Oprah Winfrey, Miley Cyrus, Dzhokhar Tsarnaev (Boston bomber that made the cover of Rolling Stone Magazine), John Lenin, Angela Davis, Jimmy Carter, Janeane Garofalo, Van Jones, Elizabeth Warren, Peter Jennings, Robin Roberts, Anderson Cooper, Whoopi Goldberg, Joy Behar, Rosie O'Donnell, Susan Sarandon and Tim Robbins, Joe Biden, Roman Polanski, Woody Allen, Woody Harrelson, Pee-wee Herman (Paul Reubens), Sesame Street, PBS, Joseph Stalin, Karl Marx, the opium smoking caterpillar in Alice In Wonderland sitting on a magic mushroom (saw it on a teacher's car in a school parking lot and the principal quipped that it was just a cartoon character), Leon Trotsky, Michelle Obama, Bill Ayers, Bernardine Dohrn, Islam, Al Sharpton, Louis Farrakhan (Screwy Louis), *ad infinitum, ad nauseam*. Think these an exaggeration? Google any one of these with "text books", "schools", or "Leftist icon". That will settle your skepticism.

---

[413] http://thetruthwins.com/archives/6-videos-of-school-children-singing-songs-that-praise-barack-obama. Accessed 10/04/2015.

Here is a sample of how far the Left is willing to go in corrupting our children *Against GOD*:

> Obama's Safe Schools Czar Advocated 'Queering Elementary Education'. Kevin Jennings, Obama's Assistant Deputy Secretary for Education who heads the Office of Safe and Drug-Free Schools, began the foreword to *Queering Elementary Education: Advancing the Dialogue about Sexualities and Schooling*. The book for which Jennings wrote the foreword includes essays from gay and lesbian educators that advocate teaching acceptance of homosexuality in elementary school and kindergarten. He also wrote, "Allowing children freedom to develop their sexual identities absent guilt or conditional love is an important attribute of queer households (and classrooms)."
>
> In Chapter 8, Eric Rofes, who taught at Bowdoin College, writes about whether he influenced any of his elementary students to become gay. He was only able to locate eight former students from an elementary class he taught 20 years earlier. He found that these students were not gay.
>
> But he said an openly homosexual teacher can encourage a new generation of activists. "Finally, the greatest influence of openly lesbian, gay and bisexual teachers may be on students' relationships to political activism, and social movements," he wrote. "By witnessing up close the importance of political advocacy on a teacher's job security and social position, children's understanding of the importance of activism and its relevance to their lives might be enhanced."[414]

Our public school system is a cesspool of Leftist radicals whose whole agenda in life is to indoctrinate our children in Leftist Groupthink. Now I want to make a special note here that there are a number of non-Leftist school teachers in our public schools. However, like the

---

[414] Lucas, Fred; cnsnews.com; *Obama's Safe Schools Czar Advocated 'Queering Elementary Education'*; October 27, 2009 9:34 PM EDT.

Nazi concentration camp guards, they are guilty before GOD if they "go along to get along". I will restate an earlier point and tie it to our school children:

> To not actively oppose Evil and the Left in our schools is to tacitly give aid to the Enemy in the Left's War on our children. Evil triumphs when good men do nothing. Jesus speaking as our GOD and King said of this, "Verily I say unto you, Inasmuch as ye have done it unto one of the least of these my brethren, ye have done it unto me"[415]. Just in case you think GOD left you room to wiggle Jesus also stated it in the reverse concerning inaction, "Verily I say unto you, Inasmuch as ye did it not to one of the least of these, ye did it not to me"[416]. GOD takes *inaction* against Evil *personally*!

Hillary Rodham-Clinton with her euphemism of "It Takes A Village" to raise a child, betrays the Leftist agenda to coopt our children. Here is who Hillary Rodham-Clinton thinks owns your child:

> "How did we end up at a point where we are so negative about the most important **non-family** enterprise in the raising of the next generation which is how our kids are educated?"[417]

According to Hillary Rodham-Clinton, children's education in public schools is a "**non-family**" issue. Clinton believes that only the government can successfully educate children when the family is barred from influence. This is reminiscent of Hitler's words "This new Reich will give its youth to no one, but will itself take the youth and give to youth its own [Nazi] education and its own [Nazi] upbringing"!

The cop murdering Bill Ayers and colleague of Barack Hussein Obama who taught our children to "kill your parents" as a college professor gives us the Left's motivation for public education as:

---

[415] The *Holy Bible*: Matthew 25:40.
[416] The *Holy Bible*: Matthew 25:45.
[417] Hillary Clinton's campaign roundtable on education at Kirkwood Community College in Monticello, Iowa; April 14, 2015.

Teaching has always been, for me, linked to issues of social justice. I've never considered it a neutral or passive profession.

The Left's goals and use of the public educational system in America is *indistinguishable* from those of Nazi Germany. Alan Bloom wrote in *The Closing of the American Mind* of education:

> "The political corollary is that he is not open to negotiation. ***The opposition between good and evil is not negotiable and is a cause of war***. Those who are interested in "conflict resolution" ***find it much easier to reduce the tension between values than the tension between good and evil***. Values are insubstantial stuff, existing primarily in the imagination, while death is real. The term "value," meaning ***the radical subjectivity of all belief about good and evil***, serves the easygoing quest for comfortable self-preservation.
>
> Value relativism can be taken to be a great release from the perpetual tyranny of good and evil, with their cargo of shame and guilt, and the endless efforts that the pursuit of the one and the avoidance of the other enjoin. ***Intractable good and evil cause infinite distress—like war and sexual repression—which is almost instantly relieved when more flexible values are introduced***. One need not feel bad about or uncomfortable with oneself ***when just a little value adjustment is necessary***. And *this longing to shuck off constraints and have one peaceful, happy world is the first of the affinities between our real American world and that of **German philosophy** in its most advanced form*"[418]. (emphasis added)

Make no mistake Leftist school teachers are now, and as demonstrated in Nazi Germany, have always been the Stormtroopers in conquering our schools for the implementation and indoctrination of the radical Left! Our education system is where Leftist radicalization begins in *the Left's War Against GOD*.

---

[418] Bloom, Allan; *The Closing Of The American Mind*; 1987; pg. 142.

19. FASCISM AND THE LEFT IN AMERICA: KINDRED SPIRITS AND FAMILIAR BEDFELLOWS:

Chapter 19

This chapter will focus primarily on the frightening parallels between the rise of the Fascist Nazi Party of Hitler and that of the Democrat Party in America today. The platform of the Democrat Party today is fundamentally *indistinguishable* from that of the Über-Left Nazi Party of pre-WWII Germany. In the same way that 20th Century Nazi Fascism had its minor variants from Italian Fascism, so today does modern 21st Century Democrat Leftist Fascism have minor, contemporarily necessary, variances from its Nazi forefathers. Just as in Nazi Germany the Leftists used staged violence to coopt power in the Democrat Party in America. At the 1968 Democrat Party convention in Chicago the Left wrested away control of the Democrat Party from the less radical Party leaders. Now we see the Democrat Party planning and funding inner-city riots across America! Make no mistake the Left is using the Nazi playbook in attempting to seize control of America! In Nazi Germany the violent purge of less radical Party elements began with the Beer Hall Putsch in Munich and culminated with the *Nacht der langen Messer* (the Night of the Long Knives) during which all of the Nazi Party homosexual "Fems" were murdered by the Nazi Party homosexual "Butches" primarily targeting Ernst Röhm the leader of the Nazi "Fems", thus giving it the name the *Röhm-Putsch* or Röhm Purge. As we will see the parallels between the rise of the Nazis of Germany are virtually indistinguishable from rise and takeover of the of the Democrat Party by the Left in America today.

Fascism is nothing more than another manifestation of the ancient Evil Leftist plague. Fascism in the German/Italian sense has only minor variants in the modern American Leftist manifestation. But make no mistake at its core the Left in America today is a direct descendant of the same Evil Anti-GOD Nazi philosophy! It has been a smoke and mirrors illusion of the Leftist propaganda machine to reinvent Fascism as an expression of the Right; when in absolute fact Nazi Socialist Fascism is the great-grandfather of the New Left in America today! In a very literal sense, the Left in America is much more closely linked to Nazi Socialist Fascism than even to Communist Socialism. What most people have missed is China's transition from Communism to Fascism. In an ironic twist, even modern Communist China has reinvented itself into a Fascist system! And the Left Stream Media has uttered nary a peep! Fascism is State sponsored crony-capitalism where the State decides which companies will compete and whose leaders always in turn support the State. Pure Communism will always lead to a bankrupt economic catastrophe just as China had experienced with the starvation of tens of millions of its citizens. Pure Communism, as evidenced in China, always collapses around itself in economic bankruptcy and mass deaths. Always! China in the past several decades has adopted the crony-capitalism of Fascism where the Chinese economy now thrives, at least for the State sanctioned elite.

Fascism is at its core a Totalitarian collectivist system equivalent to Socialism and Communism as born in the Fascist slogan: "The common good before the private good" popularized by Rudolf Jung popularized it in his book *Der Nationale Sozialismus* (National Socialism), 1922, 2nd edition which was recognized and implemented by Hitler himself. This aptly describes every one of the incarnations of the Leftist movements throughout history beginning at the ancient Tower of Babel (from which GOD scattered and confounded the peoples of the earth!) through the Progressive Movement in America today. Evil never sleeps nor does it give up on its Utopian dream for control of the world's people in its *War Against GOD*. The names change, but the devils remain the same.

The 1940's Fascism is virtually *indistinguishable* from the Left in America today. Here is how Mussolini in 1925 defined Fascism: *Tutto nello Stato, niente al di fuori dello Stato, nulla contro lo Stato*, translated "Everything in the State, nothing outside the State, nothing against the State" which exactly defines the intolerant Politically Correct "cradle-to-grave" philosophy of the Left today!

The term used by the Left today is not original to them but was the gateway to the Fascism of Italy and Nazi Germany:

> "Long before the Nazis, too, the German and Italian socialists were using techniques of which the Nazis and fascists later made effective use. The idea of a political party which embraces all activities of the individual from the **cradle to the grave**, which claims to guide his views on everything, was first put into practice by the socialists. It was not the fascists but the socialists who began to collect children at the tenderest age into political organizations to direct their thinking. It was not the fascists but the socialists who first thought of organizing sports and games, football and hiking, in party clubs where the members would not be infected by other [non-Leftist] views. It was the socialists who first insisted that the party member should distinguish himself from others by the modes of greeting and the forms of address. It was they who, by their organization of 'cells' and devices for the **permanent supervision of private life**, created the prototype of the totalitarian party. By the time Hitler came to power, liberalism [classic liberalism/Conservatism] was dead in Germany. And it was socialism that had killed it[419]". (emphasis and clarifications added)

The Nazis also had their Politically Correct term for "cradle-to-grave" Leftism: *Gleichschaltung*:

> *Gleichschaltung* (German pronunciation: [ˈɡlaɪçʃaltʊŋ], meaning "coordination", "making the same", "bringing into line"), is a Nazi term for the process by which the Nazi regime successively established a system of totalitarian control and coordination over all aspects of society. The historian Richard J. Evans translated the term as "forcible-coordination" in his most recent work on Nazi Germany. Author Claudia Koontz

---

[419] Hayek, Friedrich A.; *The Road to Serfdom with The Intellectuals and Socialism* (Readers Digest Condensed version); 1945; pgs. 43-44.

uses the term to explain the transformation of ordinary Germans, who had not, before 1933, been more prejudiced than their counterparts elsewhere, into indifferent bystanders to and collaborators with persecution. Among the goals of this policy were to bring about adherence to a specific doctrine and way of thinking and to control as many aspects of life as possible[420].

Does this not precisely reflect the Left's Politically Correct forced adherence to its Leftist ideals in America today? The American Left is on the *same* path as the pre-Fascist Nazis of Germany!

Friedrich Nietzsche was the undisputed philosophical forefather of German Fascism and epitome of the Left in America today. Nietzsche was rabidly Anti-GOD, anti-Jew, anti-Christian, openly homosexual, preached eradication of the "weak" in society, created the Darwinian archetype for the Nazi *Übermensch* or Race of "Supermen", and screamed for the elimination of all Christian moral restraint in order to move *"Beyond Good and Evil"*[421]. Nothing differentiates Nietzsche and his Evil Utopian designs from the modern Left in America today! Nothing!

As was pointed out in the chapter *The Progressive Face of the Left*, the Nazi movement named the *Nationalist **Socialist** German Worker's Party*, or the *"Nazi Party"* as is its conjunctive in English, was a Leftist **Socialist** party! It was unequivocally neither Right, nor Conservative, but very much a Leftist **Socialist** movement. To argue otherwise is blatantly absurd and without *any* historical support. All one has to do is recall who the angst of German Evil was aimed at, which was the Jews and Christians who were the very embodiment and defining characteristic of what *is* the Right! Any denial of these facts is Leftist subterfuge and double-speak meant to hide the evil that lurks behind the Left.

---

[420] Wikipedia, Gleichschaltung.
[421] Nietzsche, Friedrich; *Beyond Good & Evil: Prelude to a Philosophy of the Future*; 1886.

(Let's settle this point here: So called "white supremacists" are *NOT* a manifestation of the Right! White supremacists fashion themselves after the Nazi's, and the Nazi quest for their super-race! White supremacists are Fascists, and Fascists are Socialists, and Socialists are Leftists, and *white supremacists are Leftists*! These white supremacists also hate Jews and Christians. The same as all other Leftists. The ultra-racist Ku Klux Klan was a monster harnessed by the Democrat Party as the enforcement wing of the Democrat's racist policies! The Left tries to associate white supremacists with the Right just as the Left tries to associate Nazism with the Right. Both are a *Lie* and a cover-up of the Left. White supremacy and Fascism are manifestations of the Left!)

Fascism is a form of militant *Socialism* that is dictatorial by nature and is characterized by a form of crony-capitalism by which the state finances the construction of an envisioned Leftist Utopia. In a Fascist system certain State-cooperative companies are given preferential treatment by the State, they are protected by laws written specifically to benefit these state-allied companies over competitors, and rewarded with contracts in return for the companies' financial and moral support for the State. The only real difference between Communism and Fascism is that Fascism harnesses the power of Capitalism, albeit a corrupted crony-capitalism, and Communism outright rejects Capitalism in any form.

In short, Fascism, or National Socialism as the Nazis called it, is simply a more financially expedient form of Communism in harnessing crony-capitalism to finance a Leftist Utopian fantasy. The Nazis called it *corporativism*. The Left today calls it the New Left as embodied in the Democrat Party!

Fascism is the natural result of the collapse of a republic into dictatorship. A cult of personality rises up making promises of a Utopian future if only the population falls into step with his vision. The band *Living Colour*, who hardly qualifies as holding a Right or Conservative mindset, offers a rather astute analysis of the Leftist agenda and names several specific identities among the Left's icons of the *Cult of Personality*. The song *Cult of Personality* identifies the

Utopian trap by which *Evil* vicariously deceives its victims through the Left:

Lyrics for Cult Of Personality by Living Colour[422]

> Look in my eyes, what do you see?
> The cult of personality
> I know your anger, I know your dreams
> I've been everything you want to be
> I'm the cult of personality
> Like Mussolini and Kennedy
> I'm the cult of personality
> The cult of personality
> The cult of personality
>
> Neon lights, a Nobel Prize[423]
> Then a mirror speaks, the reflection lies
> You don't have to follow me
> Only you can set me free
> I sell the things you need to be
> I'm the smiling face on your T.V.
> I'm the cult of personality
> I exploit you still you love me
>
> I tell you one and one makes three
> I'm the cult of personality
> Like Joseph Stalin and Gandhi
> I'm the cult of personality
> The cult of personality
> The cult of personality
>
> Neon lights a Nobel Prize
> A leader speaks, that leader dies
> You don't have to follow me

---

[422] Cult of Personality; Living Colour; 1988; © Sony/ATV Music Publishing LLC.
[423] It is interesting to note in an almost prophetic fulfillment the Leftist Nobel Foundation awarded Obama the Nobel Prize only days after taking office with absolutely no notable accomplishments.

Only you can set you free
You gave me fortune
You gave me fame
You gave me power in your own god's name
I'm every person you need to be
Oh, I'm the cult of personality
I'm the cult of, I'm the cult of, I'm the cult of, I'm the cult of
I'm the cult of, I'm the cult of, I'm the cult of, I'm the cult of
personality
Look in my eyes, what do you see?
The cult of personality
I know your anger, I know your dreams
I've been everything you want to be

In the lyrics of this song there is a subtle acknowledgement of the Evil behind the "cult of personality" which is easier to comprehend when it is read in print. The lines give away the hidden "power" of the "god" behind the man to which only Lucifer can make such evil claims: "I've been everything you want to be"; "I **am** the cult of personality"; "Then a mirror speaks, the reflection lies"; "Only you can set me free"; "I sell the things you need to be"; "I exploit you - still you love me"; "A leader speaks, that leader dies"; "You gave me power in your own god's name"; "I'm every person you need to be".

Author and historian Jonah Goldberg makes a keen observation, "there is a sense in which Hitler was a reactionary insofar as he was trying to overthrow the entire millennium-old Judeo-Christian order to restore the paganism of antiquity - a mission shared by some on the Left today but none on the right today"[424]. I would add that this idea of overthrowing Christianity is shared by most on the Left and is certainly a prerequisite for a leadership role in the Leftist, Democrat machine. Leftism is *paganism* in its crudest form whose only natural enemy is Christianity, and by default also Jews in general. Even the symbolism of Nazism reflects the paganism of Hinduism. The Nazi

---

[424] Goldberg, Jonah; *Liberal FASCISM: The Secret History of the American Left From Mussolini to the Politics of Meaning*; 2007; pg. 60.

swastika is actually an ancient religious symbol representing the Hindu god *Skandanava*, also called *Ganesha*, the elephant-headed, child-god of Hinduism, the Tibetan god of fire Agni, and used intermediately as the hammer symbol of the Pagan Norse god *Thor*[425]. The Swastika can be found in the Pagan religious art of the Egyptians, Persians, Greeks, Romans, Celtics, and Native Americans, as well as Hindus, Jains and Buddhists and in hundreds of other historic cultures. The swastika is still used as a religious symbol in India, Tibet, China, Korea, and Japan. The reoccurring theme demonstrates the resiliency of Evil to endure transformations through time as the same Evil simply renames and assimilates itself into a "new" false "god". The names change but the devils remain the same!

What the Left in America today has carefully hidden in its revisionist history is that it was not just the Jews which Hitler murdered, but even *more* so... the Christians! Most today would be stunned to learn that the Nazis under Hitler murdered 5 million Jews, but over 7 million Christians! And 7 million Christians is a very cautious estimate with some estimates as high as 15 million! In fact after the defeat of Hitler, the Russians found enough poison gas pellets to kill an additional 20 million people and production of the Zyklon-B poison gas crystals was still under full production at the time of the Nazi defeat. Here is what the acclaimed author and historian Max Dimont discovered: "The chilling reality is that when the Russians overran the concentration camps in Poland they found enough Zyklon B crystals to kill 20 million people"[426]. This discovery was just in Poland. How much more vast were the poison gas reserves throughout the rest of the Nazi-occupied territories? There were fewer than 9.3 million Jews worldwide[427] who survived the Pagan inspired German Holocaust, so who were the intended victims of the tens of millions of surplus poison gas pellets? The answer is that Hitler as he promised intended to kill every remaining Christian on earth in the name of his Leftist Pagan *Religion*!

---

[425] Wikipedia.org, Thor.
[426] Dimont, Max I.; *Jews, God and History*; 1962; Simon & Schuster, New York; pg. 389.
[427] United States Holocaust Memorial Museum, Washington, DC; www.ushmm.org; Accessed 1/6/2015

The Left has reconstructed history to match its *Lies*. The Left now teaches that Hitler and Nazi Germany were Christian. However, Leftist revisionist history cannot change historical fact. Hitler and his Nazi Germany were *not* Christian, but a form of early German Paganism mixed with ancient Hinduism[428]. As thoroughly documented by William Shirer who lived in Germany as a War correspondent and later documented the Nazi régime in *The Rise and Fall of the Third Reich*, Hitler fully intended to annihilate every Christian along with Christianity from the earth:

> "...backed by Hitler, the Nazi regime intended eventually to destroy Christianity in Germany, if it could, and substitute the old paganism of the early tribal Germanic gods and the new paganism of the Nazi extremists. As Bormann, one of the men closest to Hitler said publically in 1941, 'National **socialism** and Christianity are irreconcilable'"[429]. (emphasis added)

Hitler called Martin Bormann "my most loyal Party comrade"[430]. Bormann was Hitler's primary enforcer of *Kirchenkampf* which was the Nazi *pogrom* to destroy the Christian Church beginning in Germany and then use this as a template to destroy the Christian Church worldwide. Hitler further ordered that:

> "...the [Nazi] National Church will clear away all from its altars all crucifixes [and] Bibles" and "On the altars there must be nothing but Mein Kampf" Hitler's own self-aggrandizing autobiography and "the Christian Cross must be removed from all churches... and it must be superseded by the only unconquerable symbol, the swastika"[431].

Hitler was profoundly anti-Christian and openly attacked Jesus Christ:

---

[428] See the further discussion in the following chapter: *Fascism*.
[429] Shirer, William L.; *The Rise and Fall of the Third Reich: A History of Nazi Germany*; Simon & Schuster; Reissue edition (October 11, 2011); pg. 240.
[430] http://www.jewishvirtuallibrary.org/jsource/biography/Bormann.html; Accessed 1/6/2015.
[431] Ibid pg. 240.

Hitler himself said that he and the Nazi Party were fighting against "the God of the deserts, that crazed, stupid, vengeful Asiatic despot with his powers to make laws! ...That poison with which both Jews and Christians have spoiled and soiled the free, wonderful instincts of man and lowered them to the level of doglike freight"[432].

Need more convincing?

"... a 108-page outline prepared by O.S.S. (a predecessor to the C.I.A.) investigators to aid Nuremberg prosecutors. The outline, 'The Persecution of the Christian Churches,' summarizes the Nazi plan to **subvert and destroy German Christianity**, which it calls '**an integral part of the National Socialist scheme of world conquest**.'"[433]. (emphasis added)

Still need more? Remember this from *The Left Is a RELIGION!*?:

According to the Diaries of Joseph Goebbels, one of Hitler's most ardent followers and Nazi Reich Minister of Propaganda in Nazi Germany from 1933 to 1945: *"The Fuhrer is deeply religious, though completely anti-Christian"*[434]. Goebbels wrote in an 8 April 1941 diary entry, "He hates Christianity, because it has crippled all that is noble in humanity"[435]. Hitler himself comments on Christianity: "You see, it's been our misfortune to have the wrong religion"[436], referring of course to Christianity in pre-Fascist Germany. The Left is, and always has been a "religion" of Evil set specifically on eliminating its one and only true enemy... Christianity![437] (emphasis added)

---

[432] Kennedy, D. James and Newcombe, Jerry; *The Gates of Hell Shall Not Prevail*; Thomas Nelson Publishers; 1996; pg. 180.

[433] Sharkey, Joe; *Word for Word/The Case Against the Nazis; How Hitler's Forces Planned To Destroy German Christianity*; New York Times online; January 13, 2002

[434] Bonney, Richard; *Confronting the Nazi War on Christianity: The Kulturkampf Newsletters, 1936–1939*; Bern, Switzerland; Peter Lang Publications; 2009; pg. 20.

[435] Taylor, Irene, and Alan; *The Assassin's Cloak: An Anthology of the World's Greatest Diarists*; 2002; pg. 184.

[436] Speer, Albert; *Inside The Third Reich Memoirs By Albert Speer*; Translated from the German by Richard and Clara Winston; The Macmillan Company; 1969.

[437] For more see: *Fascism and the Left in America: Kindred Spirits and Familiar Bedfellows.*

Separation of Church and State was an early guise of Hitler to divide and conquer the German Christian churches and implement a single State Religion of Fascist Paganism:

> "According to Baldur von Schirach, the Nazi leader of the German youth corps that would later be known as the Hitler Youth, **'the destruction of Christianity was explicitly recognized as a purpose of the National *Socialist* movement'** from the beginning, though "considerations of expedience made it impossible" for the movement to adopt this radical stance officially until it had consolidated power, the outline says."[438]. (emphasis added)

This is today the guise of the Left in America behind the infamous Leftist platform of the contrived "separation of Church and State". The 1947 US Supreme Court decision establishing the "Separation of Church and State" *Lie* was decided by one of the most, if not the most, activist and politically Left Supreme Courts in the history of the United States. The Nazi's had only 12 years to implement their Fascist agenda whereas the Leftists in America have been diligently at work for over 70 years! The Left in America has succeeded in America in ways of which Hitler had only dreamed. Democrat and fellow Leftist Franklin Roosevelt himself privately acknowledged that:

> "What we were doing in this country were some of the things that were being done in Russia and even some of the things that were being done under Hitler in Germany. But we were doing them in an orderly way[439]".

That so many liberals today find that not only forgivable but laudable should tell us something about their ambition. After all, the FDR myth remains liberalism's most "usable past"[440].

---

[438] Sharkey Joe; *Word for Word/The Case Against the Nazis; How Hitler's Forces Planned To Destroy German Christianity*; New York Times online; January 13, 2002.
[439] Goldberg, Jonah; Claremont Review; *The Raw Deal A review of The Forgotten Man: A New History of the Great Depression by Amity Shlaes*; January 14, 2008.
[440] Ibid.

It should also be carefully noted here that Obama claimed Democrat President Franklin Delano Roosevelt as one of his political idols which has also been widely recognized in the media as such[441]. This connection will be more fully vetted later in this chapter and elsewhere in this book.

Obama even tried to emulate the Italian Fascist Prime Minister Benito Mussolini who would appear in newspapers and periodicals shirtless to show the Pagan "back-to-nature" aspect of Italian Fascism. Obama tried the same shirtless photos in a PR campaign in 2010. Obama was swooned over by Leftist publications, news, and media outlets, but laughed to hysteria by Americans as a whole. Even Michelle Obama in 2015 tried to resurrect the dead and get in on the hype releasing a shirtless photo of Obama, but to no avail. Americans were still laughing. Obama has not attempted his shirtless and tasteless escapade since. Imitation is not always the best form of flattery! Oops! Sorry Benito!

The Left in America today is diligently at work to eliminate Christianity from all vestiges of American life and influence. Recall the 2012 floor fight at the National Democrat Party convention over eliminating "God" from the Democrat Party platform. It is no coincidence that the resistance effort to stop "God" from being reinserted into the Democrat platform was the Muslim contingent. The Democrat attack was not on a generic "God" but upon The GOD of the Christian and Jewish faith!

The most fundamental and frightening link between Nazi Germany and the New Left at work in America today is *Evil*. Do you doubt this? Consider this then: As previously discussed, Saul Alinsky, who is considered the founder of the New Left in America, dedicated the Left's philosophy to **Lucifer**. Both Barack Hussein Obama and Hillary Rodham-Clinton are devotees of Saul Alinsky! As we all

---

[441] Washington, Ellis; *The Progressive Revolution: Liberal Fascism through the Ages, Vol. II: 2009 Writings*; Oct 8, 2013; pg. 204.

know through practical experience, we are known by the friends we keep!

Do you think the link from Alinsky to Obama and Hillary to Lucifer is a stretch? Ask yourself this, if you knew of a person who wrote a book advocating Evil and dedicated his book to Lucifer, would you ever look up to this man as a mentor and social engineer to whose ideas you would entrust the future of your children? No one in their right mind would!

Hitler also had dedicated himself to Lucifer: Hitler's primary mentor was a Russian occult spiritualist named Madame Helena Blavatsky (1831-1891). Blavatsky concocted the idea of an Aryan race of Supermen from a series of "ecstatic visions". Blavatsky also extensively used the Swastika as her personal occult symbol and as a talisman of her occult practices predating the Nazi régime by over 50 years! Blavatsky wrote a book titled *The Secret Doctrine* in 1888 in which she glorified Lucifer as the god of this world. Blavatsky founded both the *Lucifer Magazine* and the *Luciferian Society* to promote the worship of Lucifer. Hitler was heavily influenced by Blavatsky's *The Secret Doctrine*:

> "Among the books was one that Hitler often kept by his bedside, the occult standard "The Secret Doctrine" by Madame Helen P. Blavatsky (Kubizek). Hitler kept a copy of Blavatsky's 'The Secret Doctrine' by his bedside, ever since being introduced to its teachings by Dietrich Eckart and Karl Haushofer (Adolf Hitler, The Occult Messiah, Gerald Suster, 1981).[442]"

---

[442] Rohmer, Ulrich R.; *The Blavatsky Effect: How Madame Influenced Modern Concepts of God and Jesus.*

Madame Helena Blavatsky (1831-

Even more frightening is the result of Hitler's indoctrination by way of Blavatsky:

> "Hitler rightly believed he had established communication with Lucifer, from whom he openly coveted possession.[443]"

It is important to note that while many Christians in Germany stood up against the Leftist P.C. campaign of the Nazi's, many Christians and most Jews capitulated to the German *Zeitgeist* or literally translated "the [demon] spirit of the times" and were unceremoniously murdered right alongside those who resisted. As will be driven home numerous times throughout this book, Evil has only one goal which is to "steal, kill, and destroy"[444] and the Left as the personification of Evil will use any political *Lies*, treachery, and deceit to reach that end!

Let's take a moment to examine the American Left's brotherhood with Fascism…

Obama openly claims Franklin D. Roosevelt as one of his primary political icons. Here is Roosevelt's political ideology:

> The Nazis saw the similarities [between FDR and Hitler] as well. "There is at least one official voice in Europe that

---

[443] Cumbey, Constance; *The Hidden Dangers of the Rainbow: The New Age Movement and Our Coming Age of Barbarism*; 1983; pgs. 100-101.
[444] The *Holy Bible*: John 10:10.

expresses understanding of the methods and motives of President Roosevelt," began a New York Times report in July 1933. "This voice is that of Germany, as represented by Chancellor Adolf Hitler." The German leader told the Times, "I have sympathy with President Roosevelt because he marches straight toward his objective over Congress, over lobbies, over stubborn bureaucracies." In July 1934 the Nazi Party's newspaper, *Völkischer Beobachter*, described Roosevelt as America's "absolute lord and master," a man of "irreproachable, extremely responsible character and immovable will"... Roosevelt's books *Looking Forward* (which, as mentioned earlier, had been favorably reviewed by Mussolini himself) and *On Our Way* were translated into German and received lavish attention. Reviewers were quick to note the similarities between Nazi and [Roosevelt's] New Deal policies"[445].

Do the words of Adolf Hitler not ring absolute for Obama and the Left today, "I have sympathy with President Roosevelt because he marches straight toward his objective over Congress, over lobbies, over stubborn bureaucracies."!? How close could you get to FDR's book name, as approved by Mussolini, *Looking Forward* to Obama's 2012 campaign slogan of *Forward*?!

Did you *ever* hear Obama apologize for, let alone admit to, *any* errors? Italian Fascist dictator Mussolini had Italy plastered with posters which read "Mussolini *ha sempre ragione* (Mussolini is always right!)". Obama's favorite response was "I make no apologies...".

The Left today utilizes the same *methods* and *phrases* of their Fascist pre-incarnations and forefathers. Obama's "Summer of Recovery", which Biden announced on June 17, 2010, was an identical campaign used by the Fascist Italian dictator Mussolini, copied by FDR, and now employed by Obama:

---

[445] Goldberg, Jonah; *Liberal FASCISM: The Secret History of the American Left From Mussolini to the Politics of Meaning*; 2007; pgs. 295-296.

It's difficult to exaggerate the propagandistic importance FDR invested in the Blue Eagle. 'In war, in the gloom of night attack, soldiers wear a bright badge on their shoulders to be sure their comrades do not fire on comrades,' the president explained. 'On that principle those who cooperate in this program must know each other at a glance.' In a fireside chat in 1933, **Roosevelt** called for a great **Mussolini-style 'summer offensive against unemployment**.' Hollywood did its part. In the 1933 Wamer Brothers musical Footlight Parade, starring James Cagney, a chorus line uses flash cards to flip up a portrait of Roosevelt, and then forms a giant Blue Eagle. Will Rogers led a Who's Who roster of stars in Blue Eagle and NRA radio broadcasts[446]. (emphasis added)

Roosevelt's "Blue Eagle" campaign was propagandized as designed to "bring the free falling economy under control"[447]. This was exactly the same rationale which Obama used in his 2010 "Summer of Recovery" with its secret intended equal results of no recovery and more government control over the economy.

Obama even made an overt, albeit tacit, admission that he is in fact a Fascist. Obama proclaims in an address to the Young Leaders of the Americas Initiative Town Hall on March 25, 2016 in Buenos Aires after his "historical" trip to Havana, Cuba:

> "So often in the past there has been a division between left and right, between capitalists and communists or socialists, and especially in the Americas, that's been a big debate. Those are interesting intellectual arguments, but I think for your generation, you should be practical and just choose from what works. You don't have to worry about whether it really fits

---

[446] Goldberg, *Jonah; Liberal FASCISM: The Secret History of the American Left From Mussolini to the Politics of Meaning;* 2007; pg. 154.
[447] Wolfgang Schivelbusch; *Three New Deals: Reflections on Roosevelt's America, Mussolini's Italy, and Hitler's Germany, 1933-1939;* 2006; pg. 86.

into socialist theory or capitalist theory. You should just decide what works.[448]"

The amalgamation of Capitalism, Communism, and Socialism is… FASCISM! Fascism *is* Crony-Capitalism bent to the benefit of the Socialist State and enforced by the Communist fist. Obama was preaching his belief in Fascism with flowery metaphors.

That was not an isolated comment by Obama. Obama praised Cuba's Communist dictatorship and its Communist based Centralized "Healthcare" and free Centralized "Education". Obama commented that Havana "looks like it did in the 1950's" because the *economy* is "not working". Obama's solution to Communism's economic shortfalls is *Fascism*. Obama's metaphoric description of Fascism was "And so you have to be practical in asking yourself how can you achieve the goals of equality and inclusion, but also recognize that the market system produces a lot of wealth and goods and services". Again, Fascism *is* Crony-Capitalism bent to the benefit of the Socialist State and enforced by the Communist fist. Obama *is* a self-avowed Fascist!

Hillary Rodham-Clinton's infamous and ominous threat delivered to Americans at a Democrat fundraiser in California in 2004 "We're going to take things away from you on behalf of the **common good**" reflects the Nazi Fascist slogan *Gemeinnutz geht vor Eigennutz* "The **common good supersedes the private good**". Collectivism is a common Fascist value of *all* Leftists. Collectivism only sees individuals as a dispensable mechanism for the advancement of the State and advantage of the Leftist elite. This is what Hillary Rodham-Clinton meant in her book *It Takes A Village*. She attributed the title of her book to an African proverb: "It takes a village to raise a child". For the Left only the community or "Village" matters. The community represents the collective Fascist machine where individuals are nothing more than dispensable cogs for the benefit of that faceless

---

[448] https://www.whitehouse.gov/the-press-office/2016/03/23/remarks-president-obama-young-leaders-americas-initiative-town-hall.

machine. This euphemism of a "Village" is used to subtly disguise the inherent Evil in the deception of the Leftist collectivist movement!

Remember Hillary Rodham-Clinton's directive to "**Let us be willing to remold society by <u>redefining what it means to be a human being</u>**"? This is nothing short of the Nazi Fascists attempt to re-create, or redefine, mankind into a race of super-human beings, as Nietzsche declared and was the archetype for the *Übermensch* or new Race of "Supermen". The *Übermensch* was the Fascist justification for the extermination of over 13 million Christians and Jews specifically because these two groups fundamentally opposed the actions and the Evil foundations of the Left! Hillary Rodham-Clinton is a Fascist. Hillary Rodham-Clinton uses the Nazi playbook and tactics as translated by Saul Alinsky in *Rules for Radicals*. Hillary Rodham-Clinton's goals and aspirations are identical to the Nazi's. Hillary Rodham-Clinton is a Fascist.

The implementation of the Nazi Super-Race was sold as an implementation of unquestionable "science". The Left's reliance on pseudo "science" as the supposed final arbiter on all matters is, and always has been, intentionally misleading and despotic in nature. By no coincidence, "science" was the foundational rationalization for virtually every evil and despotic act of Nazi Germany. Of course like Nazi Germany the Left picks and chooses its "science" often just creating "scientific facts" out of thin air. The Left's sacred mantra of "The science is clear" is stated with such authority that it denies any question to their agenda. The Nazi's assured the world that "The Science Is Clear" on German racial superiority. The Nazi's assured the world that "The Science Is Clear" on the degenerative nature of the world's Jews. The Nazi's assured the world that "The Science Is Clear" on the undesirability of the Polish people. The Nazi's assured the world that "The Science Is Clear" on the undesirability of the Czech people. The Nazi's assured the world that "The Science Is Clear" on the undesirability of the world's population of Christian people!

Today the American Leftist elite use the same deception of "The Science Is Clear" as a mandate to further their takeover of American politics and every facet of American life. The Left assures America that "The Science Is Clear" on Global Warming. The Left assures America that "The Science Is Clear" that the Keystone XL pipeline is bad. The Left assures America that "The Science Is Clear" on the evil of fossil fuels. The Left assures America that "The Science Is Clear" on the unreliability of the *Bible*. The Left assures America that "The Science Is Clear" that an unborn baby is just a lifeless blob. The Left assures America that "The Science Is Clear" that science invalidates Christianity, and all things associated with Christianity.

What is the motivation behind this mantra? The Left itself betrays and answers the question: "The science is clear. *We have to act*"[449]! It is yet another excuse to further the Leftist agenda! This is the same style tactic of the Left in creating a crisis in order to create the environment in which to introduce Leftist solutions, which otherwise would never be accepted by the American people[450]. One of the biggest institutionalized Leftist arms is the Environmental Protection Agency (EPA). EPA Administrator Gina McCarthy pronounced before a Congressional committee, "The science is clear. The risks are clear. And the high costs of climate *inaction* are clear. **We must act**"[451]. Notice the pattern? Let's take the leap from frightening to horrifying…

The EPA's annual $8 billion budget finances an army of more than 1,000 attorneys, which makes the EPA one of the largest law firms in the United States! The EPA calls for "environmental justice" though grants to raise awareness of "climate change". After all, "the science is clear". However the EPA has been discovered to have created its own independent special ops army equipped with the most advanced military arsenal which includes automatic weapons, ammo, body armor, camouflage equipment, unmanned aircraft, amphibious assault ships, radar and night-vision gear and other military-style weaponry

---

[449] Ball, Jeffrey; newrepublic.com; *National Climate Assessments Scientific Obfuscations About Warming*; May 8, 2014. Comment by Dan Utech, Obama's special assistant for energy and climate change. (emphasis added).
[450] See Chapters: *Tactics for the Left's Subversion/Takeover* and *Emotion Based Politics*.
[451] Adams, Chris; McClatchy Washington Bureau; *EPA chief defends power plant rule against GOP charges of overreach*; July 23, 2014. (emphasis added).

and surveillance equipment, according to a report by the watchdog group *Open the Books*. And according to *Investor's Business Daily* the EPA appears "to be preparing to use **deadly force** to enforce EPA edicts"[452] against the American populace and the "EPA's enforcement division employs well-armed 'special agents' who appear to be conducting SWAT-type operations on American businesses and households it suspects of wrongdoing". The Left is not playing games but fully intends to use **deadly force** against its opponents on the Right of the American populace who resist *The Left's War Against GOD*, America, and all that is GOOD!

Still think this might be an exaggeration?

There was an unprecedented arming of Federal agencies under the Obama Administration ordering billions of rounds of ammunition along with machine guns and other elite military equipment. These Federal agencies include:

> the U.S. Postal Service, the Social Security Administration (174,000 rounds), the Department of Agriculture (320,000 rounds), the Department of Homeland Security (450,000,000 rounds with plans to purchase 1.2 billion additional rounds of military hollow-point bullets and has already amassed a stockpile of 2,000,000,000 rounds enough to have fought the Iraq War for 24 years! DHS also purchased 2,700 Armored vehicles called Mine Resistant Armor Protected Vehicles (MRAP) for urban combat in the streets of America's "Homeland"!), The National Oceanic and Atmospheric Administration (72,000 rounds), The National Weather Service (46,000 rounds), and the Department of Education (thousands of rounds of ammunition and over $80,000 on Glock pistols and over $17,000 on Remington shotguns).

What in GOD's name do these non-military Federal agencies need with *billions* of rounds of ammunition, military handguns and

---

[452] Moore, Stephen; Investors.com, *Investor's Business Daily; Does EPA Need Guns, Ammo And Armor To Protect The Environment?*; 10/08/2015 05:51 pm ET.

machine guns, unmanned aircraft, amphibious assault ships, thousands of armored vehicles, radar and night-vision gear!?! What in Hell's name does the Department of Education need to be armed for?! The answer to this question about any of these Federal non-military agencies can only be horrifying in its conclusion! Still think that there is an exaggeration in the earlier statement that: The Left is not playing games but fully intends to use *deadly force* against its opponents on the Right of the American populace who resist the Left's coup attempt *Against GOD*, America, and all that is GOOD!?

For the "it could never happen here in America" crowd, you should know that the US Department of Defense (DOD) began teaching US Army Reserves that "Evangelicals" and "Catholics" are "extremist groups" at the heart of terrorism in America today![453] Todd Starnes of *Fox News* reports that a Ft. Hood US Army briefing where soldiers were told that *evangelical Christians* and Tea Party supporters are a threat to the United States and are "tearing the nation apart". Soldiers were told that *they could be charged with committing a **military crime** if they supported or donated to such organizations*![454]

The US Air Force has removed "God" from its Air Force Rapid Capabilities Office logo and "so help me God" from its enlistment oath.

Further, The Department Homeland Security document called: *Rightwing Extremism: Current Economic and Political Climate Fueling Resurgence in Radicalization and Recruitment* labels the following as terroristic organizations: Veterans, those opposing "illegal immigration", those opposing the Left's attempts to establish a "New World Order", anyone believing in [*Biblical*] "end times" prophecies, those using the "exploitation of social issues such as abortion" (anyone who is Pro-Life), and those who are opposed to

---

[453] Markay, Lichian; *The Washington Free Beacon*, Friday April 5, 2013.
[454] Klukowski, Ken; *Breitbart*; 23 Oct 2013.

"same-sex marriage"[455], among others. Even though the report stated that there was "no specific information" to suggest that these Right-wing organizations had any terroristic acts. Even CNN reported the day after its issue that Homeland Security Secretary Janet Napolitano restated that she was briefed before the release of the controversial "intelligence assessment" and that she *wholeheartedly* stood by the report which specifically targeted Christians[456].

Department of Defense (DOD) training documents teach that Conservative groups are "hate groups" and suggest the colonists who fought against British for American independence rule were "extremist". Included in the DOD documents is a Defense Equal Opportunity Management Institute "student guide" titled "Extremism" identifying "the colonists who sought to free themselves from British rule" as an example of "extremist ideologies and movements".[457] The Left sees the Right in America today in the same light as the Founding Fathers of these United States and the supportive American colonists as enemies of the Leftist Totalitarian State! This is *The Left's War Against GOD*!

An article by Joseph Klein titled *Obama's War on the Christian 'Extremist' Threat*, summed up Barack Hussein Obama's outright hostility and accompanying *War Against GOD and Christianity*:

> A *concerted campaign to portray Christians as domestic enemies* comes to light.
> This bias appears to reflect the Obama administration's thinking at the highest levels. Indeed, as reported by Breitbart News, *rather than embrace an amendment passed last June in the House Armed Services Committee protecting religious speech of service members in the military, the White House*

[455] Department of Homeland security; *Rightwing Extremism: Current Economic and Political Climate Fueling Resurgence in Radicalization and Recruitment*; Prepared by the Extremism and Radicalization Branch, Homeland Environment Threat Analysis Division. Coordinated with the FBI.; April 7, 2009
[456] Meserve, Jeanne; CNN.com; *Napolitano Defends Report on Right-Wing Extremist Groups*; updated 5:11 p.m. EDT, Wed April 15, 2009.
[457] Hawkins, Awr; Breitbart, breitbart.com; *DOD Documents Suggest Colonists Were 'Extremist' for Fighting British Rule*; 23 Aug 2013.

released a Statement of Administration Policy with a threat to veto the bill if it passes the full House and Senate. "In other words," Breitbart News concluded, "***Obama says he will veto any bill that forbids his appointees or officers from telling a soldier that he cannot mention Jesus during prayer or have a Bible on his desk***, *or that keeps those appointees from telling a chaplain (who is an ordained clergyman) what religious teachings he is allowed to give in worship services, or what spiritual counseling he can give to another soldier*"[458].

In 2008 as a Presidential candidate Barack Hussein Obama told the American people:

> "We cannot continue to rely on our military in order to achieve the national security objectives we've set. We've got to have a **civilian national security force** that's just as powerful, just as strong, just as well-funded."

This is *exactly* what the Nazi's did in Germany under Hitler before their takeover followed immediately by the confiscation of all guns from non-Nazi Party citizens who were not loyal members of the Fascist "**civilian security force**"! Hitler's Nazi "civilian security forces" included the most vicious and murderous organizations including the Brownshirts, Stormtroopers, and the infamous Gestapo. Obama, like Hitler, worked to establish a secret military force through which to usurp total and absolute power in America!

Terrified of the Left yet? Well read on it gets worse…

Still think this conclusion is a stretch? Really? The Left and the Democrat Party have already been coordinating violence and hiring thugs and anarchists to physically attack Conservatives in the streets and on campuses! Obama's Organizing for Action, billionaire George Soros' network of paid agitators, the DNC paid agitators, Robert

---

[458] Klein, Joseph; Front Page Magazine, frontpagemag.com; *Obama's War on the Christian 'Extremist' Threat, A concerted campaign to portray Christians as domestic enemies comes to light*; October 24, 2013.

Creamer's organizations Democracy Partners and Mobilize paid thugs to infiltrate Trump and Tea Party rallies and pose as Conservatives and incite violence, Antifa (short for anti-fascism which actually promotes Leftist Fascism!), anarchists, ANSWER (Act Now to Stop War and End Racism), Black Lives Matter, the New Black Panther Party, La Raza, SEIU and other unions, Occupy Movement… the list is nearly endless. It is by intentional imitation that Antifa wears black shirts and bandanas just as Mussolini's "Blackshirts" who wore black shirts and uniforms and who terrorized anyone opposed to Italian Fascism! The Fascist Blackshirts killed thousands in its seize of power. It was the Blackshirts who organized its violent armed March On Rome from 27 to 29 October 1922 that brought the Fascist Mussolini into power.

Here is the obvious question for today: Why are the Antifa terrorists today not shot by police in the streets while committing their brutal crimes? Humm… let's see what cities the Fascist Antifa commit their assault and batteries and arsons: Washington, DC; University of California at Berkeley; Berkeley, California; Kansas City, Missouri; Portland, Oregon; Charlottesville, North Carolina; *et al*… all of which are Leftist-Democrat bastions! Evil protects evil!

Mark Bray, a Dartmouth lecturer who has defended antifa's (sic) violent tactics, recently explained in *The Post*, "Its adherents are predominantly communists, socialists and anarchists" who believe that physical violence "is both ethically justifiable and strategically effective."[459] In other words, Antifa are Fascists by design and actions!

The Nazi's had their own paramilitary youth brigades called the Brownshirts who also brutalized opponents killing thousands and terrorizing the masses into submission. The Left has been positioning to create their "civilian national security force" just as the Nazis and Italian Fascists did in order to forcefully seize national power!

---

[459] Thiessen, Marc A.; Yes, antifa is the moral equivalent of neo-Nazis; Washington Post online; August 30, 2017

Think this an exaggeration? Read on. Congressman Maxine Waters openly supported the riots in Los Angeles in 1992 calling them an "insurrection" and "a milestone in the history of black people demanding justice.". The 1992 riot saw 58 people murdered, thousands injured, and over a billion dollars in property damage! Maxine Waters supported Damien Williams the infamous Crips gangbanger thug who hurled a chunk of concrete at truck driver Reginald Denny's head and performed a victory dance over this innocent man's unconscious body. Maxine Waters even visited Damien Williams' mother to offer her support of Williams. After Williams was released from prison, he went on to murder another person. When other rioters went free Maxine Waters joined in the celebration. Maxine Waters still stands by her support of the murdering rioters, is still in Congress, and continues to spew her vile language against the Right in support of violence! To add to her crimes Democrat Congressman Maxine Waters said "I will go and take Trump out tonight" implying the assignation of President Donald Trump! This woman should be tried for treason and crimes against humanity and summarily shot!

The Left, just as Hitler and the Nazis did, has so successfully vilified the Right to their minions who *are* now mindlessly going out attacking, beating unconscious, murdering, and attempting to murder people for just for being Conservative and/or Republican! An exaggeration? There are dozens of examples throughout this book. Let's just review a few of the thousands of such examples:

Republican Congressman Steve Scalise was targeted by Left-wing activist James Hodgkinson for death. Hodgkinson shot Scalise with a military-style rifle on a baseball field where Hodgkinson also targeted many other Republican Congressmen and aides. Hodgkinson specifically asked before opening fire if the players on the field "were Republicans"! According to news accounts, Hodgkinson was all things Left: a Bernie Sanders volunteer, an Occupy Movement activist, a Republican hater, and especially a Trump hater. Hodgkinson had Facebook likes for Soros' MoveOn.org and Media Matters, CNN's Rachel Maddow, the repugnant Bill Moyers, the ACLU, the terrorist-like Southern Poverty Law Center, and had a tshirt associating himself with the militant thugs of the SEIU union. There are dozens of examples of Leftist sympathizers violently attacking Conservatives just for being Conservative! Or how about the Pennsylvania Democrat strategist Jim Devine whose response to the gunning down of Republican Congressman Steve Scalise was to tweet #HuntRepublicans and #HuntRepublicanCongressman!

On the heels of the Congressman Steve Scalise assignation attempt, on June 18, 2017 Johnny Eric Williams an associate college professor from Trinity College in a Facebook rant said "It is past time for the racially oppressed to do what people who believe themselves to be 'white' will not do, put end to the vectors of their destructive mythology of whiteness and their white supremacy system. #LetThemF–ingDie" and "The time is now to confront these inhuman assholes and end this now.".[460]

The Leftist-Fascists of Nazi Germany and Italy controlled the entertainment industry. In the beginning the Fascists cowed all actors, comedians, and entertainers through PC intimidation. As always, eventually the Fascists only allowed entertainers that towed the Party line! Deviants to the Left were arrested, tortured, and even executed! While we are not yet seeing executions, we are clearly seeing this trend today. Leftist entertainers regularly call for the execution of non-conformers. Several Hollywood "entertainers" have called for the execution of President Donald Trump! The entertainment industry in the United States is thoroughly controlled by the frothing Left!

The Left also hides behind the "comedian" label. The Leftist Democrat "comedian" Kathy Griffin holds up the ISIS-style severed head of President Trump and then amid the backlash she says that it was a misplaced attempt at "humor". Really? Griffin even loudly played the victim because she was being investigated by the Secret Service for threatening the President. Maycie Thornton of *BuzzFeed* declared in an inter-office online exchange that she hopes that "maybe someone will assassinate [Trump]"! Newsweek tried to write the

---

[460] Ernst, Douglas; The Washington Times online; *Trinity College professor calls white people 'inhuman': 'Let them f-ing die'*; June 21, 2017.

declaration off as a "joke" saying "The joke is flippant and not especially original. It's not even much of a joke".[461] The Left uses the "comedy" defense to dismiss vile rhetoric and calls for violence and murder against Republicans! Dozens of "comedians" advocate for violence against those on the Right and then indignantly state that they are protected because they are "comedians". Really? Where are comedians mentioned as a protected privileged-class in the *U.S. Constitution* or in the law? Others who hold up the strawman of "comedy" include, but are certainly not limited to, Wanda Sykes (wishing for the death of Conservative Rush Limbaugh while then President Obama applauds), Jon Stewart, John Oliver, Trevor Noah, Stephen Colbert, Conan O'Brien, George Lopez, James Corden, Jimmy Fallon and Seth Meyers to name a few of the more obvious.

If a Conservative "comedian" called for the beheading or death of a Democrat the shrieking hysteria from the Left would be deafening!

Leftist Democrat "entertainers" regularly spew vulgarities and call for violence against Conservatives. Some of the more obvious are Madonna, Whoopi Goldberg, Robert De Niro, Leonardo DiCaprio, Ashley Judd, Samuel L. Jackson, Alec Baldwin, Joy Behar, Rosie O'Donnell, Johnny Depp, and on-and-on! In 2017 the Left proudly displayed a rendition of *Shakespeare In The Park* where a character dressed as President Trump was assassinated nightly. A Trump lookalike as the Julius Caesar character and Brutus is portrayed as a black Congressman. It's no coincidence that after James Wilkes Booth assassinated Republican President Abraham Lincoln, Booth referred to himself as "Brutus"!

Where is the outrage on the Left or on the Right for that matter?! If they had chosen to mock assassinate Obama or Hillary Rodham-Clinton do you think that the reaction would have been more immediate and deafening?! The only reaction from the Left is moral indignation at being called out by Conservative protestors taking the

---

[461] Nazaryan, Alexander; Newsweek.com; *Right-Wing Media Critics Slam Buzzfeed Over Trump Assassination Joke*; 5/4/17.

stage to say that portraying violence against the Right is unacceptable. Me thinks that the Left doth protest too much!

"Comedic" actor Johnny Depp on June 22, 2017 openly called for the assassination of President Trump. Depp said comparing himself to stage actor John Wilkes Booth, the assassin of President Abraham Lincoln, "when was the last time an actor assassinated a president?... it has been a while and maybe it is time". Depp the next day issued an "apology" saying "I apologize for the bad joke I attempted last night in poor taste about President Trump". Joke? If you threaten someone's life make sure that you cover it as a "joke"! The Left Stream Media is trying to write it off as a bad attempt at humor.

Black female rapper Azealia Banks advocated on her Twitter post on April 3, 2017 that Sarah Palin should be gang-raped by a group of black men, filmed, and put it on the internet! Where is the outrage?

At the particularly violent riots at Berkley in February 2017 in response to speaker Milo Yiannopoulos attempt to speak at a University sanctioned event, Conservatives were attacked by Leftist groups where many Conservatives were severely injured and some Conservatives were beaten unconscious. In response Leftist Hollywood writer, director, producer, actor, and "comedian", Judd Apatow, defended the violence against conservatives with this tweet, "This is just the beginning. When will all the fools who are still supporting Trump realize what is at stake?". The Left in Hollywood support, condone, and encourage violence against the Right!

Do you think that these calls for violence are limited to Democrat "comedians" and "entertainers"? These crimes reach all the way to the top of the leadership of the Democrat Party! I will cite only a few of the myriad of examples of the Nazi-like calls to violence to make the point.

Nebraska Democratic Party official Phil Montag was recorded saying about the shooting of Republican Congressman Steve Scalise, "Let me tell you, that motherfucker, the one that was shot... this motherfucker, like his whole job is to like get people , convince

Republicans to fuckin' kick people off fuckin' healthcare". Montag summed up his feelings on Scalise being gunned down as, "I'm fuckin' glad he got shot!" and "I wish he was fuckin' dead!". Another Nebraska Democratic Party official Black Caucus Chair, Chelsey Gentry-Tipton wrote in a Facebook post about the shooting of Republican Congressman Steve Scalise, "Watching the congressman crying on live tv abt [sic] the trauma they experienced. Y is this so funny tho [sic]?"

In the wake of the riots in Charlottesville, VA in August 2017 a Missouri Democrat state senator Maria Chappelle-Nadal, called for the assignation of President Trump! Her exact quote was on Facebook was "I hope Trump is assassinated!". Neither President Trump, any Trump associate, nor any Republicans had any association with the Leftist march. It was a Nazi promoting group. Remember that the Nazis were and are a manifestation of the Left! The Nazis are a Leftist *Socialist* organization! It is therefore no coincidence that the organizer of the Charlottesville march Jason Kessler was an Occupy Wall Street activist and a Barack Hussein Obama supporter! This is how the Left pretends to be Right while causing havoc and the Left Wing Media then vilifies Conservatives for action in which the Right had no part. Remember Robert Creamer, a Democrat strategist and husband of Illinois Democrat Congressman Jan Schakowsky, who was paid by the 2016 Hillary Rodham-Clinton presidential campaign and the Democrat National Committee to place Leftist infiltrators inside Trump rallies causing violence while pretending to be Trump supporters?[462] The strategy of *Lies* and deception worked in the short term as the Left and the Leftist Media publically blamed Republicans for what Democrats had actually done!

In January 2017 on MSNBC Leftist Democrat **U.S. Senator Tim Kaine**, Hillary Clinton's 2016 presidential running mate, sent out a clarion call to fellow Democrats:

---

[462] Diaz, Daniella and Griffin, Drew; CNN online; *Dem operative 'stepping back' after video suggests group incited violence at Trump rallies*; Tue October 18, 2016, 10:04 PM ET.

"So, the way we get outside the bubble is we take advantage of this tremendous public outcry against the [Trump] administration. What we've got to do is **fight** in Congress, **fight** in the courts, **fight in the streets**, **fight** online, **fight** at the ballot box, and now there's the momentum to be able to do this".

The Left has attempted to play down the violent implications of **U.S. Senator Tim Kaine**'s declaration, but not only is "fighting" a very specific call to violence, the more specific call to "fight in the streets" cannot be separated from the Democrat led violent street riots that have blown up since President Trump was elected. How else can you explain the term "fight at the ballot box"? Note that this is not "fight for the ballot box" but "fight **at** the ballot box". The only modern fight at the ballot box in recent memory was the New Black Panther Party in 2008, in support of Leftist Barack Hussein Obama, trying to stop Republican and white voters from voting "at the ballot box". Kaine is specifically calling for violence against Republicans and Conservatives!

(Even U.S. Senator Tim Kaine's son Linwood Kaine apparently followed his father's advice recently when he was implicated in a violent assault upon Trump supporters in March of 2017 at a pro-Trump rally in Minneapolis. Several assailants dressed all in black, the dress of the anarchists terrorizing college campuses copied from Italian Mussolini Fascists of the 1940's, assaulted Trump supporters with Tasers, pepper spray, smoke bombs, and fireworks. Several Trump supporters had to be treated by paramedics. Linwood Kaine was arrested trying to flee the scene. He was charged with fleeing on foot, concealing identity in a public place, and obstructing the legal process by interfering with a peace officer. A spokesperson representing the Kaine family also issued a statement on their behalf saying, "Tim and Anne **support** their son and hope the matter is resolved soon".)

Not long after Tim Kaine's call to violence, über-Leftist **Loretta Lynch, former President Obama's U.S. Attorney General**, released a video declaring:

"It has been people, individuals who have banded together, ordinary people who simply saw what needed to be done and came together and supported those ideals who have made the difference. **They've marched, they've bled and yes, some of them died.** This is hard. Every good thing is. **We have done this before. We can do this again.**"

This video by Lynch calling for violence was then proudly posted by Democrats on the official U.S. Senate Democrat Facebook page as "words of inspiration"! There is a clear reference to "fighting in the streets" where "they've marched". The Left is calling for violence in the streets where people are to bleed and die in "resistance" to Trump, Republicans, and the Conservative Right!

Do you remember this one? At a campaign event in Philadelphia in June 2008, Then U.S. Senator Obama told supporters, "If they bring a knife to the fight, we bring a gun"? Obama with the "we" included himself in the gun comment! In September 2008 Obama also told supporters, "I want you to argue with them, get in their faces! You guys are the ones who can make the change". "Change" through confrontation, intimidation, and violence is at its core Fascism!

As President Obama in a 2010 midterm campaign message to Latinos on Univision, Obama pressed Hispanics to "punish our enemies". In a wider quote Obama says, "If Latinos sit out the election instead of saying, 'We're going to punish our enemies and we're gonna [sic] reward our friends who stand with us on issues that are important to us". This is Fascism 101! Fascism is violently built on the stick-and-carrot means of "punishing your enemies and rewarding your friends"!

Obama as President fostered acts of violence against Republicans, whites, and police in his open promotion of the violent Black Lives Matter groups. Obama hosted Black Lives Matter activists at the White House who openly called for violence against Republicans, whites, and police officers. Obama protected New Black Panther activists in Florida who openly called for the murder of white babies!

One quote is from New Black Panther self-aggrandized as "King Samir Shabazz" who advocated that blacks "kill cracker babies"![463] There was never a Justice Department investigation of these black criminals under Obama. Obama also had the absentia convictions overturned against the New Black Panther Party members, including King Samir Shabazz, who openly intimidated and threatened Republican and white voters in Philadelphia in the 2008 general elections.[464] The call to violence, encouraging to violence, and the rewarding of violence then and now goes all the way to the top of the Democrat Party leadership!

There are thousands of more examples, but these samples should be enough to frighten any sane person as to the Left's true hidden violent agenda inspired by the Nazi Fascist model. The Left is the embodiment of Evil and the Left uses tactics inherited from Fascism and the Nazis' violent playbook!

Let's return now to the broader "the science is clear discussion". Where the Left is concerned "science", when it agrees or can be made to appear to agree with the Leftist ideology, *ALWAYS* demands *action* in favor of the Leftist agenda! The hidden agenda is Leftist control of every American from cradle-to-grave. This is the hidden agenda in the Left's implementing the so called "Carbon Tax" that would cripple American industry and our American economy, which would in turn give the Leftist State almost total control over Americans' lives. Americans would become dependent on the government for their living and very survival from "cradle-to-grave"!

The Left speak their *Lies* with such dogmatic absolutes as, "The science is clear: The earth is round, the sky is blue, and #vaccineswork. Let's protect all our kids. #GrandmothersKnowBest", declared Hillary Rodham-Clinton in a Tweet on government *enforced* children's vaccines. And on absolute scientific authority of being a

---

[463] Ahlers, Mike M.; CNN.com; *Official Alleges Racially Selective Enforcement of Voting Rights Cases*; September 25, 2010 12:10 p.m. EDT.
[464] Ahlers, Mike M.; CNN.com; *Official Alleges Racially Selective Enforcement of Voting Rights Cases*; September 25, 2010 12:10 p.m. EDT.

"grandmother" to boot! To question the wisdom of the Leftist *Lies* is to question that "the earth is round and the sky is blue"!

The zealots of the Left bludgeon Americans with their *religious* fervor using so-called "science" as a weapon as if the truthfulness of their decrees were beyond question:

> "[The Left will] invoke with divine reverence "science" and the laws of economics the way a temple priests once read the entrails of goats, but they have blinded themselves to their own leaps of faith, they cannot see that morals and values cannot be derived from science. Morals and values are determined by priests, whether they wear black robes or white lab smocks"[465].

The Left today, just as it did in Nazi Germany, has politicized a false "science" for the advancement of the Left's own political agenda. This politicization of science is then the demand upon which "we must act now!". This is the same deceitful method of gaining control as über Leftist Rahm Emanuel described when he exposed the Left's Alinsky tactic of "You never let a serious crisis go to waste. And what I mean by that it's an opportunity to do things you think you could not do before." (See the discussion in the chapter *"Understanding The Battle"*.)

It is also interesting to note that in "the science is clear" argument, that "natural law", as accepted by all science, bases science on GOD's natural laws which GOD established at creation in nature and in man as an inalienable guiding truth. Natural Law testifies to the existence of the One True GOD. Natural law can neither be eradicated nor weakened by simply ignoring or disregarding it, any more than one can choose to live as if gravity did not exist. The consequences of which, as you can imagine, would be laughable!

---

[465] Goldberg, Jonah; *Liberal FASCISM: The Secret History of the American Left From Mussolini to the Politics of Meaning*; 2007; pg. 131.

I have often wondered, as many historians have, how pre-Nazi Weimer Germany fell through the looking-glass, down the rabbit hole, and landed in the Fantasy-Land of Fascism. James Kalb, who is a prolific author on the dangers of the Left, stumbles into a working definition which literally defines the Fascistic nature of the modern Left. Kalb describes the Left in America as:

> So great is the power of modern technocracy, and so close is the connection between liberalism [Leftism] and power, that liberalism [Leftism] comes to seem irresistible, almost a law of nature. All classes favor it. Political elites like what favors their power, the rich what secures and increases their wealth, experts what makes their expertise the key to social functioning, idealists what conforms social functions to abstract rational principles, social climbers what makes them respectable, and almost everyone what makes for comfort[466]. (clarifications added)

President Ronald Reagan, in a 1975 interview with *60 Minutes* remarked, "You know, someone very profoundly once said many years ago that if fascism ever comes to America, it will come in the name of liberalism.". Reagan adding, "What is Fascism? Fascism is private ownership, private enterprise, but total government control and regulation. Well, isn't this the liberal philosophy?"

When a society loses sight of a transcendent viewpoint, that is an eternal viewpoint, they can see no further that their own selfish interests and fleshly desires. This leads to the abandonment of all Right thinking even to the exclusion of the futures of its own children!

In 1886 in a publication titled *El Liberalismo es Pecado*, *"Liberalism Is a Sin"*, Dr. Don Felix Sarda Y Salvany wrote of pre-revolutionary Spain:

---

[466] Kalb, James; *The Tyranny of Liberalism: Understanding and Overcoming Administered Freedom, Inquisitorial Tolerance, and Equality by Command*; 2008; pg. 29.

The theater, literature, [and] public and private morals are all saturated with obscenity and impurity. The result is inevitable; a corrupt generation necessarily begets a ***revolutionary*** generation. (emphasis added)

The result of Sarda's unheeded warning was the Spanish Revolution in which the Fascist Francisco Franco aided by Fascist Italy and Nazi Germany conquered Christian Spain. This coup of the Left aided the Fascist Axis powers against America and her Allies. Today America stands at the same crossroads of Evil Against GOOD. Today in America: "The theatre, literature, [and] public and private morals are all saturated with obscenity and impurity. The result is inevitable; a corrupt generation necessarily begets a [Leftist] *revolutionary* generation". This is the corrupt "revolutionary generation" in America today. What will America do? What will *you* do? This is a *War* and you must choose sides. To not choose GOOD is to choose to side with Evil. As Jesus espoused, "He that is not with me is against me"[467]. Choose you this day whom ye will serve[468]! There simply is *no* neutral ground in *The Left's War Against GOD!*

Nazi and American Left Comparisons:

- Abortion
- Abortion/Euthanasia & Nazi Ideology Of *Lebensunwertes Leben* (Life Unworthy Of Life)
- Animal Rights
- Anti-Christian
- Anti-Semitism/Anti-Israel
- Corporativism
- Creating Opportunity For Radical Actions
- Drugs
- Education and Schools
- Environmentalism/Fanatical Environmentalism

---

[467] The *Holy Bible:* Matthew 12:30.
[468] The *Holy Bible:* Joshua 24:15.

- Equal Rights: As A Way of Enslaving Women
- Euthanasia T4 programs (See: Abortion/Euthanasia)
- Evolution as an Alternative to GOD
- Feminism (see Equal Rights)
- Gun Control
- Healthcare/Universal Healthcare
- Homosexuality
- Media Control
- Occultism
- P.C. Enforcement
- Pagan Morals
- Progressive Income Tax
- Propaganda Machine/Media
- Racial Supremacy White then Black now
- Religion (See: Christianity/Religion)
- Removing Christian symbols
- Savior/Messianic Delusions
- School Teachers' Unions
- Separation of Church and State
- Tolerance
- Vegetarianism/Veganism
- Welfare

Abortion:

> A positive and utilitarian attitude toward homosexuality, euthanasia, and **abortion** would therefore [then as now] be a **left-wing *regressive* orientation**, and a **typical Nazi** [Fascist] **profile**.[469] (emphasis added)

Hitler was an enthusiast for abortions of all non-Aryan peoples and codified into *law* his abortion agenda:

---

[469] Lively, Scott and Abrams, Kevin; *The Pink Swastika: Homosexuality in the Nazi Party*; pg. 144.

They may use contraceptives or **practice abortion--the more the better**. In view of the large families of the native population, it could only suit us if girls and women there had **as many abortions as possible**. Active trade in contraceptives ought to be actually encouraged in the Eastern territories, as we could not possibly have the slightest interest in increasing the non-Germanic population[470]. (emphasis added)

Abortion was encouraged and in most cases *mandated* in Nazi Germany and its occupied territories for all non-Aryan women but *strictly illegal* for Aryan women. At least two major Nazi figures, Goering and Greifelt, were executed, at least in part, as a result of their convictions at the Nuremberg trials for their promotion of abortion, both voluntary and compulsory, under the Nazi Fascist régime[471]. How far has America fallen when Americans now embrace abortion which was a fundamental Nazi Fascist principle of one of the world's most evil Leftist régimes!?

Planned Parenthood and its harvesting baby parts is an abomination *Against GOD* on par with the butcher of Nazi Germany Joseph Mengele! It's a science-fiction nightmare… without the fiction! It is absolutely representative of the most grotesque atrocities of the Nazi murder machine! Obama's then White House spokesman Josh Ernest on July 17, 2015, defended Planned Parenthood's selling of aborted baby parts saying that Planned Parenthood follows "the highest ethical guidelines" on scientific "medical research". (Again, the Left's "the science is clear"!)

The deranged "butcher of children" Nazi physician Joseph Mengele was nothing more depraved than Planned Parenthood practitioners in America today! Planned Parenthood says that as of 2015 about 10% of their abortions are done on babies that were already born alive! That is an unarguable murder of a baby! All but the most depraved can easily see that! Mengele committed horrendous atrocities against

---

[470] Poliakov, Leon; *Harvest of Hate: The Nazi Program for the Destruction of the Jews of Europe*; 1954, pgs. 273-274.
[471] Tuomala, Jeffrey C.; Liberty University School of Law at DigitalCommons@Liberty University; *Nuremberg and the Crime of Abortion*; 1-1-2011.

mankind in the name of "science". This is the same barbaric excuse that Planned Parenthood is using to hide behind as it butchers babies and sells the resultant baby body parts and organs for "science"! Every person involved in Planned Parenthood's murder of babies should be held legally responsible for murder and prosecuted to the fullest extent of the law! (Here the Leftist reading this will be aghast at the suggestion of executing a convicted serial murderer, while at the same time applauding the execution of our unborn and born children! The Left is Evil! If you were just offended… you are Evil!)

On Sep 21, 2015 Planned Parenthood CEO Cecile Richards testified before Congress that 86% of Planned Parenthood's revenue is from abortions! The U.S. House of Representatives Oversight and Government Reform Committee member Rep. Cynthia Lummis (R-Wyoming) aptly pointed out to Planned Parenthood: "You Say 3% Of Procedures Are Abortions, Yet 86% Of Your Revenue Is From Abortions?". While abortions only account for 3% of Planned Parenthood's total procedures, abortions account for 86% of Planned Parenthood's revenues. As the *Bible* tell us "For the love of money is the root of all evil: which while some coveted after, they have erred from the faith, and pierced themselves through with many sorrows[472]"!

Some here who find themselves falling for the Leftist narrative of "Yes, but abortion is legal", should also remember that it was also "legal" under Nazi "law" to murder born and unborn babies. Few would argue that the Leftists responsible for the atrocities of the Nazi-Fascist régime should have not been held to a higher legal standard than the one created by themselves to excuse their crimes against humanity! No one lamented the execution of those responsible for one of the largest genocides in human history committed by the Nazi-Fascists of World War II who were responsible for the deaths of up to 50,000,000 human souls. The butchers of the Left in America today has reached over ***60,000,000*** murdered babies, yes that is SIXTY MILLION babies (A six with seven zeros… equivalent to almost 20% of the current population of America!), and according to the US

---

[472] The *Holy Bible*: 1 Timothy 6:10.

Center for Disease Control (CDC) the number is still climbing at a rate of almost 750,000 per year! (It is telling that the Leftists in the US government have chosen to categorize abortions as a "Disease" to "Control" in an effort to disguise and excuse the murder of our children!) In 2013 according to their own report Planned Parenthood performed 327,653 abortions which was 94% of women seeking "pregnancy services". So 348,567 women who went into a Planned Parenthood "clinic" for pregnancy services 327,653 ended in the murder of either a born or unborn baby! Mengele would be proud! How then can anyone excuse contemporaries for committing the *same* atrocities against humanity today by the modern Leftist-Fascists in America today? America has either to apologize to those megalo-criminals of Nazi Germany who were prosecuted as *war criminals* for crimes against humanity and summarily executed, or put those on trial in America today for their equally atrocious atrocities against American humanity!

It should not be lost that every discussion of "science" in the videos collected from the Center for Medical Progress exposing Planned Parenthood is dominated by financial profit! Planned Parenthood has nothing to do with "Parenthood" as they themselves tell us that their main "services" are preventing and *eliminating* "Parenthood" through abortions and contraceptives[473]. This practice in Nazi Germany has been universally decried as barbaric and EVIL; the current practice in Planned Parenthood "clinics" in America today is equally barbaric and founded in EVIL! There simply is no other way to describe the total depravity of murdering the born and unborn babies for any reason in general, and specifically for "scientific research", but absolute *EVIL*! As stated elsewhere, the Left likes to hide behind their mantle of "the science is clear"!

Even after these ongoing revelations of the Evil nature of Planned Parenthood practices the Leftist elite have lined-up to support and violently defend their Evil sanctuary of baby murder! Those include Barack Hussein Obama, Hillary Clinton, Nancy Pelosi, up-Chuck

---

[473] The author believes in the use of contraceptives but not the Leftist endorsed forced use of contraceptives as in Nazi Germany and Fascist Italy.

Schumer, Bernie Sanders, Al Gore, and *ALL* the Leftist Democrat Leadership *ad absurdum*! Some of these Leftist megalomaniacs have even called for an investigation and prosecution of those who exposed these Evil practices of Planned Parenthood! That goes beyond simply defending Evil but attempting to destroy anyone who opposes or exposes their Evil designs! An Obama appointed Federal judge, Judge William H. Orrick, III, who also donated nearly a quarter of a million dollars to Obama's political campaigns, even issued a restraining order against the Center for Medical Progress in an anti-First Amendment criminal ploy to silence the opposition of the Evil of murdering babies. This Leftist *bastard* excused his unconstitutional injunction against Free Speech because the exposure of the Left's Planned Parenthood videos was a form of "harassment, intimidation, violence, invasion of privacy, and injury to reputation". This judge should be put on trial for his crimes against humanity!

Abortion/Euthanasia & the Nazis Ideology Of *Lebensunwertes Leben* (Life Unworthy Of Life):

Abortion was made a matter of decision for a medical review board. Obamacare medical review boards were aptly identified as "death panels". The Left always makes evil sound so "good". Here is how Yahoo puts a smiley face on death panels for Obamacare and end of life counseling:

"Medicare will consider a change for 2016. Such [end of life] counseling would be voluntary, aiming to make patients **aware of their options** so they can determine the type of care they want at the end of life. It's an idea that has wide support in the medical community, and some private insurance plans already pay for such counseling. Supporters say counseling would give patients more control and free families from tortuous decisions. Before former Alaska Gov. Sarah Palin ignited the "death panel" debate in 2009, there was longstanding bipartisan consensus around helping people to better understand their end-of-life choices and decisions. In 2008, a year before debate over the Obama's health overhaul spiraled into tea party protests, Congress overwhelmingly passed legislation requiring doctors to discuss issues like living wills with new Medicare enrollees. That history dissipated almost instantly when Palin said the end-of-life counseling provision in the legislation would result in bureaucrats deciding whether sick people get to live. The language, modeled after a bill by Rep. Earl Blumenauer, D-Ore., was ultimately removed. Now the administration is dipping its toe in the water again[474]".

What kind of "counseling" would be indicated here other than encouraging someone to "choose" to *die* in a form of State-sponsored euthanasia?! (Remember as stated before that the Left's programs are always voluntary until the Left gains enough power to force absolute compliance!) Notice the very "caring" language used. When the "options" are to get healthcare or die. If you are dead your family need not bother itself with those pesky "tortuous decisions". To the Left death, read State-sponsored suicide, is so humane that it becomes a choice of complete selflessness! Before "Sarah Palin ignited the 'death panel' debate" the Left could pressure as many as possible to choose death, that is until the Left was publically confronted with the truth that there really *were* death panels in Obamacare! How inconvenient for the Left. Obama here was the real victim in the eyes of the Left as "Obama's health overhaul spiraled into tea party protests". (Notice the subtle change of "Tea Party" to "tea party".) Poor, poor, Obama. Maybe we can give him another bogus Nobel Prize, maybe for "Eugenics", to placate his mind after suffering such a loss!

While the Nazi Fascists called it *Lebensunwertes Leben* or "Life Unworthy Of Life", the Left likes to euphemize murder calling it "euthanasia". And what should be carefully noted here is that the Fascists once they gained absolute power in Germany quickly expanded the *Lebensunwertes Leben* to the infamous *Aktion T4* or "Action T-4" Programme which murdered between 275,000 to 300,000 innocent souls!

---

[474] Yahoo News; yahoo.com; Medicare weighs paying for end-of-life counseling; October 31, 2014.

[The] T4 Euthanasia Program, Nazi German effort—framed as a euthanasia program—to kill incurably ill, physically or mentally disabled, emotionally distraught, and elderly people. Some physicians active in the study of eugenics, who saw Nazism as "applied biology," enthusiastically endorsed this program.[475] (Notice the same language used by the Left today saying that abortion consideration should be based in part on the "quality of life" Another code phrase for the Nazi "Life Unworthy Of Life"!)

The name "T4" was an abbreviation of *Tiergartenstraße* 4, which was the address of a villa in the Berlin borough of Tiergarten which housed the T-4 Programme. Many contemporary Leftist physicians active in the study of eugenics considered it the "science" of "applied biology". And who could argue with "science", as "the science is clear"! Once implemented the T-4 programme swiftly expanded to include over 15,000,000 of the "enemies of the Nazi State" including Christians, Jews, and all opponents on the Right!

It should also be noted here of another parallel to the Left today with German Fascism is the naming of fascistic programs using "noble" sounding titles. The Left calls murdering unborn children "Pro-Choice". The Nazis called it *Lebensunwertes Leben*. Hitler's campaign to reduce and eliminate the non-Aryan Polish population by pushing women to get abortions was called "*Auswahlfeiheit*" or "Freedom of Choice"! The Left today calls their baby extermination *pogroms* "Pro-Choice" and their death chambers "clinics"! The German name of the Fascist organization which instituted and implemented the T-4 Programme was the *Gemeinnützige Stiftung für Heil und Anstaltspflege* which translates literally as "*The Charitable Foundation for Curative and Institutional Care*". How "charitable" does that system of "care" sound? Notice the resemblance to "Obama*care*" as the "Affordable Care Act" which is neither "affordable" nor holistic "care" in any sense in which it was promoted by the Left.

---

[475] www.britannica.com/event/T4-Program.

The T-4 Programme was the direct prototype of the Holocaust extermination *pogrom* that would eventually claim the lives of more than 7 million Christians and at least 5 million Jews. History teaches us that the Left *always* ends in the mass extermination of those on the Right by the then empowered Left. *Always!* The T-4 Programme was instituted as a "choice" and a "humane" alternative to those nagging *quality-of-life* "options". Soon however the choice was removed by the Nazi's and the decision was made and enforced by the State. This is the same language and deceit as the Obamacare "choices" and "options" that have been touted by the Left promising to "give patients more control and free families from tortuous decisions"[476]. Those who today cry "it could never happen here!" merely echo the exact sentiments of millions of naïve and soon murdered souls in pre-Nazi Germany.

Lest we forget virtually every person on Obama's White House Cabinet and staff were and are supporters and proponents of State-sponsored murder of the unborn, elderly, infirm, unwanted, or just plain "unworthy". As an example, former Cabinet member "science czar" John Holdren advocates massive "population control" including China-like *forced* abortions, killing of imperfect infants, "compulsory sterilization", and euthanasia! He proposed a "planetary Regime"[477] which would oversee human population levels and control all natural resources as a means of "protecting the planet" with life and death power over all American citizens:

- Women could be forced to abort their pregnancies, whether they wanted to or not[478].
- The population at large could be sterilized by infertility drugs intentionally put into the nation's drinking water or in

---

[476] http://www.nbcnews.com/id/33866692/ns/health-health_care/t/few-americans-make-end-of-life-wishes-known/#.W42X2clnbBQ

[477] Holdren, John P., Ehrlich, Paul R. and Anne H.; *Ecoscience: Population, Resources, Environment*; 1978; pg. 942.

[478] Holdren, John P., Ehrlich, Paul R. and Anne H.; *Ecoscience: Population, Resources, Environment*; 1978; pg. 837.

food[479].

- Single mothers and teen mothers should have their babies seized from them against their will and given away to other couples to raise[480].
- People who "contribute to social deterioration" (i.e. undesirables)
  "can be required by law to exercise reproductive responsibility" – in other words, be compelled to have abortions or be sterilized[481].
- A transnational "Planetary Regime" should assume control of the global economy and also dictate the most intimate details of Americans' lives -- using an armed international police force[482].

John Holdren is just a sample of the Anti-GOD and anti-Right agenda of the Left as epitomized by the former Obama Administration. There is simply not enough space here to review all of the Über-Leftist members of Obama's shameless and GODless Administration. Simply Google "controversial Obama cabinet members" and you can review the ultra-Leftist agenda of Obama and his appointees that continues to thrive in the remnant Deep State today!

Animal Rights:

The Nazis were adamant animal rights adherents who not just protected animals but elevated their worth *above* that of humans. It is interesting to note a further modern comparison to the New Left in America is that the Nazis went as far as to consider medical experimentation on animals as unacceptable barbarity while the Nazis tortured and maniacally performed medical experimentation on humans including small and unborn children. This is the same mindset

---

[479] Holdren, John P., Ehrlich, Paul R. and Anne H.; *Ecoscience: Population, Resources, Environment*; 1978; pgs. 787-788.

[480] Holdren, John P., Ehrlich, Paul R. and Anne H.; *Ecoscience: Population, Resources, Environment*; 1978; pg. 786.

[481] Holdren, John P., Ehrlich, Paul R. and Anne H.; *Ecoscience: Population, Resources, Environment*; 1978; pg. 838.

[482] Holdren, John P., Ehrlich, Paul R. and Anne H.; *Ecoscience: Population, Resources, Environment*; 1978; pg. 942-943.

found in the animal rights movement that is rampant in America today. Ingrid Newkirk, the president of People for the Ethical Treatment of Animals (PETA), famously declared, "When it comes to feelings, a rat is a pig is a dog is a boy. There is no rational basis for saying that a human being has special rights"[483]! The undercurrent is even more sinister than a superficial reading lends. The meaning here is that animal lives actually have a higher place than a human life! Abort babies, experiment on children, mutilate babies, euthanize the elderly, but for Gaia's sake protect animals from unnecessary "cruelty"! Drown a bag of puppies go to prison, kill millions of babies and get a standing ovation! This absolute insanity speaks for itself. The Left today mirrors the Pagan animal rights protection of Nazi Germany on a level of that of a soulless animal! GOD Himself sanctioned eating meat, so the Left, as an enemy of GOD, *must* assume the opposite stand.

A National *Socialist* German Workers' Party (Nazi Party) press release states:

> "The Prussian minister-president Goering has released a statement stating that starting 16 August 1933 vivisection of animals of all kinds is forbidden in Prussia [greater Germany]. He has requested that the concerned ministries draft a law after which vivisection will be punished with a high penalty. Until the law goes into effect, persons who, despite this prohibition, order, participate or perform vivisections on animals of any kind will be deported to concentration camps."

> Among all civilized nations, Germany is thus the first to put an end to the cultural shame of vivisection! The New Germany not only frees man from the curse of materialism, sadism, and cultural Bolshevism [Soviet Communism], but gives the cruelly persecuted, tortured, and until now, wholly defenseless animals their rights. Animal friends and anti-vivisectionists of

---

[483] Goldberg, Jonah; Liberal FASCISM: *The Secret History of the American Left From Mussolini to the Politics of Meaning*; 2007; pg. 387.

all states will joyfully welcome this action of the National Socialist [Nazi] government of the New Germany!

What Reichschancellor Adolph Hitler and Minister-president Goering have done and will do for the protection of animals should set the course for the leaders of all civilized nations! It is a deed which will bring the New Germany innumerable new elated friends in all nations. Millions of friends of animals and anti-vivisectionists of all civilized nations thank these two leaders from their hearts for this exemplary civil deed!

Buddha, the Great loving spirit of the East, says: "He who is kind-hearted to animals, heaven will protect!" May this blessing fulfill the leaders of the New Germany, who have done great things for animals, until the end. May the blessing hand of fate protect these bringers of a *New Spirit*, until their god-given earthly mission is fulfilled![484] (emphasis added)

R.O. Schmidt

Notice the connection here between "Buddha", who was a Hindu and created his own version of Hinduism now called Buddhism, and the elevation of the sacredness of animals over human beings? Buddhism and Hinduism are Pagan and therefore GODless religions followed by the Nazis then, and the Left today! The Left's *Re-Name-Game* is always in play but the Evil "New Spirit and god" behind the Left remains always the same! Animals are by the Left randomly assigned "rights" which only belong to human beings as GOD's highest creation. The "New Spirit" is capitalized as the identifying name of a religious Hindu/Buddhist entity, whom the *Bible* identifies as Lucifer, the Pagan "god" of this earth: "Wherein in time past ye walked according to the course of this world, according to the prince of the power of the air, *the spirit* [Lucifer] that now worketh in the children of disobedience"[485] and "In whom *the god of this world* [Lucifer] hath blinded the minds of them which believe not, lest the light of the

---

[484] *Die Weisse Fahne* (The White Flag); 1933; 710-711.
[485] The *Holy Bible*: Ephesians 2:2.

glorious gospel of Christ… should shine unto them"[486]. The target of the Left is always total rebellion against all that GOD teaches, and this rebellion *Against GOD* is the epicenter of *the Left's War Against GOD!*

Here is another example among thousands:

> "The preoccupation with animal protection in Nazi Germany was evident in other social institutions and continued almost until the end of World War II. In 1934, the new government hosted an international conference on animal protection in Berlin. Over the speaker's podium, surrounded by enormous swastikas, were the words "Entire epochs of love will be needed to repay animals for their value and service" (Meyer 1975). In 1936 the German Society for Animal Psychology was founded, and in 1938 animal protection was accepted as a subject to be studied in German public schools and universities"[487].

At the end of the nineteenth century, kosher butchering and vivisection were the main concerns regarding animal protection in Germany. These concerns continued among the Nazis. According to Boria Sax, the Nazis rejected anthropocentric reasons for animal protection—animals were not to be protected for human interests—but for themselves. In 1927, a Nazi representative to the Reichstag called for actions against cruelty to animals and kosher butchering. Of course "kosher" is unique to the Jewish food cleanliness laws found in the *Bible*!

In 1931, the Nazi Party proposed a ban on vivisection. In early 1933, representatives of the Nazi Party to the Prussian parliament held a meeting to enact this ban. On April 21, 1933, almost immediately after the Nazis came to power, the parliament began to pass laws for the regulation of animal slaughter. On April 21, a law was passed concerning the slaughter of animals. On April 24, Order of the

---

[486] The *Holy Bible*: 2 Corinthians 4:4.
[487] Arlukea, Arnold and Saxb, Boria; *Understanding Nazi Animal Protection and the Holocaust*; pg. 9.

Prussian Ministry of the Interior was enacted regarding the slaughter of poikilotherms[488]. Germany was the first nation to ban vivisection[489]. A law imposing total ban on vivisection was enacted on August 16, 1933, by Hermann Göring as the prime minister of Prussia. He announced an end to the "unbearable torture and suffering in animal experiments" and said that *those who "still think they can continue to treat animals as inanimate property" will be sent to concentration camps*. On August 28, 1933, Göring announced in a radio broadcast:

> An absolute and permanent ban on vivisection is not only a necessary law to protect animals and to show sympathy with their pain, but it is also a law for humanity itself.... I have therefore announced the immediate prohibition of vivisection and have made the practice a punishable offense in Prussia. Until such time as punishment is pronounced *the culprit shall be lodged in a concentration camp*.

Göring also banned commercial animal trapping, imposed severe restrictions on hunting, and regulated the shoeing of horses. He imposed regulations on the boiling of lobsters and crabs. In one incident, *he sent a fisherman to a concentration camp for cutting up a bait frog*.

On November 24, 1933, Nazi Germany enacted another law called *Reichstierschutzgesetz* (Reich Animal Protection Act), for protection of animals. This law listed many prohibitions against the use of animals, including their use for filmmaking and other public events causing pain or damage to health, feeding fowls forcefully and tearing out the thighs of living frogs. The two principals (*Ministerialräte*) of the German Ministry of the Interior, Clemens Giese and Waldemar Kahler, who were responsible for drafting the legislative text, wrote in their juridical comment from 1939, that by the law the animal was to be "protected for itself" ("*um seiner selbst willen geschützt*"), and made "an object of protection going far beyond the hitherto existing

---

[488] Cold blooded animals.
[489] Animal experimentation.

law" ("*Objekt eines weit über die bisherigen Bestimmungen hinausgehenden Schutzes*").

On February 23, 1934, a decree was enacted by the Prussian Ministry of Commerce and Employment which introduced education on animal protection laws at primary, secondary and college levels. On 3 July 1934, a law *Das Reichsjagdgesetz* (The Reich Hunting Law) was enacted which limited hunting. On July 1, 1935, another law *Reichsnaturschutzgesetz* (Reich Nature Conservation Act) was passed to protect nature. According to an article published in *Kaltio*, one of the main Finnish cultural magazines, Nazi Germany was the first in the world to place the wolf under protection.

In 1934, Nazi Germany hosted an international conference on animal protection in Berlin. On March 27, 1936, an order on the slaughter of living fish and other poikilotherms was enacted. On March 18 the same year, an order was passed on afforestation and on protection of animals in the wild. On September 9, 1937, a decree was published by the Ministry of the Interior which specified guidelines for the transportation of animals. *In 1938, animal protection was accepted as a subject to be taught in public schools and universities in Germany.*[490]

Goebbels wrote on 29 December 1939: "Both [Judaism and Christianity] have no point of contact to the animal element, and thus, in the end they will be destroyed. The Fuhrer is a convinced vegetarian on principle".

The Left's "animal rights" agenda in America today mirrors that of Nazi Germany under Adolf Hitler. This is not coincidence. The same Evil Left which gave animals "rights" above humans by the Nazis is still the same Evil Left in America today. You can be arrested and imprisoned today in America for "animal cruelty" and killing animals, animals without eternal souls, and are applauded for murdering babies in the Joseph Mengele-like butcher shops of Planned Parenthood's

---

[490] Wikipedia; Animal welfare in Nazi Germany.

abortion rituals. This is a world turned upside down by the Evil of Leftism!

Anti-Christian:

The anti-Christian commonalities between Nazi Fascism and the Left in America has been discussed at length elsewhere in this book. I will add only a few additional points of interest.

> *We are the happy Hitler Youth;*
> **We have no need for Christian virtue;**
> *For Adolf Hitler is our intercessor*
> *And our redeemer.*
> **No priest, no evil one**
> *Can keep us*
> *From feeling like Hitler's children.*
> **No Christ do we follow**, *but Horst Wessel!*
> *Away with incense and holy water pots.*

How about the song taught to elementary school children to sing the praises of then President Obama to the tune of the Christian song *Jesus Loves the Little Children*:

Mm, mmm, mm!
Barack Hussein Obama

He said that all must lend a hand
To make this country strong again
Mmm, mmm, mm!
Barack Hussein Obama

He said we must be fair today
Equal work means equal pay
Mmm, mmm, mm!
Barack Hussein Obama

He said that we must take a stand
To make sure everyone gets a chance

Mmm, mmm, mm!
Barack Hussein Obama

He said red, yellow, black or white
All are equal in his sight
Mmm, mmm, mm!
Barack Hussein Obama

Yes!
Mmm, mmm, mm
Barack Hussein Obama

Notice the lines,
He said red, yellow, black or white
All are equal in *his* sight
These lines make Obama to be a Jesus Messiah from the original Christian song: Red and yellow black and white We are precious in His (Jesus') sight!

In a speech in 1941 Harold L. Ickes, United States Secretary of the Interior under Roosevelt, made the following statement:

> "Nazi hate has spilled over into the Christian camp. On their way to destroy Christianity, the Nazis first besmirched and assaulted Judaism. They believe that they will destroy Judaism if they crush the Jews. But Judaism is not Hitler's ultimate or exclusive enemy. His real enemy is the Nazarene Carpenter who was never anything else but a Jew. It is He who is the actual objective of the brown-shirted disciples of hate who run like a swarm of evil streptococci through the blood stream of our Western civilization... If anyone has any doubt that Hitler's ultimate aim is to destroy both the Jew and the Christian, between whom Christ is the link of imperishable steel, he should turn to an official publication which has been referred to as a text-book of the debasing Nazi philosophy... I read this: 'The mission of German nationality...'"[491]

---

[491] The Wisconsin Jewish Chronicle; April 11, 1941; Page 20.

Here is a wider reading of the above referenced Nazi tract:

> "Through the German soul and through unadulterated German blood, the world will be able to return to a state of health, but **only after it has been freed from the curse of Judaism and of Christianity.... The mission of German nationality in the world is to free this world of Jews and Christians**....It is the very essence of Christianity...for all people to become "united in brotherhood." To achieve this, all barriers of race must fall. The maintenance of such barriers means the preservation of national individuality, **which is essentially irreconcilable with the Christian aim of universal brotherhood**... Because this disintegration of racial culture has been consciously and systematically pursued by Christianity, and is still being pursued today, it is race defilement"[492]. (emphasis added)

Guido von List directed *his* hatred more specifically against Christians, and developed an elaborate mythology to justify attacks against Christianity. Goodrick-Clarke explains List's ideas:

> [List developed] a conspiracy theory that identified Christianity as the negative and destructive principle in the history of the Ario-Germanic race. If it could be shown that Christian missionaries had been intent upon the destruction of Armanist culture, its actual non-existence in the present could be related to empirical events...List's account of Christianization in the historic German lands reiterated the debilitation of Teutonic vigour and morale and the destruction of German national consciousness. He claimed that the Church's gospel of love and charity had encouraged a deviation from the strict eugenics of 'the old Aryan sexual morality'...it was he who had demonized the Church as the

---

[492] Hutton, Dietrich; *Defilement of Race*, publisher: Duetsche Revolution; Duesseldorf, Germany; pg. 3.

sole source of evil in the pan-German scheme of belief (Goodrick-Clarke:68f)[493].

Adolf Brand, a Nazi protagonist, homosexual activist, and anarchist called Christianity "barbarism" and "expressed his desire to fight 'beyond good and evil', (a reference to Nietzsche's book of the same name). Brand's and the Nazi's fight was not for the sake of the masses, since the happiness of 'the weak' would result in a 'slave mentality', but for the human being who proclaimed himself a god and was not to be subdued by human [Christian] laws and ethics"[494].

In March of 1935 seven hundred Protestant pastors were arrested by the Gestapo in Prussia "for issuing condemnations of neo-paganism from the pulpit", and later a similar number of clergy in Wuerttemberg had their teaching credentials stripped for "'violating the moral instincts of the German race' by references to Abraham, Joseph and David in the course of their teaching."[495].

According to the Goebbels Diaries: "The Fuhrer is deeply religious, though completely anti-Christian"[496].

Goebbels wrote in an 8 April 1941 diary entry, "He hates Christianity, because it has crippled all that is noble in humanity"[497].

Martin Bormann and the Nazis realized that the only way for Hitler's total takeover of Germany was the total destruction of the Christian Church: "To an ever increasing degree the people must be wrested from Churches and their agents, the pastors... But never again must

---

[493] Lively, Scott and Abrams, Kevin; *The Pink Swastika: Homosexuality in the Nazi Party*; pg. 105.
[494] Lively, Scott and Abrams, Kevin; *The Pink Swastika: Homosexuality in the Nazi Party*; pg. 105.
[495] Lively, Scott and Abrams, Kevin; *The Pink Swastika: Homosexuality in the Nazi Party*; pg. 107.
[496] Bonney, Richard; *Confronting the Nazi War on Christianity: The Kulturkampf Newsletters*, 1936–1939; Bern, Switzerland; Peter Lang Publications; 2009; pg. 20.
[497] Taylor, Irene, and Alan; *The Assassin's Cloak: An Anthology of the World's Greatest Diarists*; 2002; pg. 184.

the Church regain an influence in the leadership of the people. This must absolutely and finally be broken".[498]

"When in the future our youth no longer hear anything about this Christianity, whose doctrine is far below our own, Christianity will automatically disappear." Martin Bormann, Reich Leader; 1942; From *Kirchliches Jahrbuch fur die evangelische Kirche in Deutschland*, 1933-1944, pp. 470-472.[499]

Hitler on Christianity: "You see, it's been our misfortune to have the wrong religion"[500].

By 1939 the use of the word "Christmas" was banned in Nazi Germany. The offense against the Left's Paganism is the six-letter word "Christ". In America today there is again an open Fascistic assault from the Left on the use of the word "Christmas". The Left will use any Leftist euphemism to avoid having to spit out that word "Christmas" (containing "Christ") including: Happy Holidays, Winter break, Winter solstice (a Pagan religious term), and many others. This aversion to the word Christmas has infiltrated every Leftist institution of the Leftist controlled government, including both Houses of Congress, the Democrat-held White House, and every public school and University.

The modern Fascist ban has filtered down by modern Leftist Politically Correct enforcement to even most shopping retailers whose very existence depends on a successful "Christmas" shopping season! What could be so offensive to the Left in the name "Christmas"? It is rooted in what the *Bible* calls the most powerful weapon against the Left and Evil is the Person and *name* of *Jesus* the Christ! Pagan Rome, the Jewish Sanhedrin, Jacobean France, and Nazi Germany all beat and martyred Christians for speaking in the *name* of *Jesus* the

---

[498] Mosse, George L.; *Nazi Culture: Intellectual, Cultural, and Social Life in the Third Reich*; University of Wisconsin Press; 1 edition (October 15, 2003); pg. 247.
[499] Mosse, George L.; *Nazi Culture: Intellectual, Cultural, and Social Life in the Third Reich*; University of Wisconsin Press; 1 edition (October 15, 2003); pg. 245.
[500] Speer, Albert; *Inside The Third Reich Memoirs By Albert Speer*; Translated from the German by Richard and Clara Winston; The Macmillan Company; 1969.

Christ[501]. Why? Because a person becomes a Christian in the *name* of *Jesus* Christ[502], Evil is defeated in the *name* of Jesus[503], and Evil will be made to bow before Jesus Christ having been judged and condemned just before they are cast into Hell for punishment in the torments of eternal fire[504]. Evil instinctively knows that their only mortal enemy is in *Jesus* the "Christ" and the power of speaking His *name* by Christians![505] (Why else would the Obama Administration have issued an edict to chaplains forbidding them from praying "in Jesus' *name*"?) The Left's assault in America today against Christmas, which bears the name of Christ, is a tacit admission of *the Left's* open hostility in *the Left's War Against GOD!*

At the Democrat National Convention of 2012, the Democrats first voted, behind closed doors, to remove any references to GOD and Israel from the Democrat Party Platform. This action was sanctioned by Obama, the Democrat Party, and the Congressional Democrats. When this was discovered through Conservative talk radio however, a firestorm erupted. Even the Left Stream Media picked-up on it. With all of the backlash the Leftist dominated Democrat Convention was forced to vote to reinstate GOD and favorable references about Israel back into the Party Platform! When the vote was taken live on television the vote was still overwhelming to keep GOD and Israel out of the Platform. A second vote was called for with the same results, except this time the floor director announced that the vote was in favor of restoring GOD and Israel. It obviously was not. There had been orders from the top to force inclusion of the amendment because of the damage that was being done to the public perception of the Democrat Party. In public the Left feigns appearances of supporting GOD and Israel, but this is a false narrative, a *Lie!*, for public consumption. Like Jonathan Grubber said of Obamacare, "if the public knew what was in there they would never have allowed it to pass"!

---

[501] The *Holy Bible*: Acts 4:18.
[502] The *Holy Bible*: Acts 2:38; 1 Corinthians 1:2; 6:11.
[503] The *Holy Bible*: Acts 9:29; 16:18.
[504] The *Holy Bible*: Philippians 2:10.
[505] The *Holy Bible*: 1 Corinthians 5:4.

Do you think that eliminating GOD from the Democrat platform was their endgame? Hardly... Since the Democrats have retaken control of the US House of Representatives in 2018 Democrats have removed "God" (The Christian GOD) from almost every government function and document! The Democrat Left's endgame is to eliminate GOD from every government agency in the United States and then remove Christians just as the Nazis did so effectively before them!

The Left is openly hostile *Against GOD* and, by extension, all things Christian. The Left attempts to keep its hostility towards GOD and Christians hidden from public view in order to keep winning elections at least until the Left has acquired enough power to seize total control the way it did in Nazi Germany. Make no mistake, without exception history teaches us that once the Left has acquired the power it turns quickly from being "Anti-Christian" to "eliminate the Christians". This is *the Left's War Against GOD!*

Anti-Semitism/Anti-Israel:

There is little doubt that the former Obama Administration in particular, and Democrats in general, are militantly *Anti-Semitic*! To be Anti-Semitic is to be Anti-Jewish and Anti-Israel. The Left goes to great lengths to hide their Anti-Semitic beliefs, but as always, actions speak louder than words... At every turn the Left works to marginalize Israel and advance Israel's Muslim terrorist adversaries.

In a January 2010 the Egyptian Foreign Minister acknowledged in a "... Nile TV broadcast in which Egyptian Foreign Minister Abul Gheit said on the 'Round Table Show' that: he had had a one-on-one meeting with **Obama who swore to him that he was a Moslem**, *the son of a Moslem father and step-son of Moslem step-father, that his half-brothers in Kenya were Moslems, and that he was **loyal to the Moslem agenda***. He asked that the Moslem world show patience. Obama promised that once he overcame some domestic American problems (Healthcare), that **[Obama] would show the Moslem world what he would do with Israel**"[506]. (emphasis added)

Anti-Semitism is as old as Jews themselves who began with their father Jacob whom GOD renamed "Israel", from who all Jews descend, and after whom the Nation of Israel is named. Evil has been obsessed in eliminating Israel as a nation and Jews as a people since Jacob walked the earth some 4,000 years ago. The natural question is... Why? In a nutshell the *Bible* tells us that Jesus cannot return to earth to claim all Christians, including all Old Testament saints, until Israel with one voice cries out and acknowledges Jesus as the Christ. The title "Christ" of the Greek New Testament is in the Hebrew language "Messiah". Satan's only "hope" of warding off his judgement and eternal damnation to Hell is to somehow prevent the Jews from one day realizing that Jesus is the Messiah or the Christ. What better way to prevent that from happening, but to kill every Jew alive on earth? If there is no Jew alive to cry out in acknowledging Jesus as the Christ then by GOD's own word Satan could never be judged and damned. It is a futile endeavor, but it is a desperate Devil's only longshot "hope"! It is Satan's "final solution" to his eternal dilemma! With this in mind, we can at least understand Evil's obsession with exterminating all Jews on earth. As Evil's manifestation in the Left of America today, the Left carries this obsession with Anti-Semitism.

There are few of us who do not have at least a minimal knowledge of the Nazi's obsession with the extermination of the Jewish race. The Nazis murdered at least 5 million Jews in this quest. It was so horrific, even by historical standards, that it has been given its own name, we call it the *Holocaust*. The word Holocaust is derived from the from the Greek holókaustos: hólos, "whole" and kaustós, "burnt", signifying the method by which the Fascists of Nazi Germany intended to "burn" or incinerate the "whole" of Jewish humanity in the ovens of Auschwitz, Belzec, Chelmno, Janowska, Majdanek,

---

[506] Brown, Patrick; Western Journalism; *Egyptian Foreign Minister: Obama told me himself, "I am a Muslim"*; June 14, 2010 at 12:30pm.

Sobibor, and Treblinka. To say that the Nazis were Anti-Semitic is a gross understatement of epic proportions.

However, we do not always stop to think of how this Fascist atrocity began. The Germans were not always so virulently Anti-Semitic. The path to the "final solution" was well planned, methodical, and fueled by greed. The Nazis had to take the German people from indifferent to the "Jewish problem", to complicit to the Nazi's "final solution" in the extermination of Jewish men, women, and children. Perhaps surprising to some, the process did not take that long. The engine of the murderous Nazi Anti-Semitism required two primary steps.

First, it required the *removal of GOD* from the public discussion, a step in which the Nazis were masters through the codification into law of the "separation of Church and State" and its replacement of Christianity with Nazi Paganism. The lead-up to which was what is now academically referred to as the era of the "German High Criticism" religious movement of the middle to late 1800's, which removed all of the supernatural from Biblical consideration, including the reality of the miraculous, most significantly the inspiration of the Scriptures, Jesus' virgin birth, miracles, sinless life, substitutionary death, and Jesus' self-perpetuation in raising Himself from the dead. In short, German Higher Criticism movement sought to theologically remove all that is unique to the *Bible* among religious texts, and necessary to Christianity. Without these unique supernatural aspects, the *Bible* loses all connection to a supernatural GOD and renders Christianity indistinguishable from any other hopeless religion.

Second, which will be more fully discussed in this chapter's following subsection **Welfare**, it was necessary for the Nazis to appeal to the base instinct of human *greed*. The German people in large part turned a blind eye to the Nazis "final solution" because the Nazi government gave, or sold at minimal prices, the plunders it acquired from killing the Jews and confiscating their wealth and property. Because the Nazis plundered the wealth and property of the Jews, as well as the millions of Christians, it allowed the Nazi régime to bribe the German populace into silence and even pacification on the issue of the "Jewish

Solution" and its murderous consequences. For twenty pieces of silver the Germans sold out the Jews, their own souls, and GOD!

Obama has been dubbed "the most anti-Israel president in the history of the USA" by many including in the Jerusalem Post[507]. This dubious distinction has been ingloriously earned. Israeli Ambassador Michael Oren said in 2010 of Obama's behavior towards Israel, "Israel's ties with the United States are in their worst crisis since 1975 ... a crisis of historic proportions". Obama took every opportunity to weaken Israel and expose Israel to every Leftist Evil. The examples are almost innumerable. Here are just a few:

- Obama referred to ISIS (*Islamic* State of Iraq and al-Sham) as "ISIL". This is a direct attack on Israel in calling for Israel to be conquered by ISIS. ISIS calls itself the *Islamic* State of Iraq and al-Sham. Why are these facts important? Because al-Sham is an ancient reference to Syria. ISIL is Obama's renaming ISIS to the "Islamic State of Iraq and the *Levant*". The "Levant" is a referral to the entire area of the core of the Middle East *including* Israel! A reference to the old Muslim caliphate which once controlled huge swaths of land in the Middle East which included the control of all the lands of Israel. This is why Obama said that his intentions were to "contain" ISIS, an allusion to containing the Muslim Caliphate to the area of the Levant. Obama by the change of a single word subjugates Israel to Islamists whose stated goal is the annihilation of Israel! Words matter! Obama was and is militantly Anti-Israel, bent on Israel's destruction, and in totally complicit with the realization of a hegemoneous Islamic caliphate built on Israel's ashes!

- As US Senator Ted Cruz brought to our attention, Obama launched a boycott against Israel in 2014, for being the victim of Hamas rocket attacks, by boycotting American airline flights into Israel, while at the same time announcing

---

continuing funding for the anti-Israel Muslim terrorist organization Hamas.[508]

- Obama *illegally* tampered with Israeli elections in 2015 trying to unseat Israeli Prime Minister Benjamin Netanyahu. This is in gross violation of United States Federal law which strictly prohibits such activities against a foreign dignitary. Obama committed a felony in doing so.

- Obama had tried to force Israel to accept the pre-1967 borders for Israel. This would place Israel again in an indefensible position that originally provided the opportunity for Israel's Muslim enemies to have the confidence to attack Israel in 1948, 1956, 1967, and 1973. The Left has used this tactic since Leftist Democrat president Jimmy Carter tried to force it upon Israel. The Left is nearly unanimous in its objective to make Israel accept borders which would guarantee Israel's destruction.

- Obama demanded the nuclear deal with Iran, which guarantees Iran nuclear weapons, and with which Iran has promised to use on Israel. Iran is perhaps Israel's most immediate existential threat. Virtually every elected official in the Democrat Party backed the Iran Nuclear Deal which represents the gravest threat of absolute annihilation for Israel. This is the Democrat Party of the Left which publically espouses their undying support of Israel, while simultaneously working to insure Israel's destruction!

- As mentioned in the **Anti-Christian** subcategory above, at the Democrat National Convention of 2012, the Democrats first voted behind closed doors to remove any references to GOD and Israel from the Democrat Party Platform. When it was discovered through Conservative talk radio, a firestorm erupted. Even the Left Stream Media picked up on it. With all of the backlash the Leftist dominated Convention voted to

[508] http://www.cruz.senate.gov/?p=press_release&id=1593.

reinstate GOD and favorable references about Israel back into the Party Platform. When the vote was taken live on television the vote was still overwhelming to keep GOD and Israel out of the Platform. A second vote was called for with the same results, except that this time the floor director announced that the vote was in favor of restoring GOD and Israel to the Democrat Party Platform. Anyone watching could tell that the nays far outnumbered the yeas.

- In 2016 Obama orchestrated, wrote, and pushed the anti-Israel U.N. December 23 Resolution 2334 meant to cripple Israel's very existence. In a vain attempt to cover his tracks Obama ordered his U.N. ambassador US Ambassador, Samantha Power to abstain from the final vote giving the impression to the useful idiots that he was neutral on the issue.

- Obama's last act before leaving the White House was to secretly give Hamas, who vows the extermination of Israel and all Jews, 221 million dollars!

The Left in America is lunging down the same Anti-Semitic path traveled by the Nazis some 90 years ago. The Left gives lip-service to supporting Israel while acting to undermine and destroy Israel at every turn. The Left has not yet reached the place where it can begin exterminating Jews in ovens or by guillotine, but it is the unavoidable logical conclusion of which history knows no other. Anti-Semitism is but another outworking in *the Left's War Against GOD!*

Corporativism:

As discussed elsewhere, Fascism is a form of militant Socialism that is tyrannical by nature and is characterized by a form of bastardized or crony-capitalism by which the State finances the construction of an envisioned Leftist Utopia. In a Fascist system certain State-cooperative companies are given preferential treatment by the State, they are protected by laws written specifically to benefit these state-allied companies over competitors, and rewarded with contracts in return for the companies' financial and moral support for the State.

The only real difference between Communism and Fascism is that Fascism harnesses the power of Capitalism, albeit a corrupted crony-Capitalism, and Communism outright rejects Capitalism in any form.

In short, Fascism, or National Socialism as the Nazi's called it, is simply a more financially expedient form of Communism in harnessing crony-capitalism to finance a Leftist Utopian fantasy. The Nazi's called it corporativism. The Left today calls it the New Left as embodied in the Democrat Party.

As previously stated, Obama was forced to admit that since he took office in 2009, as even reported by the Leftist organization CNN, 95% of the income gains had gone to the top 1% of the richest in America[509]. What was missing was the fact that the vast majority of this wealth was filtered to Obama's Leftist cronies through government grants, favoritism to Leftist organizations, and especially the so-called *Trillion-dollar* TARP "stimulus" programs. As much as 80% of the stimulus bailouts went to Leftist organizations, especially unions, as payback for their campaign donations and PAC expenditures to support Democrats. (Is it a coincidence that the largest donor base to Democrats are unions which have donated hundreds of millions of dollars to Leftist causes and candidates?[510]) This is the defining characteristic of classic Fascism in harnessing crony-capitalism and diverting financial rewards to those businesses and businessmen who support the Leftist government in power. The Fascists called this Corporatism (also known as corporativism).

We see hundreds of examples all around under the Democrat controlled Obama Presidency and associated Congresses. Because of limited space I will only cite a few of the more obvious examples here. In the General Motors bankruptcy Obama acted illegally and unconstitutionally in forcing preferential treatment benefiting unions at the total expense of shareholders. In exchange the United States government became a multi-billion-dollar major shareholder in the

---

[509] Yousuf, Hibah; CNN.com; *Obama admits 95% of income gains gone to top 1%*; September 15, 2013.
[510] Becker, Kyle; Independent Journal Review; *The Real Party of the Rich: Democrats Have More Top Donors, Millionaires in Congress*; Jan 30, 2014.

largest automotive manufacturer in America. The government has now sold its shares but the threat of not cooperating with the Left's corporativism lives on.

The Obama Administration forced America's major "to big to fail" banks to accept "bail out" money in exchange the government received substantial portions of preferential stock, majority shares in some cases. These major banks did not need the money but were threatened behind closed doors that not accepting the blackmail money would subject these banks to overwhelming government scrutiny. Basically the threat was "accept the money or we will put you out of business". They all took the money. The Left's corporativism in America today is indistinguishable from that of the Fascists in Nazi Germany.

Creating Opportunity For Radical Actions:

Remember the words of Rahm Emmanuel Obama's White House Chief of Staff , "This opportunity isn't lost on the new president [Obama] and his team. You never want a serious crisis to go to waste. Things that we [the Leftist elite in America] had postponed for too long, that were long-term, are now immediate and must be dealt with. This crisis provides the opportunity for us to do things that you could not do before"? This is the Nazi template as used by the Democrats today.

Again, here is the template:

> 1) Use a tragedy as a crisis, or create a crisis where none exists.
> 2) Paint the crisis with as much emotion as possible, and throw logical analysis out the window.
> 3) Propose the one and only solution to the problem, which just happens to coincide with what you've wanted to implement for many years.
> 4) Paint anyone who opposes your one and only solution as evil, uncaring, not smart enough to understand the nuanced brilliance of your solution, or in the pockets of …. you pick the evil entity.

5) Force the solution on the people by any means, whether legislatively, by executive order, or through the legal system. 6) When the unintended consequences of your solution rear their ugly head, use them as a reason for more brilliant solutions to made-up crises[511].

To consolidate power the Nazis burned down the Reichstag, the National Legislature building in Berlin. The Nazis blamed an out of work drunk who they claimed was a Communist insurgent. The Nazis employed a massive propaganda campaign that effectively eliminated all Communist opposition in Germany.

Given the Left's *modus operandi* above, does this Fascist/Leftist comparison not sound like the August 2014 riots in Ferguson, Missouri: "There, Minister of Propaganda Joseph Goebbels, after conferring with Hitler, harangued a gathering of old storm troopers, urging violent reprisals staged to appear as 'spontaneous demonstrations.' Telephone orders from Munich triggered *pogroms* throughout Germany, which then included Austria.[512]"? The Left orchestrates conditions in which it can send in its Nazi-like Storm Troopers and create a "need" for government action, all the while blaming the Right for the Left's own crimes! This book is full of examples of the Left's creating crises into which it must inject itself and thereby seize control of yet another segment of American society: Healthcare, marriage, gun control, the auto industry, home ownership, banking, education, the media (e.g. The Fairness Act), energy (eliminating coal), *ad infinitum, ad nauseam*. The Left in America today creates a "crisis" in order to advance its own Evil agenda and gain control of American society and institutions just as the Nazis did in their consolidating and ultimately seizing absolute power in Germany. This is the *modus operandi* today of *the Left's War Against GOD!*

Drugs:

---

[511] Austrianaddict.com; December 18, 2012; *you-never-let-a-serious-crisis-go-to-waste*.
[512] Encyclopædia Britannica online; *Kristallnacht*; Updated 6-24-2014.

There will be a much broader discussion of Drugs in the next chapter *The Democrat Party Platform As Leftist Doctrines All OPPOSE GOD* in the "Drugs" subsection. Here it will suffice to say that the Nazis used hard drugs such as meth, cocaine, and morphine to fuel their army and its *blitzkriegs* (lightning strikes). German soldiers carried a supply of the drug *Previtin* whose primary ingredient was Crystal Meth. Hitler mainlined this meth straight into his veins. Many credit this mainlining meth as the primary factor in Hitler's plunge into the insane. Today the Left works diligently to transform Americans into accepting legalized drug use. Many states have now legalized medical and "recreational" marijuana. Obama issued Executive Orders allowing citizens to possess and use small amounts of marijuana without fear of prosecution. Obama ordered the Justice Department to release the largest number of prisoners ever from Federal prison who were serving time for drug related sentences.

It is the ultimate goal of the Left in America today to create another dependency class of drug-users who are wholly dependent upon the Federal government for their next "fix". He who controls the dispensing of legalized drugs, controls the Nation! These drug addicts, as in Nazi Germany, are the most loyal and vicious class of citizen and soldier to the Fascist State, who will commit horrific atrocities without conscience to benefit the Left's goals and ideals. GOD in His Word tells us that drugs are the gateway to the demonic. This is *the Left's War Against GOD!*

Education and Schools:

As previously stated, the Left's goals and use of the public educational system in America is indistinguishable from those of Nazi Germany:

"The political corollary is that he is not open to negotiation. The opposition between good and evil is not negotiable and is a cause of war. Those who are interested in "conflict resolution" find it much easier to reduce the tension between values than the tension between good and evil. Values are insubstantial stuff, existing primarily in the imagination, while death is real. The term "value," meaning the radical subjectivity of all belief about good and evil, serves the easygoing quest for comfortable self-preservation.

Value relativism can be taken to be a great release from the perpetual tyranny of good and evil, with their cargo of shame and guilt, and the endless efforts that the pursuit of the one and the avoidance of the other enjoin. Intractable good and evil cause infinite distress—like war and sexual repression—which is almost instantly relieved when more flexible values are introduced. One need not feel bad about or uncomfortable with oneself when just a little value adjustment is necessary. And this longing to shuck off constraints and have one peaceful, happy world is the first of the affinities between our real American world and that of German philosophy in its most advanced form"[513].

Even Leftists are making the connection to which the modern relativism of the Left and the Leftist indoctrination of America's education system which "belongs to a supple, skeptical, and hedonistic vision of university life, which is itself based on a psychology of sex and culture taken straight from Nietzsche"[514]. Nietzsche's proselytizing was the destructive relativism and nihilism on which Hitler's Third Reich was built!

As was mandated by the progressivism of the Left in 1935 mandatory school prayer was removed by the Nazis, then in 1938 Christmas carols were prohibited by law, and by 1941 all non-Nazi religious instruction was totally banned! Sound familiar? It ought to. This is exactly the same path that the Left is hurdling us down in America today in the name of tolerance and anti-discrimination!

The Left's obsession with America's youth and education system has been thoroughly documented in the chapter *Evil In Our Schools* and elsewhere throughout this book. It is the indoctrination of our youth on which the survival of the Left's Evil depends! As Hitler said:

---

[513] Bloom, Allan; *The Closing Of The American Mind*; 1987; pg. 142.
[514] Feeney, Matt; New Yorker online; *Allan Bloom's Guide to College*; April 12, 2012.

"When an opponent declares 'I will not come over to your side,'" Hitler's response was, 'Your child belongs to us already'. On May 1, 1937, [Hitler] declared 'This new Reich will give its youth to no one, but will itself take the youth and give to youth its own [Nazi] education and its own [Nazi] upbringing'. It was not an idle boast that was precisely what was happening."[515]. (clarifications added)

The Left in America today employs this same Evil in the control of our youth. The public education system will not allow any opposing influence of Christianity in our youth's education. Children in America's public schools are suspended, expelled, and arrested for violating the Left's ban on anything that pertains to Jesus, GOD, or the *Bible*. *Bible*s are banned from schools, as are Manger scenes, Christmas carols, and Crosses. Mentioning the name of Jesus in a positive light is punishable by derision, expulsion, and peer humiliation! Do you doubt any of this? Try Googling any of these and you will be mortified as to how far the Leftist takeover of our youth has "progressed" already in America today! The Left's education system is at *War* with all Christian references, symbols, icons, references to Jesus, and GOD… exactly as was Hitler's Leftist and Evil Nazi régime. It is GOD and GOOD that stand as the mortal enemy of the Left and its Fascist agenda in America today!

Environmentalism/Fanatical Environmentalism:

The Nazis were one of the first nations to create national preserves as protected lands which thereby protected Mother Nature who Al Gore now identifies as Gaia. In 1916 the United States passed the "Organic Act" under LEFTIST/Progressive President Woodrow Wilson that established America's National Park System. Under Presidents Clinton and Obama, the Organic Act has been used as a Progressive tool to set aside millions of acres of land to forbid oil exploration and thereby substantially cripple America's ability to be energy self-

---

[515] Shirer, William L.; *The Rise and Fall of the Third Reich: A History of Nazi Germany*; Simon & Schuster; Reissue edition (October 11, 2011); pg. 249.

sufficient. This tactic weakens America and before President Trump has kept us dependent on the Muslim Middle East which is one of America's biggest existential threats.

The Nazis were also one of the first to establish protected species especially indigenous species and whales.

"Himmler hoped to switch the SS entirely to organic food and was dedicated to making the transition for all of Germany after the war. Organic food was seamlessly linked to the larger Nazi conception of the organic nation living in harmony with a pre- or **non-Christian ecosystem**"[516]. Christianity is, by the doxology of the Religion of the Left, intrinsically linked to opposing Leftist environmentalism.

Environmentalism and the Environmentalist Movement elevates the worth of plants and animals above that of human life. More frightening is the fact that human life is almost always viewed by the Environmental Left as an enemy of Mother Earth and detrimental to the existence and viability of all other life on earth. Even many of the New Age Leftist movies portray Mother Earth striking back at the human race in retaliation of the many "sins" of man against the Earth: *After Earth, The Happening* (Hindu), *The Day After Tomorrow* (Hindu), *2012* (Mayan), *Frogs*, and many others. There are of course other variations on this theme such as *The Day the Earth Stood Still* where aliens from outer space come to rescue Planet Earth from the inevitable destruction of Earth by humans.

In Environmentalism there is a basic assumption that there is no GOD, and as such, life on earth is vicarious at best, and that man is indeed capable of destroying all life. Environmentalists ironically, while rejecting GOD, believe in a "god" of the earth which they name Mother Earth, or Gaia among others. This god apparently has little power since Environmentalists generally believe in a hapless and random "evolution" of the Universe and everything in the Universe. This of course would mean that Mother Earth also "evolved" into being and

---

[516] Goldberg, Jonah; *Liberal FASCISM: The Secret History of the American Left From Mussolini to the Politics of Meaning; 2007*; pg. 387.

power. How exactly did something which at one time did not exist, then through some chemical combustion excited by a lightning strike, then turn itself into a god? That is a pretty low bar for a "god". A "god" which by the way threatens to wipe out all of mankind at any moment if "she" is too offended by men and his ways. The Left laughs at the Right's Christian Faith, but the Left's faith seems much more a leap of "faith"! The Religion of the Left is the Religion of *Insanity*!

It is a major and somewhat effective weapon in the Left's arsenal to use hysteria and fear in its imagined doomsday scenarios to force compliance to its Evil agenda! To name a few of the obvious: the Nagasaki and Hiroshima nuclear bombs, the Exxon Valdez oil spill, the BP Gulf of Mexico oil spill, the Mount Saint Helens eruption in 1980, the Boston Harbor pollution, Chicago's Lake Michigan and Lake Erie (which was so polluted that they actually caught fire!), all of these were said by the Environmentalists would take hundreds of years for Earth (read: Mother Earth/Gaia) to "heal", today only a short time later, all of which are again virtually pristine environments. Most of these "clean-ups" were accomplished by GOD's built-in self-cleaning mechanisms with little or no help from men's efforts. For instance, Mount Saint Helens was a "natural" disaster and only a few years later *with no aid of man* was so restored that the casual observer could not even tell that a disaster of such monumental proportions had ever occurred. If the Left can convince enough people that Global Warming, Climate Change, industrial disasters, volcanos, nuclear holocaust, overpopulation, mass starvation, pandemics, and myriad other scare tactics, can literally wipeout life on earth, then their GODless scenario can be used to bring mankind once and for all into their clutches… for all our own "good" of course. Remember the warning of Ronald Reagan "The nine most terrifying words in the English language are, 'I'm from the government and I'm here to help'"!

The Christian GOD tells us that He Created the earth in seven literal 24-hour days. GOD being all knowing Created an earth that is resilient against anything that man would foreseeably do to the environment. GOD Created earth's environment to heal environmental degradations quickly and efficiently. GOD through His prophetic Word tells us ahead of time that man *cannot* destroy the earth and that when the end comes the earth will be destroyed by an act of GOD alone[517]. The *Bible* tells us that man was the first being on the earth, that man was GOD's reason for Creating, and that man is the most valuable entity on our planet. Man is so valuable to GOD that GOD Himself came to earth, became a man, and lived a perfect sinless life, was vicariously Crucified on the Cross for our sins, and resurrected Himself from the dead just as He promises to do for Christians after their death. Hmm? Which God seems like a personal caring GOD Who Created everything as a means of opportunity for a personal relationship with men?

Jessica Alba's *Honest Company* may not be so honest. Their "eco-friendly" SPF 30 sunscreen, with "broad spectrum, mineral-based protection" did not work and users "came out in droves" to protest that yet another Leftist-oriented product simply "does not work". You could literally say, as with all Leftist concoctions, they all got burned! Whether it be the Left's insanity in the "alternative energy" debacle, "alternative fuel" electric cars, or alternative sea-salt, whenever the Left tries to create an "alternative" to proven, real-world methods and products and substitute an "environmentally friendly" alternative... it fails... miserably. Alternative energy companies go bankrupt costing Americans billions of dollars, electric cars batteries blow up killing Americans, and sea-salt tastes horrible. There is a reason that "mental" is the root word used to define... insane![518] Remember the Leftist, murderous *Comrade* Lenin's useful idiots? But then again with the Left, truth, practical real-world experience, and common sense[519] are irrelevant and an anathema to achieving their Leftist Utopia. The Left uses the façade of "Environmentalism" as a way to seize control of every aspect of American life. All of course just as the Nazis, in the name of "science"[520].

---

[517] The *Holy Bible*: 2 Peter 3:12-13.

[518] See the broader discussion of insanity in the chapter *The Left Is a RELIGION!.*

[519] For a wider discussion of the Left's "common good" see the chapter: *Fighting To WIN!: How Do We Fight The War? The Right's RULES FOR ANTI-RADICALS! A Call To ACTION!,* Bolded Topic: *Practical War Strategies,* Bolded subcategories: *THE LEFT IS NOT ABOUT COMMON SENSE!* and *Use Common Sense.*

[520] For further discussion on "the science is clear" see the chapter *Fascism and the Left in America: Kindred Spirits and Familiar Bedfellows.*

Equal Rights: As A Way of Enslaving Women:

It may come as a surprise to many to learn that the Nazis were one of the first Western nations to implement a national campaign for "Women's Equal Rights". Women's Rights is always a red herring, a sleight of hand *Bait and Switch*. The Equal Rights Movement has been a trap for women since its inception by Satan in the Garden of Eden. (This issue will be further developed in the next chapter *The Democrat Party Platform As Leftist Doctrines All OPPOSE GOD* under the subsection "Equal Rights".)

In reality, instead of "equal pay" the Nazis, like the Left today, substituted equal pay with "compulsory employment" and "sexual liberation" which turned women into breeders for the Third Reich's Thousand Year Reign (an evil counterfeit of Jesus' Thousand Year reign of the Bible[521]).

Ending all of the moral restraints of the then dominant Christian Religion allowed the Nazis to turn women into breeding stock and laborers for the Third Reich.

The Nazis giving "Equal Rights" to women in the marketplace gave Equal responsibility in the workplace for women. Giving full work "privileges" to women devolved into every woman's patriotic "duty" to work and fuel the war machine for the Leftist Nazi War effort. Women became a form of indentured servants to the State. Girls at the age of 16, who weren't used as breeders, were shipped off to rural work-farms where they were then required to perform manual labor. This project was couched as an opportunity to get "back to nature". Ah... the Left's word manipulation, its *Bait and Switch: The Re-Name-Game*, could even make indentured servitude and forced prostitution sound noble! What is promised by the Left is *never* what you ultimately get from the Left. Remember the Left's primary marketing moniker "If they had known what was in it, they would have never allowed it".

---

[521] The *Holy Bible*: Revelations 20:4-6.

Through the modern day "Equal Rights" Movement the Left is herding women into one or all of three camps: the Sexual Liberation camp, the Homosexual camp, and the Workforce labor camp. Sexual Liberation aids the State in population growth and destroys all semblances of Christian morality, which is the biggest Enemy of the Left. Sexual Liberation began in earnest in America at what has been labeled the Sexual Revolution of the 1960's. Again the Left's wordsmiths chose their slogans well in calling women to join the "Revolution" Against Christianity and GOD! The Homosexual Agenda corrupts any Christian morals and makes lesbians totally dependent upon the State to maintain their "alternative" lifestyle. Even the moniker "alternative" shows its Rebellion *Against GOD* as an "alternative" to GOD. Otherwise who or what is homosexuality an "alternative" to? Turning the primary use of women to the workforce again makes the woman totally dependent on the State, which through materialism they have a constant need to "keep up with the Jones" or at least the men. An "Equal Rights" Workforce mandate also requires women to turn their children over to the State controlled childcare centers and public schools where their children are indoctrinated into Leftist thought control and creates a loyal Fascist-class "from cradle to grave" as the Left deceivingly promises. When children exist only in the Leftist bubble, they never know a better opportunity and they can never know GOD.

Equal Rights was sold to the women of America as a bill of goods for "equal pay". Equal Rights is a Trojan Horse to demean women, destroy the family, and de-Christianize America. Equal Rights has *never* been about equal pay for women. It has been about destroying the GOD-ordained home and corresponding family unit. The *Biblically* defined family unit has been the foundation upon which Western Civilization was built. The Left must first destroy the family unit before it can seize power in America. That Leftist goal is well under way!

We need to take a moment here to debunk the myth that women do not already get "equal pay" for equal work. There have been a number of investigations done recently on women's pay compared to men's with the surprising conclusion that, when factored equally, women actually earn more than men! To support the Left's miscalculations (read: *Lies*) the Left ignores some very important factors in the "equal pay" for equal work equation. Men tend to work longer hours, take higher paying and less family-time advantaged positions, are more likely to work the higher paying and more physically demanding jobs, and are much more likely to work significantly more overtime which typically pays double and triple time wages. And of course women are substantially more likely to take maternity leave than their male counterparts. In short the greatest contributing factor to the so-called "equal pay" for equal work discrepancy is a matter of a woman's choice and *not* a matter of men's discrimination against women!

It should also be noted that the Leftist vanguard never lives up to its own Leftist mandated standards. A review of Obama's White House staff showed that in a 2014 survey the average male White House employee was earning about $88,600, while the average female White House employee was earning about $78,400[522]. This according to the Obama White House's own data! During Hillary Rodham-Clinton's time as a US Senator, Ms. Clinton only paid only 72¢ on the dollar to women compared to men.[523] Even after this pay discrepancy was discovered, women on Hillary Rodham-Clinton's presidential campaign staff were only being paid 87¢ on the dollar as compared to men.[524] This is the Left's War On Women!

Have you ever considered that Equal Rights already exists in America? It is already the law of the land. Yet the Left constantly tells Americans that there is so much *more* that needs to be done in the Equal Rights campaign. The Left bellows that the Right has a War On Women. Really? So every Conservative is at War with their mothers, sisters, and daughters? Really? It is the basic tenant of the Right to protect and reverence women. Where is this War On Women then? It is *the Left's War on Women*! Again, as always, it is the Left who

---

[522] Goldfarb, Zachary A.; The Washington Post; *Male-female pay gap remains entrenched at White House*; July 1, 2014.
[523] Scher, Brent; The Washington Free Beacon; *Hillary Clinton's War on Women: Analysis: As senator, Clinton paid women 72 cents for each dollar paid to men*; February 23, 2015 5:00 am.
[524] Scher, Brent; The Washington Free Beacon; *Hillary Clinton's Campaign Has a Gender Pay Problem Analysis: Women made less money than men in first months of Clinton campaign*; August 6, 2015 5:00 am.

wages an all-out War On Women and use their contrived accusations to deflect their own guilt upon the Right! This is the Left's *Lies, Lies, Lies!*, the Left's own War On Women, and the Left's *Bait and Switch Re-Name-Game* in *the Left's War Against GOD!*

Evolution as an Alternative to GOD:

I repeat the points with pertinent changes from the previous discussion on Environmentalism/Fanatical Environmentalism: The Left, like the Nazis, is "Embracing Evolution as an alternative to GOD"! In Evolutionary Theory there is a basic assumption that there is no GOD, and as such, life on earth is vicarious at best, and man is indeed capable of destroying all life. Evolutionists ironically while rejecting GOD, believe in a "god" of the earth which they name Mother Earth, or Gaia, among others. This god apparently has little power since Evolutionists generally believe in a hapless and random "evolution" of the Universe and everything it the Universe. This of course would mean that Mother Earth, Eaarth, Gaia, or myriad other like-named devils, also "evolved" into a self-conscious being and somehow created its own power. How exactly did something which at one time did not exist, then through some chemical combustion excited by a lightning strike, then "evolve" itself into a god? That is a pretty low bar for a "god". A "god" which is more easily explained as coming from the imaginations of men. A "god" which by the way threatens to wipe out all of mankind at any moment if "she" is too offended by the deeds of men. The Left laughs at the Right's Faith in GOD, but the Left's faith seems much more a stretch of "faith" and a product of a desperate Anti-GOD imagination! The Religion of the Left is indeed the Religion of Insanity![525]

The Christian GOD tells us that He Created the earth in seven literal 24-hour days. He created every species and flora a literal seven 24-hour day period called Creation week. The *Bible* tells us that man was GOD's sole *reason* for Creating, and that man is the most valuable entity on our planet. Man alone, among all living creatures, was given an eternal spirit and soul. The *Bible*, GOD's literal Word, tells us that

---

[525] See the chapter: *The Left Is a RELIGION!* and the discussion on *neurosis* and *insanity*.

man is so valuable to GOD that GOD Himself came to earth His Creation, became a man Himself, and lived a perfect sinless life, was Crucified vicariously for our sins, and resurrected Himself from the dead just as He promises to resurrect every Christian after their death and take His Faithful to an eternity in Heaven with Him. Hmm? Which God seems like a personal caring God Who Created everything as a means of opportunity for a personal relationship with men?

Evolution tells us that we are all merely cosmic accidents. How hopeless is that?! Under the randomness of Evolution there can be no fixed definition of "evil". After all, if everything is merely a contrived construct of an aimlessly evolved human mind, then in effect there literally can be no "right" or "wrong" and as the Left has been preaching for years, everything then is relative, no absolute! If there is no ABSOLUTE RIGHT on which to measure Wrong, then there can be no gauge to determine Wrong, and Wrong could not therefore exist. (Remember the trick of the Devil: You never knew. That was his power. The greatest trick the Devil ever pulled was convincing the world he didn't exist!)

Let me give you a couple of examples. The only way to measure if something is a *Lie* is to have ABSOLUTE TRUTH by which to judge something that departs from ABSOLUTE TRUTH, and is therefore a Lie. In the *Bible* Light is associated with GOD and GOOD. Not coincidently, science can only measure darkness as an absence of light. Darkness has no other definition or measurability in science. If we did not have "light" there simply would be no way to determine a thing called "darkness". This is how GOD measures each person as to whom they belong... to the Light or to Darkness. If Jesus, Whom the *Bible* calls "the Light"[526], is in a person's spirit then that person belongs to GOD, however a person without GOD's Light then belongs to Darkness or Satan the Prince of Darkness. Is it any wonder then that Evil and the Left want us to believe that everything is relevant or definable at each person's whim? If you do not make a conscious decision to receive the Light, then by default you belong to the Darkness or Satan the Devil of devils! Does that strike you as harsh? This is why the *Bible*

---

[526] The *Holy Bible*: John 1:6-18.

warns us that the Devil "cometh not, but for to steal, and to kill, and to destroy"!

The Left is literally "Embracing Evolution as an *alternative* to GOD": Evolution completely devalues individual life and places the emphasis on the "greater good"[527] of society, community, or as Hillary Rodham-Clinton calls it the "Village". The Nazis called it the *Volksgemeinschaft*! The *Volksgemeinschaft* is literally translated from German as the "people's community". The Left's ideas and agendas are not "new" as the "New Left" would have us believe; their ideas are as old as Evil itself! We must also keep in mind that the Theory of Evolution is just that, a *"Theory"* that has *never* been able to be proven at *any* level. The "missing links", after 150 years of unprecedented scientific investigation and hundreds of billions of dollars of research, are still "missing". Every time a supposed "missing link" was "discovered" it was without exception later actually discovered to be an outright fraud, as in the case of *Piltdown Man*, Ernst Haekel's faked embryonic drawings, and *Archaeoraptor Liaoningensis*: the faked Dinosaur-bird "ancestor", to name a few of the more obvious. Even Charles Darwin had the integrity to admit that if these "missing links" could not be bridged that his "Theory" would collapse under its own weight. A hundred and fifty years later there are none of Darwin's bridges!

Let's look at a couple of examples scientifically of how Evolution is an *absolutely* impossible. Evolutionists tell us that it took over 4 billion years for a formed earth, having accumulated the necessary primordial ooze, for a random lightning strike at just the right moment, in just the right way, with just the right incalculable circumstances, and presto-chango… life began! Here's the rub for any reasonable and thinking person… all life requires other forms of life to sustain its own life. In some manner *all* living organisms must feed on other pre-existing living organisms to sustain life. What then did the original post-mordial organism feed upon?! So the ooze, lightning strike, agitated molecules experience mathematically impossible

---

[527] See further comments in: *Understanding The Two Faces of The Enemy* and *America's War/The Left's War Against America's Judeo-Christian Foundations*.

spontaneous life… and then quickly starve to death! THE END. Hmm, that's an insurmountable dilemma. The 4 billion years of supposed "Evolution" would come to a crashing halt and have to wait for countless more millennia for another random lightning strike at just the right moment, in just the right way, with just the right incalculable circumstances, for life to start… again. Of course, again… this new miracle organism would immediately die from lack of other preexisting living organism to feed upon! This creates a sort of primordial *Groundhog Day* scenario where life, even if it were possible to begin under this Evolutionary myth hypothesis, the imagined living organism would cease to exist as quickly as it began leaving it doomed to repeat itself in vain for eternity in a Sisyphean[528] dilemma of Universal proportions!

Now for the incurable skeptic who says wait a minute, there could have been multiple living organisms spawned from that one random lightning strike. Ok, but the same dilemma still occurs as each organism feeds upon all other available organisms until at last there is no more organisms to eat… then the last organism *still*… dies!

This one single scientific fact proves that the Theory of Evolution is… *dead*! How much more dead can the Theory of Evolution get? Dead is dead. Impossible is impossible. And *only* GOD can create life from nothing! Even the Theory of Evolution demands the existence of GOD!

This is indicative of the account of the lawyer who showed up to court without his client. When the judge asked the lawyer angrily why his client was not there as required by the law, the lawyer responded, "well your honor there are several reasons why my client is not here today. First", the lawyer began, "my client is dead…". The judge stopped the lawyer right there saying, "That is enough I don't need to

---

[528] Sisyphus was a character of Greek mythology, a sinner condemned to hell and an eternity and an unsurmountable task of rolling a boulder up a hill to its summit, only to watch in horror, despite Sisyphus' valiant but vain efforts, to watch the boulder roll back down again under the natural inclination of nature's gravity. Every time Sisyphus, by the greatest of exertion and toil, had the peak within sight, the damned thing rolled back down again. So goes the modern-day myth of the Theory of Evolution.

hear any more reasons!". That is the situation that should rule our decision-making process. Dead is dead and impossible is impossible. This is certainly a law of science. When even one absolute reason can be presented that render any theory impossible, why would any reasonable person need any more convincing of the inevitable and unavoidable conclusion?

This same scientific dilemma could be used over and over in absurd redundancy. Each example would utterly and absolutely destroy "evolving" and spontaneous life and destroy any possibility for the "Theory" of Evolution to be a working model in *any* way. For example, let's consider the presumed lightning strike in the Theory of Evolution which is taught to have agitated the chemical reaction that resulted in the first living organism on earth. An unsurmountable problem for Evolutionary Theory is that the core temperature a bolt of lightning reaches temperatures of roughly 30,000 kelvins (53,540 degrees Fahrenheit!) and would not facilitate a life-creating combustion, but would in fact instantly incinerate and thereby obliterate life! As a way of comparison, the sun's surface temperature is just 6,000 kelvins or 10,340 degrees Fahrenheit! The presumed lightning strike in the Theory of Evolution which is purported to have agitated the chemical reaction that resulted in the first living organism on earth... is impossible! Lightening only "creates" life in Frankenstein movies. Frankenstein and the Theory of Evolution have in common that they are both "science *fiction*" about creating unwieldy monsters that exist only in the imagination of their cult followers!

This one single fact again proves that the Theory of Evolution is *dead*. How much more dead can the *Theory* of Evolution get? Dead is dead and impossible is impossible!

For those who are incredibly slow at the draw, let's consider another fact that would *absolutely* disqualify the Theory of Evolution. Any organism that has a circulatory system with blood must have a clotting agent present in the blood or every organism at some point in their life would be injured and would bleed-out and die. The medical term for this condition in humans is hemophilia. Hemophiliacs in the human race can have their lives prolonged through medical intervention and medicines. However, under-"evolved" organisms from which humans supposedly "evolved" could not have had this advantage to overcome such a deadly condition. Again, all life would have come to a screeching halt almost before it started with no time to "evolve" a lifesaving clotting agent.

This one single fact again proves that the Theory of Evolution is *dead*. How much more dead can the *Theory* of Evolution get? Dead is dead and impossible is impossible!

The same reasonable and unavoidable conclusion could be drawn from tens of thousands of like examples including such obvious examples as: the digestive system, the immune system, the self-preservation instinct, brains, the eye, the ear, the skeletal system, the body's self-repair system, reproduction, *ad absurdum*. Only fully developed organisms wholly designed and functionally fully equipped can survive on earth! Only with a being on par with GOD, as Designer and Creator, is it possible to have such an intricate, symbiotic, and sustaining fauna and flora ecosystem that makes life on earth first possible, then sustainable!

The Nazis, like the Left in America today, used Evolution as a *substitute* for GOD. When people want to find an excuse to dismiss GOD from their calculations, lives, and personal responsibility almost any excuse will do, even the most untenable, self-serving, and insane… even Evolution!

Food Restrictions/Nutrition:

"Holistic" was a key cornerstone in the Nazi programs with "natural" and "organic" catchphrases while vilifying any food producers that did not conform to these Leftist standards.

Veganism and vegetarianism were pushed through government food programs. Adolf Hitler, Joseph Goebbels, Rudolf Hess, Martin Bormann, and Heinrich Himmler were all militant vegans and vegetarians. Today the Left can only be described as literal *food Nazis*.

They want to impose their Leftist Religious beliefs on everyone with no exceptions. The Left would mandate what foods we eat, in what amounts, and establish State mandated ingredients and preparation. The Left are the modern incarnation of the *food Nazis*!

Nutrition: "Himmler hoped to switch the SS entirely to organic food and was dedicated to making the transition for all of Germany after the war. [529]Organic food was seamlessly linked to the larger Nazi conception of the organic nation living in harmony with a pre- or **non-Christian ecosystem**"[530].

The Left's nutrition campaign is closely tied to their "animal rights" and vegetarian/vegan agendas. These are synonymous with the Hindu concepts of a consciously integrated living Universe under the religious views of reincarnation, Bhūmī-Devī (remember that *devī* in Sanskrit is the female equivalent in English for a devil, a literal demon!) or Pṛthvī Mātā (Mother Earth), and the submission of self to the "greater good". Hinduism, as we have shown and will continue to show, is inseparable from Nazism and the Left in America today.

A popular Nazi slogan of the 1920's was *"Gemeinnutz geht vor Eigennutz"* – "The common good supersedes the private good" – to justify the policy of sacrificing individuals' health for the sake of the body politic. In 2004, Hillary Rodham-Clinton insisted that we look at children's entertainment "from a public-*health* perspective". According to the Hitler Youth health manual, "Food is not a private matter!" and "You have the duty to be healthy![531]" This is the mantra picked up by the Left as a whole and Michelle Obama in particular through her failed school nutrition program.

Gun Control:

---

[529] For more on being GOD's see the books Postscript: *For the Sinner who finds himself on the Wrong side of GOD in The Left's War Against GOD.*

[530] Goldberg, Jonah; *Liberal FASCISM: The Secret History of the American Left From Mussolini to the Politics of Meaning*; 2007; pg. 387.

[531] Washington, Ellis; WND.com; *The Nazi cult of the organic, Exclusive: Ellis Washington compares Hitler obsessions with today's 'liberal fascists'*; 03/26/2011.

Here is Hitler's view on Gun Control:

"The most foolish mistake we could possibly make would be to allow the **subject** races to possess arms. History shows that all conquerors who have allowed the subject races to carry arms have prepared their own downfall by so doing. Indeed, I would go so far as to say that the supply of arms to the underdogs is a *sine qua non* for the overthrow of any sovereignty"[532].

In 1938 the Nazis put into effect the following "gun control" law targeting the German Jewish population which prohibited Jews from "acquiring, possessing, and carrying firearms and ammunition, as well as truncheons or stabbing weapons. Those now possessing weapons and ammunition are at once to turn them over to the local police authority"[533].

Notice that the "gun control" laws of the Left never end with just "guns" but all self-defense instruments, such as "truncheons or stabbing weapons" or knives, by which a person can fight back against an Evil State *pogrom* aimed at the destruction of Christian and Jewish populations. This betrays the Left's propaganda that removing guns is for general "safety issues" but is a means of total State control!

The confiscation of all guns from German civilians was the opening salvo of the Nazi Holocaust which claimed the lives of over 12 million Christians and Jews. The eradication of the Jews in Nazi Germany was accomplished with some ease as the disarmed Jews lacked a way to defend themselves. This was evidenced by the famous Warsaw Ghetto Uprising of 1943 in which the Jews resisted the Nazi invasion for nearly a month only because some Jews had refused to surrender their weapons.

---

[532] Hitler, Adolf; Edict of March 18, 1938; Trevor-Roper, H.R.; *Hitler's Table Talks 1941-1944*; London, Widenfeld and Nicolson; 1953; pgs. 425-426.
[533] Burleigh, Michael and Wippermann, Wolfgang; *The Racial State: Germany; 1933-1945*; NY: Cambridge, 1991; pgs. 92-96.

The continuing subjugation of nations has as Hitler said *always* involved the disarming of the populace. *Always*. In ancient Israel, the Evil Empire of Babylon kept Israel in slavery by taking every sword, spear, and implement of war, including sharpening instruments for farm implements[534].

"Gun Control" is a two-prong attack by the Left against freedom and liberty. First, the Left cannot seize total control while its citizens are armed. Second, in the Left's cradle-to-grave mantra, only the government should be in a position to "protect" Americans from criminals with guns. Criminals will always have guns. The Left demands that its citizens must always be dependent upon the State for every critical aspect of survival: food, water, protection from criminals, *et al*. Is it any wonder then that the Left seizes upon every opportunity to politicize mass shootings as a need for more gun control? Obama in reaction to the 2015 Oregon College shooting said "This is something we should politicize". Obama has advocated for an Australian-style gun confiscation by Executive Order and Imperial edict. This is yet another blatant example of the Left's Rule of "never let a crisis go to waste". On January 16, 2013 Obama issued a series of Executive Orders on "gun control", number 16 reads "Clarify that the Affordable Care Act (Obamacare) does *not* prohibit doctors asking their patients about guns in their homes". Obama issued an Executive Order on January 5, 2016 directing doctors to report "mentally unstable" patients to the FBI for gun confiscation. Remember that it is also the objective of the Left to pronounce *all* dissenters as "insane". The success of the Left's takeover of America is absolutely dependent on the confiscation of guns from all law-abiding citizens... just like Nazi Germany!

Healthcare/Universal Healthcare:

One of the first steps of Nazi Nationalization was implementing Nationalized Healthcare. This has always been a guise of the Left in seizing control of national economies and the very lives of the national populace. Americans instinctively understand this and oppose total

---

[534] The *Holy Bible*: 1 Samuel 13:19-22.

government control of peoples' lives. Remember this the next time that you might get an inkling that Nationalized Healthcare might not be so bad: with Nationalized healthcare doctors, hospitals, and all medical organizations work for and answer exclusively to the government, not to you as an individual or any individuals! The objective of Nationalized Healthcare becomes the "greater good" of the State at the expense and exclusion of individuals! When given the choice Americans have always rejected Nationalized Healthcare. Ronald Reagan twenty years before he became President was already fighting this Battle Against the Left:

> But at the moment I'd like to talk about another way because this threat is with us and at the moment is more imminent. One of the traditional methods of imposing Statism or socialism on a people has been by way of medicine. It's very easy to disguise a medical program as a humanitarian project. . . . Now, the American people, if you put it to them about socialized medicine and gave them a chance to choose, would unhesitatingly vote against it. We have an example of this. Under the Truman administration it was proposed that we have a compulsory health insurance program for all people in the United States, and, of course, the American people unhesitatingly rejected this.[535]

Controlling Americans' healthcare is *enslavement* to the State. Compromise or "moderation" with Evil always leads to incrementalism of corruption which always leads to enslavement[536]. The Devil's ways never change.

As evidenced in Nazi Germany, medical "ethics" become the sole domain and definition of the Leftist controlled State. American morals which have been traditionally understood and defined by its Christian and Biblical moorings, become not just irrelevant, but an anathema to the ruling Fascist Left. The new State "ethics" become defined almost

---

[535] *Ronald Reagan Speaks Out Against Socialized Medicine* (1961 LP).
[536] See broader discussion on compromise and moderation in the chapter *Fighting To WIN!: How Do We Fight The War? The Right's RULES FOR ANTI-RADICALS! A Call To ACTION!* and the subcategories: *Compromise Kills!* and *Moderates:*.

wholly as what opposes Christian and Biblical morals. This counter-ethics of the Left is already evidenced by the embracing of Leftist "ethics" of *everything* unGODly: Homosexuality, anti-Christian, redefining marriage, promiscuous sexual laws, racism, disenfranchising of the individual, devaluing of life, abortion, legalizing euthanasia, forced sterilization, and many, many others. This is *exactly* what happened in Nazi Germany and is precisely what is happening in America today!

Healthcare is a mechanism of the Left of controlling the masses. Every American life, at some point in your life, depends on proper healthcare. If the Left is the sole provider of healthcare, then the Left controls everyone. The Left decides who will live and who will die. Ultimately as in Nazi Germany National healthcare was a money saving endeavor. Those whom the Leftist State deems Worthy of Life will live, and those deemed *Lebensunwertes Leben* or "life unworthy of life" by the State will die. We must also remember that the Left in Nazi Germany deemed *all* Jews and Christians *Lebensunwertes Leben*. The War Against Christians and Christianity is already well underway. As well as the Left's War Against the unborn, old, feeble, and wounded war veterans whom the Left has already deemed as unworthy of life. This is the exact trajectory that the Left is on in America today. You say it can't happen here? So did the pre-Nazi Germans! As we have already meticulously documented throughout this book… It is already happening here!

Homosexuality:

Obama while running for president in 2008 stated in an interview with Pastor Rick Warren at the Saddleback Church that he believed that marriage was "sacred" and "I believe marriage is between a man and a woman. I am not in favor of gay marriage". Later Obama said that his view on gay marriage had "evolved" which of course was a euphemism for "I lied so that I could get elected" and do exactly what I promised not to do! Of course while running for the US Senate in 1996 Obama had previously said: "I favor legalizing same-sex marriages, and would fight efforts to prohibit such marriages". Homosexuality, or as the *Bible* calls it *sodomy*, is embraced in the

Leftist régime in America today as it has been throughout Leftist history. Homosexuality not only had its place in Leftist-Fascist Nazi Germany, but German Nazi Fascism was *founded* upon, by, and through the radical Leftist homosexual movement! The Germans even renamed sodomy… "homosexuality"[537] to disassociate sodomy from the *Bible's* condemnation and as an abomination before GOD!

In a foundational precursor to Fascism, Friedrich Nietzsche (1844 - 1900) was the quintessential German philosophical mentor to Hitler and most of the Nazi's leadership by which Nietzsche almost singlehandedly laid the foundation for German Fascism. Nietzsche popularized the "God is Dead" movement and was rabidly anti-Christian and an openly practicing homosexual. Nietzsche's grudge *Against GOD*, as with virtually every homosexual in history, was GOD's rejection of homosexuality as a grotesque sin against GOD and nature[538]. Nietzsche went insane after contracting syphilis from one of his many homosexual encounters and eventually died a torturous death of the then fatal disease.

It was the "rise of homosexual militancy in the [German Leftist] movement that gave Nazism to the world"[539]. Beginning in the Weimar Republic era and reaching its zenith in the Nazi era, sodomy was euphemized throughout Europe as the "German vice". Hitler was "the *condottiere* of a band of evil men who were united together by a common vice [homosexuality], [whereas] Jewish national tradition for thousands of years has been actively opposed to this particular evil"[540]. This opposition to homosexuality is equally vehement in the Christian New Testament[541] and as a Biblical extension of the Jewish Old Testament.

---

[537] The State of Germany did not exist at the time but was part of the wider Prussian Empire. Vienna born Karl-Maria Benkert a sodomite and gay activist coined the term homosexual in his correspondence after moving to Berlin as a way to speak of himself and other sodomites in code.

[538] The *Holy Bible*: Romans 1:26-32.

[539] Lively, Scott and Abrams, Kevin; *The Pink Swastika: Homosexuality in the Nazi Party*; pg. 24.

[540] Igra, Samuel; *Germany's National Vice*; 1945; pgs. 13 ff.

[541] The *Holy Bible*: Romans 1:24-32; 8:24-25; 1 Corinthians 6:9; Ephesians 4:17; Colossians 1:27; 1 Timothy 1:10; 2 Peter 2:6; Jude 1:7; Revelation 22:15.

It is also important to note that while Communism, since its very foundation from Engels and Marx, has historically rejected homosexuality in the strongest and often deadly terms[542], Fascism was *founded* upon homosexuality and openly promoted the "butch" version of the sodomite sect so infamous for its *Übermensch* or "Superman" image and its rampant sadomasochism and pederasty[543]. Like its Nazi predecessors before it, it has been a primary goal of the Left in America to legalize, legitimize, protect, and promote homosexuality in order to establish the legitimacy of their most militant supporters and modern-day Storm Troopers. These Storm Troopers who are historically unabashed for the Leftist cause in doing the Left's dirty work just as the infamous Nazi Stormtroopers who were recruited almost exclusively from the sodomite ranks[544]. Modern Leftism has intimately close ties to Nazi-style Fascism much more so than even traditional Marxist Communism.

As in Nazi Germany, the American Left's most ardent venomous supporters are drawn from the ranks of the militant homosexuals. The terms "homosexual" and "transvestite" were originally coined by German homosexual psychiatrists and activists to disassociate from the use of the Biblical term "sodomite" in the coordinated effort in repealing Germany's anti-sodomite laws (Paragraph 175 of the German legal code, which criminalized homosexuality). Homosexuality remained "illegal" on the Nazi law books, but as many crimes today such as possession of small amounts of marijuana, these laws were seldom enforced and then only selectively for the benefit of the Leftist State.

---

[542] From the earliest European homosexual rights movements, activists such as Karl-Heinrich Ulrichs and Magnus Hirschfeld approached the Left for support. During the 1860s, Ulrichs wrote to Karl Marx and sent him a number of books on Uranian (homosexual/transgender) emancipation, and in 1869 Marx passed one of Ulrich's books on to Engels. Engels responded with disgust to Marx in a private letter, lashing out at "pederasts" who are "extremely against nature", and described Ulrichs' platform of homosexual rights as "turning smut into theory". He worried that things would go badly for heterosexuals like himself should homosexual rights be gained. -Wikipedia; Socialism and LGBT rights.

[543] Pederasty is the desire to and/or practice of adult men having sexual relations with young and prepubescent boys.

[544] Knickerbocker, H.R.; Is Tomorrow Hitler's?; New York, Reynal and Hitchcock; 1941; pg. 55.

Homosexuality IS *unGodly*! This is the description of God's reaction to sodomy: "And turning the cities of Sodom and Gomorrha into ashes condemned them with an overthrow, making them an ensample unto those that after should live *ungodly*[545]". Sodom is the city from which the term "sodomite" (German: homosexual) was derived. Gomorrha, or Gomorrah, and Sodom were destroyed by God for the wickedness of sodomy, the German term homosexuality.

The vast majority of the Nazi high command were either openly homosexual, pederasts[546], or closet homosexuals[547] including: **Adolf Hitler** (*Führer*, Megalomaniac, Genocidal Maniac, Ernst Röhm's homosexual "protégé", pederast, homosexual, Occultist (See below for further details)); **Ernst Röhm** (Co-Founder of the Nazi Party, Co-founder of the *Sturmabteilung* Nazi "Stormtroopers", pederast, and close friend and possible onetime lover of Hitler); **Hermann Goering** (Hitler's 2nd in Command, founder of the *Geheime Staatspolizei* "Secret State Police" (*Gestapo*), Commander-in-Chief of the *Luftwaffe* "Air Force", "liked to dress up in drag and wear campy make-up[548]"); **Heinrich Himmler** (*Reichsführer-SS*: Commander of the *Schutzstaffel* Nazi "SS", Commander of the *Geheime Staatspolizei* "Secret State Police" (*Gestapo*), one of the ones most responsible for the Holocaust, pederast, Occultist); **Rudolph Hess** (Deputy *Führer* to Hitler and Commandant of *Auschwitz* death camp, used the pseudonym "Fraulein Anna", Hitler's homosexual lover in Landsberg prison); **Joseph Goebbels** (Hitler's Minister of Propaganda, arranged pederast/homosexual orgies for Nazi Party leadership); **Hermann Ehrhardt** (Commander in the *Freikorps* an equally vicious forerunner to the Nazi Stormtroopers); **Martin Bormann** (replaced Hess as Deputy *Führer*, vehemently anti-Christian, Hitler's private secretary, promoted the "Final Solution"). These to name just a few of the most notorious homosexuals and myriad others including: **Reinhard Heydrich** (Mastermind of the first *pogrom*, *Kristallnacht*,

---

[545] The *Holy Bible*: 2 Peter 2:6.
[546] Sexually active with young boys.
[547] Many of the Nazi homosexuals were of the "Butch" persuasion who married only for procreation and sometimes appearance purposes and either openly or secretly lived homosexual lives.
[548] Rector, Frank; *The Nazi Extermination of Homosexuals*; Stein & Day; New York; 1981; pg. 57.

the Röhm Purge, and the Concentration/death camps), **Leon Graf du Moulin-Eckart** (Chief of the Nazi Party's Information Service, and Ernst Röhm's adjutant and procurer of young boys, Stormtrooper General), **Hans Frank** (Hitler's personal lawyer, Reich Legal Director, Minister of Justice, Governor-General of occupied Poland's "General Government" territory presided over Polish mass murders and plunder), **Gerhard Rossbach** (sadist, murderer, *Rossbach's Sturmabteilung* "Rossbach's Storm Troopers", *Schilljugend* "Schill Youth" founded for pederastic purposes), **Karl Ernst** (Stormtroopers *Obergruppenfuehrer* "Lieutenant General", pseudonym "Frau Röhrbein", sadist), **Albert "Maria" Forster** (as the *Gauleiter* of Danzig-West Prussia administered the execution of Jews and Poles), **Baldur von Schirach** (Head of the *Hitler-Jugend* "Hitler Youth", Hitler's private attorney, Reich Legal Director, Minister of Justice, Holocaust-butcher Governor-General of Poland), **Walter Funk** (Reich Minister of Economic Affairs, Hitler's personal financial advisor), **Edmund Heines** (Stormtrooper, pederast, and a convicted murderer), **Captain [Paul] Rohrbein** (Karl Ernst's homosexual partner, Organizational Nazi Strategist), **Captain Petersdorf** (Organizational Nazi Strategist), **Count Ernst Helldorf** (Organizational Nazi Strategist), **Julius Streicher** (pederast, publisher of *Der Stürmer* newspaper and Nazi propagandist, Organizational Nazi Strategist), **Berthold Konrad Hermann Albert Speer** ("homo-erotic relationship"[549] with Hitler, Minister of Armaments and War Production for the Third Reich), **Emil Maurice** (Hitler's chauffeur, bodyguard, cellmate in Landsberg prison, and homosexual lover; Charter member Nazi Stormtroopers, and SS General), **Wilhelm Canaris** (Chief of *Abwehr* the German military intelligence service, Nazi Admiral, later turned against Hitler), and **Hans Blüher** (Nazi leader, author of *The German Wandervoegel Movement as an Erotic Phenomenon* and *The Role Of the Erotic In Male Society* and whose book *Volk and Führer In the Youth Movement* which was considered "a hymn to pederasty[550]".). There are indeed thousands of other examples in the militant homosexual ranks of the Nazi Third Reich, just as there are in the Left in America

---

[549] Newsweek, Oct. 30, 1995.
[550] Gilman, Sander; *Franz Kafka, The Jewish Patient*; Psychology Press; 1995; pg. 159.

today. The Fascist comparison of the homosexual agenda of Nazi Germany and the Left in America today is unavoidable as the rise of the Left through the homosexual agenda in America almost exactly parallels that of the rise of Nazi Germany. Evil does not change its tactics and strategies through time, just the names by which Evil is called!

Hitler had spent some years as a homosexual prostitute in Vienna, Austria when his aspirations as an artist failed abysmally. Austrian Chancellor Englebert Dollfuss possessed a certified document which detailed that Hitler "had been a male prostitute in Vienna at the time of his sojourn there, from 1907 to 1912, and that he practiced the same calling in Munich from 1912 to 1914"[551]. To avoid public disclosure of this career ending document, Hitler had Dollfuss murdered by a group of likeminded homosexual Fascists in Vienna led by "[Otto] Planetta who was also a well-known sex pervert". Over this incident Mussolini published a scathing indictment against Hitler through his newspaper *Il Popolo di Roma*:

"Pederasts and assassins rule in Berlin!"[552]

Hitler's immediate German predecessor Chancellor Kurt von Schleicher identified Hitler and his Nazi cadre as "This pack of scoundrels, these criminals, these **filthy boy streetwalkers!**"[553]. Desmond Seward in *Napoleon and Hitler* documents that: "the files of the Viennese police list [Hitler] as a homosexual"[554]. The German periodical *Die Fanfare*, in a 1931 article headlined: "HITLER'S LOVER COMMITS SUICIDE: BACHELORS AND HOMOSEXUALS AS LEADERS OF THE PARTY" referred to Hitler as the then "Leader of the [Nazi] Party" and specifically as a "bachelor and homosexual"[555]. As was previously documented, Hitler was "the *condottiere* of a band of evil men who were united together

---

[551] Igra, Samuel; *Germany's National Vice*; 1945; pg. 67.

[552] Lively, Scott and Abrams, Kevin; *The Pink Swastika: Homosexuality in the Nazi Party*; pg. 85.

[553] Rector, Frank; *The Nazi Extermination of Homosexuals*; New York, Stein and Day; 1981; pg. 64.

[554] Seward, Desmond; *Napoleon and Hitler*; 2013; pg. 283.

[555] Rosenbaum, Ron; Vanity Fair Magazine; *Hitler's Doomed Angel*; April 1992.

by a common vice [homosexuality]. During WWI Lance Corporal Adolf Hitler and a male senior German officer "were charged with engaging in sexual relations" by the German government. More disturbingly, Adolf Hitler continually and regularly sexually molested the young Wieland Wagner (pronounced: *Vägner*), grandson of the famous German composer Richard Wagner, while Wieland was still a prepubescent boy during the 1920's[556]. Wieland Wagner who was born in 1917 would have been very young during this 1920's timeframe. This was confirmed by Wieland Wagner's son, Wolfgang Wagner, in a *Time Magazine* interview in 1994.

Although it is documented that Hitler did have sexual relationships with several women in his lifetime, including his fifteen year old niece, Geli Raubal, whom Hitler later murdered in jealous rage over their common male bisexual lover named Emil Maurice, interestingly "a Jewish art teacher", who would later become Hitler's own personal chauffeur and bodyguard. Hitler's sporadic relationships with females always ended tragically and were fleeting at best. Hitler's relationships with women were most likely a public prop designed to conceal his true homosexual deviancies. Hitler's sexual orientation was almost exclusively pederastic and homosexual in nature.

The infamous Nazi book burning campaign began four days after Hitler's Brownshirts stormed Magnus Hirschfeld's Institute for Sexual Research in Berlin on May 6, 1933 where the records of Hitler and much of the other Nazi sexual deviancy records were stored. Magnus Hirschfeld, a "Fem" homosexual psychotherapist, was murdered by Hitler, in large part, to cover Hitler's own homosexual and sexually deviant past.

German psychiatrist Ludwig L. Lenz who had treated many of the Nazi leadership prior to the legalization of German homosexuality documented that "...not ten percent of the men who, in 1933, took the fate of Germany into their hands, were sexually normal..."[557]. (For the

---

[556] Duffy, Martha; Time Magazine; *MUSIC: Die Wagneren: A True-Life Opera*; August 15, 1994; pg. 56.
[557] Lively, Scott and Abrams, Kevin; *The Pink Swastika: Homosexuality in the Nazi Party*; pg. 21.

math-challenged, that leaves ninety-percent of the Nazi leadership as *deviant homosexuals!*) Contemporary opponents to the Nazis charged that "homosexuality [was] an essential characteristic of the fascist system"[558].

There is some confusion caused by modern homosexual activists who have attempted to rewrite history concerning the intimate ties between Nazism and homosexuality. These modern activists have asserted that homosexuals were victims of Nazi oppression on par with the Jewish Holocaust. This is a revisionist *Lie* of the Left. It is true that many homosexuals were imprisoned in concentration camps, however it was not a result of the State condemnation of homosexuality. It was in fact the result of an internal battle between two warring factions within the Nazi homosexual movement between the "Butches" and the "Fems". The Butches loathed the Fems and sought to destroy them resulting in the *Nacht der langen Messer* or "The Night of the Long Knives" and the murder by Hitler of Ernst Röhm, a notorious Nazi "Fem" and the rest of the "Fem" remnants in the Nazi leadership. The "The Night of the Long Knives", also called the "Röhm Purge", was executed: as cover to eliminate Hitler's political enemies, as revenge against the "Fems" for prior offenses against the "Butch" Nazis, and as a political move designed to convince the German people, contrary to fact and evidence, that the Nazis did not tolerate homosexuality.

The Nazi Party itself had its very beginnings in a notorious homosexual rendezvous tavern called the *Bratwurstgloeckl* where the Nazi Party was established and organized in this now infamous homosexual gathering place, roughly equivalent today to a homosexual bar combined with a homosexual bathhouse:

> "At the door of the *Bratwurstgloeckl*, a tavern frequented by homosexual roughnecks and bully-boys, Roehm (Ernst Röhm) turned in and joined the handful of sexual deviants and occultists who were celebrating the success of a new campaign

---

[558] Oosterhuis, Harry, and Kennedy, Hubert; *Homosexuality and Male Bonding in Pre-Nazi Germany: the youth movement, the gay movement and male bonding before Hitler's rise*: original transcripts from Der Eigene, the first gay journal in the world; New York, Harrington Park Press; 1991; pg. 239 notes.

of terror. Their organization, once known as the German Worker's Party, was now called the *Nationalsozialistische Deutsche Arbeiterpartei*, The National Socialist German Worker's Party — the Nazis. Yes, the Nazi [organizers] met in a 'gay' bar"[559].

The irony of the tavern's name *Bratwurstgloeckl* and its allusion to "*Bratwurst*" or "sausage", as a slang for male genitalia, was not lost on the Butch Nazi's and no doubt was a motivating factor in the tavern becoming a local "hook-up" venue for German homosexuals.

Herein also lies the explanation of the Left's and the homosexual attack on the Boy Scouts of America. In the early Nazi pederast organization the *Wandervoegel* or "Wandering Youth", there existed an effort to "revive the Greek ideal of pedagogic pederasty" ("Hands-on" teaching of man-boy homosexual relationships). In 1912, Hans Blüher, the pederast, anti-Semite, and Nazi activist who wrote *The German Wandervoegel Movement As An Erotic Phenomenon* documented the *Wandervoegel*'s recruiting of young boys into homosexuality. Not coincidently the *Wandervoegel* is where the "*Heil*" salute and the *Fuhrerprinzep* (*Führer* Principal) originated. The "*Heil*" salute (as in *Heil* Hitler!) was originally the secret salute by which pederasts and young boys acknowledged their common kinship. The *Wandervoegel* organization evolved then into the *Freikorps* or "Free Corps", then the *Hitler-Jugend* or "Hitler Youth", then into the Brownshirts, referred to as the "Brown Fairies", and into the *Sturmabteilung* or Nazi "Stormtroopers". Virtually the entire leadership of the Stormtroopers "were almost without exception homosexuals. Indeed, unless a Storm Troop officer were homosexual he had no chance of advancement"[560]. This was also the case for the general membership of the Stormtroopers who were "mostly, if not entirely homosexual"[561]. Historian Robert Waite states that the predominately homosexual *Freikorps*, "contributed thousands of their

[559] Lively, Scott and Abrams, Kevin; *The Pink Swastika: Homosexuality in the Nazi Party*; pg. 20.
[560] Knickerbocker, H.R.; Is Tomorrow Hitler's?; New York, Reynal and Hitchcock; 1941; pg. 55.
[561] Lively, Scott and Abrams, Kevin; *The Pink Swastika: Homosexuality in the Nazi Party*; pg. 80.

members to positions of power in the Third Reich. Indeed, 48.6 percent of the [Nazi] Party leadership came from the [*Freikorps*] veterans"[562]".

There again is no coincidence that the Left in America today demands and seeks to force compliance through the courts that the Boy Scouts of America be forced to accept homosexual men as troop and administrative leaders, which the Boy Scouts of America now does! The Left seeks to coopt the Boy Scouts, the largest organization for young boys in America, into a homosexual recruiting organization in its attempt to rapidly spread its ranks like a virus through America's young boys and young men!

Homosexuality was not only foundational to Nazi Fascism, but a primary dictate in carrying forward the Fascist agenda in Germany and a key factor in the Nazi's cruelty and savagery.

Here is a quote worth regarding:

> Victim-plunder ideology is at the core of "gay" political strategy. Homosexualists exploit the public status of homosexuals to impose their new definition of human sexuality upon society. "Victim ideology" and "reductionist" thinking is destroying America from within. Today's new victims see no reason to modify their own behavior. Victim psychology and philosophies undermine the legitimate workings of government and the justice, health and social systems. Like their Nazi predecessors, today's homosexualists lack any scruples. Homosexuality is primarily a predatory addiction striving to take the weak and unsuspecting down with it. The "gay" agenda is a colossal fraud; a gigantic robbery of the mind. Homosexuals of the type described in this book have no true idea of how to act in the best interests of their country and fellow man. Their intention is to serve none but   themselves.
> *The Pink Swastika* documents a hidden aspect of

---

[562] Waite, Robert G. L.; *The Psychopathic God: Adolf Hitler*; 1993.

German history. The authors contend that homosexualism, elevated to a popular ideology and combined with black occult forces, not only gave birth to Nazi imperialism but also led to the Holocaust itself. The militarists in Germany were happy with Hitler. His teachings on "total war" and of a secret Jewish conspiracy against Germany provided a good screen for their own veiled preparations. From its very inception, it was the goal of the Nazi Party, working as a front for the German military industrial complex, to overthrow the Weimar Republic by whatever means necessary. *The Pink Swastika* documents how, from their beginning, the National Socialist revolution and the Nazi Party were animated and dominated by militaristic homosexuals, pederasts, pornographers and sado-masochists.

As Igra explains in *Germany's National Vice*, "the criminals who wreaked such astounding horrors on innocent civilian populations were not acting as soldiers drunk with the fury of battle, nor as patriotic fanatics, but as chosen instruments of a satanic religion to the service of which they had been dedicated by the systematic teaching and practice of unnatural vice" (Igra: 94).

The Pink Swastika documents how the Society for Human Rights, founded by members of the Nazi Party, became the largest homosexual rights organization in Germany and, further, how this movement gave birth to the American homosexual rights movement. Its influence has grown[563].

As a group, homosexuals are one of the most vindictive, bigoted, condescending, hateful, despicable, underhanded, judgmental, self-righteous, and intolerant people. Yes, it's all true. Are there exceptions? Do some people know homosexuals who are generally decent people? Obviously so on both questions, but as a group the aforementioned characteristics are fair and true to life characterizations. Almost every person knows or has seen behavior by

---

[563] Lively, Scott and Abrams, Kevin; *The Pink Swastika: Homosexuality in the Nazi Party*; pg. 11.

many homosexuals that is typified by the above characterizations. Of course this statement will have the Left in general, and homosexuals in particular, screaming and frothing at the mouth. And of course, this just proves the point! (Me thinks she doth protest too much!)

To most it will come as a great surprise to learn that sodomy, or Homosexuality as the Germans renamed it, is the worst sin in the *Bible*[564]. Yes you read that correctly, the worst sin in the *Bible*! Sodomy is the worst sin according to GOD's Holy Word in the *Bible* even worse than robbery, rape, and yes, even murder[565]! The *Bible* is explicit in revealing that when the door of homosexuality is opened by an individual, all other sins come bolting in behind it. This explains the inclination of the Nazi Butches who delved into extreme forms of sadomasochism and vile sexual practices and why the atrocities of the Third Reich were so utterly terrifying. This explains Evil's obsession with legitimizing homosexuality in *the Left's War Against GOD!*

As an aside: There may be at least seemingly credible, *prima fascia*, evidence and certainly personal testimony that former President Barack Hussein Obama may have in his past participated in homosexual relationships. Certainly Barack Hussein Obama celebrated the legalization of homosexual marriage even going as far as to light up the White House with the rainbow colors of the radical homosexual movement. His current marriage may be, like the Nazi's of the Third Reich, for only political and procreation purposes. If true, Obama's secret life and career would certainly directly parallel the Leftist, Fascist life and career of *Herr Führer* Adolf Hitler.

Media Control:

Just as in Nazi Germany, the Left Stream Media (LSM) today in America is an organ of the Fascist Left. The LSM today is the equivalent to Hitler's *Reichsministerium für Volksaufklärung und Propaganda* or the Reich Ministry of Public Enlightenment and Propaganda. We must not give the grotesquely Leftist LSM the excuse

---

[564] The *Holy Bible*: Romans 1:24-32.
[565] The *Holy Bible*: Romans 1:27-29ff.

that they are merely cloistered in dark rooms together and do not know better than to support the Left because they don't know that the Left is Evil. The Left Stream Media like Obama, the Clinton's, and the rest of the Left, count on our always giving them the "benefit if the doubt", but they act intentionally and forcefully to *Lie* to and deceive the American people and knowingly advance an Evil Leftist agenda. The Left Stream Media is intentionally and knowingly complicit in advancing and covering for the Left's Evil!

The Left Stream Media *Lies* to cover for the Left's sins and crimes. The Left Stream Media *Lies* with false accusations and innuendos regularly perpetuating the Left's *Lies* against those on the Right. The Left Stream Media unfailingly attacks Conservatives in general, and Christians in particular. As Conservatives we must forcefully confront the Left Stream Media. As evidenced by now President Trump in the 3rd Republican debate of the 2016 Presidential race, the Left is disarmed by those on the Right who forcefully and truthfully go on the offensive against the *Lies* and manipulation of the Leftist Media.

The Right must stop falling victim to the Left's Media Propaganda Machine. There is no discernable difference between the Nazi *Reichsministerium für Volksaufklärung und Propaganda* and today's Left Stream Media Propaganda Machine in America today!

Occultism:

Occultism was the foundation of the Nazi Leftist Religion and continues to be so for the Left in America today. As discussed in the sub-chapter **Pagan Morals** a little further on, The Left has always embraced Occultism in its many forms such as witchcraft, environmentalism, Hinduism, and many false "christian" religions. Occultism is the spiritual, or religious, core of the Left's Evil Religion.

> The occult (from the Latin word occultus "clandestine, hidden, secret") is "knowledge of the hidden". In common English usage, occult refers to "knowledge of the paranormal", as

opposed to "knowledge of the measurable", usually referred to as science.[566]

The center of cultic belief is secrecy or "hidden knowledge" which supposedly only those enlightened can fully develop or understand. Throughout history the religious quest for "hidden knowledge" has been called "Gnosticism" which literally means "having secret knowledge":

> Gnosticism (from Ancient Greek: γνωστικός gnostikos, "having knowledge", from γνῶσις gnōsis, knowledge) is a modern term categorizing a collection of ancient religions whose adherents shunned the material world – which they viewed as created by the demiurge – and embraced the spiritual world.[567]

The Gnostics teach that a person can obtain "god" status by acquiring knowledge. This is the *Lie* of Evil throughout history beginning with Satan's *Lie* to Eve in the Garden of Eden that through eating of the Tree of the Knowledge of GOOD and Evil Eve and Adam could "be as gods, knowing good and evil", through the Jacobeans in the French Revolution and the Goddess of Reason, through Abraham Maslow's Pyramid of Self-Actualization in achieving godhood, to the Left's social programs designed to relieve the masses from the ignorant Christian restraints that have held man back from realizing his evolutionary destiny of self-perfection (self-Actualization into a promised godhood).

Enlightenment into the occult's spiritual aspect comes from various ways of obtaining the "hidden knowledge" that empowers a person to have extra-human abilities through the "paranormal". The *Bible* calls this demonization or a person's relationship with devils!

Hitler epitomized the Occult and his obsession with its promised "enlightenment" and empowerment from otherworldly spiritual

---

[566] Wikipedia; Occult.
[567] Wikipedia; Gnosticism.

entities. Remember that through his association with the Occultist Madame Helena Blavatsky:

> "Hitler rightly believed he had established communication with Lucifer, from whom he openly coveted possession.[568]"

The Left keeps its agenda and intentions secret because the Left's elite consider the masses to be too ignorant to understand its means and goals as being for the "better good". This goes a long way in explaining the condescending looks so infamous in people like Hillary Rodham-Clinton, Al Gore, Nancy Pelosi, Chuck Schumer, Maxine Waters, Barack Hussein Obama, and so many others in the Leftist elite today. This condescending attitude was the hallmark of Adolf Hitler and the Nazi elite. Hitler like Obama is considered one of the world's most vicious megalomaniacs because they considered themselves above reproach on their path of achieving the Leftist Utopian Paradise on earth.

As previously documented in the opening to this chapter, the subsection **Anti-Christian**, and elsewhere Hitler and the Leftist Nazis believed that Christianity held back the realization of what the Nazis called the *Übermensch*, or Superman, from obtaining his fully evolved potential of becoming his own "god", "the human being who proclaimed himself a god and was not to be subdued by human [Christian] laws and ethics"[569]. It was the Protestant pastors who were stripped of their credentials, arrested, imprisoned, and eventually executed "for issuing condemnations of [Nazi] neo-paganism from the pulpit[570].". This is what Hitler when he uttered that he "hates Christianity, because it has crippled all that is noble in humanity"[571]. The Nazi Leftists saw ancient Paganism and its imagined Arian Race as "all that is noble in humanity". The Left today disguises its Anti-

---

[568] Cumbey, Constance; *The Hidden Dangers of the Rainbow: The New Age Movement and Our Coming Age of Barbarism*; 1983; pgs. 100-101.

[569] Lively, Scott and Abrams, Kevin; *The Pink Swastika: Homosexuality in the Nazi Party*; pg. 105.

[570] Lively, Scott and Abrams, Kevin; *The Pink Swastika: Homosexuality in the Nazi Party*; pg. 107.

[571] Taylor, Irene, and Alan; *The Assassin's Cloak: An Anthology of the World's Greatest Diarists*; 2002; pg. 184.

Christian Pagan beliefs and actions behind its "common good" and "we're here to help" rhetoric.

P.C. Enforcement:

As stated in the chapter *P. C. Police*, Political Correctness is political enforcement of the Leftist Religion! It was the political enforcement of the Leftist Religion in Nazi Germany and it remains the political enforcement of the Leftist Religion in America today.

The Politically Correct Enforcement of the Left's Religious mandates is well-covered throughout this book (see the Index). The Left uses speech laws to quiet, limit, and ultimately ban opposition voices. This is exemplified in the Left's resurrection of its so-called "Fairness Doctrine"[572] which is aimed by the Congressional Democrats at silencing Conservative talk radio that has been such a successful mechanism for the Right in America.

The Nazis used P.C. Enforcement to silence their opponents. Eventually the Nazi P.C. Enforcement led to the murder of anyone who spoke out against the Fascist régime. The Left in America today has already come a long way on the road of Nazi P.C. Enforcement. P.C. Enforcement is intended by the Left to silence the Right and anyone the Left sees as a threat to the realization of the Left's Fascist Utopian nightmare.

Pagan Morals:

Paganism defines itself as "A polytheistic or pantheistic nature-worshipping religion"[573]. Simply explained "Paganism is the belief in many gods, all as god, nature is god, where anything is god but GOD".

The Nazis, as discussed throughout this book and by their own definition, practiced the most virulent form of Paganism known to man. It was under Nazi Paganism that some of the world's most vicious crimes against humanity were committed. Yet this same

---

[572] For more on the Fairness Doctrine see the chapter *The "Fairness" Doctrine*.
[573] http://www.paganfederation.org/what-is-paganism/.

Paganism has been implemented under the Left in America today. The Nazi practices of pagan Hinduism were symbolized by the Swastika. All forms of Paganism, until recently, was universally considered Pagan barbarism has now been accepted, customized, and legalized under the Left in America today, just as in Nazi Germany. These Pagan barbarisms include human sacrifice (abortion, euthanasia, infanticide, killing or suicide of undesirables, infirm, and handicapped), homosexuality, witchcraft, environmentalism (Ecology), tattoos, Christmas has become Winter solstice, Easter has become Spring equinox, Pagan god worship (e.g. Gaia), Lying as a craft, no absolute right and wrong (Relativism), legalized suicide, legalized drugs, racism, and many, many others. Think "witchcraft" is an exaggeration? Here is a brief synopsis offered by the BBC (British Broadcasting Service): "Paganism encompasses a diverse community with some groups concentrating on specific traditions, practices or elements such as ecology, *witchcraft*, Celtic traditions or certain gods"[574]. The BBC further defines Pagan groups that include: "Wiccans, Druids, Shamans, Sacred Ecologists, Odinists, and Heathens all make up parts of the Pagan community". The *Bible* calls all of this *witchcraft*[575]! The *Bible* calls the worship of these Pagan "gods", literally the worship of devils[576]. The worship of Pagan "gods" and the worship of GOD in Christianity are absolutely incompatible[577] and these two world views are at *War* for the hearts, minds, and *souls* of Americans!

The Left has facilitated the transformation of Christian America into Pagan America, with all its associated Evil and devils, just as Obama promised to "transform America". This is *the Left's War Against GOD!*

Progressive Income Tax:

The Nazi's of Hitler's régime were supporters and implementers of a progressive income tax. A progressive income tax is supposedly the

---

[574] http://www.bbc.co.uk/religion/religions/paganism.
[575] The *Holy Bible*: 2 Chronicles 33:6.
[576] The *Holy Bible*: 1 Corinthians 10:20.
[577] The *Holy Bible*: 1 Corinthians 10:21.

more money you make the more you pay to the government. The Left in America is obsessed with a progressive income tax… or so they claim. The Left wants a progressive income tax, except on its most ardent and most wealthy supporters. A well-kept secret of the Left is that there are far more Democrat/Leftist millionaires and billionaires in America than Republican/Right millionaires and billionaires. This was the core of the Nazi Fascist system that there were rich people in Nazi Germany made that way by their allegiance to the Fascist régime!

There is the same smoke and mirrors trick occurring by the Left in America today. Under Obama *only* the top 10% of Americans grew richer. Even Obama was forced to admit that 95% of income gains from 2009 to 2012 went to the top 1% of the earning population[578]. So much for the Left's deafening outcry against the evil rich "1%" who are screwing us "99%"! It is the Left who is Fascistically favoring the rich 1% and screwing the other 99%. The Left's deeds and words seldom correspond. (Interpretation: The Left *Lies!*) A Leftist "progressive" income tax is designed to stop the middleclass earner from becoming an upper-class earner, unless of course they fall lockstep, or goosestep as the case may be, into line with the political Left!

Propaganda Machine/Media:

The Left's propaganda machine today rivals Hitler's *Reichsministerium für Volksaufklärung und Propaganda* or the Reich Ministry of Public Enlightenment and Propaganda. The Left's Propaganda Machine overwhelms every aspect of American life.

The Democrat Party's Propaganda machine rivals in every way that of the Nazi's. *Lies* are the biggest commodity of the Left's Propaganda machine. The Left uses the *Big Lie* theory of Hitler in "if you repeat the *Lie* often enough and loud enough, they will eventually believe anything"!

---

[578] CNN Money (New York); *Obama admits 95% of income gains gone to top 1%*; September 15, 2013: 3:03 PM ET.

Racial Supremacy White then, Black now

Aryan supremacy was at the core of Nazi Fascism. The Fascists murdered millions in the name of racial supremacy.

Now in America the Black Lives Matter movement has turned into a black *supremacist* movement. Former Maryland Governor and Democrat Presidential candidate Martin O'Malley speaking at the über-Leftist gathering Netroots Nation on 7/21/2015 was booed off the stage for saying "all lives matter". O'Malley was responding to a black mob shouting, "What side are you on? Black people! What side are you on?" as they rushed the stage and seized the microphone. O'Malley's "offense" was not that he told the mob that "black lives matter", but that he also included in his phrasing, "black lives matter, white lives matter, all lives matter". To the new Leftist black movement *only* "black lives matter", not "white lives" or "all lives" *only* "black lives"! This goes far beyond mere racism to the Nazi-style *supremacist*! Obama as the Left's epitome went out of his way to provoke black supremacy. (For further discussion see the chapter *The Obamas: The Epitome of the Left* and the subsection *Obama as a Racist.*)

Removing Christian Symbols:

Hitler ordered that:

> "the National Church will clear away all from its alters all crucifixes [and] Bibles" and "On the alters there must be nothing but Mein Kampf" and "the Christian Cross must be removed from all churches… and it must be superseded by the only unconquerable symbol, the swastika"[579].

---

[579] Shirer, William L.; *The Rise and Fall of the Third Reich: A History of Nazi Germany*; Simon & Schuster; Reissue edition (October 11, 2011); pg. 240.

Former President Obama and the Left's ongoing hatred for Christian symbols and Jesus Christ Himself, can only be rivaled in history by that of Hitler and the Nazi régime:

> This bias appears to reflect the Obama administration's thinking at the highest levels. Indeed, as reported by Breitbart News, rather than embrace an amendment passed last June in the House Armed Services Committee protecting religious speech of service members in the military, the White House released a Statement of Administration Policy with a threat to veto the bill if it passes the full House and Senate. "In other words," Breitbart News concluded, "**Obama says he will veto any bill that forbids his appointees or officers from telling a soldier that he cannot mention <u>Jesus</u> during prayer or have a *<u>Bible</u>* on his desk**, or that keeps those appointees from telling a chaplain (who is an ordained clergyman) what religious teachings he is allowed to give in worship services, or what spiritual counseling he can give to another soldier."
>
> The White House acknowledged, for example, that it asked Georgetown University, a Catholic institution, to cover up prominent *Christian symbols* for President Obama's economic speech there in 2010. Is it any wonder that the military followed the example of its commander-in-chief in going overboard to remove anything that looked like a *Christian symbol* in the chapel at the Afghan base?[580] (emphasis added)

Obama ordered Christian symbols at the Catholic Norte Dame University covered when he spoke there in 2010. Imagine that Obama usurped the symbols of Christianity and ordered them covered as a prerequisite to his speech. Obama ousted Jesus and the Cross! Is it even fathomable to imagine Obama having requested that the symbols of Islam be removed from a mosque so that he could speak

---

[580] Klein, Joseph; Front Page Magazine, frontpagemag.com; *Obama's War on the Christian 'Extremist' Threat, A concerted campaign to portray Christians as domestic enemies comes to light*; October 24, 2013.

there?![581] *Never!* (see wider discussion in the chapter: The Obamas: The Epitome of the Left: Obama as a Muslim or Muslim Sympathizer)

This was not an isolated incident for Obama. Officials at the Jesuit Catholic Georgetown University were asked by Obama's staff to cover a monogram symbolizing the name of Jesus because it was inscribed on the stage where Obama spoke in 2009. Georgetown complied.

The Obama Administration was complicit in the U.S. Military removing a large cross that had been displayed outside a chapel at Camp Marmal in northern Afghanistan because it "violated Army regulations"[582].

The Obama Administration through the Pentagon ordered the removal of Christian symbols from the chapel at an Army Forward Operating Base Orgun-E that included specifically: a Cross and a steeple from atop a chapel and to board up Cross-shaped windows.[583] These examples go on and on. The kindred [demon] spirits between Hitler and the Nazis, and Obama and the Left in America today are undeniable!

The Left only attacks the symbols of Christianity and *ESPECIALLY* the Cross. The Left never attacks the symbols of other religions. Removing Christian symbols for the Left has nothing to do with erasing signs of religious bias, racism, homophobia, etc., but is *the Left's War Against God!*

Savior/Messianic Delusions:

There has been much ink devoted to Mussolini and Hitler's Messianic delusions.[584] I will not recount it all here. Let it suffice to say that these

---

[581] Bottum, Joseph; CBSNews/Weekly Standard; *God and Obama at Notre Dame*; May 11, 2009, 12:38 PM.
[582] Mak, Tim; *POLITICO*; *Cross Removed at Afghanistan Base*; 11/23/11 08:29 AM EST, Updated 11/23/11 07:39 PM EST.
[583] Starnes, Todd; the home page of Fox News Radio's Todd Starnes; Army Removes Crosses, Steeple from Chapel; Jan 24, 2013.
[584] A Google search of "Hitler's Messianic delusion" resulted a total of 348,000 results.

Fascist dictators epitomize the role of the Messianic Delusion in seeing oneself as a "savior" in a religious quest to implement the Leftist Utopian State.

Barack Hussein Obama has been coronated by many on the Left as a modern day "messiah". It was first pronounced that Obama was the Messiah in 2008 by Louis Farrakhan (Screwy Lewy) who called Barack Hussein Obama the "Messiah". It was quickly picked up by the Left Stream Media organs. In 2013 "Barbara Walters admitted on a broadcast appearance with Piers Morgan that… the media regarded President Obama as the 'next messiah' because of his promises and policies".[585]

In 2007 Oprah Winfrey at a campaign rally in South Carolina called Obama "The One" referring to her earlier comment of those looking for a "Savior". In 2009 an editorial in the largest Dutch newspaper *Politiken* declared "Obama is, of course, greater than Jesus".[586] There was also the 3rd grade school lesson approved by Common Core , based on the book *Barack Obama: Son of Promise, Child of Hope* by Nikki Grimes, which portrayed Obama as the "messiah".[587] Then there was the disgraceful and blasphemous Jamie Foxx who proclaimed on the 2012 Soul Train Awards: "Thank god, and our lord and savior, Barack Obama!". These are just a few of the more noteworthy examples of how the Left's Messianic Delusion has not died with the Nazis, but lives on in the Left in America today. It will die for good one day when Jesus Christ, The true Messiah, finally dispatches the Devil possessed Antichrist to Hell for eternity. Until then the Left will continually resurrect the Messianic Delusion in an attempt to fulfill Satan's dream of being the false and anti-christ, the "messiah" of all that is Evil!

---

[585] Chumley, Cheryl K.; The Washington Times; *Barbara Walters admits 'we' thought Obama was 'the next messiah'*; December 18, 2013.
[586] WorldNetDaily; *'Obama is, of course, greater than Jesus', Publication deifies American president, dismisses Christ*; 12/29/2009 at 8:39 PM.
[587] WorldNetDaily; School lesson portrays Obama as messiah 'More fitting for an authoritarian regime'; 11/28/2013 at 4:45 PM.

There have been dozens of posters created illuminating Obama with haloed beams protruding from his head as a "messiah" of the Left's Religion of Evil. These posters have even gone as far as to show Obama in a "Christ-like pose with a crown of thorns" with all of its obvious connotations to Jesus Christ (remember that "Christ" is Greek for "Messiah" in Hebrew). These were not all merely an invention of disconnected, overzealous enthusiasts, but some were also created purposely by Obama's campaign staff, a staff over which Obama had direct control! Barack Hussein Obama himself openly perpetuated the idea of himself as a religious messiah! This is *the Left's War Against God!*

School Teachers' Unions:

Michelle Obama's campaign to make school lunch programs "more nutritional" was a pretense to instate the old Nazi food restrictions in America which the Nazi Third Reich had also implemented on their State-run schools. The result today is that many children simply choose to throw away the "nutritional" slop that they are given[588]. The outcry in schools from school children and their parents from around the Country has gone unheeded by the FDA and their Nazi inspired school lunch programs.

The equally sinister motivation of Michelle Obama was the unionization of the school lunch programs. Government school lunch programs require strict enforcement which can only be entrusted to the Leftist Party faithful! There is no more a faithful organ of the Left and its Democrat Party than the Service Employees International Union (SEIU) for enforcing the Leftist mandates upon our children! Do you doubt this? The Chicago Tribune reports that, "Little Village Academy on Chicago's West Side, students are not allowed to pack lunches from home. Unless they have a medical excuse, they must eat the food served in the cafeteria"[589]. A move which only benefits the Leftist SEIU cafeteria workers. There are literally hundreds of such

---

[588] Harrington, Elizabeth; The Washington Free Beacon - The Washington Times; *1M kids stop school lunch due to Michelle Obama's standards*; Thursday, March 6, 2014.
[589] Eng, Monica and Hood, Joel; Chicago Tribune; *Chicago school bans some lunches brought from home*; April 11, 2011.

examples[590]. Does that not seem to qualify as militant enough for you? Try this: A North Carolina preschooler had her lunch confiscated by a State government inspector acting under Federal regulations enacted under Michelle Obama's school nutrition campaign. The lunch of "turkey and cheese sandwich, banana, potato chips, and apple juice did not meet U.S. Department of Agriculture guidelines, according to the interpretation of the person who was inspecting all lunch boxes in the More at Four classroom that day[591]". To add insult to injury the preschooler was sent home with a bill for $1.25 for the forcibly replaced meal. Scared yet? The preschool food police is yet another step to total enforcement of the Left's goal of cradle-to-grave reprogramming of human nature to enforce the ideals of a Leftist Utopian State.

Of course this begs the question: What did Michelle Obama's children eat at their exclusive private school? A quick look at the menu posted online for Sidwell School reveals a virtual culinary delight nothing like the not so fortunate children in public schools who are forced to tolerate or go hungry. A menu for February 5, 2015 which is typical of the daily menu at Sidwell boasts:

> Calico Wild Rice Soup
> BBQ Chicken Salad
> Blackened Potato and Mushroom Salad
> Brats & Sauerkraut
> w/ Red Eye Gravy
> Roasted Apples
> Garlic Green Beans
> Creamy Mashed Potatoes
> Melon[592]

---

[590] E.g. Mientka, Matthew; Medical Daily; *School Bans Homemade Lunches, Angering Parents Critical Of Federal Nutritional Standards*; Nov 16, 2013
[591] Burrows, Sara; Carolina Journal News; *Preschooler's Homemade Lunch Replaced with Cafeteria "Nuggets": State agent inspects sack lunches, preschoolers purchase cafeteria food instead*; Feb. 14th, 2012
[592] https://www.sidwell.edu/mobile/index.aspx?v=c&mid=375&t=Lunch+Menus.

So much for the equality that the Obama's preach! As Napoleon the Fascist Pig etched the amendment to the Leftist Commandment in *Animal Farm*, "Some [of us] are more equal than others"!

In the 1980's the Left through its lobbying campaign and insider manipulation convinced the Food and Drug Administration (FDA) to drastically reduce the portion of meat, specifically beef, which the FDA recommended as healthy from the FDA's newly created "food pyramid". Their outcry was immense and succeeded in forcing the FDA to modestly increase the suggested amount of meat in the State-sanctioned pyramid[593]. However, the Left's War on meat and GOD continues.

Separation of Church and State:

The Separation of Church and State was an early guise by the Nazis to divide and conquer the German Christian churches and implement a single state Religion of Fascist Paganism. Mandatory review of pastors' sermons and outlines were instituted by the Leftist Nazi régime, "After 1937, German Catholic bishops gave up all attempts to print" their pastoral letters publicly and instead "had them merely read from the pulpits." Then the letters themselves were confiscated. "In many churches, the confiscation took place during Mass by the police snatching the letter out of the hands of the priests as they were in the act of reading it"[594].

For those naïve enough to think that it can't happen here... It *is* happening already here!

While this may sound like a bad dystopian novel, the Fascistic attempt to monitor and confiscate sermons is already happening in the United States with impunity. Über-Leftist radical homosexual Houston Mayor Annise Parker in 2014 spearheaded a Houston City "Equal Rights Ordinance" (ERO) that added "sexual orientation" and "gender

[593] Nestle, Marion; Food Politics, foodpolitics.com; *MyPyramid R.I.P.*; May 29, 2011.
[594] Sharkey, Joe; *Word for Word/The Case Against the Nazis; How Hitler's Forces Planned To Destroy German Christianity*; New York Times online; January 13, 2002.

identity" to the Houston's non-discrimination provision, which included "public accommodations" that would include public restrooms. A group of Houston pastors got together and filed a petition to overturn the Leftist homosexual biased ordinance. The referendum required 17,000 signatures, they gathered 55,000. The City's Secretary signed off on the petition to become a referendum. However, city attorney David Feldman stepped in without any legal authority and disannulled the petition and Parker and the city council rejected the petition. In retaliation against Christians Mayor Annise Parker sued several Houston pastors personally, who were not even legally involved in the petition, demanding that these pastors turn over all sermons, emails, texts, and all other forms of communications relating to "all speeches, presentations, or sermons related to Houston ERO, the Petition, Mayor Annise Parker, homosexuality, or gender identity prepared by, delivered by, revised by, or approved by you or in your possession". This is not only a subversive attack against the US Constitution, but an outright Fascist attack upon Christians in *the Left's War Against GOD!*

In a 1937 directive from Hitler, many German churches willingly entered into a concordant with the Leftist régime with this proviso: "The Evangelical Church has learned from Martin Luther to distinguish sharply between the realms of reason and faith, politics and religion, **state and Church**"[595]! (Bold added)

The mantra of the "separation of Church and State" has been a Leftist doctrine since the beginning of *the Left's War Against GOD!* It should be noted however, as discussed thoroughly in this book, that the definition of "Church" here by the Left is exclusive to the "Christian Church". What was the Left's reaction to the Muslim attack on America in 2001? Feisal Abdul Rauf a devout Muslim tried to build a Muslim mosque at ground zero! And the name of that mosque was to be called the Cordoba Mosque in honor of the mosque that the Muslims built in Cordoba, Spain in celebration of the Muslim conquering of that city from its Christian population! The Muslims

---

[595] Mosse, George L.; *Nazi Culture: Intellectual, Cultural and Social Life in the Third Reich*; University of Wisconsin Press; September 2003; pg. 243.

killed all Christians, Jews, and non-Muslims who refused to convert to Islam. Feisal Abdul Rauf stated on his website "the name Cordoba was chosen carefully to reflect a period of time during which Islam played a monumental role in the enrichment of human civilization and knowledge". Obama endorsed and celebrated the building of a Muslim victory mosque at the point of Islam's most successful attack upon America. The Left's strawman of the "separation of Church and State" is only enforced against Christians and Christianity!

The Left uses the mantra of the "separation of Church and State" to isolate Christians from politics and influence in society. Where the necessarily ensuing vacuum is created the Left steps in to fill the moral and civic void and become the savior of the crisis which the Left itself created. There are no degrees of separation between the Left in America today and the Nazis of Germany 75 years ago! The devils of the Left are the same, only the name of Evil changes! This is *the Left's War Against GOD!*

Tolerance:

"Tolerance becomes a crime when applied to Evil" - Thomas Mann. Paul Thomas Mann was a Nobel Prize laureate who escaped Germany in 1939 at the rise of the Nazi takeover. When Hitler came to power in 1933, Mann fled to Switzerland. When World War II broke out in 1939, he moved to the United States, returning to Switzerland in 1952. As thoroughly demonstrated in the chapter *Tolerance*, the Left in America today uses a bastardized and false "tolerance" to marginalize and defeat any opposition to its agenda.

Vegetarianism/Veganism:

Do you think that the link between Fascism and the American Left is a bit exaggerated? Let's talk about Nazi Germany's push to turn their country into a vegetarian paradise. Under Walther Darr, the Third Reich Minister for Nutrition and Agriculture, Nazi Germany instigated a campaign to promote a "healthier eating lifestyle". While it was voluntary in the beginning, it quickly became a State-mandated, State-regulated, and State-enforced food industry, enforced at the individual level. The Left always begins with seemingly benevolent guidelines, which quickly morph into State-enforced "guidelines" as soon as the Left has acquired sufficient power to force compliance to its Leftist agenda.

Goebbels, Hitler's Minister of Propaganda who arranged pederast/homosexual orgies for Nazi Party leadership, wrote on 29 December 1939: "Both [Judaism and Christianity] have no point of contact to the animal element, and thus, in the end they will be destroyed. The Fuhrer is a convinced vegetarian on principle".

In Nazi Germany, "Reich Minister of Food and Agriculture, Richard Walther Darré, made the official statement that, 'plant food must once again as in olden times form the main food...'"[596].

Vegetarianism **and processed food**: The Third Reich implemented a series of laws promoting vegetarianism and vilifying the meat industry. They also vilified processed food manufacturers as poisoning the population:

> Himmler was particularly vexed by the slow pace of his efforts to transform the way Germans ate: "The artificial is everywhere; everywhere food is adulterated, filled with ingredients that supposedly make it last longer, or look better, or pass as 'enriched,' or whatever else the industry's admen want us to believe . . . [W]e are in the hands of the food companies, whose economic clout and advertising make it possible for them to prescribe what we can and cannot eat . . . [A]fter the war we shall take energetic steps to prevent the ruin of our people by the food industries"[597].

---

[596] Aboul-Enein, Basil H., MSc, MPH, MA; Online Journal of Health Ethics, 9(1); *Preventive Nutrition in Nazi Germany: A Public Health Commentary*; 2013; Retrieved from http://aquila.usm.edu/ojhe/vol9/iss1/10.
[597] Goldberg, Jonah; *Liberal FASCISM: The Secret History of the American Left From Mussolini to the Politics of Meaning*; 2007; pg. 301.

Sound familiar? It should. The Left in America began in earnest in the 1960's its own food limiting campaign with the scare that salt was killing tens of thousands of Americans. Then it was eggs killing everyone. Now their campaign assaults fast food, processed food, trans-fat, Big Gulps and the Leftist is daily widening its vegetarian agenda based on Hinduism's reincarnation beliefs and protecting people from eating their ancestors. Sound extreme?

In January 2015 the Obama Administration appointed Dietary Guidelines Advisory Committee (DGAC) issued their 571-page report which recommended that the Federal government mandate to Americans "*plant-based*" and that State "trained interventionists" be used to enforce these new dietary "guidelines" in *schools*, *businesses*, and *homes*! The DGAC recommended that the government enforce "Vegan, lacto-ovo vegetarian, pesco-vegetarian, and Mediterranean diets" as the healthiest diets!

Scientists are even openly drawing positive conclusions from the Nazi nutritional guidelines and suggesting that they be adopted today in America, "Nazi public health promotion and education were involved in activities that we might today view as socially responsible within the fields of preventive medicine."[598].

The Left's vegetarianism agenda is based on the Nazi Pagan model instituted by Hitler himself and his Evil minions. The vegetarianism of the Left is closely tied to its Animal Rights and Nutrition agendas. These agendas are drawn from Paganism's Gaia worship and Hinduisms Universal Consciousness. These Hindu and Pagan beliefs are at their core Evil and the forefront of *the Left's War Against GOD!*

Welfare:

---

[598] Aboul-Enein, Basil H., MSc, MPH, MA; Online Journal of Health Ethics, 9(1); *Preventive Nutrition in Nazi Germany: A Public Health Commentary*; 2013; Retrieved from http://aquila.usm.edu/ojhe/vol9/iss1/10.

The *Bible* tells us that the *love* of money is the root of all Evil.[599] Welfare preys on that root of covetousness and causes people to always covet more and more of other people's money and property. That devil is never satiated!

Götz Aly, a German professor at the University of Frankfurt, in his book *Hitler's Beneficiaries: Plunder, Racial War, and the Nazi Welfare State* walks us down the path of the German story of self-interest which leads to an unquenchable thirst for a self-serving Welfare State[600]. Once the popular culture becomes accustomed to the government handouts of the Welfare State, they soon find themselves willing to overlook greater and greater evils in return for more government indulgences. Aly "focus[es] on the *socialist* aspect of [German Nazi] *National Socialism*" showing clearly the evil consequences of "the Nazi regime as a kind of racist-totalitarian welfare state"[601]. The German people received housing subsidies, food assistance, retirement and pension plans, universal healthcare, a barrier from inflation, a high minimum wage, and many other Welfare State perks, and all that it cost was the lives of 5 million Jews, 7 million Christians, and 100 million or so other lives worldwide!

Götz Aly does an amazing job of showing us how the average German citizen was himself, actually responsible for the Nazi atrocities stemming from the payoffs of the Nazi Welfare State. Self-interest in the *Socialist* nature of taking from others for one's own benefit, causes the recipient to turn a blind eye to all of the horrors necessary in acquiring the pillages of an unGODly War. Germans were *no* different than Americans in general are today, "Germans wanted their children to have nice Christmas gifts. They wanted to set aside money for retirement. They wanted to send a special someone back home a pretty sweater from Holland or perfumed soap from France. Citizens were sated with decent wages, generous overtime pay and innovative

---

[599] The *Holy Bible*: 1 Timothy 6:10 "For the love of money is the root of all evil: which while some coveted after, they have erred from the faith, and pierced themselves through with many sorrows".
[600] This topic is also discussed in the previous subsection **Anti-Semitism/Anti-Israel**.
[601] Aly, Götz; Translated by Jefferson Chase; *Hitler's Beneficiaries: Plunder, Racial War, and the Nazi Welfare State*; Metropolitan Books; 2007.

pension plans — that is, through the establishment of a complex…welfare state"[602]. It was these spoils of War that were plundered from murdered Christians and Jews as well as conquered countries that fortified and financed the Nazi Welfare State. Welfare is never sustainable as avarice once released from Pandora's Box is never satisfied with what it has been given!

Today the Left pillages our children and children's children to fortify and finance its unsustainable spending frenzy. We too often see only the monsters at the top of the Welfare State as the sole benefactors of their Evil. The monsters of Evil like Pol Pot, Mao, Stalin, Hitler, Kim Jong-un, and Obama are easily recognized examples of the head of the Welfare Beasts. The truth of the matter is that none of the world's Evil Leftist megalomaniacs could obtain, nor retain power without the, at the very least, tacit approval of a majority of their populace, the everyday Joe on the street, so to speak. Welfare, or the promise of State Welfare's Social largesse, has always been at the center of peoples' acquiescence to Evil as a nation.

All Leftists in history have attained power through the promise of the *Socialist* Welfare State in some form or another. Communism, Socialism, Fascism, and all other manifestations of the Left, have all promised to take from the rich and give to the poor, from the haves to the have nots. Why? Because the "have nots"[603] always outnumber the "haves". The votes to usurp power are with the "have nots". As has been aptly said, when the welfare recipients outnumber the tax payers, the nation is set in a downward spiral doomed to oblivion, as the welfare recipients always vote for more welfare and bankrupt the country. As previously noted in the chapter *Understanding The Battle*, Alexander Fraser Tytler aptly noted that history teaches us that the Cycle of Dictatorship develops this way:

> "The average of the world's great civilizations [democracies] before they decline has been 200 years. These nations have

---

[602] Aly, Götz; Translated by Jefferson Chase; *Hitler's Beneficiaries: Plunder, Racial War, and the Nazi Welfare State*; Metropolitan Books; 2007.
[603] The "have nots" is used here a bit tongue-in-cheek using the Leftist-Socialist rhetoric, which lumps all into this category who are not the very rich.

progressed in this sequence: From bondage to spiritual faith; from faith to great courage; from courage to liberty; from liberty to abundance; *from abundance to selfishness*; from selfishness to complacency; from complacency to apathy; from apathy to dependency; from *dependency back again to bondage*"[604]. (emphasis added)

To the Left a Totalitarian Dictatorship is always the means to its ends of an imagined Utopian Paradise. Socialism sometimes "imagined" by its visionaries as benevolent, most times not.

The Left in America, just as in Nazi Germany, are the proprietors of greed, avarice, and covetousness to which the Left feeds, fosters, and addicts Americans every day. The Left has been shrieking: Those greedy Capitalists! In fact Capitalists are the exact opposite of greedy! Capitalism fills the needs of people. The Capitalist's very existence depends on filling the needs of the people otherwise it goes out of business. The Entrepreneur must fill the niche in the market precisely by cost of production, fair market value, filling a consumer need. Leftist Socialism is the opposite and totally founded on human greed of taking from the rich and giving it to everyone else!

Zero Sum Game: When the Socialist Left controls the government, they always by their limiting philosophy are forced to deal with their policy of the Zero-Sum Game. Socialism determines the limited size of the pie and who gets what proportion of that pie and in what size slices it doles out. Capitalism says entrepreneurs and consumers determine not only the size of the slice but demand has Capitalists baking more pies!

As long as the Left keeps creating dependency through its give-away Welfare State, America will never be free of Evil and the downward

---

[604] Alexander Fraser Tytler, Lord Woodhouselee (1747-1813) was a Scottish lawyer, writer, and professor at the University of Edinburgh, Scotland. Tytler was an historian in Greek and Roman Antiquities and was intimately familiar with the Greek democracy and the degradation of the Roman Republic into democracy, then into dictatorship. There is some question to the origin of this quote which was first published in America on December 9, 1951 in an article by Elmer T. Peterson in *The Daily Oklahoman* and credited to Tytler. It has since been quoted and attributed to Tytler by dozens of people including Ronald Reagan.

spiral into oblivion, following quickly in the footsteps of Nazi Germany straight into the Pit of Hell! Ultimately it is Americans themselves which must bear the bulk of the responsibility for the evils done in the name of the Welfare State. Abortion, homosexuality, sexual perversions of every sort, drug and alcohol addiction, prostituting our sons and daughters, violence, and every other form of Evil all come back to our love of money and our willingness as Americans to acquiesce to Evil in the acceptance of the Left's Welfare State give-away programs. American's love of money, through the corruptions of the Welfare State, necessarily consumes everything that is GOOD and Right in America. Americans turn more and more a jaundice eye, just as the everyday Germans in Nazi Germany, to evil as they extend their hand further and further out for the blood money offered so freely by the Left. Americans are accepting payoffs from the Left for their silence, to pretend that the Devil doesn't exist and the Evil being done in America today isn't really… Evil! Welfare at its core is the love of money and the root of Evil in America today. Welfare is the Left's twenty pieces of silver for which many in America have sold their soul to the Left in *the Left's War Against GOD!*

CONCLUSION:

The Left works tirelessly against all that is RIGHT. How do they intend to implement their Fascist Utopia? Obama had called for a "civilian national security force" saying: "We cannot continue to rely on our military in order to achieve the [homeland] national security objectives we've set. We've got to have a *civilian national security force* that's just as powerful, just as strong, just as well-funded"[605]. Obama never rescinded his statement. We need not look far to discover the motive behind Obama's "civilian national security force", which was illegal and against the *US Posse Comitatus Act* and was instituted as a safeguard against an Executive takeover of the United States using American troops against Americans. The US *Posse Comitatus Act* forbids the military from "search, seizure, arrest,

---

[605] Obama speech in Colorado Springs, CO; July 2nd, 2008.

or other similar activity" by any branch of the US military. This is identical to the Hitler Nazi "national security" force called the Brownshirts or the *Sturmabteilung*, the Nazi "Stormtroopers"!

The Storm Troopers began as the *Freikorps* or "Free Corps", then the *Hitler-Jugend* or "Hitler Youth", then morphed into the Brownshirts, referred to as the "Brown Fairies", and into the *Sturmabteilung* or Nazi "Stormtroopers". The *Freikorps* or "Free Corps" was a *civilian* para-military organization used to subdue the German population under the Leftist-Fascist Nazi régime.

This was the goal of Obama and is the goal now of the Left. The Obama Administration purchased hundreds of millions of rounds of ammunition and military grade equipment for several Federal departments... Federal Departments which do not yet even own guns! Here is the logical and only reasonable answer to an otherwise puzzling question... Why?:

> It was Rossbach who formed the original terrorist organization which eventually became the Nazi Storm Troopers, also known as "Brown Shirts." Both the Rossbach Storm Troopers and the *Schilljugend* were notorious for wearing brown shirts which had been prepared for German colonial troops, acquired from the old Imperial army stores (Koehl:19). It is reasonable to suppose that without Rossbach's Storm Troopers, Adolf Hitler and the Nazis would never have gained power in Germany.[606]

These conclusions are no longer a "far-fetched conspiracy theory", but an undeniable fact as verifiable by the words and actions of those on the Left. If it quacks like a duck... This is the quackish Vast Left-Wing Conspiracy! Still doubtful? Remember when Obama used his union thugs from the SEIU to literally beat up and intimidate opponents and tear down their tents and booths? That is exactly how the Nazi Storm Troopers began their reign of terror. Obama attempted

---

[606] *The Pink Swastika*; pg. 40.

to create his own private police force to enforce the demands of the Left.

Still skeptical? Really? How about the Obama established FEMA Corps? What you ask. The Obama Administration through the Department of Homeland Security created a paramilitary "youth" organization that trains teenagers in military tactics and operations. The word "corps" signifies a military organization trained in weapons and crowd control among other things. Are you scared yet? As Yoda famously said while pointing his crooked finger… You will be! (The reference to Star Wars is intentional, including the Evil Empire's Storm Troopers, to show the similarity with this subject and a science fiction novel which is hard to believe until it actually happens!) The Federal Emergency Management Administration (FEMA) is responsible not just for response to national disasters, but frighteningly to any "possible" event that leads to Marshal Law!

Marshal Law can only be declared nationally by the President of the United States. On March 16, 2012 Obama signed an Executive Order giving himself as President sweeping and absolute dictatorial powers in case Martial Law "may" need to be implemented. The Executive Order 13603 gives the sitting President full control over all resources including confiscation of all property and the allocation of *all medical, food, and water resources*. Scared yet? Executive Order 13603 was signed by President Barack Hussein Obama only a few months before Obama's election for a second term. The *National Defense Resources Preparedness* Executive Order gave Obama power over "resources and services needed to support such plans and programs". Scared yet? You should be!

Barack Hussein Obama signed the National Defense Authorization Act of 2013 passed by the Congress, which gave Obama legal authority to *indefinitely* imprison any American, any time, and without any legal basis! Still not scared? Could this chain of events be purely coincidental? Yes, and pigs can fly and Pearl Harbor was a purely coincidental accident! The time-tested wisdom of Ockham's Razor teaches us that when faced with multiple choices in finding a solution to a seemingly complex question, "The simplest solution is almost always the right one". The *Holy Bible* tells us that all solutions associated with GOD's GOOD are simple[607], simple enough for a child to understand[608]! The simple and only reasonable conclusion to which we are forced is that the Left has actively been pursuing Nazi-like tactics by which it intends to forcibly usurp control of America... just as Hitler did in Nazi Germany.

While Obama is gone from office, he and his minions are still working tirelessly behind the scenes through Obama's Fascist-modeled political machine Organizing for Action. This organization is so evil that even some Democrat operatives have dubbed it Obama's Organizing for Action, and ostensibly Obama himself as "The Devil"![609] Even Über-Leftist media outlets like the *Daily Beast* are reporting the use of "The Devil" as a moniker by Democrat operatives for Obama's Organizing for Action.[610] There is no doubt that Obama still harbors the ambition to be Emperor as Obama tours the world's evil empires seeking self-aggrandizement. There are legion in the evil ranks of the Left who would, or have, sold their soul for the opportunity to become the evil emperor of the world! Evil always keeps its potential antichrist in the waiting. We can either stand and *Fight* NOW or we will regret it when our children and grandchildren are marching goosestep and *Seig Heil* saluting whatever Leftist dictator is commanding America!

Today the Left ruthlessly and relentlessly attacks every vestige of the Right which still remains in America. With the only exception that the modern Left in America has replaced Nationalism with Internationalism (Obama's America is not exceptional), and replaced the National mantra of Nazi "racism" with the outright Leftist mantra of "Anti-GOD" and by extension "Anti-Christianism" as the Final Solution, the Left in America today is virtually indistinguishable from

---

[607] The *Holy Bible*: 2 Corinthians 11:3.
[608] The *Holy Bible*: Mark 10:15.
[609] Kant, Garth; *World News Daily*; Now Democrats call Obama's shadow government 'The Devil'; 02/19/2017 at 5:24 PM.
[610] Suebsaeng, Asawin; *Daily Beast*; Leaked Emails: Dem State Leaders Think Obama's New Organizing Army is 'Grade A Bullshit'; 02/17/17 1:13 AM ET.

Nazi Fascism! It is absolutely a distinction without a difference. This is *the Left's War Against GOD!*

20. The Democrat Party Platform As Leftist Doctrines All OPPOSE God

Chapter 20

The Democrat Party national Platform today is indistinguishable from the radical Leftist movement in America today which *absolutely* opposes *all* that is GOD's. As such, the Democrat Left today in America is the frontline Army of Evil in *the Left's War Against GOD!* To some this statement may seem a little over dramatic. However in this chapter we will review in a point-by-point comparison, the platform and doctrines of the Democrat Party which stands in *total* and *absolute* opposition *Against* the doctrines of GOD's *Holy Bible*. The results of this comparison will shock some and will, for various reasons, make others angry, but hopefully to the troops on the Right it will lend encouragement, equip, and invigorate us in our Battle for America against the Left in *the Left's War Against GOD!*

Quoting again the secularist commentator on the Evil of the Left, Evan Sayet notes of the modern Democrat Party in America today:

> I assume that just about everybody in this room agrees that the Democrats are wrong on just about every issue. Well, I'm here to propose to you that it's not "just about" every issue; it's quite literally every issue. And it's not just wrong; it's as wrong as wrong can be; it's 180 degrees from right; it is diametrically opposed to that which is good, right, and successful.
>
> What I discovered is that this is not an accident. This is part of a philosophy that now dominates the whole of Western Europe and the [American] Democratic Party today. I, like some others, call it Modern Liberalism. The Modern Liberal will invariably side with evil over good, wrong over right, and the behaviors that lead to failure over those that lead to success. Give the Modern Liberal the choice between Saddam Hussein and the United States, and he will not only side with Saddam

Hussein; he will slander America and Americans in order to do so. Give him the choice between the vicious mass murderer corrupt terrorist dictator Yasser Arafat and the tiny and wonderful democracy of Israel, and he will plagiarize maps, forge documents, engage in blood libels--as did our former President Jimmy Carter-- to side with the terrorist organizations and to attack the tiny democracy of Israel.

It's not just foreign policy; it's every policy. Given the choice between promoting teenage abstinence and teenage promiscuity--and believe me, I know this from my hometown of Hollywood--they will use their movies, their TV shows, their songs, even the schools to promote teenage promiscuity as if it's cool: like the movie American Pie, in which you are a loser unless you've had sex with your best friend's mother while you're still a child. Conversely, NARAL, a pro-abortion group masquerading as a pro-choice group, will hold a fund-raiser called "'F' Abstinence." (And it's not just "F." It's the entire word, because promoting vulgarity is part of their agenda.)[611].

The Democrat Party in America today stands at odds with all that is decent and GOOD. The Democrat Party is Wrong on "quite literally every issue. And it's not just wrong; it's as wrong as wrong can be; it's 180 degrees from right; it is diametrically opposed to that which is GOOD, right, and successful". The Democrat Party quite literally is Against *all* that the *Bible* teaches as GOD's Word, Will, and Nature. We will make a side-by-side comparison below of GOD's Doctrines as they stand in opposition to virtually every plank of the Democrat Party Platform and the Leftist Doctrines of which the Democrat Party so vehemently embraces.

Comparisons Between GOD's Doctrines and the Democrat Party Platform and the Democrat Party's Leftist Doctrines:

---

[611] Sayet, Evan; Speech to The Heritage Foundation; *Regurgitating the Apple How Modern Liberals "Think"*; March 5, 2007.

Abortion: (see also: Euthanasia, Infanticide, and Murder)

The Democrat Party: *Militantly* Pro-Abortion

The Democrat Party is militantly Pro-Abortion including abortion on demand, late term abortions, partial birth abortions, harvesting baby body parts, letting "accidently" born babies die, and killing babies "until they leave the hospital".

GOD: Anti-Abortion

The *Bible* is Absolutely clear that abortion is *murder*, forbidden by GOD, and specifically demonic. (Exodus 21:22-23; 2 Kings 6:33; Job 10:8; 31:15; Psalms 71:6; 94:20-21; 106:37-38; 119:73; 139:13-16; Is 43:1; 44:2, 24; Jeremiah 1:5; 7:6; 22:3; Lamentations 2:12; Romans 9:1). GOD tells us that life begins at conception. (Job 31:15)

Class Warfare:

The Democrat Party: Promotes Class Warfare

The Democrat Party's goal is to divide and conquer. The Democrat Left divides us by economic status, male and female, by race, religion, social status, *et al* and the Democrat Party are creating new groups to divide America further *every* day!

GOD: Forbids Class Warfare

The *Bible* not only Forbids Class Warfare, but demands equal treatment of all people regardless of economic status. (James 2:3-9)

Cradle-To-Grave:

The Democrat Party: Tries to Play "God" Offering Cradle-To-Grave

As documented throughout this book, the Left tries to play "God" in advocating Cradle-To-Grave "caretaking". However by historical experience the Democrat Left's Cradle-To-Grave "caretaking" always results in Cradle-To-Grave *tyranny*!

GOD: Only GOD Can Provide Cradle-To-Grave Caretaking

GOD alone can provide for His people from Cradle-To-Grave (Isiah

46:3-4)

Crime:

The Democrat Party: The Government Alone Takes Care Of

Crime

The Democrat Party wants all Americans totally dependent upon it for its livelihood, sustenance, and protection. When it comes to personal involvement in dealing with the immediate issue of crime the Democrat Left demands that you call the "authorities" and let the government deal with it, even if someone will die by waiting the individual cannot interject himself in place of authorized government authorities.

GOD: GOD Holds Persons Responsible To Deal With Crime

With GOD there is no such thing as an "innocent bystander" when you see a crime being committed. (Psalms 50:18)

Cults:

The Democrat Party: Cults Recognized as Good Religions

The Democrat Party recognizes all religions as equally acceptable, except of course Christianity which it loathes and seeks to destroy by every means possible.

GOD: Cults Condemned as Representations of Evil

GOD recognizes only Christianity as acceptable and all other religions are manifestations of Evil at War with Christianity. (Deuteronomy 8:19)

Death Penalty:

The Democrat Party: Anti-Death Penalty

It is astonishing that the Democrat Party militantly supports killing babies, killing children, killing the handicapped, supports killing the elderly, and supports assisted suicide, and yet is against the death penalty for murderers who kill. Maybe in some twisted way, the Democrat Left sees the Death Penalty as a bigger threat to them than the murderers of babies, children, the handicapped, the diseased, the terminally ill, and the elderly!

GOD: Pro-Death Penalty

GOD's Word the *Bible* clearly prescribes the Death Penalty for those who willingly and knowingly commit murder. (Genesis 9:6; Revelation 13:10) The *Bible* exempts self-defense, the police, and national military actions from being defined as murder. The Ten Commandments in the *Bible* tell us "Thou shalt not kill". This is literally translated as "Thou shalt not murder". GOD's reasoning for the Death Penalty is impossible to argue with: "Whoso sheddeth man's blood, by man shall his blood be shed: for in the image of God made he man". (Genesis 9:6)

Drugs:

The Democrat Party: Pro-Drugs; Legalization and Government Control Of:

Today the Democrat Left works diligently to "transform" Americans into accepting legalized drug use. Many States have now legalized medical and "recreational" marijuana. Obama had issued Executive orders allowing citizens to possess and use "small amounts" of marijuana without fear of prosecution. Obama ordered the US Justice Department to release the largest number of prisoners ever from Federal Prison System who were serving time for drug-related sentences. The Left *never* stops down its path to legalizing and normalizing sin. Drugs are no exception and the Left will move ever increasingly to legalize worse and worse drugs to as the *Bible* tells us "by thy sorceries [drugs] were all nations deceived"! (Revelation 8:23) Drugs are the Evil at the center of the Left's plot to rule the world!

It is the ultimate goal of the Democrat Left in America today to create another dependency class of drug-users who are wholly dependent upon the Federal government for their next "fix". He who controls the dispensing of legalized drugs, controls the Nation. As was evidenced in Nazi Germany, these drug addicts are the most loyal and vicious class of citizen to the Fascist State, those who will commit horrific atrocities without conscience to benefit the Democrat Left's goals and ideals. Drugs make you both stupid and SLAVES! GOD in His Word tells us that drugs are the gateway to the demonic. This is *the Left's War Against GOD!*

GOD: Anti-Drugs:
The *Bible* in Revelation 18:23 tells us "for thy merchants were the great men of the earth; for by thy sorceries were all nations deceived.". The word "sorceries" is translated from the Greek *Pharmakeia*, from which we get the English word "pharmacy" and pharmaceuticals or illicit *drugs*. In the end-times, merchants through drugs will control the world. *Sorceries* are directly associated in the *Bible* with Evil and *witchcraft* specifically through the illicit use of mind-altering *drugs*. *Sorceries* and *witchcraft*, which GOD calls devil worship, are synonymous in the *Bible*.

Drugs are Evil and always associated in the *Bible* as a tool of *sorcery* and *witchcraft* and the gateway to a person being influenced and controlled by the demonic.

Economics:

The Democrat Party: Anti-Capitalistic

The Democrat Party is Anti-Capitalistic and substitutes a crony or corrupted form of "Capitalism" the same as was done in Nazi Germany[612].

GOD: Pro-Capitalistic
GOD created and promoted through the *Bible* what we now call Capitalism. (Proverbs 31:18)

Education:

The Democrat Party: Government Is Responsible For a Child's Education
The Democrat Party believes that it should run education through its many organs such as the National Education Association (NEA) teacher's union, the US Department of Education, the Service Employees International Union (SEIU), and dozens of other Leftist organizations. The Democrat Left, as Hitler did, sees America's Education system as a means to indoctrinate and control our youth from cradle-to-grave.

GOD: Parents Are Responsible For a Child's Education
The *Bible* tells us that a child's education is the exclusive responsibility of his parents (Deuteronomy 4:10; Proverbs 22:6) with specific accountability before GOD. (Genesis 18:19; Ephesians 6:4)

Environmentalism (Fanatical):

The Democrat Party: *Militantly* Supports Fanatical

---

[612] For a wider discussion see the chapter *Fascism and the Left in America: Kindred Spirits and Familiar Bedfellows* and the subsection *Corporativism*.

Environmentalism
The Democrat Party militantly forces Fanatical
Environmentalism as a means of seizing control of America's
energy and food production systems. Global
Warming/Climate Change are created "crisis" whereby the
Democrat Left can terrify Americans into giving up their
freedoms up to the government. Environmentalism is the
modern manifestation of Pagan worship of the Hindu goddess
Gaia as Mother Earth who supposedly threatens a conscious
retaliation against mankind for man's defilement of "her". As
popularized in movies *2012*; *The Happening* (M. Night
Shyamalan); *An Inconvenient Truth*; *Avatar*; et al.

GOD: Opposes Militant Environmentalism
GOD commanded man to have dominion over all of the earth.
(Genesis 1:26, 28) GOD gives the responsibility to man for his
role in the earth's aesthetics, the small environmental areas
where man can have an effect. But GOD created the earth to be
resilient and naturally heal itself from *any* possible
degradation that man or nature may inflict. This can be
evidenced in man-made disasters like Lake Michigan catching
fire from pollution, the Exxon Valdez, the BP Gulf of Mexico
oil spill, and the atomic bombs that were dropped on Japan.
There is no evidence today that these disasters ever even
happened. Devastating natural disasters like the Pompeii and
Mount Saint Helen's volcanos are today invisible to the eye.

Equal Rights: (see also: Feminism)

The Democrat Party: Promotes a False Equal Rights Movement

Equal Rights for the Left is am intentional misrepresentation, a cleverly disguised *Lie*. The Democrat Left in actuality is seeking to destroy the Biblically mandated role of a husband's responsibility before GOD for the family. The Democrat Left has strived to destroy the family unit in America since the 1960's in *the Left's War Against* GOD and *Against* America's traditional Christian roots.

GOD: Equal Rights but a Biblically Ordered Hierarchy

GOD ordained equal but significantly different roles for men and women. Man was created in the image of GOD, while the woman was taken as only a part of man. (1 Corinthians 11:7-9) Some fail to notice that a woman is significantly different physically as well as emotionally from a man.

GOD created a hierarchy where children are responsible to the parents, the wife is responsible to her husband, and the husband is especially responsible before GOD for his wife and children. (1 Corinthians 11:3) The husband ultimately has the GOD-given responsibilities for protecting, nurturing, and educating the family.

Eugenics:

The Democrat Party: Advocates Eugenics

The definition of Eugenics is: *The study of or belief in the possibility of improving the qualities of the human species or a human population, especially by such means as discouraging reproduction by persons having genetic defects or presumed to have inheritable undesirable traits (negative eugenics) or encouraging reproduction by persons presumed to have inheritable desirable traits (positive eugenics)*[613].

The Democrat Left encourages murder by abortion when the baby's characteristics are not physically or mentally desired.

---

[613] Dictionary.com; eugenics.

This can include the baby being physically or mentally handicapped, have genetic markers which make a disease or illness more likely, or be as simple as an undesirable eye or hair color. This is all genetic engineering. This is the Left's attempt to play "God"!

GOD: Forbids Eugenics

Whether the genetic malformations were caused by environmental contagions or created as a direct act of GOD (Job 31:15; Isaiah 44:24), GOD considers all life sacred. GOD knows each of us while we are even still in the womb and from conception. GOD accepts us coming to him just as we are physically and mentally. GOD even uses physical and mental abnormalities to glorify Him and bring us to GOD. (Luke 1:64-66; John 9:1-39; Acts 3:1-9)

Euthanasia: (see also: Abortion, Infanticide, and Murder)

The Democrat Party: Supports and Promotes Euthanasia

Euthanasia has been publically redefined by the Democrat Left as exclusive to "mercy killing" sometimes inclusive of doctor-assisted suicide. The Left always begins with legalized "mercy killing" and always strains for the killing of the elderly, the sick (sometimes terminally sometimes not), the mentally ill, the chronically ill, and a plethora of other reasons. The Democrat Left through Nationalized healthcare becomes its sole provider and sole funder. When the State becomes the sole funding source, then decisions for who receives life-saving medical attention becomes the sole discretion of the State. Euthanasia becomes a money-saving device as epitomized in the Nazi T-4 euthanasia killing programs labeling the undesirables of the State as "life unworthy of life" or "useless eaters". Under the Nazi Left, euthanasia was employed to eradicate Christians and Jews because they were considered mentally ill by the State.

GOD: Forbids Euthanasia

GOD considers *all* human life as *sacred*, meaning belonging to GOD. The *Bible* forbids any form of Euthanasia. GOD Himself became a man because GOD so loved all men. (John 3:16)

Evolution:

The Democrat Party: Promotes the Theory of Evolution

As documented in the chapter *Fascism and the Left in America: Kindred Spirits and Familiar Bedfellows*, the Democrat Party of the Left seeks to substitute Evolution as an *Alternative* to GOD. To do this the Left has to try to discredit the *Bible*'s account of a literal seven 24-hour days of Creation and present some *theoretical* "alternative". There are only two existent theories as to the origin of the Universe and all living things, Evolution and Creation. To reject Creation is to accept Evolution, as it is to accept Evolution is to reject Creation.

GOD: Evolution Does Not Exist

The *Bible* tells us clearly and absolutely that GOD created the Universe, including the earth, and all living things in literally seven 24-hour days. (Genesis 1:1-2:4)

Family:

The Democrat Party: Anti-Family

The Democrat Party is intentionally trying to destroy the Family unit as established by GOD and substitute the State or "Village" as the nurturer, educator, and protector of people from Cradle-To-Grave. In removing the traditional Family, the Democrat Left is attempting to remove accountability to GOD from the human psyche.

GOD: Pro-Family

GOD designed the Family as the cornerstone of civilization. GOD created the Family as a hierarchy to hold people accountable to GOD. (Genesis 1:26-27; Mark 10:6-9; Col. 3:18–21; *et al*)

Feminism: (see also: Equal Rights)

The Democrat Party: Pro-Feminist

The Democrat Party supports Feminism as a means to destroy the Family unit as designed by GOD and to cause chaos in society. Feminism elevates the worth of a woman over a man and marginalizes men in society. In order to accept feminism as legitimate one must suspend rational thought and empiric observation choosing to ignore and dismiss such things as men are naturally physically stronger than women, women are more emotionally controlled than men, men are more reasoned than women, and other things such as the obvious physical differences and the unalterable reproduction roles of the sexes.

GOD: Anti-Feminist

Feminism seeks to elevate women above men. GOD established the husband and father as head of the household, so Evil must strive to destroy the *Bible*'s ordered community. (1 Corinthians 14:34; Ephesians 5:22; Colossians 3:18; 1 Peter 3:1) The *Bible* states the obvious on issues that the woman is the "weaker vessel". (1 Peter 3:7) The *Bible* calls Feminism: Rebellion Against GOD (Genesis 3:6; 1 Timothy 2:12)

Food:

The Democrat Party: Pushes Vegetarianism and Veganism

The Democrat Left pushes Food diets like vegetarianism, veganism, and non-processed food "lifestyles". The Left seeks every opportunity to discourage and even mandate no meat diets. Why? Well they say it is a healthier lifestyle, but it is not. Many vegetarians and vegans experience serious health issues from not eating meat, some to the point of death, just as the *Bible* said would happen. (Psalms 107:18) The Democrat

Left seldom acknowledges this in public. The reason that the Democrat Left pushes these dietary regimens is that the *Bible* associates Vegetarianism (and Veganism) with the Anti-GOD Paganism. (Acts 10:15; Romans 14:20; 1 Timothy 4:3-5) The Democrat Left will *always* assume the opposite stand as the *Bible*.

GOD: Vegetarianism and Veganism Is Anti-GOD; Eat Meat

The *Bible* tells us that Vegetarianism (and by association Veganism) is Anti-GOD (Acts 10:15; Romans 14:20; Colossians 2:16-17; 1 Timothy 4:3-5) and that GOD Himself first provided meat for men's healthy diets in a fallen world.

GOD:

The Democrat Party: Anti-GOD

The Democrat Left will tell you that whatever or whomever you think is "God" is alright with them. This with the exclusion of the One true GOD of course. The Democrat Left will even tell you that you are an as yet, unrealized "god". The Democrat Left even will tell that no "god" is alright with them. Again, anything is acceptable to the Democrat Left as "God" except the LORD GOD Jehovah of the *Bible*.

GOD: Only GOD Is GOD

GOD Himself in the *Bible* tells us emphatically and repeatedly that there is only one GOD (Deuteronomy 6:4), there is no GOD but GOD (Isaiah 44:8), we are to worship only GOD (Matthew 4:10; Luke 4:8), and that worshipping anything else is idolatry and the worship of devils (1 Corinthians 10:19-21).

Government:

The Democrat Party: Everything From, For. And To the State

The Democrat Party believes that the government is their tool to bring about the Democrat Left Socialist Utopia. Government for the Democrat Left is a means to an end. The Democrat Left harnesses government on every level to destroy the Judeo-Christian foundations of America and replace it with their own Religion of the Left.

GOD: GOD Established Government for GOOD

Government was established By GOD. Government was intended by GOD to operate on GODly principles and promote GOOD. When all the peoples of the world united under a wicked Leftist-Socialist government, GOD confused them into many languages and displaced them across the world. (Genesis 11:1-9) Jesus condemned government corruption. (Mat 23:25)

Gun Rights:

The Democrat Party: Anti-Gun Rights

The Democrat Party is *violently* Anti-Gun Rights. The Democrat Left's unspoken reason for their fierce stance against gun ownership coincides exactly with Hitler's words, "The most foolish mistake we could possibly make would be to allow the **subject** races to possess arms. History shows that all conquerors who have allowed the subject races to carry arms have prepared their own downfall by so doing. Indeed, I would go so far as to say that the supply of arms to the underdogs is a *sine qua non* for the overthrow of any sovereignty"[614].[615] The Jews who were under the control of the Philistines were disarmed and kept in subjection because they lacked the weapons with which to fight. (1 Samuel 13:19-23) To take control of America the Left must first disarm Conservative Americans.

GOD: Pro-Gun Rights
Jesus Christ tells everyone to arm themselves against a hostile government and for self-defense. (Luke 22:36)

Homosexuality:

The Democrat Party: Militantly Pro-Homosexual (Pro-Sodomite)
The Democrat Party is *militantly* Pro-Homosexual. Remember that Obama lit up the White House with the "rainbow colors" of the Militant Homosexual Movement. Almost without exception the Democrat Party is a militant supporter of the Homosexual agenda. There is a growing segment within the Democrat Party that even supports the NAMBLA (The North American Man/Boy Love Association) which as discussed in the chapters *Fascism and the Left in America: Kindred Spirits and Familiar Bedfellows* and *Tolerance* and the discussion of "bullying" is behind the Left's campaign to force infiltration into The Boy Scouts of America.

GOD: Anti-Homosexual (Anti-Sodomite)
Homosexuality in the *Bible* is called "sodomy" after the ancient city of Sodom which GOD destroyed for the same sin of sodomy. The *Bible* also refers to Homosexuality as

---

[614] Hitler, Adolf; Edict of March 18, 1938; Trevor-Roper, H.R.; *Hitler's Table Talks 1941-1944*; London, Widenfeld and Nicolson; 1953; pgs. 425-426.

[615] For a wider discussion of the Left's Anti-Gun Rights obsession see the chapter *Fascism and the Left in America: Kindred Spirits and Familiar Bedfellows* and the subsection *Gun Control*.

"uncleanness", "vile affections", "against nature", as being of a "reprobate mind", "unseemly", (Romans 1:29-32) and wicked and sinners before the LORD exceedingly (Genesis 13:13). Homosexuals in the *Bible* are referred to as "abominations" (Leviticus 18:22, 26, 27, 29, 30; 20:13; Deuteronomy 23:18; 1 Kings 14:24; Ezekiel 16:50. An "abomination" in the Bible is the association with devils (demons) Deuteronomy 18:9-10; 2 Kings 23:24; Revelation 17:4-5) and on the level of filthy and rabid "dogs" (Deuteronomy 23:17-18; Revelation 22:15).

GOD tells us that in His eyes Homosexuality is the worst sin that a person can commit (Romans 1:24-32). Yes, worse than rape, and even murder! Homosexuality is associated with the worst devils! These homosexual devils bring with them the devils of "unrighteousness, fornication, wickedness, covetousness, maliciousness; full of envy, *murder*, debate, deceit, malignity; whisperers, backbiters, *haters of GOD*, despiteful, proud, boasters, *inventors of evil things*, disobedient to parents, without understanding, covenantbreakers, without natural affection, implacable, unmerciful" (Romans 1:29-32). Again, GOD is not anti-Homosexual because He wants to repress mankind, but to protect man from Homosexuality's associated Evil and its destructive and deadly consequences!

Infanticide: (see also: Abortion, Euthanasia, and Murder)

The Democrat Party: Pro-Infanticide
The Democrat Party is militantly Pro-Infanticide supporting embryotic testing to kill handicapped babies in the womb, they support all forms of abortion including partial birth abortion, and the Democrat Left even supports killing babies after they are born as a result of a "batched" abortion or simply at the wish of the mother.

GOD: Anti-Infanticide (see also: Abortion)

GOD calls Infanticide *murder*, an abomination, and a vile sin before GOD. (Exodus 21:22-23; 2 Kings 6:33; Job 10:8; 31:15; Psalms 71:6; 94:20-21; 106:37-38; 119:73; 139:13-16; Is 43:1; 44:2, 24; Jeremiah 1:5; 7:6; 22:3; Lamentations 2:12; Romans 9:1). GOD tells us that life begins at conception. (Job 31:15)

Israel:

The Democrat Party: *Militantly* Anti-Israel

The Democrat Party has demonstrated over and over its Anti-Israel racism and bigotry. The Obama Administration consistently sided with the mortal enemies of Israel supplying them with money and weapons to attack Israel. Obama tried to force Israel to return to the 1967 boarders which as several Wars proved are indefensible. Obama wanted to destroy Israel!

The Democrat National Convention of 2012 voted initially to remove their support of Jerusalem as Israel's capital. The Convention was forced to re-vote to reverse the initial Platform denying that Jerusalem should be acknowledged as Israel's capital.[616] The voice-vote to reinstate the language was overwhelmingly against reinstatement, but because of bad press and orders from the DNC public relations arm, the moderator called it as passing. GOD Himself chose Jerusalem as the seat of His Old Testament throne, chose Jerusalem as Israel's capital, as the seat of Jesus' Millennial throne, and in the end of time as GOD's eternal earthly throne. *The Democrat Left Wars Against GOD* opposing everything GOD has decreed and chosen!

GOD: Creator, Supporter, and Defender of Israel

GOD tells us that *every* nation's treatment of Israel they either blessed or cursed. (Genesis 12:3; 27:29; Numbers 24:9) To not

---

[616] McGreal, Chris; The Guardian; *The Democrats' misstep on Jerusalem and Israel's place in the US election*; September 6, 2012.

support Israel is to defy GOD and bring destruction upon your nation. GOD Himself established the boarders of Israel long before there was a "Palestinian" people or any Arab or Muslim nations! (Joshua 1:3) GOD chose Israel as His Nation and the Jews (Genesis 35:10), and by New Testament extension Christians, as GOD's people.

Judges:

The Democrat Party: Uses Judges for Evil
The Democrat Left uses Judges to legislate Evil in defiance of the American *Constitution* and GOD! The Left up until the recent has never been able to pass Leftist legislation legitimately. The Left has resorted to using corrupted Leftist Judges to make rulings that effectively creates law, circumventing our *U.S. Constitution* and established law. GOD calls these Judges and the Democrat Left… corrupt and Evil!

GOD: Warns Judges Against Being Corrupted of Evil
Judges are responsible before GOD to Biblically represent GOD's justice here on earth. GOD specifically warns Judges that they and their corruption will be severely judged (Psalms 58:1-2; 82:1-2).

Law:

The Democrat Party: Lawless
The Democrat Party has no respect for the rule of law. The law in America is based on Biblical Law and, as such, it is opposed at every turn by the Democrat Left. This is why the Democrat Left must "reinterpret" the *U.S. Constitution* to align with the Left's agenda and use judges to rewrite standing law. The Democrat Left defies all Biblically based laws as evidenced throughout this chapter. The *Bible* calls these men "Lawless"! (1 Timothy 1:9)

GOD: GOD's Law

The *Bible* warns lawmakers against corruption from a Biblically based law. (Psalms 94:20) GOD instituted Law throughout history. To change GOD's Law is to defy GOD.

Lying:

The Democrat Party: Proliferates Lies

The Democrat Party is the Party of Lies! This is thoroughly documented in the chapter *Lies, Lies, Lies!* The *Bible* calls perpetual Liars... the children of the Devil, the father of *Lies*! (John 8:44) The entire leadership of the Democrat Party are pathological Liars! Alinsky, the father of the Democrat Left and mentor to the Left, taught a "by any means necessary" War tactic. Lying is the Left's stock-in-trade. Because, as Jonathan Gruber so eloquently stated, the Left's position of "if the American people actually knew what the truth was behind the Left's agenda, Americans would never have voted for it or tolerated it"! GOD calls the pathological Liars of the Democrat Left... Abominations (Revelation 21:8), whom the *Bible* also describes as devil controlled (Deuteronomy 18:9-10; Revelation 17:4-5).

GOD: Do Not Lie

GOD clearly tells us that we are not to lie. (Exodus 20:16, Matthew 19:18, Romans 13:9) GOD condemns unrepentant, pathological Liars to Hell. (Revelation 21:8)

Marriage:

The Democrat Party: Seeks to Re-Define Marriage

The Democrat Party now openly works to redefine "marriage" as everything that contradicts marriage as created by GOD. The Democrat Left demands acceptance of anything but a marriage between one man and one woman, especially homosexual "marriage". Homosexuality is an Abomination before GOD. (An "abomination" in the Bible is a person who is in union with devils (demons) Deuteronomy 18:9-10; 2 Kings 23:24; Revelation 17:4-5) GOD created, defined, and ordained marriage as between one man and one woman. The Democrat Party, by their own self-definition, as the representation of Evil, *must* oppose GOD's definition of marriage.

GOD: Created, Defined, and Ordained Marriage

GOD created, defined, and ordained marriage as between one man and one woman. (Genesis 2:24; 1 Corinthians 7:2, 10; Romans 7:1-3) GOD will judge those who defile marriage by His definition. (Hebrews 13:4)

Murder: (see also: Abortion, Euthanasia, and Infanticide)

The Democrat Party: Pro-Murder:

The Democrat Party supports and promotes murder through euphemistic doctrines like: Abortion, Euthanasia, and Infanticide.

GOD: Anti-Murder:

GOD commands: "Thou shalt not kill", literally "thou shalt not murder". (Exodus 20:13; Deuteronomy 5:17; Matthew 5:21; Romans 13:9) GOD exempts Self Defense, military service, and manslaughter from Murder.

National Debt:

The Democrat Party: Militantly Pro-National Debt

The Democrat Party promotes and demands unlimited increases in America's National Debt. The National Debt allows the Democrats to buy votes in the short term and enslave Americans in the long term. Even the Über Democrat Leftist Barack Hussein Obama Jr. said that National Debt was "unpatriotic", of course after almost an additional *$11,000,000,000,000* (that's *ELEVEN TRILLION DOLLARS!*) in National Debt. The Democrat Left still demands more and more in National Debt to feed their Evil Beast!

GOD: Debt Forbidden By GOD

National Debt is forbidden by GOD (Deuteronomy 28:12), except under a national emergency such as war. GOD teaches that *fiscal debt is physical debt*! (Deuteronomy 15:6; Proverbs 22:7)

Peace Movement:

The Democrat Party: Claims To Be The Party of Peace:
The Democrat Party claims to be the Party of Peace when in actuality they promote chaos, forced servitude, and violence.

GOD: Only GOD Can Bring Peace:
The *Bible* says that only the Antichrist, the Devil incarnate, claims to be the Man of Peace. (Daniel 8:25; 11:21) The *Bible* also clearly says the men who "saying, Peace, peace; when there is no peace" (Jeremiah 6:14, 8:11) are Evil men.

Politics:

The Democrat Party: Promotes Evil and Opposes GOD:
The Democrat Party uses Politics to indoctrinate, manipulate, and force Americans into their Leftist and Anti-GOD agenda. Democrat Left politicians promote Evil and oppose GOD. The Democrat Leftist Politics, or Political Correctness, is the enforcement side of the Left's Religion of Evil.

GOD: Must Promote GOD and Biblical Standards:
Biblical Politics demands GODly standards in Politics and politicians (Exodus 18:21). Politics must represent GOD Himself as Politics is the enforcement side of all Religion including GOD's Religion.

Private Property:

The Democrat Party: Anti-Private Property:
The Democrat Party seeks to destroy all vestiges of private property. Private property is an offense to the Left as it keeps the Left at arms-length in America. The Democrat Left abhors

a citizen's Constitutional right to private property, which it sees as an obstruction to total Leftist control of Americans' lives. The Left has worked with great success to eliminate all barriers to the States ability to seize all private property, or as the Left euphemizes it, Eminent Domain. The Left sees itself as having "Eminent Dominion" over all of Americans' property.

GOD: Pro-Private Property:
Private property was a foundational command in the Old Testament, so much so that GOD codified private property in Israel by which property ownership was for all time and not transferable (Leviticus 25:1–55). There was no private property tax in Israel by which the government could confiscate private property. This is the foundation on which American private property rights were originally based.

Government confiscation of private property is considered lawlessness by GOD. (1 Kings 21:1-29)

Psychology:

The Democrat Party: Uses Psychology to Falsely Explain the Spiritual:
The Democrat Left covers over spiritual problems and renames them as "Psychological" Disorders. This is the epithet, "The greatest trick the Devil ever pulled was convincing the world he didn't exist". In order for the Left to dismiss GOD and GOD's explanation of spirituality, the Left must find a substitute diagnosis for the spiritual problems that are inherent natural consequences from sin *Against GOD*. The consequences of the sins of lying, stealing, unfaithfulness, sexual deviancy, murder, overeating, drunkenness, drug addiction, insanity, cutting, and many others, becomes a "disease" with a corresponding diagnosis of Psychology, instead of a *Bible* identified *sin* problem.

GOD: Explains Pseudo-Psychological Issues As Spiritual

Problems:

The *Bible* diagnoses many mental issues as *sin* produced. The demonic is often the true spiritual cause of many "Psychological Problems".

Bi-Polar	(1 Samuel 16:14-23; 19:8-10; 24:16-20)
Confusion	(Isaiah 41:29; James 3:16)
Cutting One's Flesh	(Leviticus 19:28; 21:5; Mark 5:5)
Gluttony (overeating)	(Deuteronomy 21:20-21)
Homosexuality	(Judges 19:22)
Insanity	(Matthew 17:15-18; Romans 1:28; 1 Timothy 4:7; 2; Timothy 1:7)
Physical Illness (Infirmities))	(Luke 8:2, 13:11; Romans 6:19
Murder	(John 8:44; 10:10)
Pathological Lying	(1 Kings 22:22-23; 2 Chronicles 18:21, 22; Micah 2:11; Jn 8:44; 1 Jn 2:22)
Phobias	(1 John 4:18)
Self-Mutilation	(Mark 5:5)
Suicide	(Matthew 17:15)

Reason and Reasoning:

The Democrat Party: Is Absolutely Without Reason and Unreasonable:

The Democrat Party feeds on *emotion* and sees Reason as an enemy of the Left. (See especially the chapter *Emotion Based Politics*.) If a person thinks logically then he most often would make decisions that align with Biblical principles, a situation which the Left cannot afford to tolerate! The Left cannot afford to be Reasonable, logical, or deal in real life issues. The Left must rely on emotion to drive its adherents and issues. The very definition of a "radical" is being emotionally driven and without Reason! The Left has no Common Sense!

GOD: Absolutely Reasonable:

GOD calls for all of mankind to "Come now, and let us reason together, saith the LORD: though your sins be as scarlet, they shall be as white as snow" (Isiah 1:18). GOD by His very Being is Reasonable, logical, and grounded in reality. Common Sense is another outworking of Reasoning.

Right To Work:

The Democrat Party: Pro-Right To Work

The Democrat Party says that everyone has the "Right To Work". However, under the Democrat Left during the last half-Century, unemployment tripled and quadrupled to historic highs. What the Democrat Left is actually implying is "a right to food, housing, healthcare, cell phones, etc.". The Left's guise of Right To Work actually encourages the lazy and those who refuse to work. This is a gimmick (a *Lie!*) to entrap all American's in the Left's Socialist and Fascistic agenda of their cradle-to-grave enslavement. The Left's Right To Work is actually a government takeover of all jobs and paychecks and make all Americans totally dependent upon the Democrat Left!

GOD: Anti-Right To Work (In the Leftist Sense)

In the Leftist sense GOD is Anti-Right To Work. GOD clearly tells us that "if any would not work, neither should he eat". (2 Thessalonians 3:10)

Self Defense:

The Democrat Party: Against Self Defense

The Democrat Party is again *militantly* Anti-Self Defense and obliges all Americans to be totally dependent upon it for its livelihood, sustenance, and protection. When it comes to Self Defense the Democrat Left demands that you call the "authorities" and let the government deal with it, even if you will be injured or die. The individual cannot Defend himself in place of authorized government authorities.

GOD: Pro-Self Defense

Jesus Christ tells everyone to arm themselves against a hostile government and for self-defense. (Luke 22:36)

Sexual Sin:

The Democrat Party: Encourages and Empowers People to Commit Sin

It is the stock-in-trade of the Democrat Left to offer the legalization and normalization of Sexual Sins in exchange for support of the régime. These Sexual Sins include Homosexuality, transgenderism, adultery (sex outside of the marriage), homosexuality, homosexual "marriage", fornication (no sexual restraint), lust, *et al.*

GOD: Forbids Sexual Sin

GOD forbids Sexual Sin not because GOD wants to keep people from having a "good time", but because Sexual Sin causes heartbreak, diseases, and death. This is the secret and hidden motivation of Evil "to steal, kill, and destroy"[617].

Adultery	Exodus 20:14; Matthew 19:18; Romans 13:9; Hebrews 13:4; James 2:11, 4:4; Revelation 2:22
Bestiality	Leviticus 18:21; Deuteronomy 24:21
Cross Dressing	Deuteronomy 22:5; 1 Corinthians 6:9
Effeminate	1 Corinthians 6:9
Fornication	Romans 1:29; 1 Corinthians 6:9; Ephesians 5:3; Jude 1:7
Sodomites (Homosexuals)	Romans 1:27-32

---

[617] The *Holy Bible*: John 10:10.

Lesbians	Romans 1:26
Lust	Matthew 5:28; 1 John 2:16
Homosexuality	Leviticus 20:13;
	Romans 1:24-32; 1 Corinthians 6:9

Taxes:

The Democrat Party: Pro-Progressive Taxes

The Democrat Party's agenda is dependent on the Socialist-based Progressive Income Tax. The Progressive Income Tax allows the Democrat Left to exclude its own lower-class voters from all income tax in exchange for securing their votes for the Democrat Party. Class Warfare is used to convince many of the lower-class voters that if they did not support the Democrats that their lives would somehow be much worse. It has been an effective, albeit a circular *Lie*! The opposite is actually true, as a Progressive Income Tax System is the process of enslavement of the lower-classes to the Left in creating a lower-class totally dependent upon the government for its very existence.

GOD: Anti-Progressive Taxes

The *Bible* treats all classes the same using a Non-Progressive Tax System. (Ex 30:15) All families were accessed a 10% Flat Tax, The government was forced to live within these means. This Flat Tax was a guard restricting the government from becoming burdensome to the people and totalitarian in nature.

It was only in a National emergency that Israel was allowed to collect a onetime tax. These however were few and far between.

Welfare:

The Democrat Party: Pro-Public Funded Welfare

The Democrat Party uses Welfare to create dependence and enslavement to the Democrat Left. When you take away someone's incentive to work you hollow out the man into a mere shell, he or she becomes a ghost. Welfare as we know it today is designed by the Democrat Left to create a dependent class, dependent on the Left for even the most basic necessities, especially food. There is no coincidence that Obama fostered an increase of over 13,000,000 food stamp recipients. That is an additional 13,000,000 million Americans depending on the Big Brother of the Left for their very survival. The Left are not interested in creating jobs, but creating dependency and securing votes for the Left.

GOD: Anti-Public Funded Welfare:
The *Bible* only allows "welfare" under extreme circumstance where the family or extended relatives are not available. Welfare in the *Bible* is only given through the Church as a private not public endeavor. (2 Thessalonians 3:10)

Conclusion:

To my horror and shock I heard Greta Van Susteren of Fox News give an "Off The Record" commentary comparing the divide between Republicans, in the Conservative and anti-Left sense, and Democrats to her cat and dog.[618] (Yes, you read that right!) Greta talked about how her cat and dog each reacted differently to a stranger's knock at her front door. Her cat ran and hid and her dog barked and charged the door. Greta's cat and dog had "adamant disagreements", which were "sometimes very heated". But Greta concluded with a photo of her cat and dog snuggling noses and the comment "why can't Republicans and Democrats who have disagreements just put all their ideological differences aside like her cat and dog and just be friends? Either Greta Van Susteren is either naïve on the level of a brick, or completely insanely delusional! Unfortunately, this insanity is not as rare as one would hope.

---

[618] Fox News Channel; On the Record w/ Greta Van Susteren; 11/6/2015.

This mentality is so prolific in the general naiveté of the public who sees the divide between the Republican Party, again in the Conservative sense, and the Democrat Party as nothing more than that between a friendly disagreement between a household's cat and dog. This misguided (or psychotic!) conclusion is *frightening* on an Epic scale! This Pollyanna attitude is literally killing our America and enslaving our children. This attitude is at best... *delusional*! The Democrat Party is a hate group! Let me emphatically restate that: The Democrat Party is by practice and definition a *hate group*! (Note this is the Democrat Party leadership and Party loyalists, not necessarily all registered Democrats. The latter are the useful idiots used as pawns for the Left's Evil agenda.) They foster violence against *anyone* who oppose them. They spit vitriol more toxic than a king cobra! This *War* is the Evil of the Democrat Left Against all that is GOOD, Right, and decent in America. This is not about kittens and puppies. The "divide" is quite literally as wide as that between GOD and the Devil! This is a *War* with the hearts, minds, and souls of every American man, woman, and child on the line! The most horrifying problem is that so few see the conflict for the Epic War that it is, *the War of Evil Against GOD!*

The Democrat Party Platform opposes GOD and *all* that GOD represents. The Left's working organs are not limited exclusively to the Democrat Party but can be seen in many other Evil organs such as the Green Party, Communist Party, Libertarian Party, and even within the ranks of the Republican Party.

The modern-day Democrat Party stands absolutely, 100%, diametrically opposed, and *Against* all that is GOD. The Democrat Party in America today exemplifies all that is Evil, Left, and Opposed to GOD!

21. THE OBAMAS: THE EPITOME OF THE LEFT:

Chapter 21

Obama has epitomized and continues to epitomize all that is Evil, Bad, and Wrong with the Left in America today. Although Obama is gone from office, he continues to undermine our American Republic both from behind the mic and behind the scenes. There is not a single Leftist cause for which Obama does not endorse and advance by any means necessary. As such we will use Obama as the personification of the Evil that represents the Left in America today.

In 2007 Barack Hussein Obama was voted the most Liberal Senator in the US Congress by the National Journal in its 27th annual ratings. (How revealing is that nefarious honor?) Obama has self-identified himself as a Liberal, a Socialist, a Communist (New Party), a Progressive, an Environmentalist, and of course a Leftist. Obama has *always* been a Leftist radical activist. *Obama is the epitome of the Left.* And since Obama was elected President in 2008, the Left has been emboldened to come lunging headlong out of the shadows. The Left has normally remained hidden behind sheep's clothing, but has now thrown aside all pretenses. The entire Leftist pack of ravenous dogs has become unleashed!

The Left's leadership knows EXACTLY what they are doing! They are not naïve nor ignorant. They've read Trump's books; they know the repercussions of their failed policies. They are pushing their evil agenda by *Lies* and coercion!

For those on the Right who squirm at these emphatically stated truths, as well as those on the Left who have mindlessly followed militant Leftists like Herr Obama[619] and the ways of the Left, let's start with a representative case example… partial-birth abortion. Obama was and

---

[619] Also refer back to the side by side comparisons of the Left's 100% Anti-GOD platform and agenda in the chapter *The Democrat Party Platform As Leftist Doctrines All OPPOSE GOD*, which aligns absolutely with that of Obama.

is both a zealous advocate and enthusiast of partial-birth abortion. When even some on the Left were reluctant to push for legalization of this horrific procedure, Obama was militant in his support. Let's begin with a quick synopsis of exactly what partial-birth abortion is. I will use brevity here to spare the gruesome details of a more full and graphic description.

Partial-birth abortion can be used on a living baby in the mother's womb up until the moment of natural delivery and has actually been used during the natural birthing process. The doctor induces labor and allows the head of the baby to be born. At this point the doctor holds the head of the baby to prevent a full birth. Now the doctor turns the baby face down, presumably to avoid face-to-face contact with his Victim. Next the doctor inserts a long knife into the soft spot on the baby's skull and proceeds to scramble the baby's brains killing the child. The doctor then pulls the dead baby from the mother and discards the body as medical waste. This is a partial-birth abortion! I can say with absolute certainty that only a truly Evil person could advocate such a heinous crime against humanity as partial-birth abortion. Obama, as a wholehearted supporter of partial-birth abortion, is the epitome of the *Evil* which manifests itself so openly in the Left today!

In further evidence, Barack Hussein Obama as an Illinois State Senator voted four times *against* the Born Alive Infant Protection Act which would have saved babies "born alive" during a botched abortion procedure attempt:

> President Obama voted against the Born Alive Infant Protection Act *four times*, horrifyingly voting against protecting babies who survived abortion and voting in favor of leaving them to die. A vote against this legislation was a vote for infanticide[620].

---

[620] http://www.jillstanek.com/2008/02/links-to-barack-obamas-votes-on-illinois-born-alive-infant-protection-act/.

How much more violent and Evil is a person than one who supports the murder of a baby "born alive"?!

How is this for an accurate analysis of the mind of Barack Hussein Obama?:

> "His primary rules [are]: never allow the public to cool off; never admit a fault or wrong; never concede that there may be some good in your enemy; never leave room for alternatives; never accept blame; concentrate on one enemy at a time and blame him for everything that goes wrong; people will believe a big lie sooner than a little one; and if you repeat it frequently enough people will sooner or later believe it"[621].

Does not this sound hauntingly familiar? We should be *terrified* as this was *not* an analysis of Barack Hussein Obama, but of wartime Adolf Hitler! This far predates even Obama's mentor Saul Alinsky, which Hitler is of course at least one of the likely origins of many of Alinsky's ideas. How frightening is it that the analysis of Hitler can be placed on Obama and we cannot distinguish between them?!

Just as the Nazis did, the Left today practices blaming Christians in America for every evil in America. A whole chorus of Leftists blamed the Islamic terrorist attack on a homosexual nightclub in Orlando in June 2016 that killed 49... on Christians! Did Obama defend Christians or decry the *Lies* of the Left Against Christians? No! Obama went on television and defended Islam! How long before the blame and *Lies* turns into action against Conservatives and Christians just as it did with the Nazis in World War II?!

Where did Obama and the Left get their ideology of "hope and 'change'"? It is a frightening look into the downward spiral of the

---

[621] Langer , Walter C.; *A Psychological Analysis of Adolph Hitler, His Life and Legend*; United States Office of Strategic Services (OSS), Washington, D.C.; WWII classified U. S. Intelligence Office report prepared by the OSS; pg. 219.

Cycle into Dictatorship[622]. We need look no further than Obama's Leftist political and religious guru Saul Alinsky in Alinsky's *Rules For Radicals* and the section titled *THE IDEOLOGY OF CHANGE*:

> This raises the question: what, if any, is my ideology? What kind of ideology, if any, can an organizer have who is working in and for a free society? The prerequisite for an ideology is possession of a basic truth. For example, a Marxist begins with his prime truth that all evils are caused by the exploitation of the proletariat by the capitalists. From this he logically proceeds to the revolution to end capitalism, then into the third stage of reorganization into a new social order or the dictatorship of the proletariat, and finally the last stage—the political paradise of communism.[623]

The Obama administration bragged about "record low unemployment" at about 5.6%. Obama emphatically stated at his 2015 State of the Union Speech:

> "Tonight, after a breakthrough year for America, our economy is growing and creating jobs at the fastest pace since 1999. Our unemployment rate is now lower than it was before the financial crisis"[624].

However, that was a blatant *Lie!* Jim Clifton CEO of Gallop Polling Group, a non-partisan organization, said this in response to Obama's claim:

> "There's no other way to say this. The official unemployment rate, which cruelly overlooks the suffering of the long-term and often permanently unemployed as well as the depressingly underemployed, amounts to a **Big Lie**[625]".

---

[622] For the Cycle of Dictatorship see a broader discussion in the chapter: *Understanding The Battle*.
[623] *Rules For Radicals*; pg. 10.
[624] NPR.org; Transcript: President Obama's State Of The Union Address; January 20, 2015.
[625] Clifton, Jim, CEO Gallop; Gallop.com; *The Big Lie*: 5.6% Unemployment; February 3, 2015.

In an interview on February 15, 2015 CEO of Gallop polling Jim Clifton told FOX News that "the number of full-time jobs as a percentage of the adult population is the **lowest ever**" in America. This is a long way from Obama's claim of an economic "breakthrough" and low unemployment, of which Obama's statements certainly qualify as an unmitigated Hitler-style "Big Lie"! Again, how frightening is it that the words of Hitler can be placed in the mouth of Obama and we cannot distinguish between them?!

Most people are unaware that Barack Hussein Obama received his training in "community organizing" from Saul Alinsky's radical Leftist Industrial Areas Foundation. But Obama did. In and of itself that marks his heritage and training as that of a radical Leftist activist.

Barack Hussein Obama openly associates himself with radicals and self-admitted and unrepentant "cop killers" along with those who openly call for killing police officers. Glorification of cop killers is a recurring theme of Obama and the radical Alinsky Left. With pride the Obamas invited rapper Lonnie Rashid Lynn, Jr., aka "Common" who raps of the killing cops to the White House for a private concert. Obama came out in support of Michel Brown who was killed while in the process of attempting to kill a Ferguson, Missouri police officer. Obama has never changed this position even after it was proven by his own radicalized Leftist US Department of Justice that Michael Brown was indeed trying to kill the police officer Darren Wilson and Officer Wilson acted wholly in self-defense against a pathological Brown!

Obama has had a long association with the self-avowed radical Bill Ayers. Ayers is a cop killer who bombed police stations with the explicit intent to "kill cops". Ayers boasted, "I don't regret setting bombs". Ayers also infamously said, "Kill all the rich people. Break up their cars and apartments. Bring the revolution home, kill your parents, that's where it's really at"!

Ayers said of his relationship with Obama:

> "We were friendly, that was true; we served on a couple of boards together, that was true; he held a fundraiser in our

living room, that was true; Michelle [Obama] and Bernardine (Ayers wife) were at the law firm together, that was true. Hyde Park in Chicago is a tiny neighborhood, so when he said I was 'a guy around the neighborhood,' that was true."[626]

Ayers and his convicted cop killing wife Bernardine Dohrn, hosted Obama's first political fundraiser in their own home in Chicago, which launched Obama's nefarious political career.

Obama while exemplary of the Left is certainly not alone is his penchant for these particular "cop killers". It was Bill Clinton who originally pardoned Bill Ayers and commuted the sentence of Bernadine Dohrn.

We began in the first chapter describing the intent of this book in unmasking the hidden agenda of the *Left* and its *War Against GOD* especially in its targeting of the Christian Faith in its attempt to *fundamentally transform America*, as Barack Hussein Obama so succinctly stated it. I will repeat again, make no mistake the Left's attempt to "transform" America is a P.C. doublespeak for destroying America as we know it! Even the über-Left political commentary site *Slate.com* reluctantly admitted that Obama's comment that he would "fundamentally transform the United States of America" was according to *Slate*, "a hint that Obama knew what he was going to do to [American] government for years and let it slip out at a campaign rally"[627]. *Slate* goes on to downplay the comment by saying that it was simply Obama using a lot of "boilerplate" material, but this is an intentional *Lie* by *Slate*. The shameless lengths to which an apologetic Leftist press corps is willing to go to cover-up for their comrades-in-arms is a personal disgrace, a discredit to the ideal of an independent Fourth Estate, and a *sin* before GOD. There may have been boilerplate material in the speech but this in no way discredits nor diminishes Obama's blatant statement that he was planning to *fundamentally transform America*!

---

[626] Klein, Aaron; WND.com; *Bill Ayers confirms what Obama has denied: Weatherman domestic terrorist finally spills the beans*; 04/07/2013.
[627] Weigel, David; *Fundamentally Transforming the United States of America*; Slate.com; October 18, 2011.

And Obama three years later again restated his intention to remake America in his speech on the deficit on April 12, 2011 at George Washington University:

> "But the way this plan achieves those goals would lead to a fundamentally different America than the one we've known throughout most of our history."

Obama's comments on his intent to "fundamentally transform America" cannot in any way be written off as a mindless "boilerplate" comment or as an offhanded remark as Obama had almost 20 years earlier said:

> "Hopefully, more and more people will begin to feel their story is somehow part of this larger story of how we're going to *reshape America* in a way that is less mean-spirited and more generous, " Obama said. "I mean, I hope to be part of *a transformation of this country*"[628]. (emphasis added)

These were *not* "misstatements", but professed revelations by Obama of his true intentions and long-term goal of destroying America as we know it, then rebuilding his envisioned Leftist Utopia upon America's smoldering ashes! (And Obama came dangerously close to accomplishing his dream!) This is frighteningly reminiscent of the Roman Emperor Nero who in AD 64 burned down Rome in order to "rebuild" a new more glorious Rome on its ashes. Nero, like Obama, also held religious animosity against Christendom and used his own self-made "opportunity"[629] to blame the his own intentionally set fire and ensuing deaths on Christians. Nero used this "opportunity" as an excuse to escalate his campaign of murder in an attempt to annihilate every Christian in the Empire. Nero is infamous for burning Christians alive as human torches to light his Pagan orgies and rituals. This fire

---

[628] *Illinois Daily Herald*; Interview of Barack Obama by Associated Press; *Harvard Student Tackles Racism At Its Core*; May 3, 1990.
[629] See "never let an opportunity of crisis go to waste" in the discussion of the Cycle of Dictatorship in chapters: *The Coalition of the Unlikely: The Tie That Blinds* and *Understanding The Battle*.

is of course where we get the phrase *Nero fiddled while Rome burned.* Obama fiddled and America burns!

Michelle Obama called for graduates at the Oberlin College commencement to join the Leftist Revolution against America as a 2015 keynote speaker saying, "rise above the noise and shape the revolutions of your time". The only "revolutions" going on in America today are the Leftist ones to overthrow what has been the traditional Right and Christian history of America. The Obama's are Evil Leftist revolutionaries in every sense of the word bent on the destruction of America! *The Obamas are The Epitome of the Left!*

Further revealing as to the depth of Obama's commitment to their über-Leftist cause are the telling comments by his Evil co-conspirator and wife Michelle Obama:

> "Barack knows that we are going to have to make sacrifices; we are going to have to change our conversation; we're going to have to change our traditions, our history; we're going to have to move into a different place as a nation.[630]"

Change what?! How exactly do you "change... our history"? History has already happened and cannot be "changed" as a matter of political convenience. This is an open admission to the Left's scheme of its continual *revisionist* history program. This is a horrifying throwback to the dystopian[631] prophecy of George Orwell's book *Nineteen Eighty-Four* (1984) where Orwell foretells the inevitable consequences of the Leftist Utopian ideal:

> "The Ministry of Truth is involved with news media, entertainment, the fine arts and educational books. Its purpose is to rewrite history to change the facts to fit Party doctrine for

[630] Michelle Obama on the campaign trail in San Juan, Puerto Rico on May 14, 2008.
[631] *Webster's* defines *dystopia* as "an imaginary place where people lead dehumanized and often fearful lives" specifically in relation to the government as a counterfeit or "anti-Utopia". Obama's and the Left's Utopia may have existed only in their collective imaginations in the past, but is quickly becoming America's dystopian nightmare today.

propaganda effect. For example, if Big Brother[632] makes a prediction that turns out to be wrong, the employees of the Ministry of Truth go back and rewrite the prediction so that any prediction Big Brother previously made is accurate"[633].

These were not random "misstatements" by Barack Hussein Obama as evidenced again by fellow Leftist sojourner Michelle Obama who confirms by her personal accounting about her and her husband's fundamental beliefs about America. Here is Michelle Obama in her own words on the campaign trail in Milwaukee, Wisconsin on February 18, 2008:

> "For the first time in my adult life I am proud of my country because it feels like hope is finally making a comeback.[634]"

And again later that same day Michelle Obama on the campaign trail in Madison, Wisconsin on February 18, 2008:

> "For the first time in my adult lifetime, I'm really proud of my country, and not just because Barack has done well, but because I think people are hungry for change[635]".

What planet does she live on? Michelle Obama feigns as if she grew up in America as a slave girl and was just at that moment emancipated to freedom at the ascension of the Messiah[636] Barack. (One man's maniacal lunatic is another's messiah!) The absurdity of her statement is obvious to all except those who find themselves severely mentally

---

[632] Today called Big Government.

[633] Wikipedia, Ministry of Truth, Role In Information; George Orwell's novel *Nineteen Eighty-Four* (1984)

[634] Tapper, Jake; *Michelle Obama For the First Time in My Adult Lifetime, I'm Really Proud of My Country*; ABCnews.go.com; Feb 18, 2008 8:24pm.

[635] Tapper, Jake; *Michelle Obama For the First Time in My Adult Lifetime, I'm Really Proud of My Country*; ABCnews.go.com; Feb 18, 2008 8:24pm.

[636] The first notable attempt at deification of Obama was a reference during the 2008 campaign trail by Jeremiah Wright, Jr. and has been followed by many sycophants like actor Jamie Foxx's comment at the 2012 Soul Train Awards: "...give honor to god and our lord and savior, Barack Obama!", BET (Black Entertainment Television used this bit of blasphemy to promote the upcoming tape-delayed show.

challenged.[637] (read: moronic imbecile!) She portrays a slave mentality as if she had been shackled under the repressive moral constraints of a white Christian America. At their core both of the Obamas' demonstrate a disdain or hatred for anyone and anything not black[638], unless, as Obama in his book *Dreams From My Father: A Story of Race And Inheritance*, those [whites] who identify themselves with Malcom X, "that some whites would be worthy allies but only if they were part of the Nation of Islam or Muslim"[639]. This would explain Michelle's and Barack's long association with Black Liberation Theology, which calls for a bloody revolt against whites as the imagined modern oppressors of blacks. Here we have it from the lips of the founder of Black Liberation Theology James H. Cone:

> "Whether the American system is beyond redemption we will have to wait and see. But we can be certain that black patience has run out, and unless white America responds positively to the theory and activity of ***Black Power***, then *a **bloody***, protracted ***civil war is inevitable***.[640]" (emphasis added)

Here is a synopsis of black author, Christian theologian, and associate professor at King's College Anthony Bradley of the *Christian Post* of Black Liberation Theology:

> "...the language of 'economic parity' and references to 'mal-distribution' as nothing more than channeling the views of Karl Marx. He believes James Cone and Cornel West have worked to incorporate Marxist thought into the black church, forming an ethical framework predicated on a system of oppressor class versus a victim much like Marxism.[641]"

The Obama's affinity with Black Liberation Theology also speaks volumes about their lifelong friendship with the radical and racist

---

[637] See the broader discussion of insanity in the chapter *The Left Is a RELIGION!*.

[638] e. g. See following comments by black author Mychal Massie on the Obamas' black racism.

[639] Massie; Mychal; Do people fully understand the type of monster Obama truly is?; referenced in Mychal's Column: *OBAMA'S WHITE BLOOD: PRIDE OR SHAME?*; date unavailable.

[640] Cone, James H.; *Black Theology and Black Power*; 1989; pg. 143

[641] Wikipedia; Black Liberation Theology, Criticisms.

"pastor" Jeremiah Wright, Jr. of the Chicago Trinity United Church of Christ "church" where the Obama's faithfully attended as members for *over 20 years*! The Obama's were married there and they and their two daughters were also baptized there by Wright. Who in their right mind would set their children under the teaching of a black racist preacher who called for the violent overthrow of "white America" by blacks?! This is a telling fact about the radical Leftist and Anti-GOD beliefs held by the Obama's!

The natural outworking of Black Liberation Theology, adapted almost in whole by the black community, is the thug mentality so pervasive in today's black "culture". The black "gangsta" is the mold by which black youths in mass seek to fashion themselves. This mentality is prevalent throughout all of the black pop culture and dominates their music which is the largest influence in the black communities. Those blacks who reject this life of violence and counterculture are ridiculed and attacked as "not being black enough". The pressure to conform to this violent Black Liberation Theology is overwhelming today in the black community. This was Barack Hussein Obama's struggle which Obama describes of his own life in his autobiography *Dreams From My Father: A Story of Race And Inheritance*. This autobiography of Obama chronicles what Obama describes as his "struggle" to find his place and calling in the world. Obama uses the term "struggle" no less than **33 times** throughout his book *Dreams From My Father*.

Would not Obama's book *Dreams from My Father: A Story of Race And Inheritance* be better summed up with the alternate title: *My Struggle*? Obama himself has referred to his book as a chronology of his life's "struggle" to find meaning and place. It seems a not so strange coincidence that there was another author who did write a book titled "*My Struggle*" which was first printed with the German title *Mein Kampf*. That author's name was Adolf Hitler! Like Hitler, Obama had to "struggle" to find the "meaning" of his life. Again, and not so coincidently, they both arrived at nearly identical Über-Leftist conclusions. What they were both so profoundly struggling against was their loathing and hatred for their contemporary Christian foundations of the country in which they each lived!

Why does the Left hate America? This hatred manifests from the Left in many ways: America in unexceptional, Imperialistic, energy mongers, Earth killers, racists, phoebes of every imaginable conception, and many other delusions... *ad infimum*. The core of the Left's hatred stems from the GOD-centered issues that defined the success of America that made it an example to the world as President Ronald Reagan referred to America as the Shining City on the Hill.

This is why Obama made little more than a faint gesture to deal with the plight of violence so pervasive in black culture. Chicago black on black murder and violence was then and is now the worst murder and violence rate in America today! To do so would make Obama "unhip" and ostracize Obama from the core of the black community. As Obama makes clear in his autobiography, his black identity is what he has fashioned his life and self-worth upon. Obama and the Left need a dysfunctional and dependent black base from which to wield their power. We will further explore Obama's Racist biases in the upcoming subsection to this chapter titled *Obama as a Racist*.

The danger of Obama's Fascistic ideologies and consequent actions cannot be overemphasized. As noted earlier in the chapter *Fascism and the Left in America: Kindred Spirits and Familiar Bedfellows*, Obama had direct connections to the Nazi/Fascist ideals through many Leftists including Obama's self-acknowledged political icon Franklin Roosevelt. This as the collective group-thought of the Left as the 1933 *New York Times* article attests:

> New York Times; BERLIN, July 9, 1933 – **Chancellor Admires Roosevelt for Marching to Objectives Over Congress and Lobbies:**
> There, is at least one official voice in Europe that expresses understanding of the methods and motives of President Roosevelt. This voice is that of Germany, as represented by Chancellor Adolf Hitler. When asked in an interview what he thought of the messages of the President to the London Economic Conference, Herr Hitler replied: "I have sympathy with President Roosevelt because he marches straight toward

his objective over Congress, over lobbies, over stubborn bureaucracies"[642].

Is this an exaggeration of Obama's extremism? How else do you explain even the simple things like the Obamas' Christmas ornament on the official 2009 White House Christmas tree with the picture honoring the Leftist mass-murderer Mao Zedong? Mao was a fellow sojourner with Obama's Leftist ideology and one of the greatest mass-murderers in the history of the world, all in the name of creating the Leftists' Utopian Paradise! An Exaggeration? Hardly!

The Left likes to employ "the science is clear" argument, but only when it benefits the Left. So let's see how the Left fairs under their own criteria using Obama as the poignant Leftist representative example. We will start with the assumption that Obama is not a stupid man in general and therefore not stupid when it comes to policy decisions specifically. (A point on which the Left and Right can generally agree.)

So then, ruling out stupidity, there are only three basic alternate conclusions for the consistent policy decisions that Obama made: Obama was either making decisions intentionally, ignorantly, or naïvely. Those who assume the latter two generally conclude that Obama was "in over his head" (ignorant) or "Obama just didn't understand for lack of experience" (naïve). Using the *science* of mathematics and employing the "science is clear" theology of the Left and using the *Law of Statistics* and the *Law of Probability* we can *prove* that Obama was and is neither ignorant nor naïve, but just a radical Leftist and whose actions were and are all *intentional* and determined by his preexisting Leftist ideology.

Both the mathematical Laws of Statistics and Probability require that ignorance and naïveté on Obama's part would result in his making random policy decisions, some Left and some Right in roughly equal percentiles. For instance, these same Laws when applied to a repetitive coin toss show that it is essentially mathematically

---

[642] McCormick, Anne O'Hare; *The New York Times*; July 10, 1933, Page 1.

impossible to toss heads 100 times in a row without tossing a tails; a constant condition of always having the same result 100 times in a row by random chance. Science tells us the mathematical chances of a consistent heads in a coin toss happening 100 times in a row are: $(1/2)100 = 1/7.9 \times 1031$ or: One in 79 million, million, million, million, million. (That's 79 with 30 zeros after it!)

Predictive results using statistical and probability calculations are extremely accurate with a remarkably low margin of error. Any chance of errors becomes infinitesimally smaller the larger the repetition, such as used in this coin toss calculation with larger calculations. This almost perfect predictability theorem of conforming to the means is known in theoretical science as *Borel's law of large numbers*, which says that the more repetitions the more likely the outcome conforms to the mean, or 50%.

The notion that random results can always, or nearly always, come down on a single side becomes infinitely more absurd when applied to an individual, such as Obama, in finite time and space whose very thoughts influence the outcome through prejudice, bias, or ideology. Keep in mind that these statistics are based on random outcomes that are by definition not influenced by any prejudice, bias, or ideology.

In the real world, the science of statistics tells us that all mathematical probabilities are absolutely weighted to the middle at a rate of 51% to 49% in either direction. (100 coin tosses would result in a 51% to 49% heads to tails, or *vice versa*, outcome.) However, Obama *always*, that is *statistically always*, came down on the side of the extreme radical Left. If Obama were ignorant and/or naïve, and not simply an über-Left revolutionary, Obama would at least come close to the statistically mean average of 50% in his decision-making process of Left verses Right. Obama's decisions, if random and unintentional, would *not* be weighted towards either outcome of Left or Right and would over time remain almost inerrantly at the mean 50%, especially given that Obama had made far in excess of a mere 100 policy decisions. It is from the fact that Obama *always*, that is *statistically always*, decided to act in favor of the extreme radical Left that science proves his intentional Leftist radical bias which is neither the result of ignorance nor naïveté! There can be no question as the Left and Obama love to say... *the science is clear...* Obama was and is by choice, intention, and calculation an acting Leftist radical and does not act out of ignorance, inexperience, nor naïveté!

It is a tragic mistake, which many on the Right make, to attribute the seemingly nonsensical actions of the Left to something other than cold and calculated moves to advance the Left's agenda. Many Conservatives have attributed Obama's actions to nothing more than "inexperience" and being "in over his head". After all, they reasoned, Obama had no real political experience prior to being elected president. The frightening fact is that Obama had, as has all the Left, calculated every move to advance the Left's agenda, and the Right has unwittingly assisted in the cover-up of Obama's Evil actions.

Even a secularist comedian like Sayet can recognize the inherent problem of Evil in the Left's agenda and thought pattern, but still miss the Evil of the Left: "If it were just stupidity [the Left] would be right more often[643]"!

Here is Obama in his own words nearly seven full years into his presidency, "I know what I'm doing and I'm fearless". Does it get any clearer than that? Obama was and is acting *intentionally* to advance the Leftist agenda at *every* move.

So *PLEASE*, those of you on the Right who are commentators, pundits, activists, and armchair quarterbacks... *STOP* equivocating and giving Obama, and ALL Leftists, the "benefit of a doubt". Obama was and is an über-Leftist who's *every* action and inaction is determined by the ideology of his radical Leftist ideals! Obama did not act or not act from ignorance or naïveté, but from an *intentional* Leftist radical motives concerning foreign policy, the economy, social welfare, gun control, attacking and/or not defending Christians and Christianity, refusing to confront and even tacitly supporting the Islamic extremists, attacking Israel, the environment, global warming

---

[643] Sayet, Evan; *Regurgitating the Apple: How Modern Liberals "Think"*; Lecture #1020 on Political Thought, The Heritage Foundation; May 10, 2007.

(climate change), abortion, supporting the homosexual agenda, equal rights, indoctrinating children, school nutrition, attacking the Right, dismantling the military, legalizing drugs, race baiting… and the list goes on and on… *ad nauseam. ACTIONS HAVE CONSEQUENCES!* By refusing to call Obama what he was and is, an *intentionally* acting Über Leftist, the Right empowers Obama's and the Left's radical deception of "transforming America" into an envisioned Leftist Utopia! Obama and the Left are Hell-bent on *intentionally* destroying America as we have known and loved it! You cannot Fight, let alone defeat, an enemy that you cannot see, identify, and understand! Obama and his Leftist cohorts are not naive, ill-informed, or blundering… they are *intentionally EVIL*!

OBAMA AS A RACIST:

Even some blacks have openly acknowledged that Barack Hussein Obama is a racist[644]. Black commentator Mychal Massie recently wrote a piece commenting on the following *words of Obama*: "If [black] nationalism could create a strong and effective insularity, deliver on its promise of self-respect, then the hurt it might cause well-meaning whites, of the inner turmoil it caused people like me, would be of little consequence.[645]" Massie comments, "For those who miss the exact point [Obama] was making, [Obama] was saying that he would sacrifice his white mother and white grandparents on the altar of Black Nationalism[646] [Black Liberation Theology]"!

Massie, again himself a black man, continues:

> "I also wrote in the same article, **'There resides within Obama a hatred of white people** that explains in part why he is so conflicted. In his book 'Dreams [From My Father],'

---

[644] i.e. Massie; Mychal; *OBAMA: A LENINIST AND A RACIST*; September 1, 2014; WND.com, Commentary.

[645] Obama's Autobiography Dreams From My Father: A Story of Race And Inheritance, paperback edition; pg. 284.

[646] Massie; Mychal; WND.com, Commentary; *OBAMA'S WHITE BLOOD: PRIDE OR SHAME?*; June 24, 2013.

> **[Obama] opines that**, as was the case with Malcolm X, if [I] were able '**I would purge the white blood from my veins**'[647]. Obama by his own admission, referred to blacks who dated whites and blacks who spoke without slang as 'Uncle Toms.' [Obama] by his own admission called black students who associated with white students 'half-breeds.'" (emphasis added)

Obama's Harvard Law School Education was paid for by Muslim Saudi Prince Alwaleed bin Talal, the world's 19th wealthiest person, and a worldwide radical Muslim. The money was funneled through Khalid Abdullah Tariq al-Mansour a radical Muslim and a *black nationalist* and *mentor to Black Panther fanatics*.

It bears worth repeating here from the previous section:

> At their core both of the Obamas' demonstrate a disdain or hatred for anyone and anything not black[648], unless, as Obama in his book *Dreams From My Father: A Story of Race And Inheritance*, those [whites] who identify themselves with Malcom X, "that some whites would be worthy allies but only if they were part of the Nation of Islam or Muslim"[649]. This would explain Michelle's and Barack's long association with Black Liberation Theology, which calls for a bloody revolt against whites as the imagined modern oppressors of blacks. Here we have it from the lips of the founder of Black Liberation Theology James H. Cone:
>
> > "Whether the American system is beyond redemption we will have to wait and see. But we can be certain that black patience has run out, and unless white America responds positively to the theory and activity of *Black*

---

[647] Obama's Autobiography Dreams From My Father: A Story of Race And Inheritance, paperback edition; pgs. 101-102.

[648] e. g. See following comments by black author Mychal Massie on the Obamas' black racism.

[649] Massie; Mychal; Do people fully understand the type of monster Obama truly is?; referenced in Mychal's Column: *OBAMA'S WHITE BLOOD: PRIDE OR SHAME?*; date unavailable.

> ***Power***, then ***a bloody***, protracted ***civil war is
> inevitable***.[650]" (emphasis added)

Here is a synopsis of black author, Christian theologian, and
associate professor at King's College Anthony Bradley of the
Christian Post of Black Liberation Theology:

> "...the language of 'economic parity' and references to
> 'mal-distribution' as nothing more than channeling the
> views of Karl Marx. He believes James Cone and
> Cornel West have worked to incorporate Marxist
> thought into the black church, forming an ethical
> framework predicated on a system of oppressor class
> versus a victim much like Marxism.[651]"

The Obama's affinity with Black Liberation Theology also
speaks volumes about their lifelong friendship with the radical
and racist "pastor" Jeremiah Wright, Jr. of the Chicago Black
Liberation Theology "church" where the Obama's faithfully
attended as members for *over 20 years*! The Obama's were
married and they and their two daughters were also baptized
there by Wright. Who in their right mind would set their
children under the teaching of a black racist preacher who
called for the violent overthrow of "white America" by
blacks?! This is a telling fact about the radical beliefs held by
the Obama's!

The natural outworking of the Liberation Theology, adapted
almost in whole by the black community, is the thug mentality
so pervasive in today's black "culture". The black "gangsta" is
the mold by which black youths in mass seek to fashion
themselves. This mentality is prevalent throughout all of the
black pop culture and dominates their music which is the
largest influence in the black communities. Those blacks who
reject this life of violence and counterculture are ridiculed and

---

[650] Cone, James H.; *Black Theology and Black Power*; 1989; pg. 143.
[651] Wikipedia; Black Liberation Theology, Criticisms.

attacked as "not being black enough". The pressure to conform to this violent Black Liberation Theology is overwhelming in the black community.

Obama uses race baiting in accusations of racism in an attempt to deflect his own gross racism.; Here in Obama's own words:

> "Of course, a more common mistake is to suggest that racism is banished, that the work that drew men and women to Selma is complete, and that whatever racial tensions remain are a consequence of those seeking to play the "race card" for their own purposes. We don't need the Ferguson report to know that's not true. We just need to open our eyes, and ears, and hearts, to know that this nation's racial history still casts its long shadow upon us. We know the march is not yet over, the race is not yet won, and that reaching that blessed destination where we are judged by the content of our character – requires admitting as much"[652].

Obama used the phrase "Selma is now" to show that his racism of yesterday would be forever used by racists to drag up long dead racist ghosts of the distant past. Obama plays the "race card" while condemning those who he imagines doing so. (Only the Left plays the race card. The Left is at their heart... *RACISTS*!) This is not simply hypocritical, but an intentional manipulation of words using the Left's *doublespeak* of *Lies*! Obama is a racist at heart and racism is an integral part of who he is at his core.

Obama himself admits that he is a racist. At a memorial for five slain police officers killed by a black supremacist, Obama said, ""If we're honest, perhaps we've heard prejudice in our own heads and felt it in our own hearts... Although most of us do our best to guard against it and teach our children better, none of us is entirely innocent"".

Obama in his book *Dreams From My Father: A Story of Race And Inheritance* identifies himself with Malcom X, "that some whites would be worthy allies but only if they were part of the Nation of

---

Islam or Muslim"[653]. Obama only identifies with "*Race*", specifically the *black Race of* Obama's *Father*! Obama is a black racist!

Obama ordered the US Justice Department to dismiss charges filed by the Bush Administration against New Black Panther Party members who were videotaped intimidating voters at a Philadelphia polling station during the 2008 election. There already existed a default judgement against these Black Panthers.

As previously noted, Obama's Race baiting is another prime example of how the Left accuses the Right for what they are in fact guilty of in order to claim the "moral" high ground. Obama in his speech in March 7, 2015 Selma, Alabama spoke accusingly of "those seeking to play the 'race card'", while Obama was himself "playing the race card"! Let's take this a little further. Obama himself describes the last reason racism still remains in America as what he describes as "whatever racial tensions remain are a consequence of those seeking to play the 'race card' for their own purposes." Obama by his own definition is a primary example of someone who is responsible for "whatever racial tensions remain"! Obama by his own definition is a racist!

Perhaps the most condemning and telling example that convicts Obama as a racist is that if Obama's words were said in reverse by *any* white man, they would be excoriated and universally condemned as an unrepentant and subhuman *racist*! *Barack Hussein Obama is a racist* in the most insidious terms as Obama falsely accuses others of racism, especially those on the Right, as Obama himself is a racist who vomits his own racist ideology!

Obama as a Muslim or Muslim Sympathizer:

As was noted in the chapter *The Left Is a RELIGION!*, there is a direct...

---

[653] Massie; Mychal; Do people fully understand the type of monster Obama truly is?; referenced in Mychal's Column: *OBAMA'S WHITE BLOOD: PRIDE OR SHAME?*; date unavailable.

… association of Islam or "Muhammadism" to Hindu Paganism and as such is wholly at *War* Against Christianity. This brief explanation will go a long way in understanding why with one voice Islam cries for the destruction of Christianity and daily executes Christians worldwide for no other crime but for rejecting Islam for their faith of Christianity. "Allah" is *not*, contrary to what the Muslims would have us deceptively believe, equivalent to the Christian GOD JEHOVAH. Allah was a carryover from the official Pagan "Moon god" of Muhammad's tribal Religion. Notice the symbol of Islam, found on all Muslim flags and symbols, is the Crescent Moon. The Muslim calendar is constructed around the lunar (Moon) cycle. The Muslim year begins with the first appearance of the "crescent Moon", the 'hilal' in Arabic, heralding the beginning of Ramadan and ends with the Muslim holy day celebration of *Eid ul Fitr*, the "day of the full moon". The most sacred site of all Islam is Mecca to which all Muslims are *required* to make a pilgrimage at least once in a lifetime. The center of this worship in Mecca, which all Muslims gather around to worship Allah, is a building which houses a "sacred rock", taught by Islam to be a piece of the Moon! Islam is nothing more than a degenerated form of Hindu Paganism!

With this in mind we will see the undeniable connections and grave dangers in Barack Hussein Obama's , and the Left's, association to Islam which is violently non-American, murderously non-Christian, and a Pagan Religion based on *deceit* and world *conquest*.

Here is what the Islamic State (ISIS) leader Abu Bakr Al-Baghdadi said about the nature of the Religion of Islam:

> "Islam was never a religion of peace. Islam is the religion of fighting. No-one should believe that the war that we are waging is the war of the Islamic State. It is the war of all

Muslims, but the Islamic State is spearheading it. It is the war of Muslims against infidels"[654]. – May 2015

Islam was the self-made creation of its "prophet" Muhammad whose design was to conquer all of his neighboring tribes and beyond. Muhammad was successful in this beyond his wildest dreams in establishing and expanding his Muslim Theocratic dictatorship by military force inspired by his self-created Religion of Islam, which by Muhammad's own Islamic edict executed all who stood in his way in the name of the Moon god Allah. Al-Baghdadi was historically correct when he said, "Islam is the religion of fighting" and "It is the war of Muslims against infidels". Infidels are all those who are not Muslim, with a special animosity, as has been clearly demonstrated, against Christians and Jews by the televised execution of Christians by Muslims in the name of their Pagan Moon god Allah!

In *every* country where Islam is the State Religion, it is blasphemy punishable by death to convert from Islam to Christianity. *Hundreds of thousands* have already been executed by the mandate of the Koran, another invention of Mohammad, for this "blasphemy" in the name of Islam and its "prophet" Muhammad. Some try to use apologetics in saying that it is only "Muslim extremists" that carry out Muslim extremism. While not all Muslims are terrorists, statistically speaking all terrorists are Muslims! Coincidence? Hardly! Where in the world is Islam itself not extremist? We hear daily of these executions not just by ISIS, but the government sanctioned Muslim countries of Pakistan, Saudi Arabia, Iran, Iraq, Kuwait, Lebanon, Syria, Libya, Indonesia, Nigeria, Somalia, Yemen, Afghanistan, Algeria, Tunisia, Morocco, North Sudan, and the list goes on and on! Where exactly are these "peace loving Muslims" at? Remember we are told that "Islam is a Religion of peace". Really? Where? A recent poll of Muslims in America found that 51% supported installing Islamic Sharia Law as the supreme law in America! Remember also that Sharia Law contains the blasphemy laws and calls for jihad, open murder of non-Muslims

---

[654] British Broadcasting Corporation, BBC.com; *Islamic State releases 'al-Baghdadi message'*; 14 May 2015.

in the name of Allah, against all non-Muslims worldwide by beheading all who refuse Islam, Allah, and Muhammad, just like ISIS!

For a flagrant example we need look no further than San Bernardino, California 2015 where Syed Rizwan Farook got into an argument at a Christmas party with a Jewish Christian, Farook disputing that Islam was a "religion of peace". Farook became furious because the Jewish Christian dared to question the peaceful aspect of Islam, so Farook went home got his wife, two automatic rifles, 2,000 rounds of ammunition, some pipe bombs, and body armor that these "peace loving" Muslims just happened to have laying around, and these "peace loving" Muslims came back and murdered the Jewish Christian and 13 other people and wounded 17 others. So much for Islam as the "Religion of peace"!

Let's give a few high-profile examples of State sponsored Muslim terrorism against apostates to make the point.

> In 2010 a Pakistani Christian woman, Aasiya Noreen, also known as Asia Bibi, was sentenced to be hanged for apostasy against Islam. What was the crime so heinous against the State of Islam? She drank water out of the same cup used by her Muslim co-workers! Islam is a Religion of demonic insanity!

> In 2014... a pregnant woman in Sudan, Meriam Yehya Ibrahim, was sentenced to death by hanging because she refused to renounce Christianity for Islam... Meriam Yehya Ibrahim, who was eight months pregnant, was convicted under the Islamist-led government on charges of apostasy - the crime of abandoning or criticizing Islam - which is punishable by death in several Muslim-majority countries.[655]

> And remember Salman Rushdie and the Islamic "blasphemy" case brought against his book against Islam *The Satanic Verses*? On Valentine's Day 1989, the dying Ayatollah

---

[655] Smith, Alexander; NBC News; *Pregnant Christian Woman in Sudan Sentenced to Death for Apostasy*; May 15 2014, 7:41 am ET.

Khomeini, head of Iran's Muslim religious order, ordered a fatwa against Rushdie which included a one million dollar bounty on Rushdie's head!

These are only a few of hundreds of thousands of examples of the murderous nature of Islam. So much for Islam as the "religion of peace"!

I find Ann Coulter's quip from September 13, 2001 particularly poignant: "We should invade their countries, kill their leaders, and convert them to Christianity". Harsh? Hardly. When a group attacks you because you are not their religion, you can either capitulate and start buying fezzes, or you can obliterate their brand of Evil from the earth! We did it to Nazi Germany and their Pagan Religion… and we should do it again! There is simply no third way. Not so oddly this has always been the plan of *the Left Against GOD* and the Right. There is no appeasing Evil. Greta Van Susteren, who as we have seen is not exactly a "far Right" journalist, calls Muslim leadership EVIL![656]

In our following discussion, I will first state the obvious: **Barack Hussein Obama is *not* a Christian**! Wise up people, the Emperor has no clothes! As the *Bible* clearly states, *Faith without corresponding action is dead*!:

> Even so faith, if it hath not works, is dead, being alone. Yea, a man may say, Thou hast faith, and I have works: shew me thy faith without thy works, and I will shew thee my faith by my works. Thou believest that there is one God; thou doest well: the devils also believe, and tremble. But wilt thou know, O vain man, that faith without works is dead? - James 2:17-20

By the authority GOD and GOD's own Word, **Obama is *not* a Christian**! There is *no* Christian Faith without corresponding Christian deeds. Obama has *NO* Christian deeds!

---

[656] Fox News Insider, July 1, 2015.

However, Obama does and has had innumerable Muslim deeds, proclivities, and biases![657] From a Biblical perspective it would be easy to deduce that Obama *is* a Muslim. Jesus and the *Bible* tell us that we do not judge people on what they say, but how they *act*. If Obama were to claim to be an "ostrich", for example, we could clearly see that by his *actions* that Obama is not an ostrich. Jesus in Matthew 7:15-20 states with absolute certainty that "Ye shall know them by their fruits… a corrupt tree bringeth forth evil fruit". Obama always brings forth Evil fruit! For those who claim that "only God knows what is in the heart", they clearly contradict Jesus Himself, GOD incarnate! Jesus in this text also clearly identifies people like Obama as those "which come to you in sheep's clothing, but inwardly they are ravening wolves"! In other words Barack Hussein Obama comes pretending to be a sheep, a Christian, only to destroy GOD's own true flock, the Church, as an Evil devouring "wolf in sheep's clothing"!

As a matter of pure *survival* are forced to constantly judge others. If we see that the driver of the oncoming car seems to have fallen asleep and is careening head-on for us, we must judge that that person is putting our life in immediate danger and react accordingly. According to the Left to judge that person would be wrong. Or if we are walking down the street and someone runs at us screaming "Allah Akbar!" and has explosives strapped to their chest we immediately judge that person as a matter of self-preservation. They might not have our best interests in mind! But again, according to the Left that judgement would be intolerable! The *Bible* never says "not to judge", but the Bible instructs us not to "pass judgement" as that is GOD's place alone. Many like to condescendingly misquote the *Bible* as "judge not" but conveniently leave out the rest of the text which says "that ye be not judged. For with what judgment ye judge, ye shall be judged: and with what measure ye mete, it shall be measured to you again". This clearly is not meant as "not to judge", but not to enter into the act of "passing judgement", which is assigning eternal punishment for what is judged. To pass judgement is to administer the punishment that we not GOD deem appropriate. This however is the foundation of the Left's doctrine. Contrary to the Left's deception, Christians are actually

---

[657] See the discussion in the chapter: *The Obamas: The Epitome of the Left.*

commanded of GOD to judge *all* things[658]! These are little known facts that the Left hides because it is not convenient to their cause. Of course none of this is "Politically Correct", but neither is the *Bible* nor GOD in any sense of that phrase! Here is a good place to re-emphasize that: Leftist Politically Correct enforcement is the Muslim equivalent of Blasphemy Laws! If a person violates Islam's blasphemy laws, they are severely publically punished, usually with a public execution!

At the very least Barack Hussein Obama is and was a Muslim sympathizer, at worst a Muslim infiltrator and saboteur for Muslim extremism in America. Barack Hussein Obama is and was the Muslim Ambassador of Evil. Sound a bit exaggerated? Let's consider just a few of the undeniable facts:

- Obama only trusts **Muslims**: Obama himself wrote in his book *Dreams From My Father: A Story of Race And Inheritance*, more aptly titled *Nightmares From My Father*, that Obama identifies himself with Malcom X in, "that some whites would be worthy allies but *only* if they were part of the **Nation of Islam** [black Muslim followers of "screwy" Louis Farrakhan] or *Muslim*". (emphasis and brackets added)
- Obama, in his first foreign speech after becoming president, chose to give his "Apology Tour" against Christian America in Muslim Cairo, Egypt, apologizing to the Muslim world for Obama's *imagined* historical crimes committed by Christian America against Muslims.
- Obama said that what he considered the most beautiful sound in the world is the "Muslim call to prayer".
- Obama's father Barack Hussein Obama, Sr. was a strict Muslim.
- Obama's step-father, Indonesian born Martodihardjo who chose the Muslim name Lolo Soetoro, was a Muslim who greatly influenced Obama to Islam.
- In a January 2010 the Egyptian Foreign Minister acknowledged in a "... Nile TV broadcast in which Egyptian

---

[658] The *Holy Bible*: 1 Cor 2:15.

Foreign Minister Abul Gheit said on the "Round Table Show" that he had had a one-on-one meeting with ***Obama who swore to him that he was a Moslem***, *the son of a Moslem father and step-son of Moslem step-father, that his half-brothers in Kenya were Moslems, and that he was **loyal to the Moslem agenda**.* He asked that the Moslem world show patience. Obama promised that once he overcame some domestic American problems (Healthcare), that he would show the Moslem world what he would do with Israel"[659]. (emphasis added)

- Obama was raised as a Muslim in Indonesia, a Muslim country, during Obama's most formative years.
- Obama's Harvard Law School Education was paid for by Muslim Saudi Prince Alwaleed bin Talal, the world's 19th wealthiest person, and a worldwide *radical* Muslim. The money for Obama's education was funneled through Khalid Abdullah Tariq al-Mansour a *radical* Muslim, a *black nationalist*, and mentor to the murderous Black Panther fanatics.
- Obama bowed to the Wahhabi Muslim Saudi King Abdullah on April 1, 2009 in London which is a Muslim show of reverence and submission before another Muslim.
- Obama said, "In the wake of 9/11, my meetings with Arab and Pakistani Americans... that I will stand with [the Muslims] should the political winds shift in an ugly direction". -Obama, Barack Hussein; *The Audacity of Hope*; 2008; pg. 261
- Obama celebrates the Muslim-Iranian National holiday *Nowruz* even in the American White House. Remember that it was the Iranian Muslim activists that took the American hostages in 1978 beginning the Iranian Muslim caliphate that is now Muslim terrorist Iran! What *non*-Muslim, especially an American, would celebrate such Muslim atrocities against America in standing in solidarity with a Muslim Terrorist Nation that has murdered thousands of Americans!?
- Obama celebrated the Muslim holy days of Ramadan and gave Presidential decrees in the support of Islam. *Ramadan is*

---

[659] Brown, Patrick; Western Journalism; *Egyptian Foreign Minister: Obama told me himself, "I am a Muslim"*; June 14, 2010 at 12:30pm.

observed by Muslims worldwide as a month of fasting to commemorate the first revelation of the Quran to Muhammad according to Islamic belief. **Only Muslims** are allowed to participate in the Ramadan holy days observances, to which *violations of non-Muslims is punishable by death according to Islamic Law*! This annual observance is regarded as one of the Five Pillars of Islam. The month lasts 29–30 days based on the visual sightings of the crescent moon.[660] Remember, as discussed elsewhere, that the Moon is the symbol of the Muslim god Allah as worshipped by Muhammad's tribal Pagan ancestors.

- Let's not forget Obama's middle name is *Hussein*! "Hussein" is recorded by Islam to have been first used by the Islamic prophet Muhammad when he named his grandson Husayn [Hussein] ibn Ali.[661]

- In *May of 2012*, Obama's (admitted) Marxist pastor for over 20 years, the "Reverend" Jeremiah Wright, said that Obama, was "raised as a Muslim", was "steeped in Islam," and "knew very little about Christianity".

- "The president, his entire life his whole influence has been Islam. His mother has been married to a Muslim. His father is a Muslim. Then she married a man from Indonesia. He was raised in Indonesia. Went to Islamic schools. I assume she was a Muslim as *required* by Islamic law under threat of death. So, his whole life experiences have been surrounded by Islam. He only knows Islam. And, he's given a pass to Islam. He's refusing to accept and understand the evil that is in front of him"[662]. -Reverend Franklin Graham

OBAMA WAS INTENTIONALLY AND PURPOSELY EMPOWERING ISLAM AND ITS MUSLIM TERRORIST IDEOLOGY:

---

[660] Wikipedia, Ramadan.

[661] Wikipedia, Hussein.

[662] Rev. Franklin Graham; Fox News; On the Record interview with Greta Van Susteren; 2/17/15.

- Obama forced a treaty upon America with Muslim Iran that ensures that Iran gets nuclear weapons with nuclear warheads that can reach the United States and gives $150,000,000,000.00 ($1,5000,000 in cash) to the largest sponsor and funder of Muslim terrorism in the world!
- Obama arranged the Iranian nuclear deal to help create an unconquerable Muslim caliphate in the Middle East whose sole intention is to obliterate America and Israel.
- In response to the November 13, 2015 Paris terrorist attacks by the Islamic State (ISIS) which killed 129 French civilians and wounded hundreds more, Obama *the next day* released 5 Muslim terrorists from the Guantanamo Bay Prison in Cuba. The French killed 7 of the ISIS terrorists in the attack, and it has been aptly noted, Obama replenished the Muslim losses in the terrorist ranks with the 5 Muslim terrorists released from Guantanamo!
- Obama refused to call the ISIS terror attacks in Paris a Muslim or Islamic terrorist attack. Remember that ISIS is the "*Islamic* State of Iraq and al-Sham".
- ISIS cuts off the heads of 21 Egyptian Coptic Christians and Obama barely acknowledges it and refuses to call it Islamic terrorism, Islamic extremism, or Islamic *anything*. ISIS in the video declared "War on the Cross" that would continue until we "Lay down Jesus" and all Christians convert to Islam!
- Obama said that ISIS, the *Islamic* State of Iraq and al-Sham, is not Muslim. What?! Even Obama acknowledged that ISIS is the "*Islamic* State of Iraq and al-Sham"! Islamic is the first word in their name!!!
- Obama refers to ISIS (*Islamic* State of Iraq and al-Sham) as ISIL. This was a direct attack on Israel in calling for Israel to be conquered by ISIS. ISIS calls itself the *Islamic* State of Iraq and al-Sham. Why are these facts important? Because "al-Sham" is an ancient name of Syria. ISIL was Obama's renaming ISIS to the "Islamic State of Iraq and the *Levant*". The "Levant" is an historical reference to the entire area of the core of the Middle East *including* Israel! Obama by the change of a single word subjugates Israel to Islamists whose stated

goal is the annihilation of Israel! Words matter! Obama was and is militantly Anti-Israel, bent on Israel's destruction, and is totally complicit with the realization of a hegemoneous Islamic caliphate built on Israel's ashes!

- In Cairo in June 2009, Obama vowed to establish "a new beginning between the United States and Muslims". And "I consider it part of **my** responsibility as president of the United States to fight against negative stereotypes of Islam wherever they appear."
- Obama called the Fort Hood Muslim terrorist attack "workplace violence" refusing to acknowledge that it was a Muslim jihad attack where the Muslim attacker killed 13 and wounded 30 Americans while yelling "Allahu Akbar" which means "Allah is great"!
- Obama endorsed and celebrated the building of a Muslim victory mosque at the point of Islam's most successful attack upon America, the 911 ground Zero in New York City. The mosque was to be named the Cordoba Mosque after of the mosque that the Muslims built in Cordoba, Spain in celebration of the Muslim conquering of that city and subsequent Muslim occupation over 95% Spain's Christian population! All inhabitants were required to convert to Islam or die by beheading!
- Obama ordered NASA to become a "Muslim outreach" organ.
- On the day that Netanyahu was elected, Obama in a video to Iran, blamed American and Israeli hardliners for the problems in the Middle East intentionally ignoring that it is exclusively the Muslims which are the source of hatred and violence in the Middle East.
- The "Arab Spring", which would have been more appropriately called the "Muslim Uprising", was supported and helped by Obama. Obama gave 100's of millions of U.S. dollars in military and economic support to radical Muslim coups in the Middle East. Twelve countries fell to Islamic terroristic organizations.

- The "Arab Spring" was one of Obama's many contributions to insure the creation of an Islamic caliphate in the middle East and North Africa.
- Obama illegally interfered in the 2015 Netanyahu elections in support of a more pro-Muslim candidate.
- Obama's Red Line in Syria was a head fake that Obama, as in all of his "threats" against Muslim States, never intended to enforce.
- Obama pulled all American combat troops out of Iraq opening the way for the rise of the Muslim terrorist organization ISIS whose goal was to establish a Muslim caliphate and destroy America and Israel.
- Obama pulled virtually all American troops out of Muslim Afghanistan, a Muslim country which supports the Taliban and its ISIS counterparts.
- Obama supported the Muslim Brotherhood, an original Islamic terrorist organization, in its takeover attempt in Egypt as part of Obama's attempt to establish a Muslim caliphate in the Middle East which Obama the intentionally and deceivingly called the "Arab Spring".
- Obama refused military aid in Benghazi to save the lives of five Americans, including an American Ambassador, against their Muslim jihadist attackers.
- Obama in Libya unilaterally bombed Kaddafi and let ISIS take over.
- Obama touted Yemen as an example of his foreign policy success and shortly thereafter Yemen fell to Islamic radicals.
- Obama had dozens of "Muslim outreach" conferences at the White House. Did you ever hear of an Obama White House "Christian outreach" conference? Never!
- Obama conspired to overthrow longtime American ally President Mubarak in Egypt and replace with Muslim Brotherhood Mohammed Morsi.
- Obama supported Mohamed Morsi and Muslim Brotherhood in its takeover of Egypt. There is convincing evidence that Barack Hussein Obama not only supported the takeover of the Muslim terrorist organization the Muslim Brotherhood in

Egypt, but conspired in secret to put the full weight of the American government behind the Muslim terrorist organization to insure its success in replacing Mubarak . Hillary Rodham-Clinton as Secretary of State was the go between in the Obama Administration's conspiracy.

- Obama was *charged* by the Egyptian judiciary courts of conspiracy to support the terrorist organization the Muslim Brotherhood.
- Obama was hostile to Egyptian President Abdel Fattah Al-Sisi who kicked out the radical Muslim Brotherhood from Egypt.
- Obama praised the Islamic Society of North America, an American chapter of the Muslim Brotherhood terrorist organization, in April of 2014.
- Obama celebrates the Muslim holiday of Ramadan in the White House, while for years Obama refused to acknowledge Christmas and Easter the two most Holy days on the Christian calendar! NO Christian celebrates other religions' holidays, as it is forbidden by the *Bible* as an abomination!
- August 2010 – Obama went to great lengths to speak out on multiple occasions on behalf of building an Islamic mosque at Ground Zero, while at the same time he was silent about a Christian church being denied permission to rebuild at that location.
- April 2010 – Christian leader Franklin Graham is disinvited from the Pentagon's National Day of Prayer Event because of complaints from the Muslim community.
- April 2010 – The Obama administration requires rewriting of government documents and a change in administration vocabulary to remove terms that are deemed offensive to Muslims, including jihad, jihadists, terrorists, radical Islamic, *et al*.
- Obama refused to support Iran's Green Revolution which sought to overthrow the terrorist Muslim clerics who finance and promote radical Muslim terrorism worldwide and who are directly responsible for the deaths of hundreds of Americans!
- Obama boasted, "The future must not belong to those who slander the prophet of Islam". –Obama, Barack; White House

Press Office; Remarks by the President to the United Nations General Assembly; September 25, 2012

- Obama in his September 2014 speech before the United Nations praised the Muslim cleric Sheikh Abdallah Bin Bayyah who publically supported a fatwa calling for the murder of U.S. soldiers in Iraq!

- Obama defended Islamic terrorists in a bizarre attempt of creating some kind of moral equivalency between Islamic terrorists and Christianity by saying that Christians also had 1,000 years before "committed terrible deeds in the name of Christ" during the Crusades, leaving out of course that the Crusades were a defensive war against the invading Muslims which the Muslim Moors had already invaded and conquered *95%* of Christian Spain and was attempting to conquer all of Europe! –Obama, Barack; White House Press Office; Remarks by the President at National Prayer Breakfast; February 05, 2015.

As to Barack Hussain Obama's attempted deflection comparing Muslim Crusades happening today, to the 10th Century Catholic Crusades of 1095-1291. First, I refute that the Crusades was a "Christian" endeavor, but as history clearly bears out, the Crusades were a Catholic Church undertaking, and perpetuated by a succession of Catholic Popes. The Muslim Crusades against the Christian West are being implemented today... right now. The Catholic Crusades occurred over *700 years ago*! To say that American Christians today somehow bear responsibility for the actions of Europeans over 700 years ago is tantamount to Obama having blamed you for your great, grandfather's actions! This is *insane*! (Of course Obama and the Left blame you today for your great, great, great, great, great, great, great, grandfather's contribution to slavery over 160 years ago! Equally *insane*! Not to mention that many of our ancestors were not even in America then and those that might have been probably fought to overturn slavery in the American Civil War, in the streets, and in numerous legislatures.)

- Obama refused to name Muslim terrorists as Muslims but referred specifically to "Christians" as terrorists during the "Crusades" and the *Spanish* "Inquisition".

- Obama claimed, "I also know that Islam has always been a part of America's story," Obama said in a June 4, 2009 speech in Cairo, Egypt. "Islam has always been part of America," he said in an August 11, 2010 statement marking the start of Ramadan. And in a 2014 statement marking *Eid*, Obama said the holiday "also reminds us of the many achievements and contributions of Muslim Americans to building the very fabric of our nation and strengthening the core of our democracy". "Islam has been woven into the fabric of our country since its founding." - February 18, 2015. Hey Barrack did you know that the biggest threat to our brand-new Republic was going to war with the Muslim Barbary Coast Pirates who were seizing American merchant ships, stealing the ships and cargo and enslaving the American sailors. Wow that is what you call the Muslim contribution in building the fabric of America?!

- Obama gave money and spearheaded a campaign headed by Obama supporters in Israel to turn out the Muslim vote in the 2015 elections in an illegal attempt to bring down the Israeli government.

- Obama said, "We will convey our deep appreciation for the Islamic faith, which has done so much over the centuries to shape the world — including in my own country." (Humm... Obama neglected to mention what those imagined instances were.)

- Obama supported Islam saying, "These rituals remind us of the principles that we hold in common, and Islam's role in advancing justice, progress, tolerance, and the dignity of all human beings." What planet does he live on?

- Obama himself admitted, "So I have known Islam on three continents before coming to the region where it was first revealed".

- Obama equated his love for Islam as the same as his quest for black superiority saying, "Ramadan is a celebration of a faith known for great diversity and racial equality".
- Obama regularly quoted the Quran and credits the Quran for giving him inspiration in his life.
- Obama's obsession in closing Guantanamo because it offends Muslim terrorists.
- Obama's secret trade of 5 Muslim terrorists for Sargent Bergdahl a confirmed U.S. Army deserter and Muslim convert.
- The Obama Administration blasted Israel as having been in "an *occupation* [of Muslim lands] that has lasted for almost 50 years must end" and "Israel cannot maintain military control of another people [Muslims] indefinitely". These remarks were given by Obama's White House Chief of Staff Denis McDonough in a speech on March 23rd, 2015 at the notoriously Leftist and anti-Israel J Street lobbyist forum. This was done not only because Obama is himself anti-Israel but equally to support the Terrorist state of Iran and provide cover for Obama's negotiating to give Iran the ability to build nuclear weapons which Iran has pledged to use against both Israel and the United States. If Obama had disagreed in any sense with these words, Obama most certainly would have immediately fired McDonough!
- In February/March 2015 Obama released Top Secret documents on Israel's nuclear program as a cover and justification for pushing a nuclear deal with Muslim Iran which would allow Iran to build nuclear weapons. Again, this with the backdrop that Iran through its Islamic mullahs has pledged to use any acquired nuclear weapons to annihilate both Israel and the United States.
- Obama and Obama's Secretary of State John Kerry strove in negotiations to accommodate Iran getting nuclear weapons, even as a top ranking Iranian Muslim general reiterated Iran's promises to destroy Israel "Israel's destruction is non-negotiable" (3/31/2015), and the Iranian Muslim Supreme

Leader Ayatollah Ali Khamenei was filmed chanting "Death To America" (3/21/2015).

- In 2012 Obama released classified information about Israel's funding and training of Iranian opposition forces, the *Mujahideen-e-Khalq,* working inside Iran to overthrow the Muslim Terrorist régime. This move was designed to protect the Muslim régime and weaken Israel's ability to stop Iran from acquiring nuclear weapons.

- The Obama Administration sanctioned the pre-deployment briefing at Fort Hood in which army pre-deployment soldiers were told that evangelical Christians and members of the Tea Party were a threat to the nation and that any soldier donating to those groups would be subjected to punishment under the Uniform Code of Military Justice. The Obama Administration *never* issued a likeminded warning against Muslims in the military *even* after the many Muslim terrorist attacks inside its ranks!

- There are literally *thousands* of additional examples, but these should suffice to document that Obama was and is in the very least sense a Muslim sympathizer and most probably a Muslim infiltrator!

Remember the Law of Large numbers from earlier in this chapter? Every action taken by Obama grossly favors Islam and the creation of a Muslim caliphate. *Every action.* What some might say were steps against ISIS and terrorist Islam like "bombing" ISIS, is nothing more than a head fake to make it appear as if Obama were actually confronting Islam. The "bombing" of ISIS is a joke as more than 75% of the bombing sorties returned without dropping a single bomb! How else could France, after a year and a half of US "bombing", immediately after the Muslim Paris attack bomb ISIS's capital city of Raqqa Syria? Shouldn't that city presumably already be "bombed" into oblivion?! The Law of Large Numbers demands that Obama's favoring of Islam, even in the face of *insidious* Muslim terrorist events, that Obama was and is in fact at the very least, a Muslim sympathizer! Probably much worse. It might not necessarily be completely accurate to say that Obama was and is sleeping with the enemy, but it would be absolutely accurate to say that Michelle Obama was and is sleeping with the enemy!

Conclusion:

If America and especially the leadership of the American Right are not currently willing to publicly call Obama what he was and is - a Leftist subversive radical bent on the *intentional* destruction of America as we know it and all things Christian - What exactly would Obama have to do in addition to the already committed atrocities to cause the Right to wake up and enjoin the *War* that is raging for the souls of all Americans?! Barack Hussein Obama Jr was and is *the Epitome of the Left* and the face of Evil in America today!

22. IGNORANCE IS NO EXCUSE FOR THE LAW

Chapter 22

Some may be thinking to themselves at this point, "I have considered myself a Liberal, but I had no idea that what has been revealed in this book and elsewhere, was the agenda of Evil that Liberals really stood for. Am I responsible for what I did not know about the Left and things that I may have supported without knowing the truth?". GOD's answer is... Yes. GOD clearly states that an individual who has reached the age of accountability[663] is responsible to GOD for their actions and inactions as measured by GOD's Word[664]. To restate an earlier point, Jesus as GOD Himself warned all of mankind that there is NO gray area[665], "He that is not with me is against me"[666]. Notice there are no "gray areas" in GOD's eyes, there are only two categories: those "for" GOD, and those "*Against*" GOD! The Left includes all those "*Against*" GOD. You do not necessarily have to be an activist of the Left to be "*Against*" GOD, you simply have to be not "for" GOD, which as Jesus tells us is actually "*Against*" GOD. Unquestionably GOD condemns those who vote for and support the Left are themselves *Against GOD*!

Satan would have us believe that everything is relative, that everything is in a "gray area". However you categorize it, whether Leftist, gray areas, progressive, liberal, Fascist, atheist, agnostic, or non-committed, it is all rebellion *Against GOD*!

The GOOD news is that every person has the ability to learn from GOD's Word and repent from this and all their sins *Against GOD* and receive forgiveness. However, this is an all or nothing offer from GOD. A person must accept Jesus as his GOD and Savior and acknowledging he is a sinner, ask Jesus to save him, and surrender his life to GOD. It is a simple but life altering commitment. For a fuller explanation of

---

[663] The Biblical age of accountability is when a person is old enough to recognize right from wrong. The maximum age is 21 years old. See The *Holy Bible:* Numbers 32:11; Deuteronomy 1:39; Ezra 3:8.
[664] The *Holy Bible:* Leviticus 4:13 (vv. 1-35); 5:17-18; Luke 12:48.
[665] The subject of "gray areas" will be addressed more fully in the later chapter Shades of Gray.
[666] The *Holy Bible:* Matthew 12:30.

how to commit yourself to GOD and GOD's side, see the Postscript: For the Sinner who finds himself on the Wrong side of GOD in *The Left's War Against GOD* at the end of this book.

23. FIGHTING TO WIN!: HOW DO WE FIGHT THE WAR? THE RIGHT'S RULES FOR ANTI-RADICALS! A CALL TO ACTION!

Chapter 23

The timeless *War* of Evil *Against GOD* has been won in Eternity by Jesus Christ, but the temporal Battle For America rages on. Will GOOD or Evil prevail in America? Only GOD knows the answer to that question. But the question we can and must answer is: Are we willing to cede our Country in a surrender to Evil or simply sell out to Evil for twenty pieces of silver because the struggle seems insurmountable? I for one believe that the principles on which America was founded are worth fighting for... whatever the cost. *This is an all or nothing Fight*. Either GOD wins the Battle for America or Evil wins. There is no ceasefire or armistice with Evil. Evil never sleeps. Evil is itself in a Battle for its own survival. The only way for Evil to survive is to continually replicate itself and thereby subdue its opponents. This is the *Left's War* to "Transform" America!

Get *ANGRY*! I am talking about *Righteous Anger*! We own the term. *Righteous* belongs to GOD alone. Jesus knocked over a few tables of the Left in the Temple, maybe it's time to follow Jesus' example and get *Angry*!

Again, this is not necessarily a treatise on Christianity, but without the guidance and direct intervention of GOD, and GOD through His people the Christians, the *War* against Evil cannot even be engaged, let alone won! To illustrate this point the *Bible* relates a story of when seven non-Christian Jews tried to perform an exorcism on a demon-possessed man by using the name of "Jesus", the demon in the man replied, "Jesus I know... but who are ye?". The demon-possessed man then proceeded to beat these seven well-meaning men, but wholly unequipped men, senseless until they ran away "naked and wounded"[667]. This is an apt picture of non-Christians taking on Evil

---

[667] The *Holy Bible:* Acts 19:13-16.

and their defenselessness against Evil. There is no authority against Evil without GOD living in the individual. *Only* Christians can wield the Name of Jesus. This is why Christians and Christianity are necessary to the discussion. To go into the Battle against Evil without GOD would not just be spitting into the wind, but more akin to spitting into the nuclear fission reaction of an exploding thermonuclear bomb in hopes of extinguishing the resultant fireball! The reason the Right has suffered such loses and setbacks is that we all too often go marching into battle seven abreast and completely unarmed! Remember the Road to Hell is paved with "good intentions"!

The most obvious point which must be understood is that THIS IS A *FIGHT*! If you are not fighting you are losing! If you are fighting to make a point and they are fighting to kill you, you have a problem! This is the collective problem of the Right. The Right does not take the stakes seriously. Christians must wake up and realize that this is a fight to the death! The Right thinks that winning an argument will win the Battle. The Left thinks that seeing you dead will win the Battle. Who do you think will win the day under these conditions? When you actually stop to think about the Battle in its base terms, it quickly becomes a no-brainer! Chamberlain tried reasoning with Hitler to avoid World War II and we all know how that turned out. You cannot reason with Evil! Do you remember how the Democrat strategist Chris Lehane explained the Leftist strategy in Fighting the Left's War Against GOOD: "Everyone has a game plan until you punch them in the mouth. So let's punch them in the mouth"[668]. Try reasoning with someone like that and you will end up unconscious and out of the Fight!

Yet this is the very strategy of the Left:

> A complacent society tolerantly views the turbulent atmospheric noise of Liberal [Leftist] minds with the old childhood slogan of "Sticks and stones may break my bones, but names will never hurt me." Let the Liberal [Leftist] turn to the course of action, the course of all Radicals, and the amused

---

[668] Nagourney, Adam; The New York Times online; *Everyone Has a Game Plan Until You Punch them in the Mouth*; February 26, 2014.

look vanishes from the face of society as it snarls, "That's radical!" **Society has good reason to fear the Radical. He hits, he hurts, he is dangerous**. Conservative interests know that while Liberals [Old School Liberals predating the 60's] are most adept at breaking their own necks with their tongues, **Radicals are most adept at breaking the necks of Conservatives**[669]. (Brackets and emphasis added for clarity)

The Right plays by "the Rules" of the Left and aids and abets the Left in its Evil deeds. For instance, the Left will oppose the appointment of any nominee by a Right or Right leaning President, while the Right follows the miss-stated standard of "if they are qualified". *NO LEFTIST NOMINEE IS EVER QUALIFIED!!!* Virtually every Leftist nominee gets approved with the consent of the Right and virtually every nominee of the Right is rejected or substantially hindered and falsely discredited by the Left. The inevitable discreditization of the Right's appointees by the Left for political reasons, severely hinders the future ability of a Rightist to effectively serve. This is an intentional and well-developed strategy of the Left and has worked very effectively against the Right for decades in America! Wake up Right!!!

Compromise Kills!

Call it what you will: compromise, capitulation, appeasement, or any other euphemism, compromise by the Right always plunges headlong down the road to defeat! It is far past time to stand up and *FIGHT* the Left's forest fire with a napalm backfire! Evil through the Left *ALWAYS* seeks to destroy anyone who stands against it! I'd rather go down fighting than be shot in the back running away! Compromise, capitulation, and burying our head in the sand only empowers and advances the Left's cause through incrementalism, a favorite guise of the Left. Compromise makes you more like the Enemy every time you compromise until you are no longer a Conservative but a "moderate" which is a Liberal [Leftist] by any other name! (See continued discussion later in this chapter and in the Chapter PRACTICAL WAR

---

[669] Alinsky, Saul; *Reveille for Radicals*; 1946; pg. 29.

STRATEGIES: The Right's RULES FOR ANTI-RADICALS! A Call To ACTION! in the subsection "Moderates".) "In time liberalism [Leftism] remakes conservatism in its own image by forcing it to give up everything distinctive for the sake of consensus"[670]. The Left understands this and has been winning the Battles one compromise at a time. Remember Jesus' words you are either for GOD or Against Him; GOOD or compromised by Evil. Compromise is the corruption of Evil in degrees. If you are fighting on the battlefield as an American soldier, how much can you "compromise" with the enemy until you are considered a traitor guilty of treason?

There is a reason that the Left is *always* calling for compromise: compromise *always* favors the Left! Compromise is nothing more than incremental shifts *to* the Left. *Right* is *Right*, compromise corrupts that which was *Right* and is *NOT* any longer Right! Remember anything that is not *Right* is *WRONG*. If $2 + 2 = 4$ then that is *Right*, then what is a compromise on that? Compromise renders the truth irrelevant! Did you ever notice that a call for "compromise" from the Left always involves concessions from the Right?

Once the Left gets the proverbial foot-in-the-door the rest of the body is *always* soon forced through the breach! Every time! *Guaranteed!* Remember the Left only "compromises" until it has incrementally received enough power through capitulation of the Right to seize absolute power. Every major issue that the Left has won started with just a little acceptance through "compromise", then the whole vulgarity comes rushing in and militantly demands that the Right relinquish all rights of opposition to the Left's agenda… health care, homosexuality, gay marriage, deficit spending, evolution, global warming, trans fat, *et al*, *ad absurdum*! The next battle on the horizon is total legalization of drugs. Skeptical? It's already begun. Obama issued a proclamation that possession of "small" amounts of marijuana will not be prosecuted by the Federal government. This will incrementally increase until one day all drugs will just be decreed legal either by a usurpation of the Leftist courts or by a Leftist

---

[670] Kalb, James; Modern Age Quarterly; *The Tyranny of Liberalism: The Iron Heel of Freedom*; Summer 2000.

presidential dictate. Taxable of course, but legal. This is the inevitability of appeasement by the Right given to the Left!

Even secular institutions recognize that Middle-of-the-Road Policies Lead to Leftist Socialism as outlined by the Austrian School of Economics. Ludwig Von Mises pointed this out as early as his lecture before the University Club of New York, April 18, 1950 in his speech titled, not so coincidentally, "Middle-of-the-Road Policy Leads to Socialism"[671]. Every compromise "To-The-Middle" is nothing more than an incremental move to the Left! It is no wonder that the Left thunders that "politics is built on compromise!". So-called Republican "moderates" are nothing more than "compromised" to and of the Left! Would you agree to "compromise" on how much cyanide poison you would allow someone to put in your children's drinking water? NO! Of course not! Never! Yet this is exactly what the Left has been doing to the Right in America for decades! The Right has now drunk so much of the Left's cyanide laced Kool-Aid that we have almost killed ourselves and America with us!

Compromise, capitulation, and appeasement kills the necessary zeal of the individual and movement to *Fight* and Win the Right's Battle Against Evil. The Tea Party's[672] zeal frightens both the Leftists and "moderate" Republicans. The Left fears the true Right because of the serious threat the zealous Right poses against Evil by those who are ready, willing, and able to effectively *Fight* the War Against Evil. The so-called Republican "moderates" hate the Tea Party and their zeal because it exposes the complete ineffectiveness of "moderation" against Evil. The Tea Party's mission-mindedness makes them far less willing to compromise with Evil.

When you concede ground to the enemy, you only empower the enemy and cede what belongs to you, in a vain effort to satiate Hell's insatiable appetite! Hell *never* has enough to satiate Its horrific appetite. Hell continually enlarges Itself to accommodate newly

---

[671] Mises Institute Austrian Economics, Freedom, and Peace; Mises Daily; December 2, 2006.
[672] This is not a blanket endorsement of the Tea Party. However there are many in the Tea Party who are Right and bearers of the Truth. Generally the Tea Party possesses the necessary zeal and persistence to effectively Fight the Battle Against Evil.

acquired souls and territory[673]! Compromise only gives the Left the opportunity to retrench, regroup, and reequip. Ultimately appeasement becomes a slow and painful suicide by a thousand cuts of death! America is in its death throes! Trump is nearly the only active, outspoken, and zealous opponent of Evil in America today. It's time for the army of the Right to unite, stand, and *Fight*!

When even the archangel Michael, the most powerful angel of GOD, was contending for the body of Moses, Michael dared not directly argue with Satan[674]. Evil gets in your head. Evil twists your thoughts. We cannot take on Evil in its own arena. This is what we do when we allow Evil to set the stage for debate. Michael's response to Satan's attempt to define the perimeters for debate was to rebuke Satan in the name of GOD! This is our only winning strategy against Evil. We too must identify Evil… as *Evil*! The American people must see the true face of the Left as the *Evil* it really is. Americans must see that the only outcome of playing with the Devil is death and destruction[675]. The American people must learn to recognize the Evil behind the schemes of the Left. *The debate must always be turned to an open debate of GOOD Against Evil*! When the Left offers free cell phones, the Right must show them that this is nothing more than a lure to *enslavement*. Bobbles in trade for their soul. If something can be given it can just as easily be taken away. This is the road to Hell paved in dependency!

Arguments must show the natural *consequence* or *logical conclusion* of that path dangled by the Left. Public school sex-ed programs result in mass teen pregnancy. Condoms handed out in school results in teen sex. Abortion results in the murder of a totally innocent unborn baby. Homosexuality results in a complete abandonment of GOD and a horrifying death from AIDS. *Actions have consequences!* These consequences are the logical conclusions of accepting the Left's arguments.

---

[673] The *Holy Bible*: Isaiah 5:14; Habakkuk 2:5.
[674] The *Holy Bible*: Jude 1:9.
[675] The *Holy Bible*: John 10:10.

Turn around the Left's arguments Against them. When the Left screams that Roe v. Wade is the law of the land and as such must stand, we respond that the Left must be against black civil rights because at one time that was the law of the land! Every Leftist argument can be turned around against them.

There are American folk songs that talk about dueling with the Devil and winning, but these are mere human fantasies no doubt encouraged by the Devil to lure the unsuspecting and unprepared into defeat and annihilation. There are no true-life stories about winning against the Devil without direct intervention from GOD!

We must *confront* Evil at *every* turn. The Left establish the narrative which allowed the Left to promote the *Lie* of a false narrative. (a "false narrative" is a cleverly disguised *Lie!*) On a Fox News program a roundtable of commentators was discussing "immigration", in itself a false narrative, a *Lie*, and the Leftist commentator spoke of the "undocumented citizens" of America and neither the Fox anchor nor the two supposed Conservative co-commentators challenged or even acknowledged the false narrative as a *Lie*, thus seeming accepting the *Lie*! Conservatives *cannot* win a War in which they not only refuse to Fight, but surrender without even feigning a disagreement!

The Left just keeps spewing "false narratives" (*Lies!*) until their masses of useful idiots believe their *Lies*. The Right must confront every *Lie* as it is spewed, before it can take root in the weak-minded!

It's time to destroy those who seek to destroy our Constitutionally guaranteed freedoms! Evil cannot be placated! Like every attempt to placate evil in history (Nazi Germany, Soviet Union, Communist China, etc.), Evil uses the time to fortify, regroup, and reattack at its earliest opportunity. A very important note must be made on the War Against Evil which is that: you cannot merely Fight to stem, or contain the tide of Evil in America, but we *must* Fight to reverse, dislodge, and annihilate the gains and footholds that the Left has already established in America today! The Left has successfully lodged in the minds of Americans the idea of "compromise". Compromise with the Left is only the incremental surrender of the Right… to Evil!

We on the Right are in a literal existential War Against the Left! Our very existence depends on the willingness of the Right to rise up and Fight! The Left as Evil incarnate will always exist in America, but if the Right is defeated by this existential threat then all that is GOOD in America will be destroyed and lost forever!

24. PRACTICAL WAR STRATEGIES: THE RIGHT'S RULES FOR ANTI-RADICALS! A CALL TO ACTION!

Chapter 24

I would be woefully remiss if after defining the *War*, that I did not also then follow-up and offer pragmatic, and even *emotionally* pragmatic, proposals for Winning the Battle for America. You cannot out-Liberal the Liberals! But you can use their tactics against them!

Here is a general condensed list that will be elaborated upon in the bulk of this chapter:

• **Couch the Issue In Terms of Evil vs GOOD**

• **Use Emotion!**

• **Shout Them Down!**

• **Use Name Calling!**

• **Use Their History!**

• **Forget Reasoning With Them. They are far beyond reason! - Reason with the audience!**

Specific Tactics:

1. Action, ACTION, ACTION!
2. ATTACK!!!
3. CALL THEM LIARS! Challenge the Left on its Lies. And back it up!
4. Challenge The Left's Labels
5. USE *EMOTION*! Challenge Directly the Emotional Arguments. Use emotion back and even first, but based in Rightness. Use Common Sense with Emotion!

6. The old adage "if it feels good, it must be right" is a *Lie* of the Devil! But we can take what is Right and make it feel good!
7. THE LEFT IS NOT ABOUT COMMON SENSE!
8. Use Common Sense
9. Sticks and Stones: Words matter! Words ARE Dangerous and Deadly!
10. The Left Does *NOT* Play By the "Rules"... Confront Lawlessness!
11. Don't Play Their Game!
12. Don't Play by the Left's Rules and Mandates!
13. Racism is a Leftist/Democrat Manifestation
14. Clearly Illustrate Your Points with Relatable Story Images (Reagan)
15. Make the Leftists Answer to the Point
16. Take Back Our Churches
17. Use the Hitler/Nazi Analogy Often as it Best Reflects the Tactics, Ideology, and Actions of the Left
18. K.I.S.S.! (Keep It Simple Stupid!)
19. Demonize the Enemy!
20. Be Positive!
21. Combat the Leftist contrived Euphemism of the "Separation of Church and State".
22. Be **BOLD!** Unabashed!
23. OWN IT!
24. Public Debates and Winning the Uncommitted.
25. Persuade the Audience NOT the Leftist!
26. *REFUSE* to Comply!
27. The Law of Diminishing Returns
28. Use the logical conclusion for Leftist ideals. (See Working Draft: *Reductio ad absurdum*) Compare and contrast what would happen if the voters are given everything they think they wanted. Higher taxes vs self-sufficiency, etc.
29. Offer Real HOPE!
30. Moderates

31. People are convinced by either *compassion* (a form of love) or *fear*[676]. USE BOTH: The Right is a friend of the people and the Left is to be feared.
32. Organize, ORGANIZE, ORGANIZE!
33. Never "negotiate" with the Left
34. The Science is Clear Nazi Straw Man
35. Unified Front
36. The Individual verses the State
37. Quit Holding Our Own To A Perfect Standard

1. Action, ACTION, ACTION!

Here is a little adapted anecdote which adequately describes the Right's dilemma of inaction:

> This is a story about four Conservatives named Everybody, Somebody, Anybody, and Nobody.
> When there was a job to be done these had to decide which of the four Conservatives would do it.
> Everybody assumed that Somebody would do it.
> Somebody assumed that Anybody would do it.
> Everybody was angry that Anybody didn't just do it.
> Anybody figured that it was Everybody's responsibility to do it.
> Who finally did it?
> … Nobody!

The radical Left lives for *Action*! The Left instinctively understands that to not be *Acting* is to be losing ground! The Right must realize that Evil wins when GOOD men do nothing. We must *continually* Fight! Wendell Phillips astutely noted that "Eternal vigilance is the price of liberty". Calvin Coolidge added "There is no substitute for a militant freedom. The only alternative is submission and slavery". And Milton Friedman concluded "Maybe I did well and maybe I led the battle but nobody ever said we were going to win this thing at any point in time. Eternal vigilance is required and there have to be people who step up to the plate, who believe in liberty, and who are willing to fight for it". Only the *Action* of the Right in eternal vigilance

---

[676] The *Holy Bible*, Jude 1:22-23.

ensures that we keep our GOD-given liberties which we have enjoyed these 240 years. Millions of men before us were willing to lay down life and limb in the defense of America against the tyranny of the Left. Are you willing to give up your sports time, your drinking nights with your buddies, your book club, and your spa time to ensure that ours, and our children's freedoms are not taken from us by the Left? If not you, who? If not now, when? Will *Nobody* do it? ***Inaction is surrender and suicide!***

Here are a few bits of wisdom to leave you with on the subject of *ACTION*:

"The battle, sir, is not to the strong alone; it is to the vigilant, the active, the brave." — Patrick Henry

"The land of the free will cease to be when it's no longer the home of the brave." — Rick Gaber

"Perhaps the meek shall inherit the Earth, but they'll do it in very small plots . . . about 6' by 3'." — Robert A. Heinlein

"The Romans used to say that courage is not the only virtue, but it's the only one that makes the other virtues possible." — Benjamin Netanyahu to Brian Lamb on C-SPAN's Washington Journal, Sept. 21, 2001

"One man with courage makes a majority." — Andrew Jackson, 1832

"God grants liberty only to those who love it, and are always ready to guard and defend it." — Daniel Webster (1834)

"The tree of liberty must be refreshed from time to time with the blood of patriots and tyrants. ... God forbid we should ever be twenty years without such a rebellion; what country can preserve its liberties if their rulers are not warned from time to time that their people preserve the spirit of resistance? Let them take arms." — Thomas Jefferson to William Stephens Smith, 1787

"War is an ugly thing, but not the ugliest of things. The decayed and degraded state of moral and patriotic feeling that thinks that nothing is worth war is much worse. The person who has nothing for which he is willing to fight, nothing which is more important than his own personal safety, is a miserable creature and has no chance of being free unless made and kept so by the exertions of better men than himself." — John Stuart Mill

"Live free or die." — Gen. John Stark, the hero of the battles of Bennington and Bunker Hill. Now the motto of the State of New Hampshire

"Guard with jealous attention the public liberty. Suspect everyone who approaches that jewel. Unfortunately, nothing will preserve it but downright force. Whenever you give up that force, you are ruined." — Patrick Henry, Virginia's Ratification convention, 1788

"Better to die on one's feet than to live on one's knees." — Mordechai Anielewicz, 1943, Warsaw Ghetto, Poland

"A society of sheep must in time beget a government of wolves." — Bertrand de Jouvenal

"When they took the 4th amendment away, I was quiet because I didn't deal drugs. When they took the 6th amendment away, I was quiet because I had never been arrested. When they took the 2nd amendment away, I was quiet because I didn't own a gun. Now they've taken away the 1st amendment, and all I can do is be quiet." — Fred Albury

"No man is entitled to the blessings of freedom unless he be vigilant in its preservation." — General Douglas MacArthur

"The spirit of resistance to government is so valuable on certain occasions, that I wish it to be always kept alive." — Thomas Jefferson to Abigail Adams, 1787

"I know not what course others may take but as for me: give me liberty or give me death!" — Patrick Henry

"Rebellion to tyrants is obedience to God." — John Bradshaw (1602-1659)

2. ATTACK!!!

The Right is really good at forcing the Right to incremental retreats and the measured surrender of compromise. Take up the Left's tactics and use those tactics against them! The *Bible* is full of examples where GOD gave Heavenly tactics to defeat GOD's enemies of the Left and Evil. Those who are too timid or too nervous to fight the Fight have no place in the Battle! This may sound cold and calculating to some, but those are the very ones who should not be the Right's leaders or soldiers in this *War*!

It has been sadly noted that when a Republican and a Democrat square off it's like Godzilla verses Bambi. They call us racists, sexists, homophobes, and otherwise selfish pigs and we call them... liberals. Who's going to win that argument?[677] The Battle for America *cannot* be won *without* a committed and sincere *BATTLE*! Contrary to Disney's animated movie, Evil is not defeated by the haphazard, lazy, unprepared, and unequipped Panda!

Here's how the Leftist strategist Chris Lehane explained his operating principle in fighting the Left's *War* Against GOOD:

> "Everyone has a game plan until you punch them in the mouth. So let's punch them in the mouth"[678].

---

[677] Horowitz, David; *Take No Prisoners: The Battle Plan For Defeating The Left*; pg. 109.

[678] Nagourney, Adam; The New York Times online; *Everyone Has a Game Plan Until You Punch them in the Mouth*; February 26, 2014.

Who's going to win that argument?! Who's going to Win that Battle?! Lehane is a self-righteous and unapologetic Leftist. Here is how even the Leftist publication *The New York Times* proudly describes Lehane:

> "He spent six years working in the Clinton White House, battling the ethical scandals that seemed to confront the administration every day — typically by **discrediting the accuser** or leaking a document to undercut an impending news story critical of the president or the first lady. Now Lehane uses similar strategies — opposition research, attention-grabbing **antics**, the **crafty manipulation** of old and new media... [Lehane] takes the relentless **molding of public opinion** and **scorching tactics** of the Clinton White House to a **new extreme**. This '**warrior mode**,' as Lehane calls it"[679]. (emphasis added)

Again, who's going to win the argument?! Who's going to Win that Battle?! Wake up Conservatives! This is not a simple "argument" without consequences, but a *War* for the very survival of what is GOOD and Right in America. A *War* for the very hearts, and yes *souls*, of *every* American!

3. Call Them *LIARS*!:

As thoroughly documented in the chapter *Lies, Lies, Lies!*, the Left survives only on *Lies* and deceit. The Right instead of calling the Left Liars when they Lie, Conservatives almost always resort to using almost indefinitive terms such as disingenuous, equivocate, not completely forthcoming, fabricate, not transparent, false narratives, fake news, et al. Conservatives even, and often, fall into the Leftist line against those few brave Conservatives who occasionally call a *Lie* a *Lie* like Congressman Joe Wilson which incident has previously been noted. Congressman Joe Wilson should have gotten the Congressional Medal of Honor!

The Left must be challenged *every* time that they *Lie*! Call them what they are: idiots, half-wits, liars, and thieves! The Right must focus

---

[679] Nagourney, Adam; The New York Times online; *Everyone Has a Game Plan Until You Punch them in the Mouth*; February 26, 2014.

with laser accuracy and in *unison* on the Left, as the Left has done in painting the Right as "the Party of the rich", etc. The Right must turn around the tactics of the Left against them. The difference is that the Right can do it while still being totally honest and forthright.

The Left uses words like "complex" to cover their *Lies*. "It's not what it seems, the situation is complex". For the Left making a cup of coffee can be described as "complex" if it suits their cover-up for the *Lies* that they regularly spew. The Right must go beyond simply pointing out the *Lie* and show how accepting that *Lie* has enormous *bad* consequences for all Americans! It is past time for those on the Right to grow a pair and *remove* those who refuse to also do so. Hand-wringing is nothing more than a symptom of a losing strategy! *Inaction is surrender and suicide!* To survive the Right *must* institute the Left's strategy of *Action, Action, Action*!

4. Challenge The Left's Labels:

It used to be the worst thing you could call someone was a Liberal. Now the Left has created new labels that in general most Americans do not understand and certainly most Americans misunderstand. The Left will self-identify with the label *Progressive*. As discussed in the chapters *The Progressive Face of The Left* and *Bait and Switch: The Re-Name-Game*, the Left's use of the term *Progressive* is nothing more than a reincarnation of a long list of Leftist characterizations such as Jacobin, Leftist, Communist, Marxist, Socialist, social justice, Luciferian, labor movement, and Liberal, among many others. We must educate the man on the street of the meaning and consequences of the Left behind their misleading labels and how it affects him and his family.

When the Left mislabels the Right we must also react, and react *strongly*! As an example, when the homosexual created and motivated "anti-bullying" campaign began, we should have had a campaign to expose the Evil behind their deceptive narrative. When the Left created the narrative that the Colorado abortion clinic shooting was the result of "incendiary language" of the Right's Pro-Life Movement, the Right should have risen in mass in protests, media assaults, lawsuits, and online attacks against this *Lie*! (Remember that what the

Left calls the "incendiary language" of the Right, the United States *U.S. Constitution* calls Free Speech.) When the Left said that the Right "targeted the Left" after the Gabby Giffords shooting, we should have flooded the media with targeting symbols. *Absurdum infimum* neutralizes nonsense!

The Left should be afraid of the backlash of the Right before they can launch their campaign of *Lies*! If the Right is not willing to counter the Left with at least as much vigor as the Left now exerts, then the Right has already lost the Battle for America!

5. USE *EMOTION*!:

The Right far too often relies on Common Sense, Logic, and Reasoning alone to Win the debate and Battle against Evil in general and the Left in particular. With some this will work, but as we have seen, not very often and not in large enough numbers. The Left has changed America and it's past time that the Right takes notice! Take a tactic out of the Left's playbook… USE EMOTION! Make American's FEEL and understand you really CARE about them! (Because we do!)

The Right can use emotion and still tell the reasoned truth. Truth without Emotion is flat and un-motivating. You wouldn't tell your wife, "you have to love me because it is the right thing to do". You *show* your wife that you love her with *demonstrations of emotion* and she responds positively, not because she "has to" or simply because it's "the right thing to do", but because she becomes *emotionally* vested in the marriage. Don't be fooled, emotion without the truth eventually is discovered. America must discover the emotional *Lies* that the Left uses to manipulate Americans for the Left's own advantage!

Remember this insightful axiom:

> *A person may not remember what you have said to them, but they will never forget how you made them feel!*

6. The age-old adage "if it feels good, it must be right" is a *Lie* of the Devil!:

The age-old adage "if it feels good, it must be right" is a *Lie* of the Devil!... But we *can* take what is Right and make it feel good! Generally people like to do the right thing. The euphemism "if it feels good do it!" is a Leftist contrived excuse to sin *Against GOD*. The Right must show the consequences of simply doing whatever "feels good". This Leftist mirage results in drug and sexual enslavement, broken homes and marriages, incarceration, mental illness, bankruptcy, abortions of unwanted babies, untethered morals, and ultimately... enslavement to the Left!

7. THE LEFT IS *NOT* ABOUT COMMON SENSE!:

How many times have you heard those on the Right claim that the actions on the Left "just don't make sense"? But of course, their actions make total sense to those who understand the Lefts motivations. The Left actions often make no sense according to the Left's publically stated goals, but their actions make total sense according to the Left's hidden agenda! The Right is just viewing the motivations of the Left, from the Right's perspective. The Right assumes the actions of the Left are with "good intentions" which from that tainted perspective the Left's actions appear to make absolutely no sense. Remember that the Left's holy book, *Rules for Radicals*, teaches the Left to hide its real motives of Evil!

Common Sense assumes that there are definitive lines between right and wrong. For the Left, right is wrong and wrong is right. This is the Orwellian double-speak by which the Left has mastered deceit. To engage the Left with Common Sense is a *fool's game*! The Left could care less about Common Sense as Common Sense opposes the goals of the Left!

The Left needs a permanent dependency class just to survive. The Left's biggest philosophical enemy is a Common Sense, free thinking, and independent individuals. The Left's "useful idiots" must intentionally suspend all rational thought and throw themselves into either an emotional frenzy or completely block all reasoned thought. These are the *Kookaphants* of the Left today!

The Left suffers from a form of *Evil Insanity*[680]! Anyone who expects the Left to possess or use Common Sense is suffering himself from a self-delusion. The Left is **rabidly emotional** in its missional zeal to destroy anything Right and Traditional in the foundational Judeo-Christian sense in America!

It is stunning the amount of times you can hear a pundit on the Right say with exasperation in his voice that the actions of the Left "just don't make sense". Until the Right gets a grip on the true nature of Evil which *senselessly* drives the actions of the Left, the Right will remain clueless and unarmed to Fight the Enemy of Left and Evil! As the saying goes: "It is what it is". So quit trying to make Sense out of the Left and their actions and *FIGHT*! Now grow up, get over it, quit whining, get into the Fight, and deal with it the way it is!

On what planet does any of the Left's "nonsense" make "sense" other than on the Leftist imaginary planet of Utopia? Utopia we know only exists in the minds of the deluded Left, or as Marx himself, and later Vladimir Lenin, called them the *useful idiots*! These are the *Kookaphants* of the Left today! For some of the Left's useful idiots the term "educated idiot" should actually be "educated stupid" (idiot can be fixed, stupid lacks that ability!) but the latter lacks a certain linguistic ring to it. An accumulation of knowledge does not make one smart; it is the ability to reasonably arrange knowledge for actionable intelligence that makes one wise! That wisdom is the very definition of Common Sense. By its very definition, an idiot is someone incapable of judging truth from fiction and imagination. The Left without question are collectively: nonsensical, insane, and *useful Idiots*!

8. Use Common Sense:

How do you generally tell if something is a *Lie*? You generally know it's a *Lie* if doesn't make "sense". Explain things using "Common Sense" when appealing to the masses. (As noted above, using Common Sense on frontline Leftists is a fool's game!)

---

[680] See the broader discussion of insanity in the chapter *The Left Is a RELIGION!*.

"Common Sense" emphasizes the individual, and the Left's "common good" emphasizes the State at the total exclusion of the individual! Common Sense is Law; common good is baseless and wildly flailing *emotion*! The "common good" has no immovable foundation and can therefore be redefined at will to advance the Leftist agenda. By definition you cannot "do good" in the name of the "common good", humanism, or any other non-Christian religion (including the Left's Religion of Evil), because ultimately, aside from GOD, there is *no good* and all attempts at "good" are self-centered, which the *Bible* defines as *self-righteousness*! Remember this quote from the *Bible* in the opening chapter: "For they being ignorant of GOD's righteousness, and going about to establish their own righteousness, have not submitted themselves unto the righteousness of GOD"[681]. GOD compares man's attempts to be *Righteous* outside of GOD, as works equivalent to "filthy rags"[682]… or a used, bloodied Kotex!

To the Left the phrase "that doesn't make sense" becomes irrelevant. Common Sense is steadfastly anchored in an immovable foundation based in GOD's Natural Laws and is the process which helps us analyze and discover untruths. It is a process that helps us tell if someone is telling us a *Lie*. If consecutive or sequencing statements don't make sense (Common Sense), we automatically and rightly deduce it as a *Lie*. It is a process by which we discover if something is the Truth or a *Lie*. It's what the *Bible* calls *reasoning* through[683]. (No wonder the Left is so rabidly and unreasonably opposed to reasoning!)

People instinctively recognize Common Sense as Truth. This is the moral behind the story *Emperor Has No Clothes* children's tale. When someone finally has enough courage, or in the case of the little child in this children's story just plain *Common Sense*, people recognize the *Lie* and change their minds and behavior accordingly. It's past time for the Right to start shouting the Common Sense that the Left's *Emperor Has No Clothes!*

---

[681] The *Holy Bible*: Romans 12:3.
[682] The *Holy Bible*: Isaiah 64:6.
[683] The *Holy Bible*: Isaiah 1:18.

Common Sense is generally the way to lead the uninformed from the Left and Evil, to the Right and GOOD. Common Sense as previously discussed must be properly seasoned with emotion to connect to the hearts of all Americans. Until the Right stops the fools-game of trying to use Common Sense on the Leftists and employ Common Sense with the masses, the Right cannot hope to influence a majority to the Right!

9. Sticks and Stones: Words matter! Words ARE Dangerous and *Deadly*!:

There has been a sustained effort to subtly rename the "Democrat Party" as the "Democrat*ic* Party". (Yes, it is registered as the Democratic Party but is done as a deception) Democrats themselves use "Democrat" as adjective which is a noun-as-adjective misuse of the word. The Left Stream Media consistently refers to this noun-as-adjective deception using the "Democrat*ic* Party". As though the Democrat*ic* Party is the sole upholder of a "democratically free society", when in fact the Democrat*ic* Party is *public enemy number one* to a free society! The Left does represent what Robespierre implemented as a "pure democracy"[684] which became known as the French *Reign of Terror*! We all know of the murder, and pain inflicted in the name of "pure democracy" in Robespierre's Revolutionary France. In this sense the Democrat Party is "democratic", but certainly *not* in the sense of democracy as colloquialized representing America's Constitutional Republic! The Right must begin to challenge the Left's word misrepresentations at every opportunity. Remember words do hurt... and eventually left unrestrained are *always* deadly!

Don't Play the Left's *Re-Name Game*. We absolutely *must* expose the Left's *Re-Names* and Call them what they are. For example, we can call Obamacare Abomination Care; The Dream Act is The Health Nightmare Act; Pro-Choice is Anti-Life Baby Killing; Democracy is Mob Rule; Anti-Bullying is Pedophilia; "Gay marriage" is Anti-Marriage. You get the point. We *cannot* allow the Left to use their word-games to deceive Americans and usurp control. This *Re-Name*

---

[684] See the discussion in the chapter: *Understanding The Battle*.

Game must be confronted at every opportunity! We *cannot* allow the Left to determine the battlefield and rules of engagement!

10. The Left Does NOT Play By the "Rules"… *Confront Lawlessness!*:

Obama said at least 25 times that he did not have the legal authority to simply sign an Executive Order to bypass Congress and the *U.S. Constitution* on dismissing deportation of illegal aliens. But that is exactly what Obama later did. The Left does not play by the rules. The Left is *lawless*! Anyone expecting the Left to stay within the confines of the law is delusional. Unless the Right is willing to stand up against the deceit of the Left's lawlessness America has no hope!

Pursue any and ALL legal avenues of prosecution against the Left in its breaking of the law! Thousands of Leftists have acted with total disregard of the law. Yet very few have *ever* seen prison time, or *any* consequences for that matter, for their crimes! Yet republicans are convicted of such heinous crimes as toe tapping under a bathroom stall partition! Prosecute the lawless like Hillary Rodham-Clinton for her illegal activities, such as the email crimes and treason, and *put them in prison*! Not acting only encourages other Leftists to higher and higher violations and crimes. If we do not stop this lawlessness in its tracks now, we have already lost the Battle!

11. Don't Play Their Game!:

As demonstrated in the 3rd Republican Presidential Debate of the 2016 election cycle, when the Right opposes, exposes, and attacks the Left's political games, the Right WINS! Go Trump!

12. Don't Play by the Left's Rules and Mandates!:

The Left's drumming home of "we must respect the office of the President" when it is a Democrat President is a *Lie* even they do not believe. It is interesting to note that this "rule" only applies to Leftist Presidents and is abandoned by the Left when there is a Republican President. As far as Christians go, we are under *no* Biblical obligation to respect a President who does the bidding of Evil! For this to be true it would be equally true that Christians would one day be required to "respect" the *Antichrist* even though the *Antichrist worships and is possessed by Satan*! The absurdity of this to any non-idiot is obvious. The Right's behavior should *never* be allowed to be mandated by the Left!

Quit letting the Left tell us what we must do and how we must act! It is *all* a trap! *We* define what we must do and how we must act by the mandates of GOD and GOOD! Our actions should be guided by Right and not Wrong!

13. Racism is a Leftist/Democrat Manifestation:

The Democrats in the 60's were the racists who fought against black civil rights. Democrat Robert Byrd of West Virginia who was a US Representative and US Senator was the former Grand Wizard of the Ku Klux Klan! The Democrats today are the racists! The Left practices total degradation of minorities, especially blacks, through Leftist/Democrat promoted programs! Former Vice President and über-Left Democrat Joe Biden is a racist! Biden was amazed that there even was a black man who was clean and could speak proper English. Of course, Biden was talking about Obama in 2008. Democrats are the last true racists! It was almost solely the Republicans in the 1960's whose leadership was responsible for the ultimate passing of the Civil Rights Act of 1964. Today the Democrats are Masters (Yes as in Plantation Masters!) at giving minorities lip-service while working to destroy them through policies and Nazi-like pogroms that keep minorities under their thumbs and in the ghettos! It is no coincidence that the word Ghetto was originally used by the Nazis as the name of the neighborhood where the Nazis forced the Jews before packing them up for concentration camps and exterminating them! Welfare, Food Stamps, abortion, and even "free" cell phones are the trinkets by which the Left controls and subjugates minorities. Uncle Toms like Jesse Jackson, Louis Farrakhan, and Al Sharpton sell out the black community into perpetual poverty for their own gain.

The Right wants to free minorities by giving them training and jobs so that they can support themselves with dignity. President Abraham Lincoln was the first Republican President of the United States. Lincoln went to war with the predominately Democrat controlled South to free the slaves! Yet somehow many believe that Republicans are the racists. Republicans have been afraid to challenge this Leftist created propaganda. The age-old adage "sticks and stones may break my bones but names will never hurt me" is a *Lie* straight out of the Pit of Hell, and the Right had better wake up and start using Battle words of their own!

14. Clearly Illustrate Your Points with Relatable Story Images (Reagan):

President Ronald Reagan was a master at relating issues with real-life stories. This has become a lost art in communicating the message of the Right. We must learn to relate the impact of political decisions Left and Right upon the common man. Without this emotional appeal people *cannot* connect themselves with the issues of the day.

15. Make the Leftists Answer to the Point:

Make the Left answer to the point! The Left when it does not want to be accountable for their stands and actions, they simply refuse to answer to the question by changing the subject and/or talking over the point and the Conservative! America when confronted with the hidden truth of the Left will reject them and their beliefs and actions every time.

We must learn to instantly recognize and publicly refute the tactic and bring them immediately back and make them publicly accountable for their beliefs and actions!

16. Take Back Our Churches:

Christians need to take back our churches and kick out the heretics! It may violate the IRS code to promote a politician by party, but as most people are ignorant, Conservatives in churches can promote a candidate for being *Right* and out a politician for being *Left*, or *Wrong*! If we must give up the Leftist inspired bobble of the Church's non-profit tax deduction to retain our Country and ultimately our freedom… so be it! It's a small price to pay for GOD and Freedom!

The Right has been cowered by the Left though the media, Church heretics, academia elites, and even in seminaries to believe that we must accept all people regardless of their opposition to GOD and GOOD. The Left simply and continuously espouses Evil presumptions so often that they simply become accepted as "truth" in the Church, which of course is what Hitler called the Big *Lie* which is a *Lie* that if repeated long and forcefully enough it becomes accepted as truth. Fight back hard and continuously against the Big *Lie* of the Left *Against GOD*'s churches!

Our Churches belong to GOD! We as Christians are the stewards of GOD's Church and churches! The Left is the *Enemy* of GOD! So *what* makes us cower in submission before the Left and Evil?! What makes us think that anything that the Left does in relation to Christianity and the Church is not an attempt to neutralize and destroy GOD's Church? The Left demands that Christians accept Feminism, homosexuality, Gay "marriage", homosexual membership and leadership, and many other evils in GOD's Church. Why? As in Nazi Germany, the churches in America today are the first and last bastions of defense and vanguards Against Evil and the takeover of the Left. Hitler had to first destroy all of the Church's influence before he could usurp total control over Germany. Likewise, the Left today must *destroy* the churches before the Left can usurp total control over America! We either take back our churches or we surrender America to Evil! As for me and my house, we will serve the LORD[685]!

17. Use the Hitler/Nazi Analogy Often as it Best Reflects the Tactics, Ideology, and Actions of the Left:

The Left constantly uses the Hitler/Nazi analogy against the Right, but screams bloody murder if it is ever used against them. Why?... because, me thinks she doth protest too much! The Left is *always* guilty of what it accuses the Right of doing! Hitler and Nazism are Leftist manifestations. The only "difference" between Nazism then and the Left in America today is the Nazis were Nationalists and the Left in America today are Globalists. It is a difference without any real distinction!

In the very least sense, employing the Hitler/Nazi accusation against the Left disarms and neutralizes the Left's use of the bastardized terms. Overuse colloquializes and neutralizes terms. In the strongest

---

[685] The *Holy Bible*, Joshua 24:15.

sense, Nazism and Fascism are manifestations of the Left and the Left *must* be properly identified and defined as such!

18. K.I.S.S.! (Keep It Simple Stupid!):

The *Bible* tells us that all GOD relates to humanity through His Word is *simple* and only Evil uses complexity to confuse, manipulate, and subdue mankind[686]. The message of the Right, to be authentic, must be *simple*. Simple enough for a child to understand![687]

The law of Occam's Razor, in Latin *lex parsimoniae*, says: "The simplest solution is most often the correct one". Occam's razor is the philosophical law of simplicity. Additives, assumptions, and complications tend to corrupt and lead us away from the truth. *Lex* is Latin for the English word *law*. The English word *parsimony* is derived through the Latin *parsimoniae* which Webster's tell us means: "economy in the use of means to an end; *especially*: economy of explanation in conformity with Occam's razor"[688]. **Language matters**! The Left always confounds and confuses with its language "tricks" using its *Re-Name-Game*. If words do not have *absolute* meaning, if everything is relative, if there is no *absolute* truth, then nothing can make sense. Confusion is the work of Evil and the Left! Simplicity is the work of GOD and the Right!

19. Demonize the Enemy!

The Left will chastise us that the Right should never use "personal attacks", yet this is at the heart of the Left's tactics against the Right. However, it is the Left that is personally associated with Evil! Remember that the Left credits Lucifer, the head demon, as their foremost radical! We **MUST** identify, and quite literally, demonize the Left and clearly identify the Left's associations with Evil. It is imperative that Americans learn to recognize Evil, and the Left as they represent Evil. After all, it is the Left who uses demonology in claiming Lucifer as their power and inspiration. How can the right be fearful of "demonizing" an Enemy who claims themselves as demon empowered?!

---

[686] The *Holy Bible*, 2 Corinthians 11:3.
[687] The *Holy Bible*, Mark 10:14.
[688] www.merriam-webster.com/dictionary/parsimonies.

20. Be Positive!

Be Optimistic! Ronald Reagan's "Morning In America" speech inspired Americans to believe in America's inspired foundations. We too must again inspire Americans to believe in America's "City On A Hill" status for the world to aspire to. America is exceptional! We *must* be positive in our message that we *can* Win the War Against the Left and its innate Evil. The Left is depressive in its outlook for the future.

According to the Leftist mantra, *everything* is going to destroy civilization as we know it... Global Warming, Climate Change, environmental disasters, guns, processed food, salt, pollution, Right-Wing "incendiary language", talk radio, high-power electric lines, cell phone radiation, microwaves, the list goes on and on.

The Right can offer hope through a positive message because we have already been there and done that! The Right's message is time proven. So be positive and Win America!

21. Combat the Leftist Contrived Euphemism of the "Separation of Church and State":

The Leftist contrived euphemism of the "Separation of Church and State" is a guise to destroy the Christian influence on government until the State has amassed enough power to destroy Christianity itself in America. This is *exactly* the same guise Hitler used in Nazi Germany! Of course Hitler did not begin by revealing his ends which was the extermination of 7 million Christians and would have accelerated if Hitler had not been defeated. (See the chapter: *Fascism and the Left in America: Kindred Spirits and Familiar Bedfellows*.) The supposed "separation" only goes one way. While the Church is ordered to stay *totally* out of government this has now been extended by the Left to all public displays of Christianity. However, the Left is free to interfere in every way with the Church and Christians public and private. (Remember Hitler first brought the German Church under Nazi State control, then went in and removed the crosses and *Bible*s and replaced them with swastikas and *Mein Kompf*, then murdered all the Christians!)

22. Be *BOLD!* Unabashed!

Take a lesson from President Donald Trump. Americans want someone who is unabashed and angry at the Left's taking away our Country! Trump called a reporter "dishonest" to his face in an interview. Trumpism: if Donald Trump has taught us anything it is: *DON'T PLAY BY THE LEFT'S RULES*! Be BOLD, Be Angry, Be Anti-P.C., PUNCH BACK *harder*, Be Confrontational Against the Leftist Media! Trump also unabashedly espouses Conservative ideals without calling himself a Conservative, thus avoiding the negative connotations that the Left has spent decades demonizing. Reagan was successful because he was bold in his defiance of the Left. Regan demanded in the face of an enemy armed with nuclear weapons: Mr. Gorbachev, TEAR DOWN THIS WALL! And they did! Americans and the world respond when Right American leaders vehemently stand up for what is Right!

23. OWN IT!

Say it like it is and STICK to it! The Right *must* confront Evil. To defund Planned Parenthood, let the Left shut down the government and then use both barrels to blame them for what in fact *the Left* has done. Boehner is a Leftist who stonewalled passing a budget defunding Planned Parenthood. Get rid of the Leftist leadership from the Republican Party. Americans want the Right to own their agenda. Nobody wants a whining and apologetic Party that always apologizes for their convictions. Say what you mean and mean what you say! Own It!

The Right is anti-Obamacare… own it! Don't back down, let the Left shut down the government if necessary. If the government must be shut down do it in a way that makes the Democrats obviously responsible! The same can be said of many other issues. The Right needs do the Right thing and make sure that Americans know that the Democrats are responsible for the Wrong thing! It's time the Right got a backbone and a brain! No more Cowardly Lions and Brainless Scarecrows in The Republican Party! Eliminate and replace the moderates who draw back from what is Right! Even Ronald Reagan, the author of the Republican 11th Commandment, threatened to personally fund and campaign against any fellow non-standard bearer Republican that were RINOs (Republicans In Name Only). Own It! And those who won't, eliminate and replace them with Conservatives who will!

24. Public Debates and Winning the Uncommitted:

Quit wasting time trying to convince committed Leftists they are Wrong and convert them. Well over 99.999999% of the time you cannot convince a Leftist of the Right. Even if you can get them to see the Right and Wrong of an issue they simply do not care. Concentrate on the "middle-ground" people. For example, the Right-minded Koch brothers donated 25 million dollars to a NY hospital and the nurse's union demanded that the hospital give the money back, regardless of the good that could have been done for people, simply because the Koch brothers are on the Right side of politics. Committed Leftists are only interested in the Leftist cause. Period!

Use Public Debates to Convince the Uncommitted! Public debates should concentrate not on converting the Leftist, but on convincing the uncommitted as to the Evil, Evil intentions, and terrifying consequences of the Left's agenda! The committed Leftist has already sold his soul to Evil. Leave the conversion of those sold-out to Evil to preachers and evangelists. Win the winnable!

25. Persuade the Audience NOT the Leftist!:

In general terms you cannot debate the Left as a debate assumes a basis of logic, reason, and truth. The Left uses *Lies*, deception, and emotion. The mistake of most political debates is that the person of the Right tries to win over the Leftist opponent rather than represent the Right to the audience. The goal of the Right in a debate should be to persuade the audience and not the Left's representative! The audience needs to be shown that all the Left has to offer is ridicule, failed policy, and *Lies*! The "hope" of the Left needs to be exposed as "hopelessness"! The Utopian illusion needs to be exposed for the smoke and mirrors being manipulated by the man behind the curtain!

26. The Law of Diminishing Returns:

Concentrate on the reachable and quit trying to reach the unreachable. The Right has for too long tried to reach the unreachable. We have spent vast amounts of money and resources on trying to convert the unconvertible. We need to focus on the marginal masses who do not understand the delusion of the Leftist Utopia for which they have fallen and been enslaved. We need to first forge a solid majority and then build upon that solid foundation. Mass education can only occur once you are in the majority!

Living the Leftist delusion is like having your mind enslaved in the Utopian fantasy world of *The Matrix*, while your body exists in the real world but is totally disconnected from this reality. Some find the Utopian Fantasy-world so compelling that even if they were to be made aware of the illusion, they would refuse to even recognize the self-deception. Many on the Left live today in a self-indulgent and delusional Leftist mindset and refuse to be interrupted with reality. These are the Leftist Faithful, the unmovable 15%, who have sold their minds to Evil and are for the most part unredeemable. The Right needs to concentrate on the vast majority of Americans who are still redeemable. It is through this group through which America can once again rise up again from the ashes and once again become the Great Shinning City on the Hill.

27. Use the *Logical* Conclusion For Leftist Ideals: *Reductio ad absurdum:*

There are many techniques by which to Battle the Left. One such technique is *reductio ad absurdum* which is Latin for "reducing [the opponent's argument] to absurdity". Here is how it is defined by Wikipedia:

> "*Reductio ad absurdum* is the technique of reducing an argument or hypothesis to absurdity, by pushing the argument's premises or conclusions to their logical limits and showing how ridiculous [or disastrous] the consequences would be, thus disproving or discrediting the argument."

The Left likes to pretend that it is possible to live in the unproven or the theoretical world of their collective utopian imagination. However, as we all learn by practical experience, Never-Never Land does not exist and it never-never will exist! All those who would attempt to reproduce Hollywood's fanciful flight of Peter Pan's pixie dust induced flight by launching themselves off a building would be quickly introduced to the practical world reality of the hard ground... no matter how many happy thoughts they can muster!

The Right, as expressed through Conservativism, demands the accountability of the government to the people, whereas Leftism demands the accountability of the people to the government! William Blackstone, author of the most comprehensive law reference books *Blackstone's Commentaries*, states the underlying truth of governments thirst for power, "power, when undefined, soon becomes unlimited"[689]. The law for Leftists is that there are no limits. The Right always wants less for the government and the Left always demands more. With Leftism subjection of the people and totalitarianism is inevitable! These are the realities of the logical conclusion that must be related in everyday, understandable, simple language that reaches Americans at their gut level!

28. *REFUSE* to Comply!

When the US Supreme Court issued its edict of "legalized abortion" Alexander Solzhenitsyn, an immigrated Soviet dissident refugee, asked the obvious question of Americans, "Why did you not refuse to comply?"! Solzhenitsyn asked himself the question "Resistance! Why didn't you resist?" speaking of arrests of dissidents in the former Soviet Union. We cheered the lone resister in Tiananmen Square who on June 5, 1989 stood singlehandedly before a column of Communist Chinese tanks. This one man stood in defiance of the Leftist régime's brutal crackdown on the Freedom movement and against the Chinese Leftist oppression and suppression. Why then do we hesitate to cheer those who today stand to defy the Leftist takeover of America?! And some who claim to be Right even dare to criticize those who would

---

[689] Blackstone, Sir William, St. George Tucker, Edward Christian; *Blackstone's Commentaries: With Notes of Reference, to the Constitution and Laws, of the Federal Government of the United States, and of the Commonwealth of Virginia*; 1803; pg. 154.

make a stand against the Evil of the Left. Better yet, why are *you* not standing in defiance of the Leftist implementation of their Evil Empire yourself?! Even better yet: Why are *you* not leading a charge of fellow Rightists against the Left and the Gates of Hell?! This is what GOD applauds! This is what GOD calls *Faith*! The *Faith* that moves GOD to act! The *Faith* that removes the mountains of Evil.

This is clearly a GOD-given absolute when the *Bible* commands us to, "Resist the devil and he will flee from you"[690]! The Left always acts as the rebel in refusing to uphold the law, so why then when the Left rewrites the law and renders the law unconstitutional and Anti-GOD, does the Right cow down and follow an UnConstitutional and unGODly law?!

Alexander Solzhenitsyn: When we ask, "How could this happen?", we cannot do anything better than quote Alexander Solzhenitsyn, who said of the cruel rise of brutal and tyrannical communism in his native land, "We have forgotten God. That's why all this has happened." To comply with the Left is to be complicit in the Evil of the Left! We need to refuse to comply with the UnConstitutional and UnGODly usurpation of power by the Left!

29. Moderates:
So called Republican "Moderates" make Conservatives as a whole look and sound *schizophrenic*! There is no such thing as a "moderate". (See larger discussion earlier in this chapter under section *Compromise Kills*!) Claiming to be a moderate is like saying about your marriage: As far as marriage goes, I'm Conservative on financial matters and Liberal on the whole monogamy thing". Not only will your friends look at you a little crazy, but when your spouse finds out you will not have a marriage, or worse (remember Lorena Bobbitt!). Conservative and Liberal, Right and Left, are *irreconcilable* and *incompatible*!

---

[690] The *Holy Bible*; James 4:7.

Moderates are RINOs: Republicans In Name Only. Literally "moderate" means compromised with Evil! Compromising with the Left is *literally* making a *Deal With the Devil*! A "moderate" cannot exist. How does one moderately become compromised with Evil and still remain on the Right? It simply cannot happen. Moderates are nothing more than a Leftist parading as a Conservative! RHINOs like former Senator John McCain[691] and Senator Lindsey Graham have been Leftists who like the military. So were the Nazis! RHINOs like former Senator McCain and Lindsey Graham[692] were Leftists who supported crony-capitalism. So were the Nazis! McCain was a decorated war hero. Being a war hero does not necessarily qualify one as a Conservative or a good politician. Hitler was a decorated war hero! What makes one a Conservative is full adherence to Right issues and corresponding Right actions!

Again, some things are worth repeating, "In time liberalism [Leftism] remakes conservatism in its own image by forcing it to give up everything distinctive for the sake of consensus". Again, compromising with the Left is *literally* making a *Deal With the Devil*! Politicians like former Senator McCain and Senator Graham have often been referred to by the Left Stream Media as "consensus" minded politicians. Fundamentally, they were either mindless oafs or they are being intentionally deceitful.

Most so-called Republican "moderates", such as former Senator John McCain, are nothing more than Leftist Nationalists as opposed to the Leftist Globalists of the Democrat Party. The primary differentiation is that the Republican "moderates" believe in a militarily strong Leftist America whereas Democrats believe in a strong One World Leftist Utopia, a distinction without a meaningful difference in *The Left's War Against GOD!*

A Republican who claims to be a fiscal Conservative and a social Liberal is just trying to be on both sides of the fence at the same time,

---

[691] For specific examples of the dangers of "moderates" see the discussion of McCain's appearance on the *Ellen DeGeneres Show* in the chapter: *Legislating Morality*.

[692] Senator Lindsey Graham has veered greatly to the Right since McCain's death. It begs the question if Graham was overly influenced by the Leftist tendencies of McCain?

using the Right while whoring around with the Left. (Those of us who have seen someone or experienced coming down with one leg on either side of the fence know what a painful experience that can be! A that's how painful we need to make "moderates"!) By its very definition: A moderate is a *schizophrenic*[693]. That is, moderates are *insane* in holding conflicting and irreconcilable beliefs. The self-labeled "moderate" Republican is just a chameleon, either self-deluded or a Leftist with evil political intentions masquerading as a Conservative! This is why, ultimately you cannot trust a so-called "moderate" because you can never tell what side of any issue that they will come down on. It's like being able to trust a double-agent, you never know where their loyalties truly lay, and when you figure it out you may already be dead! This is also why "moderates" are always changing their positions because they have no moral anchor to keep them from jumping ship. An "R" behind a politician's name does not necessarily make him a Conservative. However, a "D" behind a politician's name virtually assures his alignment with the Left. Have you ever noticed that there are no "moderate" Democrats? The Democrats are too smart for that as they understand that a "moderate" Democrat would be wholly untrustworthy and unreliable in the Left's quest in *the Left's War Against GOD!*

The Right must Expose and Depose all so-called Republican "moderates"! We must Expose them as Leftist infiltrators and depose them from leadership. Ann Coulter cuts to the chase: "Moderate Republican' is simply how the [Leftist] blabocracy flatters Republicans who vote with the Democrats".[694]

30. People Are Convinced to the Right By Either *Compassion* (a form of love) or *Fear*. USE BOTH: The Right is a friend of the people and the Left is to be *feared*:

The *Bible* tells us that people are either motivated by *Compassion*, a form of love, or *Fear*[695]. Conservatives must use both in our campaign

---

[693] Mayo Clinic defines *schizophrenia* as: A brain disorder in which people interpret reality abnormally.
[694] Coulter, Ann; Slander: *Liberal Lies About the American Right*; 2003; pg. 15.
[695] The *Holy Bible*, Jude 1:22-23.

Against the Evil of the Left. Americans must have a feeling of Compassion from the Right and Fear of the Left.

Unfortunately, the concept of "Compassionate Conservatism" has been adulterated by Leftist Republicans like George W. Bush. Compassion from Conservatives was redefined as compromise to Leftist ideals. True *Compassion* is the opposite of compromise with the Left. *Compassion* is understanding the evils of the Left and helping people to understand and escape the inevitable evil consequences of Leftism. (see above discussion: Use the Logical Conclusion For Leftist Ideals: *Reductio ad absurdum*)

The American people must also *Fear* Leftism. The Right must educate the people to the evils of the Left. The Left parades as compassionate, but is the opposite in its quest to subjugate all Americans under its totalitarian régime that they euphemistically refer to as a Utopian Paradise on earth. *Fear* and *Compassion* are the two necessary compelling means in Winning the Battle for the American minds and hearts!

31. Organize, ORGANIZE, ORGANIZE!
Fight fire with Fire! It lets Americans of like mind know that they are not alone, but the real majority and gives them strength to stand up on their own!
> Organize locally, State-wide, and Nationally
> Organize Online Protestors
> Organize Boycotts
> Organize Public Protests
> Organize Resistance Movements
> Organize, Organize, ORGANIZE!

32. Never "Negotiate" with the Left:
Negotiation is *NOT* a weapon of any positive effect in the Right's arsenal against the Left. All that negotiation accomplishes is surrender in increments! Negotiation *assumes* compromise[696]. Negotiation also

---

[696] See broader discussion in the chapter *Fighting To WIN!: How Do We Fight The War? The Right's RULES FOR ANTI-RADICALS! A Call To ACTION!* and the subcategories: *Compromise Kills!* and *Moderates:*.

assumes that both parties are honest and reasoned arbiters of the truth. Otherwise what we have seen virtually every time is when the Left and Right making promises of compromise, supposedly towards the "middle", only later the Right will fulfill its commitments and the Left will *always* weasel its way out of fulfilling its commitments! *Always!* In addition, the Left later *always* uses any compromise against the Right. Remember George H. W. Bush's compromise on his "no new taxes" pledge? The Left lured Bush into a compromise and later turned it around on Bush and used it to end Bush's political career! Countless players on the Right have been lured into the "compromise" trap and always with devastating consequences. Remember Neville Chamberlain and his "compromise" with Hitler? How'd that work out for him? Negotiation with the Left always leads to compromise and self-destruction!

33. The Science is Clear Nazi Straw Man:
We must confront the deception of the Science Is Clear strawman. As discussed elsewhere, the Nazis were emphatic that the Science was clear on a myriad of deceptions including the Life Unworthy of Life and the Nazis Final Solution of killing all Christians and Jews in the world. The Left in America today uses the same Nazi tactic in persuading Americans of their Leftist and Evil agenda. The Right must confront the Left on its *Lies* when they use the Science Is Clear arguments. Climate Change, abortion, the unreality of GOD and the *Bible*, are just a few examples where the Right must challenge the Left with *real* Scientific Facts! We must educate ourselves in the real scientific facts and viciously engage the Left and expose them for their cloaked Nazi agenda. The Right cannot Win without total engagement Against the *Lies* of the Left.

34. Unified Front:
There must be a unified front of the Right against the Left. Just as in conventional warfare, not all of your allies will be in total harmony on every philosophical belief. But the enemy of our enemy is our friend. In the 1980's the Moral Majority united religious groups that had various conflicting theologies but could agree on basic moral issues in defense of the American way of life. It was effective because their common enemy was Evil.

Conservatives Win when they use the tactics of the Democrats and unite without compromising for a stated unifying *common* cause. The Contract with America from over 300 Republican candidates was wildly successful in 1994 in electing a majority of US House of Representatives for the first time in more than 40 years! Why? Because the Conservatives were united in their Fight Against the Left. President Ronald Reagan threatened to campaign against any US Senator who did not fall into step with the Conservative Republican agenda and forced unity of Republicans. Unity in the public eye is necessary for Victory. Let's get United!

35. The Individual Verses the State:
The Right is about the individual, whereas the Left is about the collective community in creating the Leftist Utopian Paradise or the "Village" as Hillary Rodham-Clinton defines it. The Right strives to empower the individual and the Left strives to empower the State. Constantly emphasize the difference between the Democrats who want the State to run Americans' lives, and the right who believes that the individual should run his own life!

36. Quit Holding Our Own To A Perfect Standard:
It has become the common sacrament of the Left to intentionally act in *Wrong* ways and simply apologize after the fact and the Left Stream Media uses the apology as cover for their actions. The apology is always enough for the Leftists. How many recent headlines attest to this fact? However, no such cover is accorded for any on the Right. No matter how genuinely remorseful the Right is, the Left-Wing uses it as an opportunity to demean and destroy their opponents on the Right. Leftist Congressman Barney Frank's homosexual boyfriend Stephen Gobie, whom Frank first had hired as a male prostitute, ran a homosexual prostitution ring out of Frank's own basement. Frank apologized and serves for another two decades as a Democrat leader in the US Congress. Whereas a Republican Congressman accidently taps his shoe against another man's shoe under an airport bathroom stall and the Left runs him out of office in disgrace. Barack Hussein Obama details how he ate dogs in Indonesia and is applauded for his candor by the Left-Wing, while Obama excoriates Mitt Romney for

strapping a dog carrier to the top of his SUV to take his dog on vacation with him. The Left Stream Media joins the chorus against Romney totally ignoring Obama's eating dogs!

Alinsky laid down the Leftist mechanism over 30 years ago on how to hold the Right to humanly unattainable standards and thereby destroy those on the Right making them seem at the least hypocritical, "The fourth rule is: Make the enemy live up to their own book of rules. You can kill them with this, for they can no more obey their own rules than the Christian church can live up to Christianity". (Notice that even Alinsky draws a connection between the Right and "Christianity".) The *Bible* makes it clear that GOD instituted the Laws of the Old Testament in order to show humanity that no one was capable of living up to those standards and could only achieve GOD's standards vicariously through Jesus' perfect life[697] as GOD on earth. So Conservatives for GOD's sake, *stop* trying to make those on the Right live up to what even GOD calls unattainable standards! I am not suggesting that the Right never judge their own as the Left does. What I am suggesting is that *the Right stop eating their own*! The Right needs to circle the wagons when our own come under attack from the Left. This has been a trick of Evil and the right must stop falling prey to the tactics of the Left!

The next time the Left mounts a campaign to castigate someone on the Right for falling short of a perfect standard, the Right *must* in unison start listing equal and worse instances by Democrats for whom the Left *never* called for equal, or any punishment. Throw the hypocrisy of the Left back into their faces and deny them their victory!

We must also remember that this is an effective way for the Left to both silence the Right and strike fear into the hearts of those on the Right to ever even consider speaking out against the Left. Why should we on the Right ever cower in fear and silence over the Left trying to hold the Right accountable for what the Left finds a horrifying standard to which they would never be held accountable! No one on the Right is perfect and it is high time to stop playing into the hands on Evil and the Left. The hypocrisy here is totally with the Left and

[697] The *Holy Bible*: Acts 15:10; Romans 3:19-20; Galatians 5:18.

their hypocrisy must be shouted from the mountain tops at every opportunity! The Left simply cannot hold someone accountable to a standard to which they themselves refuse to be held accountable!

CONCLUSION:

The panic that the publication of this material will instill in the Left is predicable. It is the equivalent of flashing the Cross in the face of Dracula, the *lord of the damned*, who is personification of Evil in American folklore. The Left can ignore this book (The greatest trick the Devil ever pulled was convincing the world he didn't exist.), they can ridicule it as a misguided fantasy, or most likely attack some obscure or irrelevant part. To be sure the Left will never willingly debate the truth of these issues openly nor will the Left discuss the premises of the blood-tie and blood-oath of the brotherhood between the Left and Evil.

We can take an historical lesson in War from Alexander the Great who was arguably the greatest military strategist the world has ever known. Alexander against Persia in the Battles of Granicus, Issus, and Gaugamela allowed the Persian armies to take the battlefield first, then when the Persians were set in their position, Alexander would exploit the weaknesses of the Persian defenses and easily win the victory. The Left has set itself in Battle Against the Right. We must exploit their obvious weaknesses and Win the victory! If those on the Right are not even willing to Fight with our natural advantage, the Battle will remain lost.

Alexander always fought the Persians with a notable numerical disadvantage in troop size. We on the Right have allowed our troop numbers to be whittled away to a significant disadvantage, but unlike Alexander we have GOD on our side, GOD Who is, or at least should be, the Captain and Power of the Right's Army. GOD not only leads and empowers the Right's battles, but provides military intelligence to His troops. The problem of course is that the Right in large part has refused to see this Battle as an actual Battle of *the Left's War Against GOD!*

The spiritual and the natural (political) dimensions of this War must both be acknowledged and enjoined by the Right. By stealth the Left already employs both! For the Right, one without the other renders the Battle futile at best. The Right has been shamed by the Left into abandoning the necessity of GOD's presence in the Fight. The Left's decades-long campaign in America to remove GOD from the public conversation has effectively *disarmed* the Right. This Leftist strategy in suppressing GOD's influence in America is intentional and well planned in *the Left's War Against GOD!* If we are to Win the Fight, we must Fight to Win! Equivocating, compromise, and inaction are formulas for absolute and abysmal defeat! Unfortunately for decades these have been the long-held losing strategies of the Right against the onslaught of the Left. The Battle *Against* the Right has been death by a thousand cuts which in large part have been either unanswered, or at best apologetically and shamefully answered. It's far past time for the Right to stand up Against the Left and Fight Hell-fire with GOD's all-consuming Fire and take back America and Win this Battle!

25. RULES FOR ANTI-RADICALS: SPECIFIC WAR STRATEGIES:

Chapter 25

1. **Call the Left what *They Are!*** Call the Left what *They Are*: *Liars*, Intolerant, Bigots, Racists, Nazis, Fascists, Baby Butcherers, Hetero-Phoebes, Thieves, Psychopaths, Insane, Nonsensical, Irrational, Schizophrenic, and especially... Evil! Make it plain and simple. Expose the Left for who they *really* are! The Right has been cowed into timidity which stops us from calling the Left by the names which represent the reality of the Left's Evil. If we don't call them what they *are*... who will?! This is why Americans in-mass don't see the Left as Liars, Bigots, Racists, etc. If we don't identify the Left to America for what they really are, Americans will not see them for who they really are! This is particularly true of what has been aptly called the "low information voter". For example, *don't* use indistinct half-terms like "disingenuous"... call them *Liars*! How many Americans can even define "disingenuous"? The term "disingenuous" is ambiguous at best and undefinable at worst. The same can be said of all the half-terms that the Right has been cowed into using by the Left. This is why many Americans don't identify the Left for the Evil that defines the Left.

   For example: The Left screams that the Right are "bigots". If you Google "bigot" the definition is "a person who is intolerant toward those holding different opinions". "Intolerance of those holding a different opinion" absolutely defines the Left! The Left ARE the bigots!

   We on the Right *must* realize that no matter the language that we use the Left will hate and attack us. So *quit* attempting to not offend the Left!!! The Left will not be satisfied until the Right is absolutely and totally silenced! So quit worrying about how the Left and the Left's Media

Machine will react and label us! (Newsflash.... The Left already calls us those names!) What the Left calls us will *never* be GOOD! Call the Left what they *really* are and in absolute, *unequivocal* terms so that Americans can see the Evil of the Left!

2. **QUIT APOLOGIZING!**
The Right *must* Quit Apologizing for being Right! The Left cows the Right at every turn and effectively neutralizes the Right by continually demanding that the Right apologize for its make-believe "offenses" against the Left. That is as nonsensical and suicidal a behavior as imaginable in a *War*! Start standing up for what is Right and demand that the Left apologize for its Evil: bigotry, *Lies*, corruption, infanticide, eugenics, racism, and every other sin for which the Left is guilty!!!

3. **Oppose and Remove UnConstitutional Judges!** Oppose *all* Leftist Judge Appointments by *all* legal means at our disposal! Remove Leftist judges for unConstitutional activities. Hold them to their own unattainable standards!

4. **Protest Loud, Often, and in Mass!** This tactic has been amazingly successful for the Left in silencing the Right and it should be turned around against the Left. Protest must be *loud* and *in their face*. Pay protesters! Protest in front of Leftist judges, activists, organizations, and politicians' homes and offices. Protest in mass in front of Leftist organizations like Planned Parenthood, TV stations, ACLU, NAACP, Daily Kos, Fact Check, *et al.* Send Letters to constituents alert them of the Leftist actions and remedies to remove the judges, discredit the activists, and vote out the politicians! Get Leftist donor lists of the Left and protest in front of their homes and businesses and print them online and in newspapers!

5. **Boycott!** American patriots *must* hit the Left's businesses, organizations, and leaders *in their pocketbooks*! Money

talks and blood-money funds the Left's crimes *Against* America. We *must* organize and unanimously support boycotts against the Left's organizations, businesses, and funding centers. We *must* boycott companies that donate to and support Leftist causes like Planned Parenthood, United Nations front groups, "Environmentalist" front groups, Climate Change, Tides Foundation and Tides Center, Ford Foundation, Rockefeller Foundation, EMILY's List, American Civil Liberties Union, Democrats and the Democrat Party, various illegal "immigrant" organizations, pro-abortion organizations, anti-Israel and pro-Arab/Palestinian organizations, many "education" organizations, etc., etc., many of which are covert front groups masquerading as non-Leftist organizations. If you support businesses that support Evil… You support Evil! If you vote for politicians who support Evil…You support Evil! If you donate to politicians and organizations that support Evil… You support Evil! We must interrupt and extinguish the funding sources of the Left!

Boycotts work! In 2015 Macy's closed 36 stores and eliminated over 4,500 positions. Was it due to "unseasonably warm weather and lower spending by international tourists" or was it due primarily to Donald Trump calling for a Macy's boycott and to cut up Macy's credit cards? We must replicate this across the Left's corporate and business concerns! Bankrupt the Left and take away their ability to propagate their evil!

We must also disrupt and expose these Leftists and Leftist organizations. They simply must no longer be allowed to do "business as usual"!

6. **Put Leftist Traitors on Trial!** The Left is seldom, if ever, held accountable for their crimes. This must end. Obama, the Clintons, Pelosi, Reed, and all of the others must be made accountable and examples that Americans will *not*

tolerate the systematic destruction of America perpetuated by the UnConstitutional and illegal actions of the Left! Prosecute the Leftist criminals!

7. **Remove the so-called "moderate" Republicans.** As discussed throughout this book, "moderates" are schizophrenic at best, and imbeciles and Leftist infiltrators at least. Republican "Moderates" are *enemies* in our camp and to our cause affecting division, capitulation to the Left, and ineffectiveness in our ranks and our mission. We must identify and eliminate "moderates" from our Party, ranks, and organizations!

8. **ONLY support Republican leadership who truly represent Right politics.** As has been clearly evidenced with Left-oriented "moderate" leadership in the Republican Party and Congress, Leftist-moderate leadership within the Republican Party leads *only* to the wholesale disarming of the Right, our cause, and our mission. Nothing Right comes from a "moderate" leadership. The Left-moderate leadership must be purged and wholly eliminated from the Republican Party and Republican elected offices!

9. **Start a "Truth Campaign".** Start a "Truth Campaign" to expose and remedy Leftist strongholds and political offices. Create Conservative media groups that would specifically target Leftists and Leftist Organizations to expose their Evil deeds and ideals. Confront the Media bias and *Lies*! This includes the Left Stream Media, online "fact checkers", Leftist commentators, Newspapers, *et al*. Left-Wing "fact checking" organizations that find their way to the top of Google searches and *Lie*… Fact Check, PolitiFact, The Washington Post's Fact Checker, Snopes, *et al*. There is a recognizable move by Google to eliminate many Right oriented websites and commentary and give first listing to Leftist oriented sites, commentary, and revisionist history telling (*Lies!*). Create and support non-

Left biased search engines. This is a good place to implement Rule #4 and boycott Google and like Leftist-minded media organizations. The Right *must* expose the Left for its *Lies* and Evil bias and educate Americans in the Truth!

10. Oppose and *Remove* All Leftist Educators and Leftist "Educational" Curriculums.

Turn around the Left's weapons against them!

Oppose and Remove Leftist Educators and "Educational" Curriculums at all levels including primary, secondary, high school, University, and trade levels. We must reinstitute core curricula of civics and factual history and eliminate Leftist indoctrinations of Environmentalism, Climate Change, Evolution, Pro-Abortion, Sex "Education", Self-Esteem, Hinduism, Anti-Bullying, Homosexuality, *et al*. We must *identify* and *remove* all Leftist Indoctrination that parades as "education" and Leftist educators who indoctrinate and manipulate our children to accept and support Evil and the Left!

Force National legislation that would tie Federal Funding for State schools to teach prescribed texts including real history, civics, social studies, math and eliminate all Leftist indoctrinations such as evolution, self-esteem, Pagan religious studies, *et al*. We can avoid the Left's screeching accusations by not shutting down the Department of Education and accomplish Right school standards. Those States who refuse to comply will be totally cutoff from Federal funding! This is exactly what the Left now uses against the Right and should be turned around against the Left. This is the only way to take back the Leftist States from the Left by educating the youth to the *Lies* of the Left!

11. Take Back Our Election Process. Enforce Voter ID
Laws: If the Federal Government will not recognize your
State's Voter ID Laws Enforce the ID laws on the State
level. Go after organizations like ACORN and its
reincarnated organizations that foster voter fraud to
advance their Evil agenda. Identify and support Right
candidates for office!

If any of these remedies seem a bit extreme, just remember that the
only and last alternative to civilized opposition to the Left in their
takeover of our great Country is full-blown open revolutionary War!
All other opposition seems reasonable given the alternative!

26. CONCLUSION

Chapter 26

There is a *War* raging for the soul of America… and the Right is losing abysmally! We must ask ourselves… Why?! The Right has truth, success, and history on our side. So why then, can the Left waltz in and steal, kill, and destroy our Country out from under us? It is the Right's own fault! We have no one to blame but ourselves! The first step to getting back in the trenches is to take responsibility for our prior failings in our conduct of this *War*! We are one election away from the irreversible destruction of our Great Republic!

The Right surrendered the Battle beginning in earnest in the 1960's at the outset of America's "Cultural Revolution". The Right gave up its role as the defender against Evil and succumb to the Left's blind ideal that the Devil was not real and that Evil was simply an illusionary construct of the weak minds of the uninitiated masses. (Let me translate the Left's strategic *Lie*: "Only an idiot could believe that there actually is a Devil".) Don't you find it amazing that while the Left ridicules the belief in Evil in general, and the Devil in particular, that the Left in its icons like Saul Alinsky and Alinsky's disciples Hillary Rodham-Clinton and Barack Hussein Obama through Alinsky, do homage to the Devil as the source and inspiration of the Leftist radicalism?! You cannot Win this *War* without first identifying the enemy, and then being convinced that that enemy is *REAL*, and that the threat posed by Evil is *real*!

As has been epitomized with Obama's refusal to identify America's enemy as militant Islam, so the Right cannot hope to Win this Battle for America unless we identify the true enemy of America, which is Evil itself! As long as the Right treats Evil as nothing more than a childhood boogieman story meant to scare children into behaving, the Right is simply, as Sheryl Crow so profoundly identified the syndrome as the futilely of "throwing punches in the air". Which is when you have no visible enemy to fight but listlessly flail at nonexistent phantoms hoping that you might hit something… anything… please!

This is why the Right so often seems so disoriented, they are being bludgeoned from every side and are helpless to strike a blow back because they cannot even identify what and who is the Enemy! It would be comical if it were not so tragic and ultimately deadly! The Right's Battle against the Left has become a laughable misdirected flailing against an imaginary enemy, rather than the real Enemy, akin to Don Quixote's blind "tilting at windmills", we have become blind to the true identity of the Enemy and the Evil behind the sneers and patronizing rhetoric of the Left. (Is it any wonder that they sneer at us?!) Let's own our mistakes and change our Battle strategy!

Unlike the Left, the Right has no comprehensive strategy for Fighting this *War*. The Right seems to swing randomly at an imagined enemy. From the American voter's point of view the Right appears as buffoons, or at best a self-centered version of the Three Stooges! Of course, the Left openly ridicules, mocks, sneers, smirks, and makes fun of the Right's whirling-dervish responses to the Left's tactics. The Right just ends up *dizzy*, the voter *confused*, and the Left *amused*!

America has paid such a monstrous price in human lives and suffering for an ill defended War by the Right. Like it or not, the Right is the only guardians of what is, or was, the uniquely American way of life and standard of justice.

The Right has been effectively marginalized by the tactics of the Left. The Left develops strategies that are impossible to counter if the Right cannot even identify the Evil behind the Left's tactics and present an alternative and effective choice to the American people!

Being Conservative is doing the Right thing. The Right thing is defined as GOD's way. Being Right, or Conservative, by definition means to make every attempt to emulate the precepts of GOD and oppose all Evil. This is why someone who proclaims to be "Conservative", but also claims to be "liberal on social issues" or a "moderate", is in fact *not* a Conservative but a Liberal with a few "right-esque" manifestations. These people are either confused, self-deluded, or intentionally trying to deceive for their own benefit! This is why so many who call themselves "Republican" or "Conservative" are confused and confuse those who try to justify them, they are *neither* Right nor Conservative.! The commentators and pundits look at every possible explanation in analyzing a "moderate", except of course the true defining characteristic, which is the defining distinction of Evil verses GOOD. It is *impossible* to be half-Right... which at the same time leaves you half Wrong, and by definition you cannot be Right, but you are contaminated by Evil! Half-wrong is *never* Right!

There is no such thing as a "moderate Conservative" any more than there is a "faithful spouse" who only "screws around half of the time"! That is an oxymoron on the level of a "righteous whore". The two just cannot coexist in the same place. One affair makes a person unfaithful! We are called by GOD to promote GOOD. Compromise always corrupts GOOD and "corrupted GOOD" is nothing more than *Evil* masquerading as GOOD. So called "moderates" are nothing more than sellouts to Evil who compromise away this Country piece-by-piece! Moderates are incremental movers to the Left and to ultimate destruction! At best they "incrementally" slow down the rate of destruction, facilitating a slower, and ultimately a more painful *death*! What we desperately need are those who refuse to compromise with Evil and not work to merely slow down the destruction, but we need those men and women who would commit to *reverse* America's downward death spiral!

Compromise is *always* at least an incremental move towards the Left and further away from what is Right. Compromise with Evil destroys souls as well as it destroys nations! How else do you explain the Left's eagerness to come to a "compromise" with its opponents? Barring of course the Left's ability to completely overrun its opponents.

If the Right cannot even recognize the real Enemy, his tactics, and his true goals, then we have already lost the Battle. The War has already been won by Christ's work on the Cross and Resurrection from the dead, but we may yet lose the Battle for America. America could become a casualty in a long historical list of national casualties with our children and grandchildren sold to the Devil and become eternal casualties condemned to Hell! The ultimate struggle is not in "creating Heaven on earth" today as the Left would have us believe, but an eternal Heaven or Hell for the souls and spirits of men. ***This is not just a struggle for an American identity, but for the minds and souls of all future American generations! We determine the heritage of our children tomorrow by our response to the threat of Evil today. The Right must again become the defenders of Right!***

The stench of the sins of America has reached to Heaven. Seldom in the history of mankind has sin reached such unGODly proportions. History is littered with the ruins of nations and whole civilizations that had not attained such perverse levels of sin as we find in America today. Sodom was burned to ash by GOD for its homosexual perversion. Their charred remains can be evidenced even today south of the Dead Sea. GOD wiped out entire civilizations because they practiced an ancient form of abortion which was identified by GOD as sacrificing babies to devils! GOD places the blood of these babies directly on the hands of the mothers[698]. The United States far eclipsed the number of babies that it has sacrificed to Evil exceeding any other nation in history. Over 57,000,000 sacrificed children and counting! That is Evil unprecedented in all of history and far surpasses that of even Nazi Germany! If GOD destroyed the Nation of Israel, His chosen people, for these same sins, what will He do to America whose sins overwhelm those of ancient Israel? Repentance from Evil is our only escape from certain judgement as a nation!

Even the Archangel Michael dared not stand directly against the persuasive power of Satan but invoked the Power of GOD to *Win* the victory[699]. Michael called upon the *Name* of GOD to repulse Satan. What gives us the audacity as mere humans to think that we can handle a pact with the Devil or stand against Evil without GOD?!

Does America love its sins more than it loves its children or its unborn babies? Like the crack addict whose children are left unprotected to die of neglect, so too are America's born and unborn children being cast away to the destruction of Evil and to Evil's Leftist ambassadors.

---

[698] The *Holy Bible:* Ezekiel 23:37, 45.
[699] The *Holy Bible*: Jude 1:9.

Try looking your children in the eye in a moment of honesty and telling them that you sold their souls to Evil for the unrestrained pleasures offered by the unrestrained Evil of the Left! Do not delude yourself, whether we want to be honest with ourselves or not, this is exactly what we are doing in America today! Regardless of how Evil tries to pervert the extent to which we identify Evil, Truth will always be Truth!

In closing I would take the liberty of quoting Ronald Reagan who was speaking of the external Leftist Evil enemy of America in 1964 and transpose Reagan's words to the internal Leftist Evil of the enemies of which we face today:

> Those who would trade our freedom for the soup kitchen of the welfare state have told us they have a utopian solution of peace without victory. They call their policy "accommodation". **And they say if we'll only avoid any direct confrontation with the enemy, he'll forget his evil ways and learn to love us.** All who oppose them are indicted as warmongers. They say we offer simple answers to complex problems. **Well, perhaps there is a simple answer—not an easy answer—but simple: If you and I have the courage to tell our elected officials that we want our national policy based on what we know in our hearts is morally right.**

> We cannot buy our security, our freedom from the threat of the bomb by committing an immorality so great as saying to a billion human beings now enslaved behind the Iron Curtain, **"Give up your dreams of freedom because to save our own skins, we're willing to make a deal with your slave masters."** Alexander Hamilton said, "**A nation which can prefer disgrace to danger is prepared for a master, and deserves one.**" Now let's set the record straight. There's no argument over the choice between peace and war, but there's only one guaranteed way you can have peace—and you can

have it in the next second—surrender.

Admittedly, there's a risk in any course we follow other than this, but **every lesson of history tells us that the greater risk lies in appeasement**... that **their policy of accommodation is appeasement, and it gives no choice between peace and war, only between fight or surrender. If we continue to accommodate, continue to back and retreat, eventually we must face the final demand—the ultimatum**. And what then—when Nikita Khrushchev has told his people he knows what our answer will be? He has told them that we're retreating under the pressure of the Cold War, and **someday when the time comes to deliver the final ultimatum, our surrender will be voluntary, because by that time we will have been weakened from within spiritually, morally, and economically**. He believes this because from our side he's heard voices pleading for "peace at any price" or "**better Red than dead**", or **as one commentator put it, he'd rather "live on his knees than die on his feet."** And **therein lies the road to war, because those voices don't speak for the rest of us**.

You and I know and do not believe that life is so dear and peace so sweet as to be purchased at the price of chains and slavery. If nothing in life is worth dying for, when did this begin—just in the face of this enemy? Or **should Moses have told the children of Israel to live in slavery under the pharaohs? Should Christ have refused the Cross?** Should the patriots at Concord Bridge have thrown down their guns and refused to fire the shot heard 'round the world? **The martyrs of history were not fools, and our honored dead who gave their lives to stop the advance of the Nazis didn't die in vain**. Where, then, is the road to peace? Well it's a simple answer after all.

You and I have the courage to say to our enemies, "There is a price we will not pay." "There is a point beyond which they must not advance." And this—this is the meaning in the phrase of Barry Goldwater's "peace through strength."

Winston Churchill said, "The destiny of man is not measured by material computations. **When great forces are on the move in the world, we learn we're spirits—not animals."** And he said, **"There's something going on in time and space, and beyond time and space, which, whether we like it or not, spells duty."**

You and I have a rendezvous with destiny.

We'll preserve for our children this, the last best hope of man on earth, or we'll sentence them to take the last step into a thousand years of darkness.

We will keep in mind and remember that Barry Goldwater has faith in us. He has faith that **you and I have the ability and the dignity and the right to make our own decisions and determine our own destiny**. (emphasis added)

To this I will add one more quote from Ronald Reagan:

Freedom is never more than one generation away from extinction. We didn't pass it on to our children in the bloodstream. It must be fought for, protected, and handed on for them to do the same, or one day we will spend our sunset years telling our children and our children's children what it was once like in the United States where men were free.[700]

It has become almost clichéd, Freedom Is Not Free, we either pay the price to regain and keep our Freedom, or pay the price for losing it! Are you willing to pay the price in the Right's War against Evil? Do you think that our Founding Fathers did not pay the price? Do you think that the US soldiers on the front lines did not pay the price in the War Against Evil in defeating the Nazi hordes in World War II? Do you think that the Evil Left in America today will be defeated until thousands on the Right stand up and actually *FIGHT* back the Left in

---

[700] Address to the annual meeting of the Phoenix Chamber of Commerce (30 March 1961).

the here and now?! Don't delude yourself, there is a reason that the Left has spent a vast amount of energy and resources convincing the Right to sit down and shut-up in their *War Against GOD* for America. The *War* against Freedom is easily won by the Left when there are few if any soldiers on the Right to Battle Against! Remember that Evil always triumphs when good men do nothing! What are *you* doing to arrest and turn back the tide of Evil in America today?!

Just a question for those of you with a Right mind but who are caught up in the doctrines of Liberal-Leftism: Are you really willing to sacrifice your children on the altar of the Left for a few pieces of silver or a moment of pleasure? The Left does not want you to face the truth of this question. They want you to continue to delude yourself with the Left's message of "live for yourself because it doesn't affect anybody else". This is a *Lie* straight from the Pit of Hell! The depraved condition of America unquestionably testifies to this. One who chooses to define his own morals in opposition to, or any variance of GOD's eternally fixed morals, has chosen to be immoral! Make no mistake this man is the Enemy of GOD. In GOD's definition of Right there is no allowance for a man's self-interpretation or deviation!

What is sold as "freedom" by the Left is the means to *enslavement* to Evil, both in the natural and supernatural realms. What may be "lawful" under the Leftist standard is not expedient for America's, or Americans', long-term survival. Just because America "legalizes" Evil, government legalization cannot make it Right or the consequences GOOD. Satan offered to make Eve and Adam to be like GOD. All we have to do is look around to see that that did not work out so well. It *never* does! It was a Leftist *Lie* of Evil then, and it remains a Leftist *Lie* of Evil today! All Adam and Eve, and consequently all of mankind, received was pain and death. Evil's apple is always delicious looking on the outside but deadly on the inside. Satan's tactics have not changed. Unfortunately neither has human nature, which left unrestrained always results in suffering and death!

The cause of Evil in the world is in the hearts of man. It is delusional to think that men with inherent Evil in their hearts can create a Utopian

Heaven on earth. *Hell does not beget Heaven*! Only Evil could propagate such a *Lie* with a straight face, while oftentimes with a sneer. Only GOD promises Heaven, not in this life but the hope of the life to come. Of course GOD's Heaven is predicated on a person choosing to wholly follow the One true GOD here in this life. In following GOD here in this world, we create the best possible life in the here and now. There will never be Heaven on earth as long as Evil and its Leftist missionaries are at work to destroy all that is GOOD. Heaven on earth comes only at the end of time when Evil is finally destroyed and condemned to Hell far away from earth. Until then *the Left's War* of Evil *Against GOD* and GOOD rages on!

If those of us on the Right will not get into the Fight then all is lost. We might as well start fitting our children for brown uniforms, closing our churches, and fitting ourselves for the guillotine! The Right is big on a strong US military defense to deter attacks from the enemy. How then can we expect to not only stem, but defeat the Left, the Left who is fighting this War as a *War*, if we refuse to even fight?!

The American voter is not stupid as the Über-Leftist strategist and demagogue Jonathan Gruber suggests, but is in large part naive, uninformed, or totally self-centered in their willingness to trade their freedom for a few bobbles dangled in front of them by the Left. The remainder of the Left are willing participants borne from Evil desires and intentions. It is our job and obligation to educate the American masses and alert them to the imminent dangers of Evil. If not you... who? If not now... when?! If no one answers the call to Freedom then it is already too late!

It is high time to begin the Counter-Revolution, Revolution! This is a trumpet call to America's Right and Anti-Rebels! Truth is the most effective weapon against the Left. As George Orwell so profoundly noted: "In a time of universal deceit, telling the truth is a revolutionary act"! Again, it is high time to begin the *Counter-Revolution*, Revolution! This is a trumpet call to America's Right and Anti-Rebels! Stand up and be an Anti-Rebel for GOD and Against Evil and the Left in America today!

If history is any indicator, it may take a full-blown economic collapse, or worse, to revive the people of their Christian moorings in America. But of course, an America once under a Leftist dictatorship may be irretrievable from the grip of Evil and the trash-heap of history!

The Right has somehow gotten the idea that the *War* can be a "clean fight". Guess what... the War is fought in the trenches where it is dirty, foul, and as far as the Left is concerned *there are no rules*! The bell rings and the Right comes out to shake hands and the Left "punches them in the face". The Right is shocked. Really!? It is said that insanity is doing the same thing over and over and expecting a different result! The Right is living in a fantasy world, and prone to insanity in its expectations of the rules of engagement in the *War* with the Left! Wake up Right Conservatives, Americans, and Christians! Wake up and get in the trenches where the Left lives and start kicking some Leftist asses!

"I am only one, but I am one. I can't do everything, but I can do something. What I can do, that I ought to do. And what I ought to do, By the grace of God, I shall do." -Edward Everett Hale

Joshua, the inheritor of Moses mantle, asked the eternal question this way:

> And if it seem evil unto you to serve the LORD, choose you this day whom ye will serve... but as for me and my house, we will serve the LORD[701]!

My family and I have personally paid a horrible price for standing up Against Evil. But through it all I have stood resolute with RIGHT and with GOD. In any war there are some who pay much bigger prices for their role in the battle. Most must fight the hand-to-hand combat down in the trenches. These are the ones who pay the biggest price, but these are the ones for whom GOD smiles upon and reserves the biggest eternal rewards. I choose to stay on the frontlines no matter how big the blows from Evil! I can withstand because I stand with GOD! I may

---

[701] The *Holy Bible*: Joshua 24:15.

die a martyr but I will die standing on my feet in a full charge against the lines of Evil! That will be my heritage! Heroes are not made outside of their fighting Against Evil. Won't you sign up and enjoin the Battle Against Evil and the Left for the deliverance of America? Won't you choose to be GOD's hero? Isn't that alone worth any price? If one person alone stands up with GOD in the Epic War of *Evil Against GOD*, they still have GOD Himself Battling alongside them, in them, and empowering them! Anyone and GOD is always a majority! Will you join with GOD's majority? GOD implores us, "Choose you this day whom ye will serve"[702]. There simply is no neutral ground in *The Left's War Against GOD*. I choose GOD, which side do you choose?

---

[702] The *Holy Bible*: Joshua 24:15.

POSTSCRIPT: FOR THE SINNER WHO FINDS HIMSELF ON THE WRONG SIDE OF GOD IN THE LEFT'S WAR AGAINST GOD:

The GOOD News for you is that there is forgiveness at the Cross of Jesus. There is a new life, a new beginning waiting for you! There is peace with GOD and an inner peace that passes all human understanding. It does not matter how deep or gross your sins have been, Jesus already paid your price of Salvation and freedom from sin on the Cross; all you must do is accept Jesus as your Savior and One and only true GOD. You must surrender your life *and* sin to Him. You cannot hold anything back, or there is no Salvation. As Jesus clearly said "He that is not with me is against me". With GOD you are either all in, or all out. There simply is no middle ground, no middle way to Salvation and to GOD. As Shakespeare quothed, "therein lies the rub". Many people want a Savior, however they do not want to wholly surrender their life to GOD, as their GOD. It is a package deal… all or nothing.

I liken the deciding moment which leads to Salvation to a man being swept down a torrential river in his canoe towards certain doom as he can see the coming waterfall and certain death awaiting him several hundred feet below his viewable horizon onto the sharp jagged rocks below. The man's boat is loaded down with every one of the man's accumulated sins which he is holding onto tightly. There is a Man standing on the shore with a rope capable of saving him from eminent death. The man in the canoe screams out to the Man on the shore, "please save me from my certain fate!". The Man on the shore throws the rope which lands across the bow of the little canoe. The Man on the shore calls out, "I will be your GOD and your Savior!". The man in the boat looks quite shocked; this is not the deal which he expected and calls back, "I just want a Savior". The Man on the shore calls back, "your grip will not hold unless you abandon all of your sins and throw yourself overboard and wholly trust in Me. Now grab hold, jump out of your boat, and I will pull you to safety".

The man in the canoe calls back, "No, I just want to be saved, but want no commitment beyond that". The Man on the shore desperately calls back to the man in the canoe headed ever closer to death, "My Father has set me here to save you, but because of the terrible price which it cost Me to be positioned here, My Father demands that you leave all behind, or you cannot be saved". Hearing this the man in the canoe turns his head away and mutters to himself, "I just wanted to be rescued, but I will not leave all of my acquired life's works behind". The man in the canoe dropped his head and blocked out the pleading cries of the Savior from the shore. The man in the canoe could not give up his boatload of accumulated sins and determined that he would hold onto them until the very end, which was fast approaching.

This is the same decision that we must all face. We have a choice between our sins… and GOD. Too many people want to be saved from the eminent doom of Hell, but still want to cling to the Evil of their sins. Sin cannot enter Heaven… into the very presence of GOD the Father. It's simply… impossible. Hell is full of those who loved their sin rather than GOD. Salvation is a package deal. You must accept Jesus the Christ as your GOD and Savior. In return you receive a package deal from GOD receiving GOD the Father, GOD the Son, and GOD the Holy Spirit. One GOD in Three Persons. It's a great deal, but there is a cost… you must wholly surrender your life.

The commitment takes less than 30 seconds. All that is required is that you believe that Jesus *is* GOD, Jesus died for your sins, and that Jesus raised Himself from the dead three days later. Then simply tell Jesus that you wholly surrender your life to Him as your Savior and GOD and that you accept His Salvation which Jesus paid the ultimate price for on the Cross to buy you back from Evil. That's it. If you've done that congratulations! You are now a Christian, and as such, a Born-Again child of GOD!

If you prayed this prayer of Salvation we would love to hear about it and share in your newfound joy! We would also like to connect with you and get you started on your new journey!:
TAFSalvationAndConnect@gmail.com

www.ingramcontent.com/pod-product-compliance
Lightning Source LLC
Chambersburg PA
CBHW062147270326
41930CB00009B/1470